Jefferson's Muslim Fugitives

Jefferson's Muslim Fugitives

The Lost Story of Enslaved Africans, Their Arabic Letters, and an American President

JEFFREY EINBODEN

OXFORD
UNIVERSITY PRESS

OXFORD
UNIVERSITY PRESS

Oxford University Press is a department of the University of Oxford. It furthers the University's objective of excellence in research, scholarship, and education by publishing worldwide. Oxford is a registered trade mark of Oxford University Press in the UK and certain other countries.

Published in the United States of America by Oxford University Press
198 Madison Avenue, New York, NY 10016, United States of America.

Library of Congress Cataloging-in-Publication Data
Names: Einboden, Jeffrey, author.
Title: Jefferson's Muslim fugitives : the lost story of enslaved Africans,
their Arabic letters, and an American president / Jeffrey Einboden.
Other titles: Lost story of enslaved Africans, their Arabic letters, and an American president
Description: New York, NY : Oxford University Press, [2020] |
Includes bibliographical references and index. |
Identifiers: LCCN 2019036456 (print) | LCCN 2019036457 (ebook) |
ISBN 9780190844479 (hardback) | ISBN 9780190844486 |
ISBN 9780190844493 (epub) | ISBN 9780190063917
Subjects: LCSH: Fugitive slaves—Kentucky—History—19th century. |
Muslims—Kentucky—History—19th century. | Slaves' writings, American. |
| Jefferson, Thomas, 1743–1826—Correspondence. |
Jefferson, Thomas, 1743–1826—Friends and associates. |
Jefferson, Thomas, 1743–1826—Relations with African Americans. |
Nash, Ira P., 1774–1844—Correspondence. |
African American Muslims—Kentucky—History. |
Slavery—Political aspects—United States—History—19th century.
Classification: LCC E445.K5 E56 2020 (print) | LCC E445.K5 (ebook) |
DDC 306.3/6209769—dc23
LC record available at https://lccn.loc.gov/2019036456
LC ebook record available at https://lccn.loc.gov/2019036457

3 5 7 9 8 6 4 2

Printed by Sheridan Books, Inc., United States of America

For
Hillary
Ezra & Eve

Contents

Prologue

On March 5, 1809, Thomas Jefferson was finally free. The day before, he had attended James Madison's inauguration, witnessing his successor take the oath of office. After two tumultuous terms, Jefferson was relieved of the presidency. And he could not wait to flee Washington. It was time to go home.

On his first full day of retirement, Jefferson wrote only one letter that has survived. Not addressed to his friends in high places, this March 5 letter was instead sent to an innkeeper in Virginia, John Benson, who had invited Jefferson to "pass a day" in Fredericksburg on his "return home" to Monticello. But Jefferson refused, offering Benson only excuses. He could not come due to the "impassable state of the roads"; and, moreover, Fredericksburg was "20. Miles" out of the way. Most important, Jefferson would not be traveling light. "I shall have a Caravan also on the road, ahead of me, which, in case of any casualty I might overtake & relieve," Jefferson informed Benson.[1] Although unburdened from office, the former president was not unencumbered in returning home to Virginia. "Three wagons" would be sent before him to Monticello, carrying all types of "property"—including, of course, enslaved persons. Jefferson was free from office; but others in his own household would stay very much in bondage.[2]

Precisely two hundred years after Jefferson's initial day of retirement on March 5, 1809, the present study took its own initial steps. On the evening of March 5, 2009, I taught a graduate seminar at Northern Illinois University and, for the first time, brought together the two topics that are synthesized in this book: Thomas Jefferson and Muslim slave writings. That evening in March, my students were assigned to read selected letters by Jefferson. During the same class session, however, I also prepared students for our next topic, introducing them to Arabic writings by enslaved Muslims in antebellum America—a subject we would be covering in depth during the very next class.[3] These disparate subjects I had deliberately set back-to-back in designing the course, juxtaposing Jefferson—famed author of US freedoms—with little-known writings by African Muslims, whose freedoms were denied in the early United States. In 2009, however, I was entirely unaware that this surface contrast hid a literal link. Exactly two centuries before our class,

Jefferson planned his escape from Washington, telling John Benson of the "Caravan" that would be sent before him, packed with possessions from his presidential years. I would later come to learn that among the many materials Jefferson accrued while in office were two little pieces of Arabic writing, penned by fugitive Muslim slaves—pieces that are published for the very first time in this book.

During the decade that has passed since 2009, it has been my own travels away from home that helped uncover the sources that sustain *Jefferson's Muslim Fugitives*. In the months that followed my graduate class on March 5, my interest in Muslim slave writings developed and deepened. Rather than teach documents already discovered, I turned to archival research, seeking to locate lost slave writings in Arabic. Visiting sites where Muslims were enslaved in the early nation, my search received critical support from the National Endowment for the Humanities (NEH), to which I now express my immense thanks. Applying in 2010 for my first NEH Fellowship, I received funding in 2011–2012 for an initiative entitled "Arabic Slave Writings and the American Canon," supporting my efforts to uncover lost Muslim sources for translation and teaching.[4] Traveling first to North Carolina and later to Georgia, my early research yielded material successes, though modest. By 2012, I had managed to recover and render just a few Arabic pieces penned by Muslim slaves that were previously unpublished.

During these first years of searching, it was what seemed missing in the South that proved just as significant as what I was able to unearth. Although African Muslims endured enslavement primarily in southern states, I increasingly uncovered hints that their Arabic writings had migrated north, ending up in leading archives from New England to Notre Dame. Buried among the papers of the most prominent early Americans, Muslim slave writings started to emerge in folders belonging to famed US politicians and professors. To locate fresh manuscripts by Muslim slaves, it became clear that *where* they were written meant far less than *why*—and for whom. The Africans who composed these documents had led lives of incarceration, or were hunted fugitives on the run. And yet, their Arabic documents enjoyed free passage, making their way into the hands of the most elite US figures— figures who themselves had private interests and personal experiences with Islam, Africa, and captivity. This realization led to repeated breakthroughs in my research. By 2013, I had begun to locate lost Muslim slave manuscripts at northern sites, experiencing success especially in early America's "capital of culture": Boston. It was at this city's Massachusetts Historical Society that

I would find the earliest extant writings by a Muslim slave after Independence, writings that have stayed hidden amid the papers of an eighteenth-century president of Yale. And it would also be at the Massachusetts Historical Society that I would later locate one of the two Arabic documents possessed by none other than a president of the United States: Thomas Jefferson.

These unexpected finds, and years of travel, not only yielded the source materials for *Jefferson's Muslim Fugitives*, but also mirror the story the book now tells—a story of improbable pursuits, spanning all corners of the country, from northern cities to the deep south, from the east coast to the far west. Straddling borders of race, religion, and region, the book pairs unknown Muslim slaves with the most celebrated early Americans, linking men on the margins to the prime centers of US power. It is a similar shift from periphery to prominence that also motivates *Jefferson's Muslim Fugitives* itself. The book aims to overturn centuries of obscurity, finally bringing to light the compositions and contributions of multiple Muslim slaves previously unknown—an aim rooted in the book's research, but which has also shaped its style. *Jefferson's Muslim Fugitives* is written not as a static study, but as a historical narrative. Dilating out from the pivotal year of 1807, the book unfolds a lost story of Arabic literacy and Muslim captivity centered in the life and legacy of Thomas Jefferson. Revealing subjects hidden in plain sight since the nation's first decades, *Jefferson's Muslim Fugitives* finds forgotten Arabic slave writings built into the very biography of one of America's most renowned founding fathers.

There are dangers, of course, in exposing such historic Muslim writings for the first time within a retelling of Jefferson's own storied career. It runs the risk, in particular, of overshadowing Muslim slaves yet again, eclipsing their experiences by placing them in proximity to a towering figure in the American mind. The intent—and the outcome, I trust—of *Jefferson's Muslim Fugitives* is precisely the opposite. There are many reasons why Muslim slaves have eluded standard accounts of US origins. Some of their Arabic writings have been physically lost; some writings that *have* survived still remain obscure due to their near illegibility—an issue that impacts the very manuscripts that came into Jefferson's hands. It is not the limitations of their Arabic authorship that have kept Muslim slaves hidden, however, but the limited audiences that have been presented with their stories. Despite heroic efforts by prior field pioneers, the study of Muslim slave writings still remains a narrow academic niche.[5] Their presence is frequently overlooked within both broad histories of early America, as well as targeted biographies of America's founders. *Jefferson's Muslim Fugitives* challenges this neglect, not only by revealing links between Muslim slaves and the nation's elite, but by presenting these links within a narrative accessible to non-specialists.

The narrative shape of *Jefferson's Muslim Fugitives* arose from its historic materials and an aim to make these materials widely available. But narratives take time. Narratives unfold through time, of course, recounting the passage of events, advancing from a beginning to an end. However, time is also the vital resource needed to craft a narrative. For *Jefferson's Muslim Fugitives*, this resource was supplied by the American Council of Learned Societies (ACLS), to which I now offer my most profound gratitude. It was an ACLS Fellowship in 2017 that released me from an entire year of teaching, allowing the time required to transform my source findings into this book's final narrative. Without ACLS support, *Jefferson's Muslim Fugitives* would not have been possible. The same could be said, however, of another institutional leader: Oxford University Press. Granted an advance contract at the very end of 2016, *Jefferson's Muslim Fugitives* received years of superlative guidance from the press's editors and readers, including Hannah Campeanu, and especially OUP executive editor Cynthia Read.

My last stages of writing *Jefferson's Muslim Fugitives* built upon years of foregoing archive research, during which I not only collected rare sources, but also accumulated countless debts of gratitude. Dozens of institutions and individuals across the country supported my search for manuscripts, welcoming my repeated visits, and later granting permissions for my quotation and image reproductions from their collections. Beginning with my earliest travels in the Southeast, I express thanks first to numerous libraries in North Carolina, especially the E. H. Little Library at Davidson College; UNC Chapel Hill's Wilson Library; UNC Wilmington's Randall Library; and Wilmington's New Hanover County Public Library. I thank also the Spartanburg County Historical Association in South Carolina for their permission to publish and translate a previously lost piece of Arabic by 'Umar ibn Sayyid during the course of my first NEH Fellowship. In Georgia, I was warmly received at Midway's Congregational Church, at the Richmond Hill Historical Society, and at the Georgia Historical Society in Savannah. My deepest debts in the Southeast were accrued, however, in Georgia's "Golden Isles." Over many years and visits, Georgia's seacoast islands have proved not only to be a rich source of research, but have also begun to feel like home. This has been due entirely to my wonderful parents, Pam and Ed, whose seasonal residence on Jekyll Island has provided not only a place to stay, but also a means of coming to know members of the Jekyll community, who generously encouraged my efforts at every turn. In the Golden Isles, I also thank Mimi Rogers, curator of the Coastal Georgia Historical Society on St. Simons Island, and, most especially, Buddy Sullivan, the region's pioneering historian who freely shared with me his peerless expertise.

As my research migrated northward, following the trail of Muslim slave manuscripts, it was Boston that became the center of my work for several years. As mentioned, first and foremost in my thanks is the Massachusetts Historical Society, where I received invaluable aid, especially from Anna Clutterbuck-Cook and Sabina Beauchard. My extended stays in the city were enriched by the Boston Athenaeum, where I was fortunate to receive a 2012–2013 Fellowship and to benefit from the guidance of Mary Warnement and Stanley Cushing. I thank also the New England Historic Genealogical Society, as well as Bentley University, and in particular, David Szymanski at Bentley's Valente Center for Arts & Sciences. During my many stays in Boston and Cambridge, countless curators and librarians at Harvard have graciously welcomed me at both the University Archives and Houghton Library. Neighboring repositories have also contributed to my work, including the Phillips Library, the Peabody Essex Museum in Salem—where I thank especially Tamara Gaydos—as well as the American Antiquarian Society in Worcester. My repeated visits to the Beinecke Library at Yale University both were warmly welcomed and became crucial to the book's contents. Outside New England, my last northern stop was Notre Dame, Indiana, where a 2015 visit yielded an unexpected manuscript find that is revealed in the final chapters of *Jefferson's Muslim Fugitives*. At Notre Dame, I thank in particular George Rugg, Curator at the Department of Special Collections at Hesburgh Libraries.

It was at mid-Atlantic archives, in between New England and the seacoast of Georgia, where I concluded my search for the book's sources, conducting research in recent years at sites with specific ties to Jefferson himself. My work received indispensable aid in Philadelphia, including at the University of Pennsylvania's Kislak Center for Special Collections, at the American Philosophical Society (APS), and at the Historical Society of Pennsylvania. Especially generous with their guidance was Mitch Fraas, Curator of Special Collections at the University of Pennsylvania, and Earle E. Spamer, Reference Archivist at APS. In Washington, DC, my research at the Library of Congress would have been impossible without the expert guidance of Julie Miller, Historian of Early America, Manuscript Division. In Charlottesville,

Virginia, I was kindly received not only at Monticello, but at the nearby Robert H. Smith International Center for Jefferson Studies, as well as at the University of Virginia's Albert and Shirley Small Special Collections Library. In Richmond, I thank the Virginia Historical Society, and especially John McClure, Director of Research Services.

As I traced the origins of the two Arabic manuscripts that came into Jefferson's possession, my research in 2016 and 2017 led me away from the east coast and into the interior, with trips to Tennessee and Kentucky. In Gallatin, I received indispensable aid from the Sumner County Archives; in Carthage, my research was facilitated by the patient guidance of John Waggoner Jr., who oversaw my review of records at the town's courthouse, searching for any final traces of two Muslim fugitives in nineteenth-century Carthage. In Christian County, Kentucky, I thank Becky Quinten, who was a joy to work with during my visit to the Hopkinsville Library, and at the Missouri Historical Society, Dennis Northcott remotely offered his invaluable expertise. Furthest west, my journeys in pursuit of *Jefferson's Muslim Fugitives* led to one final stop: California. At the invitation of the University of California–Los Angeles' Center for Near Eastern Studies, I first presented a portion of this book as a lecture delivered at the School of Law in February 2016. I thank UCLA for graciously hosting my stay, and most especially, Director of Islamic Studies Asma Sayeed.

Now, in the wake of my travels spanning the coasts, I have returned to the middle of the county—to the Midwest. It is here, at Northern Illinois University, that my debts are most extensive. I thank NIU's Graduate School for several research grants, funding summer travels essential to the book's development. Most crucial has been the support received day to day from fellow members of the faculty. I name with especial thanks Betty Birner, who has offered unparalleled support for my work over many years. I also received vital encouragement from Melissa Adams-Campbell; Lara and Tim Crowley; Ryan Hibbett and Jessica Reyman; Bil Johnson; Amy Newman; Kathleen Renk; Luz Van Cromphout; and Mark Van Wienen. Countless colleagues beyond NIU have offered essential aid during recent years; I express my particular thanks to Jeff Barbeau, Shelley Fisher Fishkin, Tariq Jaffer, Zubeda Jalalzai, David Jasper, Todd Lawson, Timothy Marr, Walid Saleh, Mustafa Shah, Fr. Isaac Slater, Shawkat Toorawa, Timothy Winter, Brian Yothers, and Eric Ziolkowski.

A decade has now passed since the spring semester in 2009, the semester that launched the journeys that have led to *Jefferson's Muslim Fugitives*. As

I write these words in 2019, I am once more in the midst of another spring semester, during which I will again teach Muslim slave writings, but with a much deeper sense of their significance and covert circulation in early America. Amid all the repetitions and variations over this past decade, however, it is the constancy of family and friends that has most sustained me, spanning south and north, from Sarasota, Florida, to Muskoka, Ontario. In Canada, I thank in particular Becky, Steve, Avery, Josh, and Rachel; Syd and Lily; and lifelong friends Andrew, Brad, James, Matt, Matthew, and Richard. I write also in memory of John Ferrari, who will be immeasurably missed. In Florida, I thank Shelley and Mike; Jerry and Peri; the entire Stein family, especially Dan; as well as the gracious community at St. Simon the Tanner Coptic Orthodox Church. It has been my own parents, Pam and Ed, who have been most impactful throughout my life; it is they who not only guided my earliest years and aspirations, but also supported my most recent steps toward completing this latest book, stretching from Jekyll's Atlantic shores to a small sandy beach on Alport Bay.

Finally, *Jefferson's Muslim Fugitives* is dedicated to the three people who have taken each of the steps charted above right alongside me. My brilliant wife, Hillary, and our beloved little ones, Ezra and Eve, are not only my perpetual sources of joy, but also my partners in the many treks that gave rise to *Jefferson's Muslim Fugitives*. In writing this book—a book based in unexpected finds and a yearning to return—it has been Hillary, Ezra, and Eve who have gifted me inexhaustible moments of wonder and the perennial promise of homecoming.

1

"A Matter of Momentous Importance"

On October 3, 1807, Thomas Jefferson's evening at the President's House was interrupted by the arrival of a cryptic note. Scribbled by a traveler from the "Territory of Louisiana," this note was a single-page petition, pleading with the president for just one thing: "an interview." I have "a matter of momentous importance to communicate," the author insisted, but added no details. At its end, the note was signed with a name unknown to the president: "I. Nash."[1]

The evening of October 3, 1807, marked the end to a long day for Jefferson—a day that had begun on the road. That morning, the president had awoken at Songster's tavern, more than twenty miles from Washington, facing the last day of his return trip from Monticello, his beloved "little mountain" home in the Virginian woods.[2] This four-day journey back to the President's House had proved more arduous, even dangerous, than expected. It was "not as free from accident as usual," as Jefferson informed his eldest daughter, Martha. On the way back to Washington, Jefferson's horse, Castor, had almost drowned in the Rapidan River. The aging animal was barely saved by the president's "servants," who braved the waters to cut the horse loose from the carriage before he was swept under. To top it all off, Jefferson had lost his "travelling money" somewhere on the way, too.[3]

Jefferson reached the President's House before noon on Saturday, October 3.[4] Any attempt to return to Washington routines, however, would be disrupted before the day was done. It had been more than two months since Jefferson had slept in his bed at the President's House; but Jefferson did not even have the chance to settle in for the night before Nash's unsettling request had arrived. A devotee of clarity and order, Jefferson had every reason to be disquieted by Nash's enigmatic note, which raised many questions. Who was this traveler—and why did he seem reluctant to write down the "matter" he wished to "communicate" in person to the president? Also troubling was the traveler's origins in "Louisiana," a vast "Territory" purchased by America four years earlier at immense cost and controversy—a largely uncharted US space whose recent upheavals had cost Jefferson sleepless nights. By the time

Jefferson opened Nash's note, night was closing in, and Saturday would soon tick over to Sunday, October 4. And yet, no Sabbath rest would be in store for Jefferson this Sunday. The mysteries of Nash's note were simply too much for the president. Not long after reading the message he received, Jefferson decided to grant the traveler's request.[5]

Ira P. Nash arrived for his desired "interview," and his note's single promise proved true; he certainly did have an urgent and significant "matter" to "communicate." Unfortunately, if Jefferson had hoped to settle matters by meeting this traveler from the "Territory of Louisiana," he would be disappointed. Jefferson had not solved a mystery by granting Nash his interview, but uncovered a whole new series of puzzles. By the evening of October 4, 1807, Jefferson held in his hands strange writings carried to him from the country's edges. Nash's "matter of momentous importance to communicate" turned out to be two manuscripts—a pair of encoded communiqués written in coiled lines, and delivered to Jefferson from deep in the American interior (Figure 1).

Astonishingly, the two pages that Jefferson held on October 4, 1807, were authored by two enslaved Africans, resisting their captivity in rural Kentucky. To receive writings by an American slave in 1807 was exceptionally rare; these writings handed to Jefferson were doubly intriguing, as he was unable to read them. Penned by literate slaves seeking emancipation, the manuscripts conveyed to Jefferson from the far West were composed entirely in Middle Eastern letters. Peering down at two pages produced in America but illegible to its president, Jefferson scanned documents in a language that he could not decipher, but which he recognized all too well. Authored by enslaved Africans held in US captivity, the pages Jefferson scrutinized were written not in English, but wholly in Arabic.

≈

Nothing extraordinary was supposed to happen to Jefferson during the first days of October 1807—and, according to the countless Jefferson biographies and presidential histories so far written, nothing extraordinary *did* happen.

A midpoint in Jefferson's second term, the opening to October 1807 is typically overlooked, seeming a brief calm amid the "Impressment Crisis" sparked earlier in the summer. On June 22, the British vessel HMS *Leopard* had attacked an American frigate, the USS *Chesapeake*, off the coast of Virginia. Suspecting that sailors on the *Chesapeake* were British deserters,

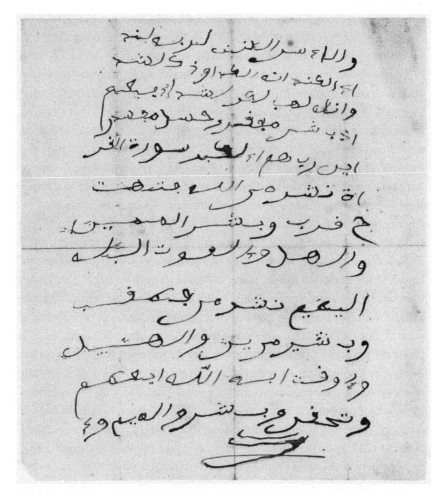

Figure 1 One of the two Arabic manuscripts delivered to President Thomas Jefferson in 1807, authored by fugitive Africans captured in Kentucky. Never before published, this image—reproducing "Page written in Arabic [October 1807]," Coolidge Collection of Thomas Jefferson Manuscripts, Massachusetts Historical Society—appears courtesy of the Massachusetts Historical Society, Boston.

the *Leopard* first bombarded the American ship and then boarded it. Killing three of the US crew, the British seized four other sailors, "impressing" them into royal service.[6] News of the "Chesapeake Affair" soon spread, provoking calls for retaliation from current Congressmen, and eliciting more nuanced responses from former US leaders. The previous president John Adams, still estranged from Jefferson after their bitter election battle in 1800, likened British impressment of deserters to the pursuit of fugitive slaves. From his unhappy retirement in Massachusetts, Adams wrote to Benjamin Rush, highlighting the hypocrisy of American outrage, noting that "our People have Such a Predilection for Runaways of ever[y] description except Runaway Negroes."[7] The current president was infuriated too, of course. But a rash response suited neither Jefferson's high office nor his cool temperament. More muted and moderate, Jefferson struck back at Britain with economic sanctions, leading to Congress's "Embargo Act," which was passed on December 22, 1807, exactly six months after the attack on the *Chesapeake*. Biding his time in between summer's open hostilities and this congressional action at Christmas, Jefferson soothed tensions at home, while seeking an apology from abroad, demanding the British admit their unjust "acts of aggression."[8]

As Jefferson pursued political solutions and slow diplomacy, October 1807 began. Often neglected by biographers as an empty interval, this month's first days saw Jefferson return from Monticello, arriving in Washington, where he would "wai[t] for a response to the protest he sent to England," in Garry Wills's words.[9] But October 1807 was no vacation nor vacuum for Jefferson. The president *did* wait in Washington for an answer from the British crown; but, instead, an entirely unexpected message arrived, which has stayed hidden for over two centuries. Sent not from a king across the ocean, the "momentous" manuscripts put into Jefferson's hands on October 4 were inscribed by Muslim slaves in America. Publicly, Jefferson sought to protect US freedoms in the autumn of 1807, ensuring US sailors were no longer detained as British deserters. Privately, at the same time, he received writings from African "runaways" wrested from their own country. While pleading with Britain to halt "impressment" of US citizens, the president was solicited by two men impressed into US slavery, who were, as Jefferson would later admit, "confined, on suspicion, merely because they cannot make known who they are."[10]

It was not the issue of "impressment" alone that made these appeals from captives in Kentucky seem especially resonant in October 1807. Also relevant to Jefferson was the authors' religious and regional origins: Islam and Africa. The first half of Jefferson's presidency had been plagued by military clashes with Muslim Africans, warring not with the British, but with the "Barbary Coast." Entering office in 1801, Jefferson prosecuted a four-year war against Muslim "pirates," combating Tripoli and Algiers, seeking to stop the plunder of American ships and capture of American sailors. The very ship at the crux of the 1807 crisis—the *Chesapeake*—had seen early service in North African waters, and was returning to patrol this same region when it was attacked by the British *Leopard*. Even the president's options for retaliation against the British were restricted by commitments on the Barbary Coast, with much of America's small navy still stationed in the Mediterranean.[11]

Such overlaps—between the national news in 1807, and the president's private receipt of writings from captive Muslims—must have been obvious to Thomas Jefferson during the first weekend of October 1807. As the president peered down at the two documents delivered by Ira P. Nash, however, a final overlap lay unrecognized. Unknown to Jefferson, these Arabic documents, like the "Chesapeake Affair" itself, owed their origins to an audacious act of navigation, undertaken during the spring of 1807. In March, as the *Chesapeake* was refitted for its mission to Muslim North Africa, the British voiced objections to this US ship's manifest, insisting that the frigate was carrying deserters. Despite warnings, James Barron took command of the *Chesapeake* in May 1807, beginning an "ill-starred" voyage that ended on June 22, when his ship soon succumbed to a broadside British attack, suffering injuries, deaths, and capture of crewmen.[12] At the same time, a very different crew piloted US waterways, braving the evident risk of attack and capture. Embarking not from the coast with fanfare, this two-man troop instead trekked furtively alongside tributaries far in the American interior. Following the sinuous bends of the Cumberland River, a pair of Muslim fugitives covertly skirted invisible borders demarcating newly born states. Driving in the opposite direction of the Cumberland's westward currents, the West Africans strove toward the sunrise, pushing slowly eastward, inching closer to the same ocean whose waters had carried them to this land of their bondage. Long before they neared Atlantic shores, however, their daring run was intercepted. Spotted by Kentuckians whose homes sparsely dotted the Cumberland River, these two anonymous Muslims were "taken up", most likely by the end of "the month of May."[13] Failing to elude the eyes of the locals, these West Africans would soon rise to the notice of the nation's capital, with news of their improbable flight, and the Arabic manuscripts inscribed by their shackled hands, carried to President Jefferson himself, ultimately reaching him five months later, during the first weekend of October 1807.

≈

Of all the moments in Jefferson's career, how could this particular moment—his receipt of Muslim slave writings—have been lost to history? Of all the pages held by America's third president, how could these two pages—authored in Arabic by fugitive West Africans—have stayed submerged for more than two centuries?[14]

It seems that every story involving Jefferson has already been told. Long before his death in 1826, Jefferson was recognized as a historic figure, celebrated as foremost among the American founders. As early as 1809, Jefferson was labeled "the first Citizen of this great Republick."[15] Even before he became the nation's first secretary of state in 1790, its second vice president in 1796, and its third president in 1801, Jefferson had forever secured his fame, authoring the Declaration of Independence in 1776. Comprehensive biographies of Jefferson abound. But so do studies dedicated to specific topics, dissecting nearly all details of Jefferson's life, from his political achievements to affairs much more intimate. "[T]here are books on every aspect of Jefferson['s] life," as John B. Boles has recently noted.[16] Jefferson's ambivalent attitudes toward race and slavery have been extensively covered, including, most infamously, the president's relationship with Sally Hemings, and reputed paternity of her children.[17] Considering Jefferson's formative role in founding the country, and his fraught stance toward American slavery, how could we forget his ownership of actual writings authored by African captives?

Such a question seems even more urgent when we consider not only the race, but the religion, of the authors whose writings reached Jefferson in 1807. The documents delivered to the US president in early October were written not only by West Africans, but by West Africans professing Islam as their religion and in the language most sacred to Islam: Arabic. Conveyed to America's "first Citizen," the words that reached Jefferson were, in fact, written in the very same Arabic dialect that first conveyed the message of Islam itself. In seventh-century Mecca and Medina, the Qur'an was revealed to the Prophet Muhammad, and publicly proclaimed to humanity. Twelve hundred years later, Qur'anic Arabic again surfaces in Kentucky, inscribed by Muslim slaves and conveyed hundreds of miles to a single man. Islam was, moreover, a topic of profound interest and deep anxiety in Jefferson's America. Anticipating the first years of the twenty-first century, the first years of the nineteenth century were occupied by US conflicts in the Muslim world. And yet, despite Islam's urgent relevance to American history—bridging 1801 and 2001, from Jefferson's presidency to 9/11—his receipt of these Muslim manuscripts, written in the Qur'an's own original Arabic, has been entirely overlooked by historians.

This neglect is especially surprising in light of the ample attention that has recently been dedicated to Jefferson and Islam, catalyzed by his early acquisition of a single book. At the beginning of another October, precisely forty-two years before Ira P. Nash reached Washington, Jefferson was still a British subject and a mere law student, enrolled at the College of William and Mary. On October 5, 1765, the twenty-two-year-old Jefferson visited his local bookseller in Williamsburg, Virginia, where he picked up a generic English translation of the Muslim scripture.[18] Entitled *The Koran, commonly called the Alcoran of Mohammed*, it was produced by a fellow lawyer in Britain, named George Sale. More important, Sale's *Koran* was the most widely available edition of the Muslim scripture in the Western world, an extremely popular rendition, remaining relevant right up to the early 1900s. Although it was entirely unexceptional at the time, Jefferson's early acquisition of *The Koran* has attracted lavish coverage by prominent sources in the twenty-first century. Reported in outlets from the *Washington Post* to *Fox News*, Jefferson's *Koran* gained traction due primarily to Keith Ellison, a Muslim congressman from Minnesota, who chose Jefferson's copy for his 2007 swearing-in ceremony.[19] Sparking commentary and criticism, Ellison helped Jefferson's *Koran* gain wide exposure, informing most recently the title of Denise Spellberg's substantial 2013 study, *Thomas Jefferson's Qur'an: Islam and the Founders*.[20] And yet, despite all the attention inspired by Jefferson's "common" copy of the *Koran*—an English edition owned by countless other book lovers in early America—the authentic and unique Muslim manuscripts that Jefferson received from fugitive slaves, written in Qur'anic Arabic, have remained entirely unknown.

For the very first time, *Jefferson's Muslim Fugitives* tells the lost story surrounding the president's private receipt of Arabic writings authored by West African Muslims fleeing their captivity in Kentucky—and suggests why such a story of "momentous importance" has remained stubbornly silent for over two centuries.

≈

One reason such a remarkable story could remain untold is its implausibility: who would believe such a thing? The idea of Thomas Jefferson receiving Arabic writings by enslaved Muslims in America sounds close to incredible. The conditions and coincidences necessary for such a story seem difficult to accept. How could two Muslim fugitives find themselves on the American frontier in 1807, without the means of making known who they were or how they got there? And, what are the chances that these same enslaved men were able to author Arabic, writing documents to be carried hundreds of miles eastward, ascending to the highest halls of US power and handed to the American president himself?

The arrival of Arabic manuscripts to Thomas Jefferson in 1807 does seem to verge on the impossible—or, at least, it seems so now. This implausibility has been exaggerated by the lapse of time. Amplified by the two centuries that have intervened, the story's unlikelihood is partly due to our own historical distance, and especially, to a single fact now largely forgotten. Millions of Africans were enslaved in the United States, and of these, many "thousands" or even "tens of thousands" were Muslim.[21] According to a recent estimate, anywhere "between less than five and up to twenty percent of the imported slaves" confessed Islam as their religion.[22] Arriving via the Atlantic slave trade to US soil, innumerable Muslims were enslaved in Jefferson's America, carrying with them not only religious convictions, but frequently a capacity to read and write. Trained in home traditions and texts, many Muslim slaves in the United States were literate, skilled in Islam's language of prayer and piety: Arabic.

Although enslaved Africans in the United States are not commonly thought of as Muslim, this fact should not come as a surprise. Africa's religious demographics, and the regions from which slaves were taken, make Muslims in early America seem not only possible, but inevitable. Islam gained a foothold in Africa during the same seventh century that the religion was first proclaimed in Arabia. Eventually supplanting Christianity in North Africa, Islam also took hold further south, advancing into sub-Saharan Africa along both coasts of the continent. By the time the African slave trade reached its horrifying peak in the eighteenth century, centers of Islamic concentration and culture were very well established in West Africa. Especially prominent in the early eighteenth century was Futa Jallon—an "Imamate" located in the mountainous regions of modern Guinea from which many of the Muslim slaves in America would come.[23]

Despite their numbers, and despite recent attempts to recover their Arabic writings, the presence of Muslim slaves in early America is still not widely known. And it might seem reasonable to assume that this was always the case. If America's Muslim slaves are rarely recognized in the twenty-first century, surely they were equally unknown in the nineteenth century, when historical hindsight was impossible. This assumption seems to be shared by many Jefferson scholars, even those interested in precisely these topics. As recently as 2013, in her *Thomas Jefferson's Qur'an*, Spellberg helpfully highlights the presence of Muslim slaves in early America, but also assumes Jefferson's own ignorance of this fact. Not only missing the president's personal receipt of Arabic writings by African fugitives, Spellberg implies that Jefferson was himself unaware that Muslims were enslaved in the United States. "The first American Muslims remained invisible" to Jefferson, Spellberg suggests.[24] The story uncovered by *Jefferson's Muslim Fugitives* shows that Muslim slave "invisibility" evaporated for Jefferson in October 1807, erased by the Washington arrival of an unknown traveler who delivered into the president's hands tangible evidence in Arabic.

This myth of "invisibility" has shielded another fact that is just as startling. Jefferson's encounter with enslaved Arabic authors may have been exceptional, but it was not unique. During the very decades that surrounded his 1807 receipt, Jefferson himself was surrounded with friends and fellow US leaders who were also acquiring manuscripts by enslaved Muslims in America. Although Jefferson was the lone recipient of Nash's Arabic delivery from Muslims enslaved in Kentucky, Jefferson was not at all alone in this type of experience. The careers of prominent politicians and professors in Jefferson's circle were also touched by surprising encounters with West Africans who were literate in Arabic. *Jefferson's Muslim Fugitives* uncovers not only the Arabic writings delivered to Jefferson, but equally historic documents hidden on the margins of his life, including a previously unseen manuscript from 1780s Georgia, which I identify as the earliest surviving instance of Arabic slave writings in the newly formed United States.[25]

This book reveals Jefferson's own receipt of Muslim slave writings; but it also tells a story that situates America's third president at the center of a forgotten tradition of literary exchange, linking Muslim slaves and the US elite. Bridging generations, while encircling all corners of the young country, this tradition spans America's rural West and urban East, stretching from Savannah in the south to New Haven in the north. Rooted in Revolutionary America, these exchanges with Muslim slaves quietly unfold up to the Civil War, echoing faintly during the decades that follow Jefferson's death, even haunting the steps of another iconic president as he ascended a stage in Pennsylvania, preparing to deliver his short eulogy over fresh graves at Gettysburg.

≈

In the first days of October 1807, Jefferson gazed down at two pages handed to him by Ira P. Nash, delivered from the edges of America—two documents that raised innumerable questions. How did two African Muslims become fugitives so far in the American interior? Who were these anonymous slaves, seeking their liberty through literal escape and literary act? What did these Arabic writings actually say? Most of all, what should Jefferson do?

The president was unable to answer any of these questions on October 4. And yet, as he scanned these foreign pages, blankly staring at strange markings twisting from right to left, an eerie sense of the familiar would inevitably have arisen. This was not the first time that Jefferson had received lines of unintelligible Arabic tangled up with American liberties. To the president, the documents delivered by Nash seemed unreadable; but the issues and identities they implied were entirely recognizable. The very ingredients that made these documents seem so alien were precisely those that made them most relevant to Jefferson. Twinning US slavery and African Islam, Muslim captivity and covert communiqués, fugitives seeking freedom and illegible Arabic letters, these manuscripts confronted Jefferson with elements intimately bound up with his own biography.

Presenting Thomas Jefferson with two manuscripts, Nash witnessed a seemingly unprecedented moment—the first moment that a US president handled Arabic slave writings. But for Jefferson, this moment in early October 1807 claimed precedents deeply rooted in his career, reaching back to the very years that followed his country's violent birth. As he received these inscrutable writings in the autumn of 1807—authored by fugitives seeking freedom, linking Islam and America—Jefferson may have been struck with an uncanny sense of déjà vu. Twenty-two years earlier, it was during the first autumn days of 1785 that Jefferson had initially read writings that wove together secrecy, slavery, and Islam. Occupying a much lower public position in a more impressive nation's capital, Jefferson opened in 1785 a petition from a captive in Muslim Africa, even as he himself was being captivated by the ineffable beauties of a European city on the brink of bloody revolt.

2

"Beyond Oure Expressing"

Paris seemed a city tailored to the tastes of Thomas Jefferson. Ambassador from the world's newest nation, Jefferson had arrived to this Old World capital in August 1784. A full year later, in the autumn of 1785, Paris still appeared inexhaustible and inexpressible. "You are perhaps curious to know how this new scene has struck a savage of the mountains of America," Jefferson wrote home in September 1785, "were I to proceed to tell you how much I enjoy their architecture, sculpture, painting, music, I should want words. It is in these arts they shine." Marveling at aesthetics, Jefferson was less impressed by the city's erotic "intrigues"; Paris was a place where "all our bad passions" are "invigorate[d]," Jefferson confessed to his friend back in Virginia.[1] And yet, if made anxious by low morals, Paris's sublime arts remained irresistible—and ineffable. It was not only the "shine" of Paris that stole Jefferson's speech, however, but its lively streets and salons. Author of the Declaration of Independence, famed for his elegant English, Jefferson was clumsy in French, even after a year of struggling with the language. This "savage of the mountains of America" found himself frequently silenced by Paris's urban din.[2]

Ironically, this same month a letter arrived to Paris posted from another American abroad, whose remote experiences faintly recalled Jefferson's own. Just a week before writing home to Virginia, confessing his "want" of "words," awed by French arts, Jefferson opened a letter that also emphasized the inexpressible, introduced with the following lines:

> We the Subjects of the United States of America Having the Misfortune of Being Captured off The Coast of Portugal the 24th. and 30th. of July By the Algerines, and Brought into this port Where we have Become Slaves, and Sent To the workhouses, Oure Sufferings is Beyond Oure Expressing or your Conception.[3]

In this breathless first sentence, Jefferson learned of another American life that was unfolding in a capital city overseas—an American life in September

1784 that was ineffable in experience, "Beyond Oure Expressing." However, it was not luxuries and liberties in Europe, but "sufferings" and slavery in Africa, that left Jefferson's fellow American in "want" of "words." The above petition—which Jefferson opened on September 24, 1785—was sent from Richard O'Brien, a prisoner in Algiers. Captain of a mercantile ship out of Philadelphia, O'Brien and his crew had been captured by Algerian pirates in the summer of 1785 and brought back to "the Barbary Coast."[4] Pleading for help, O'Brien wrote these first words to Jefferson even as he endured slavery in Muslim lands, begging for emancipation from African "workhouses."

In the autumn of 1785, Richard O'Brien was a name wholly new to Jefferson. For O'Brien, Jefferson was entirely familiar, and already long associated with capture, conflict, and escape from America's enemies. Born in Maine into an Irish family, O'Brien would eventually adopt Philadelphia as his home—the same city where Jefferson also arrived in 1775 to attend the Second Continental Congress. The War of Independence that escalated after Jefferson's famed Declaration in 1776 saw O'Brien enlist in the patriot cause, assigned as lieutenant to a Virginian brig, coincidentally named the *Jefferson*. O'Brien was on board the *Jefferson* in the spring of 1781 when it was "capturd & burnt" by the British, finding refuge in Richmond, arriving to the city just in time to spot the state's governor—Thomas Jefferson.[5] Forced to flee the *Jefferson* in flames, O'Brien had reached Richmond in the months following Jefferson's own return, after his supposed "abandonment" of the city during a raid by Benedict Arnold in January. Many years later, amid public controversy, O'Brien would recall his glimpse of Jefferson in Richmond's streets. In January 1781, Jefferson faced accusations of "timidly abandon[ing] the seat of government during Arnold's invasion"; in response, O'Brien sought to mitigate Jefferson's humiliation, attesting that the governor had returned to oversee the city in the spring, testifying that Jefferson had stood solid while in Richmond, "continu[ing] upon the spot during the whole Scene."[6]

Four years after fleeing the *Jefferson* only to glimpse another recent fugitive in Richmond, Thomas Jefferson himself, one name naturally occurred to O'Brien as he sought to escape America's new enemy. Jefferson was an obvious choice; and yet, he was also an ironic one. As an American slave in North Africa, O'Brien decided to seek aid from an American famed for his conflicted stance toward African slavery. On this issue, Jefferson was a notorious contradiction. As early as his first published work in 1774, his *Summary View of the Rights of British America*, Jefferson had advocated for "the abolition of slavery"—an advocacy that he extended at the Second Continental Congress in Philadelphia in 1775.[7] A decade later, when O'Brien's letter reached him in Paris, Jefferson's stance against slavery was still the same, although publicly rarely expressed. From Paris, Jefferson found himself in no position to influence slavery's future back home. Living abroad during the very years that America's "peculiar institution" was enshrined in law, Jefferson was out of the picture even as the US Constitution was framed during the latter half of the 1780s. In September 1785, Jefferson opened a letter from Africa, authored by an abject slave from Philadelphia, which started with the solemn words "We the Subjects of the United States." At the very same time, back home in Philadelphia, a convention was in the works that would generate the US Constitution—a Constitution whose preamble would open similarly, "We the People of the United States," and yet also affirm African slavery as an American right.[8]

In 1785, Jefferson still believed that American slavery should end. And yet, this consistent public position only made his private inconsistencies more disquieting. For Jefferson, slavery was a legal abstraction to abhor; but it was also the institution to which he was born, and which he embraced as an adult. Beginning life at Shadwell, a plantation owned by his father, Peter Jefferson, young Thomas was surrounded by slaves during his boyhood; and, at his father's death in 1757, Jefferson inherited not only Shadwell, but "fifty-two slaves" from his father.[9] By the time Jefferson departed for Paris, his own household at Monticello was sustained by "some two hundred slaves."[10] In 1784, Jefferson crossed the Atlantic *en famille*, accompanied by Martha, his elder daughter and the namesake of his deceased wife. Sailing eastward to Europe, Jefferson left behind his other daughter, Mary, but also captive men, women, and children at his Virginian home—families whose own forebears had once survived an Atlantic crossing, journeying westward to America, where their descendants would be born into bondage at Monticello.

The contradiction between Jefferson's public rejection of African slavery and his private reliance on African slaves made the letter he opened in September 1785 seem especially relevant. "Oure Sufferings is Beyond Oure Expressing or your Conception," O'Brien clumsily cries out in his introduction, appealing to America's ambassador in Paris who himself was at a loss for words. Echoing views held by Jefferson himself, emphasizing slavery's injustice and its inexpressible pain, O'Brien's letter likely touched rather close to home. Even as he read these words from an American slave in Muslim lands, Jefferson's own slaves from Monticello were never far from his mind.

Although muted in Paris, overawed by its foreign arts and expressions, Jefferson yet enjoyed some familiar company in France, and was considering additions to his little household abroad. His youngest daughter, Mary—known as Polly—would eventually join him and Martha in Paris, accompanied by a certain slave from Monticello. In 1787, Polly finally arrived, assisted by a fourteen-year-old named Sally—a slave now synonymous with Jefferson, as well as with secrecies of "Conception" that evaded his own "Expressing." Despite rumors that plagued him throughout his life and long after, Jefferson himself would always stay silent regarding the relationship begun with Sally Hemings during their time together in Paris.[11]

≈

I have received an application from the Directors of the public buildings to procure them a plan for their Capitol. I shall send them one taken from the best morsel of antient architecture now remaining.

Thomas Jefferson to James Madison
September 1, 1785[12]

O'Brien's urgent petition was not the only "application" reviewed by Jefferson in the autumn of 1785. Jefferson also received another request during this same season—not from Algeria, but from America. Three weeks before O'Brien's plea from African "workhouses" arrived, Jefferson wrote the above words to James Madison, responding to a request from Virginia, seeking help to design a new house for political work. Although living in Paris, Jefferson had been solicited to supply a "plan" for the new "Capitol" to be built in Richmond.

Jefferson was a prime candidate to assist Virginia's "Directors of the public buildings," despite his being so far from home. Jefferson was a literary architect, of course; he had fashioned American freedoms in his Declaration of Independence. But Jefferson was also a literal architect, an amateur of design, charting structures and spaces since his boyhood. Following in the footsteps of his father—Peter Jefferson had been a map-maker and surveyor—the young Thomas inherited talents for drafting and drawing, exposed to these arts from his earliest years.[13] As his own gifts matured, Jefferson turned them to domestic benefit, building and rebuilding his own home, Monticello, while also pursuing more "public" projects as well. In nearby Washington, Jefferson would eventually help renovate another residence—the president's—with his contributions still evident on the present-day White House.[14] And, in 1785, it was Jefferson's distance from home that ironically helped qualify him to sketch a new Capitol for Virginia. Jefferson was stationed in a city of stunning "arts" and "architecture," after all; listing Parisian beauties, Jefferson had prioritized its buildings, mentioning first the city's structures even before its "sculpture, painting [and] music." France had offered Jefferson ample models for American imitation, as he hinted to James Madison on September 1; and, for Richmond's newest structure, Jefferson promised to supply "the best morsel of antient architecture."

Jefferson fulfilled his pledge, but he would make Madison wait several more months. Amid his regular duties as European ambassador, as well as less expected anxieties arising from North Africa, the autumn of 1785 afforded Jefferson little time for sketching. Jefferson would not send his Capitol schematics to Madison until January, and by then, it seemed too late. Another Capitol design was already moving forward in Virginia. But his plan was superior, Jefferson argued, and should supplant "the plan begun on":

> À propos of the Capitol, do my dear friend exert yourself to get the plan begun on set aside, & that adopted which was drawn here. It was taken from a model which has been the admiration of 16 centuries, which has been the object of as many pilgrimages as the tomb of Mahomet; which will give unrivalled honour to our State, and furnish a model whereon to form the taste of our young men.[15]

Advocating his own "model," Jefferson accents its long lineage and sacred pedigree. Copied from the Maison Carrée—an ancient temple in the south of France with Roman roots—Jefferson boasts that his design had already enjoyed "the admiration of 16 centuries." Jefferson's confidence was justified; his design, which Virginia would indeed adopt, became an American precedent, with Jefferson's "Capitol" qualifying as "the first Western Hemisphere public building constructed in the classical style."[16] And yet, although derived from European antiquity, it is an Islamic analogue that Jefferson oddly invokes to advertise his plans for an American "Capitol." Naming the Muslim Prophet himself, Jefferson markets his "model" by suggesting to Madison that it has attracted "as many pilgrimages as the tomb of Mahomet." Raising a new political center in America, Jefferson recalls the grave of Islam's own founder, seeking to endow Virginia's statehouse with the same sacred pull of Muslim "pilgrimage."

Jefferson's argument proved convincing, and construction of his plan soon moved forward. Richmond's Capitol was completed just before Jefferson's return home in 1789; it would long outlive its architect, while living up to the fame he forecasted. Embellished with an allusion to the Muslim Prophet, Jefferson's urgings had won Madison over; and, his prophecy concerning the Capitol's prominence would prove true, though ambiguous. Virginia's Capitol was quickly constructed, but only with the use of slave labor.[17] And this same Capitol would eventually play a pivotal role in American's conflict over slavery, serving as the political seat of the South through the Civil War. The Capitol designed by Thomas Jefferson in the 1780s would later house Jefferson Davis's Confederate government in the 1860s. Predicted to "give unrivalled honour to our State," this classical model built by US slaves would eventually host a Confederate "State"—a "rival" faction that divided America in two, split over the same issue that Jefferson was confronting in Algiers even as he drafted the Capitol's design.[18]

Unknown to Madison, Jefferson's architectural "plans" were not the only ones he was sketching in the autumn of 1785. In Paris, as he fashioned a historic American building likened to a Muslim sepulcher, Jefferson was also quietly grappling with how to save "Subjects of the United States" consigned to live and die as slaves in Muslim North Africa.

≈

I have received your letter and shall exert myself for you. Be assured of hearing from me soon: but say nothing to any body except what may be necessary to comfort your companions. I add no more, because the fate of this letter is incertain.

I am Sir Your very humble servant.
TH: JEFFERSON.[19]

For five full days after opening O'Brien's urgent appeal from Algiers, Jefferson made no response. Life in Paris had again placed him in a speechless situation. Clean lines and simple symmetries were Jefferson's joy, including those he would sketch for his state's Capitol, seeking to rival "the tomb of Mahomet." But, in confronting O'Brien's case, Jefferson faced only dizzying inversions and confused lines of communication. What could Jefferson, the

American master of African slaves, say to console O'Brien, an American enslaved in Muslim Africa?

After five days of delay, Jefferson generated only the five lines quoted above—lines that seem little more than deferral and delay. Dated September 29, 1785, Jefferson breaks his silence, but only to encourage O'Brien to stifle his own speech. Secrecy, not "sufferings," is Jefferson's top concern; "say nothing to any body," he urges O'Brien, "except what may be necessary to comfort your companions." The fate of the American slaves seemed secondary to Jefferson's worry for "the fate of this letter," suffering anxiety for the safety of his own words. With painful irony, Jefferson ends his note by signing himself as "your very humble servant"—a conventional valediction that situates America's "minister plenipotentiary" as a powerless subordinate, in this case, while addressing an American in actual servitude in Muslim lands.

Although pointed and succinct, this five-line letter also proved predictive, not merely for what it says, but what is left unsaid. Anticipating moments later in his life, these short lines mark Jefferson's first written engagement with slavery in Muslim Africa—an engagement aptly framed by discretion and delay; silence and secrecy; intrigue and anxiety. Uneasy over the "incertain" fate of his own writing, Jefferson raises a concern that echoes throughout his career, even as Islam, Africa, and slavery repeatedly converge. But, for O'Brien, Jefferson's brisk letter would have offered cold "comfort." "Be assured of hearing from me soon" was Jefferson's single promise; and yet more than a month passed before Jefferson wrote again. In early November, Jefferson's next letter informed O'Brien of a lone emissary—John Lamb—who was dispatched from Paris to ransom O'Brien and his crew from Algerian captivity. Even in this meager effort, however, Jefferson had "no authority," he was forced to admit. Lamb's unlikely mission to save the "22. of our citizens in slavery," Jefferson confessed to O'Brien, was launched "without instruction from Congress," with no approval of funds for "redemption"; "each person" must "separately make himself answerable for his own redemption in case Congress requires it," Jefferson added.[20] Unsurprisingly, such tentative assistance was ineffective, and O'Brien's slavery in North Africa would stretch on well into the next decade. Year after slow year, O'Brien suffered in Muslim "workhouses," while witnessing many of his crewmates die in captivity.[21]

Jefferson had failed to free O'Brien. He had few words, and even less material aid, to offer this American slave in Muslim lands. And yet, Jefferson's silence forced O'Brien to rely on his own resources as he navigated his foreign captivity, listening attentively and learning all he could. Although perhaps heeding Jefferson's imperative to "say nothing to any body," O'Brien did, however, speak secretly to himself, scribbling in a private diary as his enslavement entered a new decade. Inscribed during his African incarceration, O'Brien's diary—now housed in Philadelphia—opens with the following first words, featured inside its front cover and autographed in his hand (Figure 2):

Richard OBryen his Book 1790, City of Algiers

Bismillah. In the Name of the Most Merciful God

Specifying the "city" of his captivity, these first lines of O'Brien's "Algiers" diary also emphasize identity and ownership. Himself a slave, O'Brien yet possesses at least this single item: "his Book." Opening with his own name, it is "the Name" of "God" that fills O'Brien's second line, invoking the divine as "Most Merciful," seeking heavenly compassion during earthly enslavement. Before this English phrase, however, O'Brien opens his second line with a word in a second language, naming the "merciful" Lord with a phrase he learned in cruel captivity. To begin his prayer, O'Brien inscribes "*Bismillah*"—a snippet of sacred Arabic that signifies "In the name of Allah." A formula, conventional and common, this same phrase opens every single chapter of the Qur'an, except one. Introducing his own intimate diary, O'Brien decides to use diction essential to Islam. At the head of his American chronicle of African captivity, O'Brien not

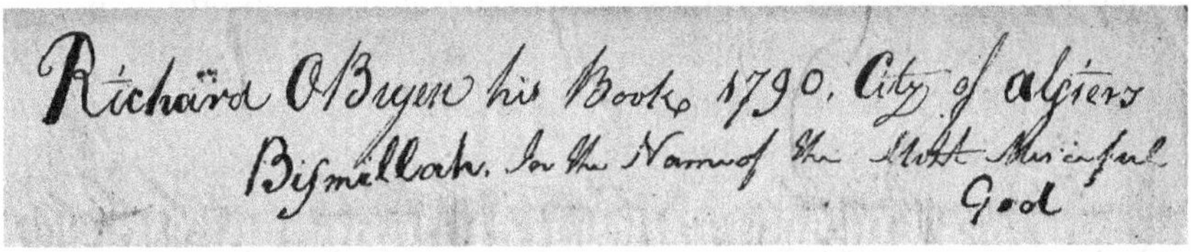

Figure 2   Penned on its inside front cover, these words form the opening to Richard O'Brien's diary, inscribed while suffering Algierian captivity in 1790. Image courtesy of the Historical Society of Pennsylvania. Material from this opening to O'Brien's 1790 diary has been previously quoted in part by Peskin (*Captives and Countrymen*, 31). Peskin does not, however, include O'Brien's transliterated Arabic (i.e., "*Bismillah*"), which opens the doxology that introduces all of the Qur'an's 114 chapters except Chapter 9 ("بسم الله," "In the name of Allah").

only writes in Arabic, but ensures that the first words of his private diary parallel Muslim prophecy.

Faced with the failure of his fellow Americans to free him, O'Brien not only endured a decade of captivity, but acclimatized to his surroundings, domesticating Islamic prayers within his own private diary. Jefferson's own incapacity to save O'Brien from bondage in Muslim lands indirectly helped bond O'Brien himself to Muslim expressions. O'Brien and his crewmates dispatched appeals for help from their very first days in captivity.[22] But, after years of receiving no mercy from home, O'Brien secretly turned to the "Most Merciful," invoking Allah with fragments from the Qur'an. No longer merely an American slave in Muslim Africa, O'Brien by 1790 had become an American bemoaning enslavement with Muslim idioms. After many years, O'Brien gained his freedom from enslavement, but would stay linked to the region, eventually serving as a lead US diplomat in North Africa. Garnering high public office abroad, at home O'Brien's two decades in Muslim lands gave rise to rumors of his Islamic assimilation. There were even reports that he had "conformed outwardly to the Mohammedan religion" while in North Africa. Jefferson's own friend, William Thornton—fellow architect, the designer of the US Capitol itself—made reference to O'Brien's supposed flirtation with Islam, bluntly labeling him in a later letter to Jefferson as "the Turk O'Brien."[23]

In 1785, despite his chilly words urging discretion, Jefferson was personally "haunted" by O'Brien and his crew's captivity.[24] Although America's "minister plenipotentiary," Jefferson found himself impotent in Paris, powerless to save a fellow American in Muslim captivity. And yet O'Brien's imprisonment would lead to outcomes not all negative for Jefferson. Many years later, when confronted by Arabic manuscripts authored by other slaves—slaves who had more authentic African roots and who also directed their prayers to Allah— Jefferson would find himself in need of help, and one name would naturally occur to him: Richard O'Brien.

≈

In the fall of 1785, Jefferson was failing to free an American slave in Muslim lands. At the very same time, however, he was winning the freedom for Americans to embrace Islam as their religion.

As October 1785 began, Jefferson's five-line note made its way to O'Brien, sent from Paris, urging silence in Algiers. As October 1785 ended, another document authored by Jefferson also advanced forward—a document marking a public victory in Virginia that Jefferson proudly trumpeted not only throughout his life but also at his death. On October 31, a bill was introduced by James Madison at the state's House of Delegates, guaranteeing religious freedom, allowing Virginians to choose their own church—or mosque. Debated and passed by the House on January 16, 1786, this bill was soon signed into law by another of Jefferson's friends, and his fellow revolutionary, Governor Patrick Henry. Known now as Virginia's "Statute for Religious Freedom," and originally drafted by Jefferson in 1777, this bill opens with the following preamble:

> Whereas, Almighty God hath created the mind free; That all attempts to influence it by temporal punishments or burthens, or by civil incapacitations tend only to beget habits of hypocrisy and meanness, and therefore are a departure from the plan of the Holy author of our religion, who being Lord, both of body and mind yet chose not to propagate it by coercions on either, as was in his Almighty power to do [. . .][25]

Linking divine "might" with the human "mind," Jefferson's statute argues for religious freedom by invoking God's own restraint, citing His refusal to control and "coerce." The "Almighty" has "power" over both "body and mind"; yet He does not "propagate" His "plan" with force. By analogy, Jefferson suggests, our creeds should not be "influenced" by civil authority; in religion, we ought to remain free from "temporal punishments or burthens."

Jefferson's statute has been justly celebrated as historic—a precedent not only for his home state, but for the whole United States. Debated in Virginia during the autumn of 1785, the bill that Jefferson drafted set a precedent for the First Amendment itself, ratified four years later to preclude any "law respecting an establishment of religion, or prohibiting the free exercise thereof."[26] For Jefferson, his original statute was not a negative "prohibition," however, but a positive "protection," covering not only Christians, but believers belonging to all sects. As is often noted, Jefferson later defined his statute as embracing "the Jew and the Gentile, the Christian and Mahometan, the Hindoo, and infidel of every denomination."[27] Aptly twinned in Jefferson's list are the two groups of religious adherents most at odds for him in 1785, during the same autumn that his statute advanced. In his legislation, "the Christian and Mahometan" are set in balance, even while, in private, Jefferson corresponded with an American oppressed in both "body and mind" in North Africa. In North America, however, Jefferson strove with success to release religious confessions from "coercion," legislating to place adherents of Christianity and Islam on the same footing, even as he witnessed a Philadelphian suffer captivity in "Mahometan" hands.

Jefferson's statute was drafted long before he left for Paris. It seems apt, however, that his bill waited for the autumn of 1785 to advance forward. James Madison spent this autumn expecting Jefferson's promised "plans," his sketch for Richmond's future Capitol predicted to rival "the tomb of Mahomet." At the same time, at Richmond's Old Capitol, Madison introduced Jefferson's new statute aligning "the Christian and Mahometan"—a statute that would be memorialized not on the Prophet's "tomb," but on Jefferson's own. Laying the groundwork for the First Amendment, Virginia's "Statute for Religious Freedom" also shadows the ground that marks Jefferson's final resting place. Pilgrims to Monticello find Jefferson's grave just west of his iconic house; featuring a five-line inscription that celebrates Jefferson's life, his grave cites just three accomplishments, his epitaph reading simply:

> Here was buried
> Thomas Jefferson
> Author of the Declaration of American Independence
> of the Statute of Virginia for religious freedom
> & Father of the University of Virginia.[28]

Although Jefferson's 1785 "Statute" invokes God as "the Holy author," his own grave names Jefferson as "Author," both of his "Declaration" and "the Statute of Virginia." As frequently noted, this memorial curiously passes over his presidency, Jefferson deliberately leaving aside his leadership of the United States, accenting instead acts of authorship and education tied to discrete freedoms: political, spiritual, intellectual. Unnoticed previously, however, is that this memorial also forgets more fraught tensions and failed hopes that linger at the margins of these three "testimonials." The middle term of his triad, Jefferson's "Statute" was lofty in public aspiration, seeking American religious liberties for all—including hypothetical "Mahometans" in Virginia. However, this "Statute" was established at the very time Jefferson was failing to free an American held by actual "Mahometans," a situation in which he urged O'Brien's silence. In the four decades that unfolded between

1786 and 1826—the year that "the Author" was himself laid in the ground under his epitaph—Jefferson's lofty aspiration to secure "Mahometan" liberties would again be tested, forcing the deceased to take to his grave another silent failure, proving unable to free actual Muslim authors enslaved in America.

3

"The Original Treaty in Arabic"

On January 16, 1786, Virginia's "Religious Freedom Act," first drafted by Jefferson, was passed by the state's General Assembly, despite early opposition voiced by Virginia's own governor: famed patriot Patrick Henry.[1] January 16, 1786, was also the date inscribed on another document—a letter addressed to Patrick Henry, which passed into Jefferson's hands in Paris. This letter's author was Thomas Barclay, but he had little time to post his own mail across the Atlantic, asking instead for Jefferson's aid, charging him with finding a "Conveyance" to bring Barclay's letter back to Virginia.[2] As America's consul in Paris, Thomas Barclay had served in France since 1781; in 1784, he had been in Paris to welcome the arrival of the nation's new minister plenipotentiary, Jefferson himself. But now Barclay was busily preparing to leave the city, departing on an overseas trip of his own. Before the end of January, Barclay would set sail from France in the opposite direction from his letter's destination, heading not westward to American shores, but eastward, toward the Barbary Coast.[3]

Jefferson was likely happy to play postman for Barclay. It was, after all, partly Jefferson's fault that his friend was in a rush, pursuing a sensitive mission in Muslim lands. A native of Philadelphia, Barclay was leaving for the same region where another Philadelphian was stuck in captivity: Richard O'Brien. Unlike O'Brien, however, North Africa held prospects of peace for Barclay, not imprisonment. Dispatched by Jefferson, Barclay was departing to secure a US treaty with Morocco, the nation often known as "America's oldest ally" in the Muslim world.[4] Confronting inverse conditions in North Africa, Barclay and O'Brien yet shared a critical link with Jefferson, and especially with his anxieties for secrecy. O'Brien's plight and Barclay's mission would both begin with Jefferson's efforts in Paris to hide his engagements with Muslim Africa. As always, the minister plenipotentiary was most worried for his own writings, fearing their potential exposure to enemy eyes.

≈

Paris Aug. 17. 1785.

I received yesterday your favor of the 7th· 1213.495.1203.770.'
339.912.1350. mr Short's of the 737.405. it 229.522.1214.970.840.706.
376.406.943.1548. therefore consider 392.820.620.' 162.629.' of 330.'
1090.810.' I write you a line at this moment merely to inform you that
1188.410.1570.1333.1053.1122. to 524.565.344.1533. the 401.401.592.481.
'1042.406.1356.1068.8.330.[5]

It was this letter that launched Barclay's mission to the Barbary Coast.
Written by Jefferson, and sent to London on August 17, 1785, this opening
seems not only elliptical, but illegible, a stream of mere digits and fragmented
diction lacking all mention of either Barclay or the Barbary Coast. And yet,
Jefferson's letter was entirely clear to its sole recipient—America's other "minister plenipotentiary" and another future US president: John Adams.

Both servants of their new nation in old Europe, Adams also shared with
Jefferson a private cipher—a key for encoding and decoding diplomatic correspondence, ensuring sensitive passages stayed secret. As a result, when
Adams opened this letter in London, it was not a jumble of integers that
he saw; instead, Adams read the following, finding Jefferson's introductory
words not only encased in code, but justifying the need for codes:

> I received yesterday your favor of the 7th· *this was 4 days later than* mr
> Short's of the *same date. it* *had evidently been opened. so we must* therefore
> consider *both govmts as possessed of it's contents.* I write you a line at this
> moment merely to inform you that *mr Barclay is willing to go* to *treat with*
> the *Barbary states if we desire it*[6]

When deciphered in London, Jefferson's first words proved to be a warning,
informing Adams that his last letter had "evidently" been "opened" on its
way from England. Delayed for "4 days"—arriving only after a letter from
Jefferson's confidant and secretary, William Short—Adams's correspondence was compromised by European intermediaries, Jefferson suggests,
prompting him to encode the above response. However, it was not European,
but North African affairs, that was Jefferson's concern, as he now wrote to
Adams in cipher. Barclay "is willing to go to treat with the Barbary states
if we desire it," Jefferson notifies Adams in covert numbers, encoding this
first mention of Barclay's acceptance of his mission to the Muslim world—a

mission that Adams himself soon approved, leading to Barclay's departure during the first weeks of 1786.[7]

Although new to espionage abroad, by 1785 Jefferson was already a veteran of writing in cipher. He had experimented with encoding his own correspondence even before leaving American shores, seeking to foil spies as early as 1783, in the months leading up to the Revolutionary War's formal cessation.[8] But it was "the Barbary states" that made Jefferson turn more earnestly to covert methods of communication. Trying to rescue O'Brien and recruit Barclay, Jefferson saw secrecy in Muslim lands as essential, with not only personal safety, but national security, at stake. And yet, little did Jefferson know that his encoded letter concerning Barclay would lead to illegible responses returned from Barclay back to Jefferson. Just one year later, it would be Jefferson who confronted an indecipherable document, staring at unreadable lines sent from North Africa—thin lines that defied his literacy, but which potentially upheld American peace.

As planned, Barclay departed at the end of January 1786, making his slow way to Morocco over the next few months. Meanwhile, Jefferson would make his own travel plans, accepting an invitation from John Adams to launch another negotiation with North Africa. In this diplomacy, however, Jefferson would not just delegate from afar. Instead, 1786 witnessed Jefferson negotiate in person with a Muslim power, traveling not to the Barbary Coast, but to the British Isles.

≈

Pappa dined with Lord Carmarthen Mr Humphrys and Mr Smith with us. At half after seven we set off again, and arrived before the Ball Room was open, which was an advantage as we could get in before the croud. At the door of the Ball room we met the Master of the Cerimonies, Mr Cottril, who was very polite and seated us in the Foreign Box. There was no person in it except the Tripolian, who I described in the Morning, the singularity of Whose appearance attracted the eyes of all the Ladies. There was a Gentleman who was an interpreter to him, for he speaks not a Word of English.

Abigail Adams, letter to her son, John Quincy
February 8, 1786[9]

For Jefferson, the sublime joys of Paris were ineffable—a feeling that Abigail Adams had slowly learned to share. Joining her husband John overseas in August 1784, Abigail came to appreciate Paris during their extended residence in the French capital. By April 1785, however, the couple had been called to London, receiving John Adams's appointment as American ambassador to the Court of St. James's. Abigail was sorry to say farewell to France in the springtime, and especially regretted the impending "loss of Mr. Jeffersons society," who had also arrived to Paris in August 1784.[10] However, by the time Abigail wrote the above from her new home in London—on February 8, 1786—England's capital city had proved more exotic than anticipated, offering Abigail experiences that also eluded her straightforward expression.

Writing home to her son in New England, Abigail offers this update to young John Quincy Adams, detailing his parents' life abroad. Describing "Pappa" as dining with a distinguished "Lord," Abigail proceeds to a more surprising encounter: meeting a man from the Barbary Coast in a London "Ball Room." For John Quincy back in Boston, his mother's portrait of this "Tripolian" was likely disconcerting; this Muslim had "attracted the eyes of *all* the Ladies," presumably including Abigail's own. Sharing intimate space, as well as diplomatic status, Abigail perhaps seems a little too eager to paint an alluring picture of Tripoli's "Ambassador," 'Abd ar-Raḥmān Aga—a man bearing an Arabic name that signifies "Slave of the Most Merciful" (*'Abd ar-Raḥmān*).[11] This African Muslim was not exotic merely to the eyes, Abigail notes, but also to the ears. Although an Ambassador to England, 'Abd ar-Raḥmān "speaks not a Word of English," Abigail emphasizes, meeting in this "Foreign Box" a dignitary whose dialogue is entirely foreign to her. Seated in close quarters, only an unnamed "interpreter" is able to break the tension and silence—an anonymous "Gentleman" who acts as a bridge between this African emissary and a future first lady of the United States.

Only one month after Abigail wrote to her son from London, Thomas Jefferson joined the Adamses in the city, drawn there partly by the same man who had "attracted the eyes of all the Ladies": Tripoli's ambassador, 'Abd ar-Raḥmān Aga. Landing in London on March 11, Jefferson stayed for more than six weeks in England—his Revolutionary foe—even as he sought to forestall America's next war, averting hostilities on the Barbary Coast.[12] Near the end of the month, Jefferson met with Tripoli's ambassador, a meeting recorded by John Adams, who had arranged their summit with the African emissary. To Abigail, 'Abd ar-Raḥmān had seemed alluring in his mysterious looks and language. For her husband, however, this Muslim envoy was no enigma, but an unmistakable threat. In his report to Congress, addressed to John Jay, Adams recalls that "[s]oon after the arrival of Mʳ Jefferson in London, We had a conference with the Ambassador of Tripoli, at His House"—a "conference" that opened with ʿAbd ar-Raḥmān demanding that America pay for "perpetual Peace" with Tripoli. Adams and Jefferson questioned the premise of this provocative demand: what were "the Grounds of [Tripoli's] pretentions to make War upon Nations who had done them no Injury"?[13]

It is the ambassador's stinging response to this question, as recorded by John Adams, that is now most remembered, cited by countless sources. Reportedly, ʿAbd ar-Raḥmān asserted that "War" against non-Muslims was scripturally sanctioned; plunder and piracy against infidels was "founded on the law of their great Profet."[14] Framing Islam not as a source of peace, but of perpetual conflict, the ambassador is quoted as justifying conquest and captivity, asserting "that it was written in the Koran, that all Nations who should not have acknowledged their [Tripoli's] Authority were sinners: that it was their right & duty to make war upon them wherever they could be found, & to make slaves of all they could take as prisoners." Justifying worldly profit by appealing to prophetic authority, ʿAbd ar-Raḥmān emerges as a fanatical extremist in Adams's report, endowed with none of the subtle "attraction" that Abigail had suggested—nor any of the language challenges she had accented either. To Congress, Adams supplied his unambiguous and alarming account of "the Koran," which is now typically quoted without question. Adams neglects to note, however, that ʿAbd ar-Raḥmān could not possibly have spoken any such sentiments without mediation. It was Abigail Adams herself who stressed that ʿAbd ar-Raḥmān was unable to utter "a Word of English"—a linguistic lack that forced him to negotiate via ad hoc interpreters, as Denise Spellberg has recently emphasized.[15] Adams, however, suppresses all mention of intermediaries in his report to Congress, placing this diatribe on "the Koran" directly into the mouth of the Muslim ambassador, citing beliefs that Adams could, at best, have received only second-hand. In her informal letter to John Quincy, Abigail had noted "the Tripolian" spoke by means of an unnamed "Gentleman"; in John Adams's official report, such a translator is not only kept anonymous, but altogether invisible.

Not softened by any deferral or doubt, Adams offers an account of ʿAbd ar-Raḥmān that seems wholly straightforward. But, if Abigail is to be believed, not one of these alarming English phrases was the ambassador's own, but represented Adams's written paraphrases from an unnamed interpreter who was charged with spontaneously relaying the ambassador's speech. Neglecting to mention this process of translation, Adams also ignores the English translation of the Tripolitan's own name—"Slave of the most Merciful" ('Abd ar-Raḥmān)—a name comically at odds with the words attributed to the ambassador. Seeming cruel as quoted in English, it is compassion that is expressed in the North African's Arabic identity. Hidden in plain sight, the Muslim name of 'Abd ar-Raḥmān mirrors another obvious incongruity in Adams's report. Writing home to John Jay, Adams protests North African imprisonment of US sailors, complaining of crimes that he links to "the law of their great Profet." And yet, the very crimes that Adams protests are precisely those endorsed by US law. The objections indignantly raised by Jefferson and Adams seem reasonable, of course, protesting the injustice inflicted on their "Nation" who had done "no Injury" to Tripoli. If this challenge appears solid, the moral standing of the challengers is shaky. Protesting to an African envoy named "Slave of the most Merciful," Adams and Jefferson defended a homeland where little mercy was offered to enslaved Africans, including countless US Muslims in captivity who bore similar Arabic names.

Writing his report to John Jay, Adams knew very well that his own country continued "to make slaves" at a rate far faster than any North African "Nation." However, another irony was implied in Adams's meeting with 'Abd ar-Raḥmān, which the American himself did not live long enough to realize. Described in terrifying terms by John Adams, the ambassador appeared much more "attractive" to Abigail as she wrote her son—her husband's namesake, John Quincy Adams. Four decades later, John Quincy would follow his father's example, meeting another African also named 'Abd ar-Raḥmān, engaging with this Muslim at yet another "conference" where America, Islam, and slavery proved to be intertwined. This meeting forty years in the future would not take place at a Muslim's "House" in a foreign capital, but at John Quincy's own residence in the American capital, the White House itself. Most important, this later Muslim hosted by the second President Adams would not merely bear the pious name "Slave of the most Merciful" but would himself be a former African slave, having endured actual captivity in America.

As they left the home of 'Abd ar-Raḥmān Aga, Jefferson and Adams carried frustrations, and little else, out into the London street. Their March meeting with Tripoli's Muslim envoy had proved less than useless. Before, peace with the Barbary Coast had at least seemed possible; now, the prospects of peace seemed slim. Adams's exasperation and anxiety bleed into the report he prepared for Congress, accenting "Musselman" aggression, while muting any complications potentially posed by translation. For his part, Jefferson remained mute altogether on this meeting, merely attaching his signature to Adams's report. Jefferson would not be able to stay a silent partner for much longer, however. Soon his autograph would be the very first required for another document, one more meaningful for America's future relations with Muslim Africa, and which was translated from an Arabic original that was anything but hidden.

≈

I do myself the honor to send you in a small Box the following Articles.

1. A Book containing the original Treaty in Arabic between the Emperor of Morocco and the United States.

2. Three translations of the Treaty in English [. . .][16]

Returning after his March meetings, Jefferson arrived home to Paris just days after his forty-third birthday on April 13, 1786. Jefferson was doubtlessly relieved to be back from Britain, but it was a cheerless beginning to his next year of life. He had left England empty-handed. By the end of the year, however, Jefferson would have his hands full. A very material success soon arrived from the Muslim mission he had initiated before leaving for London. The letter to Jefferson whose first words are quoted above came from a triumphant Thomas Barclay. Barclay had succeeded in Morocco; he had secured the desired treaty. Now, it was Jefferson's signature that was needed.

Barclay had accomplished his task with impressive speed. His trip to North Africa had taken longer than the actual time to secure the treaty. Leaving Paris in January 1786, Barclay did not arrive in Morocco until late June. By early October, an "Amicable Peace" was agreed with the Muslim "Emperor," who signed the treaty on the first day of Ramadan, the sacred season of Muslim fasting, marking the month in which the Qur'an was revealed.[17] Barclay was justifiably proud of his accomplishment; "I do myself the honor," he writes to Jefferson with a hint of self-congratulation as he sends his nation's first signed treaty with a Muslim power. If quickly acquired, the agreement Barclay was sending was not so simple. It was not a single treaty in a slim envelope, but several "Articles" in a complex container that had arrived to Paris. In his cover letter, Barclay directs Jefferson to "a small Box." Inside this box, Jefferson was to find a "Book." And inside this book was "the original Treaty"—a document, though, which was written "in Arabic," and thus still inaccessible to Jefferson. Finally, accompanying the treaty itself, Jefferson was to find multiple copies in "English," receiving no fewer than "[t]hree translations" of the treaty. Earlier that same year, Abigail Adams had met a Muslim African diplomat in a ballroom's "Foreign Box" but was unable to speak to him without an "interpreter." At the end of 1786, Jefferson found diplomacy from Muslim Africa buried in a "small box"; but again, direct access was impeded by the Arabic language. Translation would be required again to bridge the gap. Jefferson was offered the opportunity to touch the authentic and "original Treaty"; he was, however, unable to read it.

Even in his leisure hours, Jefferson only reluctantly relied on translations. When reading for pleasure, he still preferred to puzzle out "original" languages, ancient and modern, rather than trust another to translate for him.[18] In the text he received at the end of 1786, however, the stakes were higher. This was no poetical entertainment, no philosophical abstraction. Instead, the translation upon which Jefferson depended itself held in the balance real American lives and liberties. For example, in reading the translation provided by Barclay of "the original Treaty in Arabic," Jefferson found its sixth article rendered as follows:

> If any Moor shall bring Citizens of the United States or their Effects to His Majesty, the Citizens shall immediately be set at Liberty and the Effects restored, and in like Manner, if any Moor not a Subject of these Dominions shall make Prize of any of the Citizens of America or their Effects and bring them into any of the Ports of His Majesty, they shall be immediately released, as they will then be considered as under His Majesty's Protection.[19]

Seeking safeguards for US people and property, this article in 1786 champions the very freedoms abroad that Jefferson had prioritized at home a decade earlier, inscribed as part of his Declaration of 1776. And yet, this article also reflected much more recent anxieties experienced by Jefferson himself. Morocco's promise to "set at Liberty" US "Citizens" captured in North Africa mirrored back Jefferson's own inabilities to do the same, failing to rescue Richard O'Brien and his crew. Now, this article offered the prospects of freeing all Americans captured by "any Moor" brought to a Moroccan "Port." This would prove of little help to O'Brien himself, of course, who was stuck in Algiers; but how many other American crews could be saved from "Moorish" imprisonment if the Moroccans fulfilled their promise?

Jefferson was naturally eager to endorse such a treaty, with its articles pledging American liberties. And yet, one of its words—indeed, its very first noun, the word "Moor" itself—may have given him pause. Flexible in meaning, "Moor" seems a curious term in this context. Invoked to identify a people of "mixed Berber and Arab descent," "Moors" was often applied to Algerians, Moroccans, and Tunisians.[20] This word is, however, unmistakably Western in usage, implying stigmas of "foreign" religion and race. Although natural to an English translator, "Moor" is certainly not an Arabic term, nor an epithet that a North African would be likely to apply to himself. And yet, if reflecting Western translation rather than the "Treaty" itself, what did the North African "original" actually say? In December 1786, Jefferson possessed the very source that could answer such a question. Barclay had sent him a "small Box," within which was a "Book," which enclosed pages, one of which featured the authentic Article 6. But, even if he pierced these exteriors, Jefferson was unable to penetrate the final layer. The essential key he did not possess was the Arabic language itself, unable to decipher the "original" article that instead begins with the following:

مهما قبض المسلمون أهل جنسنا أو سلعتهم

وأتوا بهم لسيدنا نصره الله فإنه يسرح

Whenever the Muslims seize the people of our [American] nation, or their commodities, and bring them to our [Moroccan] Master—may Allah grant him victory!—he shall grant release[21]

If Jefferson had been able to read Arabic, he indeed would have found the word "Moor" entirely missing from the authoritative "original Treaty"; instead, the subject that starts Article 6 in Arabic is "the Muslims"—"المسلمون" ("al-Muslimūn"). Rather than promise safety from North African "Moors" merely, Morocco will save captive Americans from all those who confess Islam, the "original Treaty" promises. Perhaps most intriguing, however, the Arabic of Article 6 is written from two perspectives simultaneously, with the pronoun "our" oddly designating both Americans and Moroccans. In Arabic, the United States is named as "our nation"; immediately after, the Moroccan Sultan is heralded as "our Master"—a "Master" endowed with a Muslim benediction, blessed with Allah's "victory" entirely omitted in the English translation offered to Jefferson.[22] Incapable of reading the Arabic "Treaty," Jefferson's signature unwittingly endorsed an "original" agreement that guaranteed freedoms via a grammatical and godly synthesis, with America and Morocco merged in a first-person plural, together appealing to the singular Allah.

Although unable to detect any discrepancies in the treaty's translated words, Jefferson did, however, encounter a painful challenge in signing this document—a challenge based not in language, but in his own ligaments. Early in the autumn, Jefferson had dislocated his right wrist attempting to hop over a fence; by the end of the year, the pain had not abated, but was intensifying. As he informed Thomas Barclay in the dying days of December, Jefferson's wrist injury was "making it still painful to [. . .] write. It recovers so slowly that I am much disposed to take the advice of my Surgeon and try some mineral waters in Provence."[23] It is perhaps this wrist pain that prompted Jefferson to hold off from "writ[ing]" his name for many days after the treaty arrived, not inking his autograph at the end of this historic document until the dawn of a new year. Instead of December 1786, Jefferson waited until January 1, 1787, to trace his signature on the treaty. Mirroring the Ramadan autograph of Morocco's emperor—who had ratified the treaty on the first day of Islam's holiest month—Jefferson signaled his own approval on New Year's Day. Not a season of fasting in Paris, but a feast, the American minister signed the Moroccan treaty on a public holiday, inscribing with physical discomfort this document meant to ensure bodily relief for all Americans arriving to Morocco in captivity. The treaty Jefferson signed at the start to 1787, despite his ruptured wrist, would endure for more than two centuries, proving to be America's "longest unbroken treaty in [the] Nation's history."[24] In holding off until 1787, however, Jefferson unknowingly reached forward not two centuries in the nation's history, but two decades onward in his own biography. Authorizing a treaty whose authoritative version remained illegible to him, Jefferson forecasted events in his own life twenty years later, when unreadable Arabic would again arrive to him, sent not from North African "Moors," but West African "Muslims." As in 1787, Jefferson would in 1807 receive an encoded Arabic "original," featuring indecipherable lines that invoked Allah, while also implying the precarious character of American liberties.

4

"Written in fair Arabic Characters"

We have made an advantageous treaty with Marocco, but with
Algiers nothing is done.

Jefferson to Ezra Stiles
December 24, 1786[1]

Jefferson signed the treaty with Morocco on New Year's Day, 1787. One
week earlier, he had spent Christmas Eve, 1786, signing documents much
more intimate, writing letters to friends at home and abroad.[2] On the cusp
of Christmas and nearing the dawn of a new year, it is unsurprising that
Jefferson's thoughts turned to loved ones. However, as he wrote his letters
on December 24, Jefferson's personal updates were intermixed with practical
business; and, despite the festive season, it was not all good news to share.
On Christmas Eve, a treaty with Muslims was waiting to be signed, recalling
anxieties for Jefferson that had weighed on him throughout 1786. At year's
end, as he reflected on accomplishments, Jefferson was also aware of unfinished efforts. Pleased with the "advantageous treaty with Marocco," Jefferson
yet lamented that "nothing is done" with another Barbary power: "Algiers."
Americans still languished in captivity, laboring in African "workhouses."
No Christmas festivities would come for Richard O'Brien in 1786.

Jefferson naturally thought of old friends amid celebrations in Paris.
However, the friend he chose to send his North African update seems somewhat surprising. It was no fellow Virginian, nor a peer diplomat or politician,
but an academic that Jefferson wrote with this news: the president of Yale,
Ezra Stiles. New England's leading intellectual, Stiles was also Jefferson's most
recent American confidant in 1786. Meeting only a month before Jefferson
embarked overseas from Boston on July 5, 1784, the two men enjoyed an
immediate connection, despite their divergent roles and regions.[3] A college president from Connecticut, Stiles was also a Congregationalist minister and a pious Calvinist. Jefferson, on the other hand, was an apostle of the

Enlightenment, a Virginian who championed political rights and rejected religious dogma. Both men were polymaths, however, eager students of old classics, and amateur scientists of the new order, pursuing broad intellectual inquiry as well as meticulous measurements. Stiles's own love of detail was most apparent in the painstaking record he kept of his daily life, a voluminous diary he maintained over three decades in which Jefferson surfaces in person for the first time on June 8, 1784. Arriving to New Haven, the former Virginia "Governor" was instantly recognized by Stiles as "a most ingenous Naturalist & Philosopher." Jefferson is "a truly scientific & learned Man—& every way excellent," Stiles wrote in his diary on June 8, adding that "He visited the College Lib' & our Apparatus."[4]

As they together toured Yale, it was not only Jefferson's "ingenuity," but Stiles's own learning, that was on display—learning that proved not unrelated to Jefferson's upcoming diplomacy. A master of many disciplines, Stiles was most distinguished by a single interest in particular: his facility with Middle Eastern languages. A daring autodidact, Stiles had begun to teach himself "Oriental tongues" in the 1760s, patiently tracing the twenty-two letters of the Hebrew alphabet in his private journals.[5] Proving a quick study, Stiles soon advanced to other Semitic languages, tackling Aramaic, Syriac, and eventually, Arabic. By the time he was appointed president of Yale, Stiles was ready to share his love of Middle Eastern languages and learning; delivering his first Commencement Address in 1781, Stiles lectured to the Yale community not in English or in Latin, but in "*Hebrew, Chaldee* and *Arabic*," as he noted in his diary. Devoutly Christian, yet a diligent student of the Qur'an, Ezra Stiles was an oddity, both a leader of the nascent "Ivy League", as well as one of the few Arabists in the early Republic.[6]

Stiles's interests in the Muslim world received an indirect boost on June 8, 1784, with the arrival to New Haven of Thomas Jefferson. Recently named American ambassador, Jefferson was soon to depart overseas, where he would negotiate relationships not only with European nations, but with countries much further afield. In his new friend, Stiles found not only "a learned Man," but a minister plenipotentiary uniquely capable of keeping him apprised of global affairs. This service Jefferson did indeed provide, starting not long after he arrived to Paris. The first letter that Jefferson sent to Stiles from Europe was dispatched on July 17, 1785—a half year before he wrote Yale's president with his North African update on Christmas Eve, 1786. Still several weeks before learning of O'Brien's imprisonment in Algiers, Jefferson was already sharing anxieties with Stiles concerning Muslim captivity—captivity not of a single person, however, but of an entire nation, sharply criticizing Ottoman occupation of Greece:

> The Turks shew a disposition to go to war with [the Holy Roman Emperor]. But if this country [France] can prevail on them to remain in peace they will do so. It has been thought that the two Imperial courts [France and Holy Roman Empire] have a plan of expelling the Turks from Europe. It is really a pity so charming a country should remain in the hands of a people whose religion forbids the admission of science and the arts among them. We should wish success to the object of the two empires if they meant to leave the country in possession of the Greek inhabitants. We might then expect once more to see the language of Homer and Demosthenes a living language. For I am persuaded the modern greek would easily get back to its classical models. But this is not intended. They only propose to put the Greeks under other masters: to substitute one set of Barbarians for another.[7]

Contrasting "classical models" and Muslim control, Jefferson desires yet another declaration of independence—one not from America, but for Greece. Attacking Turkish strictures in particular, Jefferson singles out specifically their "religion," labeling Islam—erroneously—as "forbid[ing] the admission of science and the arts." Intriguingly, however, even as he yearns for the autonomy of "Greek inhabitants," Jefferson blames repression not only on Ottomans, but on "the two Imperial courts" of Christendom: France and the Holy Roman Empire. Even if Greece was freed from Muslim dominion, they would be mastered by Europeans, suffering merely a "Barbarian" substitution. Perhaps most resonant for his own looming encounter with captivity in Muslim lands, however, Jefferson's political pessimism involves not merely religion, but rhetoric. The survival of words is at stake in this current conflict between Christians and Muslims, with Jefferson glimpsing lost hopes for the revival of antique speech into "a living language."[8]

Benefiting from Jefferson's updates, Stiles kept abreast of unfolding affairs in the Muslim world, spanning threats of Turkish "war" to an "advantageous treaty with Marocco." However, it was during the very years that Jefferson sojourned abroad that Stiles himself would find more direct means to deepen his Muslim engagements, receiving not mere second-hand reports from Paris, but primary documents domestically generated by Arabic authors themselves. Rather than "a living language" from Europe, a Muslim *lingua franca* arrived to Stiles as Jefferson stayed in Paris, with Yale's president coming into "possession" of writings that reflected not "classical models," but the Qur'an itself. Anticipating future experiences of his new friend and a later US president, the president of Yale would open at home manuscripts arising from Muslim captivity, welcoming Arabic documents written by African slaves in New Haven, where just years before he had hosted "a most ingenous Naturalist & Philosopher."

≈

SIR

I take the Liberty to inform you that, yesterday at the public anniversary Commencement in this University, the *Senatus Academicus* did themselves the Honor to confer upon you the Degree of Doctor in Laws.[9]

During his New Haven visit on June 8, 1784, Jefferson had made a superlative impression, seeming "every way excellent" to Stiles. Jefferson's presence would resonate at Yale long after his departure to Paris, however. Two years later, he was again celebrated, but in absentia. Opening a letter from Stiles dated September 14, 1786, Jefferson learned that he had been conferred Yale's highest degree the day before. Adding "Doctor" to dozens of titles won throughout his life, Jefferson's New England award retains an ancient flavor, granted by the "*Senatus Academicus*" of Yale.[10] Aptly assuming "the Liberty" even while exalting the architect of American liberties, Stiles "honors" Jefferson, but not for the first time. Even before the two men met in 1784, it was Ezra Stiles who first acknowledged Jefferson in print as author of the Declaration of Independence, lauding him in a published sermon from 1783 as having "poured the soul of the continent into the monumental act of Independence," as William Howard Adams has noted.[11]

In 1786, America's minister found himself elevated once again by Stiles, learning in Paris that he had been proclaimed "Dr. Jefferson" at Yale. This new name did not reach Jefferson, however, until December 1786—the same month that his own signature was requested from North Africa. Stiles's letter arrived just days before Barclay's "Box" from the Barbary Coast; and, although coincidental in timing, these two deliveries also overlapped in concern, with Stiles raising the same issues Barclay was seeking to resolve in 1786. After announcing Jefferson's degree at home, Stiles interrogates the new "Doctor in Laws" regarding more worldly matters:

Must we also Subsidize Algiers? Why do the European Nations suffer the prædatory Wars of the Barbary States? *Delenda est Carthago.* Algiers must be subdued. In the mean Time we must expend £200,000 and subsidize that piratical State. Peace with that and Morocco, may open a Mediterranian Commerce to us of £200,000 per annum. Excuse my free Remarks. I have the Honor to be, Sir, Yr. most obedt. very hble servt.,

EZRA STILES[12]

Transitioning from collegial honors to "Commercial" tribute, Stiles queries the West's appeasement of "Barbary States." America should refuse to pay the "prædatory" North Africans; "we" should "subdue," not "subsidize," Stiles suggests. Shifting his tone and topic, Stiles also shifts tongues as well. With a classical flourish, he exclaims in Latin *Delenda est Carthago*—"Carthage must be destroyed!"[13] Quoting Cato the Elder, an ancient Roman senator and a favorite of Jefferson, Stiles frames America's struggles in historic terms, modeling the new nation on another Republic, invoking Rome's clashes with Carthage. Stiles's analogy makes sense due to another name that had changed over time. As Yale's president well knew, by 1786 the ruins of Carthage had given way to the modern-day Tunis—a Muslim city soon to be at the center of US wars to "subdue" North Africa, conducted by the very man just made a "Doctor in Laws," but who would eventually be known by a higher title: commander-in-chief.

Opening his letter to Jefferson with "Liberty," Stiles ends with "free Remarks." Amid these personal privileges, Stiles invokes "piratical" assaults on Americans, touching on the same anxieties his friend was feeling during this autumn, with Jefferson in Paris confronting reports of North African captivity. In September 1786, this link across the Atlantic was strengthened by Jefferson himself, who this same month also sent a letter to Stiles—an extended letter that took a long time to arrive, not reaching Stiles until almost a year later, on August 17, 1787.[14] This letter's deferred delivery was not entirely unusual; but it did prove unusually providential. Jefferson's delayed message to Stiles arrived even as Yale's president opened another communiqué, one that concerned not Muslim "pirates" abroad, but Muslim prisoners closer to home. Requesting news from Jefferson concerning Muslim Africa in 1786, by the time Stiles finally received his friend's long-delayed update in 1787, other letters had arrived—letters authored by Muslims detained in the New World, introducing Yale's president to a type of education he had never before imagined, but for which he was uniquely prepared.

≈

Ezra Stiles relished the rhythms and routines of university life, its semester cycles and regular vacations. Amid these variations, however, Stiles consistently kept his diary, neither resting on Sabbaths, nor pausing during the summer breaks. In 1787, the long vacation seemed to stretch on interminably as New England endured stormy heat, including "Tornadoes and Hurricanes."[15] Yet even during the dog days of August, Stiles diligently kept up his journal.

It was during this sweltering month that Stiles witnessed the end to another drought, finally receiving a long-awaited package from Paris. On August 17, 1787, a multi-page letter arrived from Jefferson, the first in many months. More exceptional than this letter from Stiles's friend, however, was an entirely unexpected arrival the next day. The mid-August entries in Stiles's diary stretching from the 17th to the 19th trace a curious sequence of events, quoted below at length:

August 17. Heb. Recitation. The 10th Inst I recd Letters from London & Paris, Gov. Jefferson & Col. Trumbull the Painter. Gov. Jefferson sent me 2 Volumes of the *Bibliotheque Oconomique*. He informs that Abbe [. . .] has made a Speculum of a Telescope with Platina, whose reflectg Power is nearly or quite equal to the common metallic specula of Telescopes, with this Advantg that the Platina Speculum will not tarnish or receive Rust more than Gold:—that an Artist at Paris presented him a polished Copper Plate, on which the Gov. wrote a Sentence, and in three Quarters of an hour the Artist bro't him a hundred Copies so well executed, that if he had written his Name it might have been applied to a Number of Bonds, and he shd have acknowledged & owned the signature:—that Pictures are now taken off from others copyg exactly not only the Outlines but the Colors without damaging the Originals: which appeared to him so like Creation that he shd not have believed it had he not seen it. He says Col. Trumbull bro't to Paris 2 Pictures or Paintings admired by the Connaiseurs, & that he is excellent in this Art. The Gov. supposes Asia peopled from America.

August 18. Thursday last Capt Todd presented me with four Specimens of Negro Writing in Arabic, written by four Negro Slaves in Trinidad in the West Indies, who were brought from the Foulie Nation in Africa, five days from the Sea Coast. I find I can read it, it being written in fair Arabic Characters: & begins بسم الله الرحم. Two of them are Mahometans & two Pagans, but all educated to write the Arabic.

August 19. Ldsdy. I attended at Chapel all day. A.M. Revd Tutor Holmes
preached an excellent Sermon Prov. xvi, 25.[16]

In run-on sentences and abbreviated words, Stiles rapidly jots down his
intimate ideas in a jargon all his own. Idiomatic in style, these entries also
shift idioms, with Stiles writing in a foreign script. Reporting news from far
and near—opening overseas letters and hearing a sermon at home—Stiles
records his August experiences, some mundane, some momentous. And
surprisingly, the most historic message Stiles received in this short span is
not from a future US president. A day after opening a letter from Thomas
Jefferson on the 17th, Stiles was handed "Negro Writing in Arabic" from the
Caribbean—"writing" which Stiles not only reads, but reproduces, copying
these "fair Arabic Characters" into his American diary.[17]

It is the making of "Copies" that oddly connects Stiles's entries together.
Opened on August 17, Jefferson's letter is eclectic, updating Stiles on a range
of innovations, scientific and artistic, from a "Telescope" to "Paintings." The
centerpiece of Jefferson's note, though, is the making of facsimiles. During
his Paris years, Jefferson was worried enough regarding the fate of his letters
to write in cipher. Jefferson's anxiety led not only to codes, however, but to
copying, searching for systems to conserve his writings. From Paris, Jefferson
tells Stiles of a new "polished Copper Plate" that cranks out "a hundred
Copies" in just "three Quarters of an hour"—a process Jefferson tests with
his own autograph. To begin 1787, Jefferson had personally signed his name
to a treaty with a Muslim nation; by August 1787, Stiles learns that Jefferson
has found a way to reproduce "his Name" endlessly, repeated so accurately
that he easily "acknowledged & owned the signature."[18] Receiving Jefferson's
letter in New Haven, Stiles copies this episode into his own diary, taking
down details on his friend's device, especially its ability to generate facsimiles
"without damaging the Originals." However, Stiles soon stops paraphrasing
Jefferson's letter, ending with a startling statement on the origins of America
itself. "The Gov. supposes Asia peopled from America," Stiles adds as his final
sentence to his August 17 entry.[19]

Shifting from reproduction to global resettlement, Stiles abruptly finishes
his entry with Jefferson's theory that "peoples" of modern "Asia" started in
America. Little did Stiles know, however, that Jefferson's eclectic concerns
would anticipate the single event that occupied the very next day: Stiles's receipt of Arabic slave writings. Jefferson's migratory link between West and
East aptly sets the scene for Stiles's own discovery, arising from a rather

different continental migration, receiving writings by Eastern "peoples" enslaved in the West. On August 18th, Stiles again becomes a copyist; but rather than Jefferson's reproduced "signature," Stiles makes facsimiles of Arabic "Originals," inscribing the very name of Allah Himself by quoting three words from the "four Specimens of Negro Writing in Arabic" received from "Capt Todd":

بسم الله الرحم

[*Bismillāh ar-Raḥīm*
In the name of Allah, the most Compassionate][20]

Copying these Arabic words from the Caribbean, Stiles reproduces in the continental United States Muslim lines composed just "five days from the Sea Coast," with phrases by "Foulie Nation" authors duplicated by Yale's president. Comprising the very first words of the Qur'an itself, Stiles's "Mahometan" quotation in his diary seems especially familiar, as it is the very same formula inscribed in the diary of an American slave in Muslim lands—Richard O'Brien. On summer break from his Yale semester, far from Muslim "workhouses," Stiles inscribes the identical Arabic invocation traced by another of Jefferson's correspondants in the 1780s. O'Brien's reliance on the Qur'an arose from his desperate enslavement, pleading to Allah for mercy; for Stiles, however, his Qur'anic copying reflects his commitment to "education." Extoling these slaves who are trained "to write the Arabic," Stiles receives support for his Middle Eastern studies from the Caribbean, these rare "Originals" helping to test Stiles's capacities to read and write Arabic. Rather than the literacy of enslaved Muslims, Stiles seems more surprised by his own skills, proudly boasting that "I find I can read it" in his private diary. Forced into servitude "five days from the Sea Coast," African slaves gain an improbable student in New Haven, with an Ivy League leader promoting his learning via the "fair Arabic Characters" written by men enduring the most hideous New World conditions.

≈

It was on August 18, 1787, that Stiles first received writings by enslaved men from the "Foulie Nation in Africa," copying their Arabic on the very day after Jefferson's letter had extolled his own autograph's reproduction. This overlap in Stiles's life—writings from Thomas Jefferson and Muslim slaves arriving at the same time—seems a mere coincidence. And yet this coincidence turns into a concrete link in the months immediately following August 1787. Stiles would soon receive more Arabic writings, which were once again authored by Muslim slaves. This time, however, these Muslim authors would be enslaved not "five days from" America's "Sea Coast," but instead just down the American coast from Stiles's home in New Haven. As he returned to open Yale's semester in autumn 1787, Stiles was only months away from receiving the earliest extant writings by a Muslim enslaved in the continental United States—a precedent never before recognized, but which would also find a secret sequel in Jefferson's experience a full two decades later, in 1807.

Aptly, it is the final detail in Stiles's August diary entries, a detail seemingly mundane, that linked him to the historic Arabic writings he would soon receive. In the last of his three August entries, Stiles records his Sabbath routines on the 19th, describing ordinary Sunday events for any clergyman, attending "Chapel all day," and hearing "an excellent Sermon." Although preached on a gloomy passage from Proverbs—"There is a way that seemeth right unto a man, but the end thereof are the ways of death"—Stiles yet cheered the "excellence" of this sermon, as well as its ambitious speaker: his former student, and a young Yale "tutor," Abiel Holmes.[21] The future father of one of the most celebrated writers of the following century, Oliver Wendell Holmes, Abiel would himself also rise later to become a leading New England minister, pastoring a church for more than thirty years in Cambridge, Massachusetts, close to Harvard. However, in 1787, this New England future was far from Holmes's thoughts. Instead he was readying to depart for a church at the opposite end of the country, planted in the furthest reaches of the US South.

The excellent preaching that Stiles praised was Holmes's farewell sermon, signaling his goodbye before he returned to Georgia. Holmes, two years before, had been ordained a Congregationalist minister, called to his first appointment in Midway, just south of Savannah. Although leaving Stiles and New Haven behind, Holmes would, however, soon be in touch once more. Impressed by his student's "excellent" sermonizing in 1787, Stiles would be sent even more marvelous writings from Holmes once he arrived again to Georgia—writings that would chart a covert parallel between this college president and a future president of the United States.

5

"I take Refuge with the Lord of Daybreak"

Parnassus Feby 22^{d}, 1788

Reverend and Dear Sir,

I have spent a day at this place and have been as much gratified as I should have been by a visit from *Clio* or *Urania*. There is a *Negro* on this Plantation who appears to me a great literary curiosity. He understands so very little of our language, however, that I cannot collect by any means so much from him as I could wish.

He was brought from *Africa* to this country about two years since. His African name is *Osamon*.[1]

On March 18, 1788, Ezra Stiles opened a letter sent north to New Haven from the seacoast of Georgia. It came from Abiel Holmes, the same young minister whom Stiles had sent south seven months before. Stiles had been anticipating a letter from Holmes, but these first words undoubtedly came as a shock.

Abiel Holmes had bid farewell to Yale late the previous summer, delivering his "excellent" sermon on a verse of biblical revelation. Now, from Georgia, Holmes reported a very different revelation. Rather than reading from a divine book, Holmes had met a celestial figure in the flesh—a "great literary curiosity," whose presence is likened to "a visit" from an ancient Greek Muse, compared to "*Clio* or *Urania*," sister goddesses of history and astronomy.[2] Familiar with such classical names, Stiles was likely unprepared for what Holmes says next. This figure compared to a mythic goddess is actually an African man—and a slave. Recently "brought" to "this country," Holmes's starry Muse is chained solidly to the Georgia soil. In a further contradiction, Holmes also notes that this "great literary curiosity" is clumsy in speech, "understand[ing] so very little of our language." Begun with divine labels—"*Clio* or *Urania*"—only the last word of Holmes's introduction reveals a human identity for this supernatural stranger. Supplying not merely a slave handle, Holmes instead offers this figure's authentic name, which is neither Greek nor pagan, but instead Arabic and Islamic. "His African name" Holmes declares "is *Osamon*"—that is, '*Usman*, a prominent name of Muslim heritage (originally, in Arabic, '*Uthmān*). A companion of the Prophet Muhammad himself, it was 'Usman who in the earliest years of Islam served as the religion's third caliph, his reign witnessing initial Muslim military forays into Europe.[3]

It is the concrete location from which this letter is written that anticipates the classical allusions Holmes invokes, as well as the dizzying contradictions he implies. "I have spent a day at this place," Holmes's note to Stiles begins, starting not with an ethereal person, but with an actual plantation, a "place" called "Parnassus."[4] Recalling the fabled mountain of the Muses, Parnassus is the historic name of a high peak in Greece, the secluded "resort" of divinities, home to gods of inspiration and illumination. A heavenly mountain and a pagan "sanctuary," Parnassus was the name ironically borrowed by planters to designate a low-lying seacoast plot just south of Savannah, not far from Holmes's church in Midway, Georgia. Precariously rooted in soggy soil, suited for the cultivation of rice, the Parnassus that Holmes visited in February 1788 was blurry in boundary, its "tidewater" shores always shifting, leaving uncertain where US land ended and Atlantic waters began.[5]

A home to contradictions, Parnassus Plantation was aptly "the place" where Holmes encountered "*Osamon*"—an enslaved African, and yet a "great literary" figure, a lowly captive trapped on a spot named for sublime heights. For Stiles, the most obvious contradiction in Holmes's letter, however, must have been its excited and exaggerated tone. Abiel Holmes had been an intelligent student, incisive but unimaginative. A young man known for prudence, not poetry or paradox, Holmes was a sober reverend as well as a budding historian, destined to author one of the first chronicles of the nation, publishing his *American Annals* in 1805.[6] But, on March 17, 1788, what Stiles heard from Holmes was not historical fact, but something that sounded like a flight of fancy. If Stiles was skeptical of Holmes's enthusiastic rhetoric, however, he would soon be convinced. From Parnassus, Holmes had sent not naked testimony, but a proof text. Behind Holmes's surprising letter, another letter, even more surprising, was enclosed. Folded in four sections, Stiles found a paper refugee sent from the resort of the Muses snugly secreted in the envelope. Evidence of Holmes's "divine" meeting, the document that Stiles unfolded was written in clear beautiful lines—lines that were never seen again, until now. On March 17, Stiles possessed plain material proof from mythic Parnassus; in his hands, Ezra Stiles held the earliest extant Muslim slave writings authored in the United States.[7]

≈

> 'Till *Georgia's* silks on *Albion's* Beauties shine,
> Or gain new Lustre from the *Royal Line;* [...]
> And when in Time the wealthy Lands increase,
> Shall bend the Curious to the Arts of Peace;
> They, with small Pain, assisted by the Clime,
> Shall pull the Anana, and unload the Lime;
> Thro' Groves of Citron breath *Arabia's* Gale,
> And parch the Berry drank in *Mecca's* Vale.
>
> "An Address to *James Oglethorpe*, Esq;
> on his settling the Colony in *Georgia*" (1733)[8]

"Parnassus" seems a lofty title for a humble rice farm nestled on Georgia's Atlantic edges. And yet, this name reflects the fabled character of the flooded coastline that surrounds the plantation. Stretching south from Savannah, Georgia's shore is shrouded in myth. Separated from the mainland by reedy marshes, Georgia's coast is known especially for its barrier islands, bearing names such as Sapelo, St. Simons, and Jekyll. These "low-country" outposts are inverse to the height of Mt. Parnassus; but, like the mountain of the Muses, these islands share not only natural seclusion, but a sense of legend.

Even before the arrival of its colonial founder—General James Oglethorpe—the Atlantic coast of Georgia was regarded as a unique sanctuary, a haven set apart. Admiring its eastward vistas, bathed in dawn light, Sir Robert Montgomery first designated this area "the Golden Isles" in the early eighteenth century—a name that still persists, applied to islands including St. Simons and Jekyll.[9] Deeming it the "most delightful country of the Universe," Montgomery appreciated the otherworldly beauty of Georgia's coastline, but also its utopian potential; he even published plans for founding an ideal community on the very site later occupied by Parnassus Plantation.[10] Montgomery's utopia was never realized; but British colonists continued to seek sanctuary in "the Golden Isles," arriving in the wake of wars in Europe, including struggles against Muslim forces. When General Oglethorpe first reached Georgia's gentle shores, this colonial founder was a hardened veteran, having vied with the Turks at the Siege of Belgrade in 1717. Blockading and eventually overcoming the Ottomans, Oglethorpe had served with the Austrian army, standing with Europeans at this pivotal victory over the Sultan's Muslim troops.[11]

A decade later, when Oglethorpe arrived in Georgia, he brought to the colony his experience combating the Ottomans. He also carried, however, companies of military men who too had recently served in lands shaped by Muslim culture and conquest. Many of Oglethorpe's men came not directly from England, but instead from Gibraltar—a Spanish isthmus under British control, whose name is itself Arabic in origin. "Gibraltar" derives from "*Jabal Ṭāriq*"—Arabic for "The Mountain of Ṭāriq"—recalling the conquest of "the rock" by Ṭāriq ibn Ziyād, an Umayyad military commander. The British colonists who arrived to occupy Oglethorpe's Georgia had just come from defending the famed "Moorish Castle," one of Gibraltar's most recognizable landmarks.[12] Among the Gibraltar veterans to arrive in 1733 was Raymond Demere (1702–1766), who came from Spain to serve General Oglethorpe in Georgia. "Demere's knowledge of Spanish, as well as his previous service in the hot climes of Gibraltar, made him a particularly desirable officer for service in the Georgia regiment that Oglethorpe recruited," as June Hall McCash has recently noted.[13] Demere's Spanish made him "valuable," allowing him to serve "as an emissary to the Spanish governor at St. Augustine"; however, Demere's arrival to Georgia would also signal the opening to another multilingual legacy. It was Demere's nephew—also named Raymond Demere (1750–1791)—who would come into possession of a coastal plantation named "Parnassus," where a West African literate in Arabic endured American slavery, even while bearing a name echoing an illustrious Muslim military past.[14]

The Islamic currents that encircled Georgia's founding swelled into celebrations of its founder. Published in 1733, the poem quoted above, "An Address to *James Oglethorpe*," concludes with gentle lines that imagine Georgia as a Middle Eastern "grove," with "*Arabia*'s Gale" wafting over this New World colony. Predicting the future "bananas" and "limes" to be planted in Georgia, these verses invoke Islam specifically, conceiving America's "low country" as "*Mecca*'s Vale," with this most sacred city of Muslim pilgrimage forming the last image in Oglethorpe's encomium. If Georgia's colonial genesis seemed a Muslim paradise, it is Muslim imprisonment that shaped this region's afterlife as a US state. Parnassus Plantation, owned by the Demere family, would be representative, not rare, in enslaving a Muslim among its West Africans. Fed by the trade in human flesh that filtered through Savannah, Georgia's southern shore became the most concentrated center of Muslim enslavement in the early United States.[15] More records of Africans professing Islam as their religion derive from this region than anywhere else in the country. Even after the Civil War, traces of Muslim culture endured here, protected on coastal outposts such as Sapelo Island, where Muslim rites and Arabic prayers were still to be witnessed a half century after slavery ended. "[T]hey still pray to the east, to the Mecca," recalled Susie Campbell Wilson, an early twentieth-century resident of the island.[16]

Founded by veterans of Europe's Muslim struggles and "Moorish Castles," Georgia's "Golden" coast would itself become a refuge for African Americans of Muslim descent. Finding havens in the same remote Atlantic outposts where their forebears were imprisoned, these later generations stayed in this region even as it underwent radical renovation, serving no longer as a secluded retreat, but as a resort, a space for the immensely rich to play and plot. By the beginning of World War I, several of Georgia's seacoast islands had become a "Southern Haven for America's Millionaires," an exclusive escape for captains of industry and finance. It was on Jekyll Island—another island occupied in the eighteenth century by the same Demere family who owned Parnassus—that the Federal Reserve was founded in 1910. A coast of contradictions, Georgia's Atlantic edge has served as a utopian paradise, and an African prison—a resort for American millionaires and a refuge for enslaved Muslims, a place for prayers to Mecca and "a mecca for vacationers."[17] Such tensions amplified over time. However, they were already evident in embryo, as Holmes wrote to Ezra Stiles in 1788, likening a Muslim slave to a sacred Muse of starry illumination.

It is illumination that has stayed consistent among this region's many contradictions. As Montgomery observed long ago, Georgia's shoreline is a marvel at dawn, with its "Golden Isles" bathed in eastern rays just as they were in the 1700s. Gilded in light, and gilded in fortune, the coast is known for its natural beauties. And yet, one man-made structure also stands from its past: aptly, a lighthouse. Built on the shores of St. Simons Island at the beginning of the nineteenth century, this lighthouse was one of the first buildings to rise from Georgia's coast, designed to outlast the Atlantic weather. Burnt down in the Civil War and then rebuilt, this icon still stands, evoking the region's visionary light and its status as a refuge.[18] However, even St. Simons lighthouse hints at the more ominous history of the Golden Isles, as well as their rich Muslim heritage. Overshadowed by its topmost beacon, the lighthouse's tower rises from grounds originally owned by John Couper—one of the region's wealthiest plantation owners, whose nineteenth-century estate was itself overseen by a Muslim slave, Bilali, himself literate in Arabic.[19] Even the material of the St. Simons lighthouse reflects Muslim cultures, its foundation constructed from a concrete mortar known as "tabby." A mixture of oyster shells, sand, and water, "tabby" merges all elements of the region—land, sea, and even marine life. Although seemingly indigenous, however, this material is not original to Georgia, but has North African roots, imported to the New World via the Spanish, who derived "tabby" from their Moorish past. The name itself is etymologically Arabic, "tabby" derived from "'attābiyya"—"عَتَّابِيّ"—a quarter in the city of Baghdad where this material was first utilized.[20]

The lighthouse of St. Simons Island still stands, a symbolic sentinel overlooking surrounding islands of wealth, whose riches derive now not from trade, but from tourism. Gleaming and whitewashed, this beacon embodies the Golden Isles in overt and covert ways, its New World lantern raised aloft, propped up by materials of Muslim heritage. A sparkling epitome of the region's hidden polarities, St. Simons lighthouse rose during the administration of a US leader himself privately invested in precisely the same contradictions. A project representative of Georgia and its coastline, the St. Simons lighthouse yet required federal investment, attracting thereby the attention of a towering identity at the intersection of American history and Arabic interiors, straddling the US elite and Muslim enslavement: Thomas Jefferson.

≈

The durability of tabby has been ascertained.

Albert Gallatin writing to Jefferson
May 25, 1807[21]

This concrete verdict was sent to Jefferson in 1807, a critical year of his presidency. Written by Jefferson's secretary of the treasury, Albert Gallatin, this testimony formed a part of his "On Proposals &c. for a light house on St. Simon's island in Georgia"—a final report to Jefferson, requesting his "approv[al]" for construction, accenting the endurance of "tabby." Built from these materials with Arabian roots, the "light house" reached up to overlook the Atlantic in 1808, exactly twenty years after Abiel Holmes had dispatched northwards from this same Georgia seacoast a rather different kind of Arabic material in 1788.[22]

Jefferson's relations with this region did not wait for his presidency, however. Reviewing Gallatin's St. Simons "proposal" in 1807, Jefferson's engagements with the Golden Isles started twenty years earlier, in 1787, when he was still in Paris. This same year saw Abiel Holmes bid farewell to Stiles in New Haven, returning south to shepherd his Midway church. From much further afield, however, Jefferson also had Georgia's seacoast on his mind in 1787. Negotiating on behalf of a famed Parisian friend, Jefferson helped none other than the Marquis de Lafayette purchase perhaps the Golden Coast's most iconic product: live oak. Famous for its own "durability," Lafayette desired lumber from Georgia for French shipbuilding, prompting Jefferson to contact Nathanael Greene, fellow American revolutionary and the latest owner of Cumberland Island, just south of St. Simons.[23] The agriculture of the Golden Isles would stay a "live" interest for Jefferson until his death. In 1825, Jefferson would again traffic with France for Georgia crops, procuring olives from Marseille. Transplanted from the Mediterranean to St. Simons Island, Jefferson acquired olive trees for the same John Couper who had supplied the ground for the island's lighthouse. Master of Muslim slaves, Couper was prompted by Jefferson to cultivate this eastern product, with olive trees still surviving on his former St. Simons Plantation in the twenty-first century.[24]

Raising up concrete and crops, giving light and life to Georgia's coast, Jefferson's associations with the Golden Isles would also have a darker side as well, arising not from the president himself, but his first vice president: Aaron Burr. Burr is infamous for assassination, of course, rather than administration. After fatally wounding Alexander Hamilton in their July 11, 1804, Weehawken duel, Burr fled his home state, heading south from New Jersey, finding a hiding place in America's region of dawning light.[25] Landing on St. Simons Island in August 1804, Burr took refuge in the Golden Isles with Pierce Butler, even while visiting neighboring properties, including the plantation owned by Jefferson's friend, John Couper. Sharing space with Arabic-literate Muslim slaves such as Bilali, Aaron Burr was hosted at Couper's plantation as he sought to evade his own capture.[26] But, even in remote St. Simons, Burr was not idle. Seeking to advance "intrigue or investment," Burr considered traveling down to West Florida, as Buckner F. Melton Jr. has emphasized; and yet, soon after he arrived to Georgia in August 1804, a severe hurricane hit, "trapping" Burr on St. Simons.[27] Stuck on the island alongside Muslim captives, Burr's ambitions soon led him toward even more audacious schemes of revenge and rebellion—schemes that would ultimately lead to his own American captivity, caught while inciting a frontier insurgency with its own Islamic intersections.

Jefferson was informed of his outlaw vice president's movements in the autumn of 1804. News of Burr's flight to St. Simons Island was sent to the president by Thomas Sumter Sr. from South Carolina, writing very near the place where the infamous fort would be built bearing his name, the same Fort Sumter that later witnessed the start of another rebellion, the Civil War.[28] Also in the autumn of 1804, Jefferson received another letter, sent from a Yankee very familiar with Georgia's seacoast—Abiel Holmes—who finally reached out to Jefferson personally, acquainting the president with his plan to publish a history of the United States, entitled *American Annals*.[29] By 1804, Holmes had himself risen to public prominence in New England, ministering in Massachusetts to Cambridge's First Church in Harvard Square. He needed the president's aid to find a few specialized US sources—aid that Jefferson eagerly provided. Approving of Holmes's project, the president expected that his "Chronological history of America" would prove "precious to the man of business."[30] Jefferson would eventually receive a copy of the published *American Annals* early in 1807, the same year that he was secretly presented with Arabic writings from Muslim slaves. Despite these historic overlaps, Jefferson would never learn that Abiel Holmes had shared the very same experience, receiving Muslim slave writings twenty years earlier in Georgia.

≈

In 1787, the passage of time was uppermost on Abiel Holmes's mind. Preparing to leave home in New England and trek south, Holmes was returning to his congregation in Midway. As a Christian pastor, eternal life was Holmes's business, of course; and yet, historical matters were his amateur passion in Georgia. Cultivating a side career as an American chronicler, Holmes enthusiastically gathered information uniquely available during his sojourn in the South. But, as 1787 melted away into 1788, Holmes found his hunt for local facts checked by a cold snap that gripped Midway as the new year opened. Even Holmes's ability to record daily temperatures was interrupted, as his thermometer had broken by February.[31]

In this same month, however, Holmes's desire to chronicle events would find an outlet, with a visit to Parnassus Plantation. Meeting there on February 21 a slave named "Osamon"—or, more accurately, 'Usman—Holmes wrote the next day to Ezra Stiles, lauding this literate Muslim with mythic hyperbole. Although ill-prepared to comprehend the historic scope of the event he had witnessed, Holmes did eagerly record the details of the "day" he "spent" at Parnassus, expressing regret only for the material he had missed. Overjoyed to encounter 'Usman, Holmes complains only in his letter to Ezra Stiles that "I cannot collect by any means so much from him as I could wish."[32] Seeking precision as always, Holmes even measured the very moments taken up by 'Usman's act of writing, noting later in his letter to Stiles that the enslaved West African

> writes with great ease and freedom, as you will readily judge from the spec-
> imen of his writing which I enclose. This he wrote in my presence in less,
> I apprehend, than the space of three quarters of an hour. He writes from the
> right to the left, after the manner of the *Hebrew*.[33]

Proficient with a pen, this Muslim slave is presented to Stiles as a marvel not only due to his literacy, but due to his manual speed. Praising 'Usman's inscription in "the space of three quarters of an hour," Holmes unwittingly echoes the last letter that Stiles had received from Jefferson in 1787—a letter in which "a hundred Copies" of Jefferson's own signature were generated in the very same time, in "three Quarters of an hour." Now, however, in 1788, this act of agile inscription seems a painful irony considering its context of enslavement. 'Usman "writes with great ease and freedom," Holmes insists, applying the language of liberty to this literary act undertaken in cruel physical captivity.

It is not 'Usman's reported speed, but the actual "specimen" that Holmes promises in his letter, that offered Stiles first-hand proof of his proficiency. On August 18, 1787, a day after Jefferson's letter arrived, reporting his copied autograph, Stiles had himself received and copied Arabic from enslaved Africans in the Caribbean; now, in 1788, Stiles found a single document, folded in fours, enclosed in the envelope that arrived from Georgia. As Holmes accurately notes, this document is indeed written "from the right to the left"; it is not, however, inscribed in "Hebrew," but entirely in Arabic (Figure 3).[34]

Ever conscious of time, Holmes noted to Stiles that this historic document was hastily inscribed by 'Usman after coming to "this country about two years since." Ironically, however, the very "country" in which 'Usman was quickly writing was itself in a slow process of composition. The same year in which 'Usman was scribbling his Arabic "specimen" for Holmes—1788—America's founding document was not yet ratified. Covering the four quarters of this

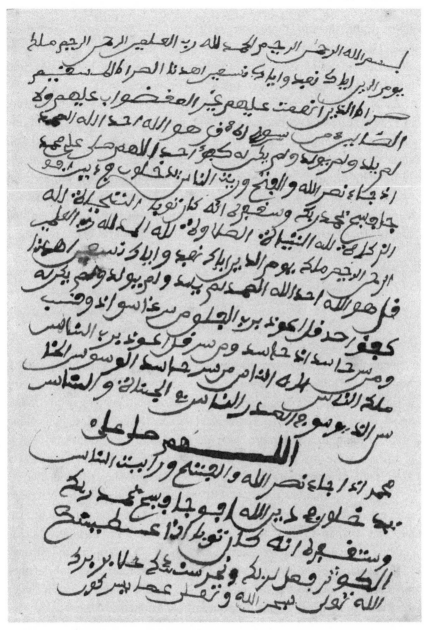

Figure 3 Opening detail from the Arabic page authored by 'Usman, enslaved Muslim from West Africa, which he penned at Parnassus Plantation, near Midway, Georgia, on February 21, 1788. This page, never before published, represents the earliest extant instance of Arabic writing by a slave in the United States after Independence. Image courtesy of the Massachusetts Historical Society, Boston.

single Arabic sheet in "three quarters of an hour," 'Usman wrote "with great ease and freedom" even as the US Constitution itself awaited approval from all thirteen states—a Constitution that tragically would value 'Usman, and his African peers, as only "three-fifths of all other persons."[35]

As he penned the page pictured as Figure 3, 'Usman was surely unaware in 1788 that he was producing a national precedent, fashioning an entirely different "founding document"—the earliest surviving Arabic writings by an enslaved African penned in the newly formed United States. And yet, if unaware of his original place in history, 'Usman aptly begins with foundational words. In his first four lines, 'Usman copies the Qur'an's own initial chapter, launching his page with the Muslim scripture's short introduction, entitled simply "The Opener" (al-Fātiḥah), the first line of 'Usman's Arabic reading:

بسم الله الرحمن الرحيم الحمد لله رب العالمين الرحمن الرحيم

[In the name of Allah, the most Merciful, the most Compassionate.
Praise to Allah, the Lord of Worlds,
the most Merciful, the most Compassionate][36]

Copying the verses that open the Qur'an, 'Usman generates the first surviving Arabic slave writings after Independence by repeating Islam's own revealed beginnings, with the Muslim canon's first words standing at the opening to this US tradition. In his 1788 cover letter, Holmes had framed 'Usman mythically, invoking "*Clio* or *Urania*" to laud him as a "great literary curiosity." But, rather than words of a pagan Muse, it is the Muslim scripture that 'Usman actually inscribes for Abiel Holmes, copying not a classical oracle, but the Qur'an's own introduction.

'Usman was doubtless unaware of the historic parameters of his composition; nevertheless, it is history, and especially the transitory nature of human life, that 'Usman stresses in the page he composed for Holmes. Quickly copying down another short selection from the Muslim scripture in February 1788, 'Usman chose to reproduce a chapter with just three verses, its brief lines mirroring our own fleeting mortality. Near its middle, 'Usman's page includes the Arabic materials that constitute the entirety of Chapter 103 of the Qur'an:

والعصر إن الإنسان لفي خسر إلا الذين آمنوا وعملوا الصالحات وتواصوا بالحق
وتواصوا بالصبر

[By Time! Indeed, mankind is in loss, Except for those who have believed and done righteous deeds and advised each other to truth and advised each other to patience.][37]

Swearing by "time" itself, these Qur'anic verses as copied by 'Usman recall the urgent condition of all human existence, marking the movement of "mankind" toward the ultimate destination of death. However, an "except[ion]" to this gloomy limit of "loss" is also proclaimed: those who practice "patience," the "believers," are consigned not to perdition, but promised eternal life. Universal in theme, it was perhaps 'Usman's own situation that prompted him to quote this "Chapter of Time" in particular. Under the watchful presence of Abiel Holmes, aspiring historian, 'Usman faced in February 1788 an observer hungry for details, as well as a document, hoping to preserve the present. Recording the precise time taken to compose this historic document—no longer than "three quarters of an hour"—Holmes is handed Arabic words that themselves meditate on "time," warning humanity to seek patiently the hereafter. As a Christian minister, Holmes might have sympathized with the Qur'an's eternal emphasis, despite his own love of chronicling. But Holmes could not read 'Usman's words, unsure even of the language that this "great literary curiosity" was writing. As for 'Usman, time constraints were not his problem. Arriving to the United States "about two years" before, an interminable prospect of slavery was now stretching out before him. Only "patience" promised release, with hopes of a world beyond.

≈

The quotations from the Qur'an chosen by 'Usman in 1788 seemed to suggest his own desperate situation; but his natural surroundings are also subtly reflected in his selections. Nearing the end of 'Usman's page appears another chapter, derived from some of the last lines of Qur'an—a chapter that opens by invoking not life's quick passing, but day's beginnings:

قل اعوذ برب الفلق

من شر ما خلق

ومن شر غاسق اذا وقب

[Say: I take refuge with the Lord of Daybreak.

From the evil of what He created.

And from the evil of the darkness as it gathers.][38]

Set down by 'Usman while stranded on American shores, these lines were first revealed in the Arabian desert, forming the opening to Chapter 113 of the Qur'an. And yet, these same words seem to portray the place in which 'Usman found himself in 1788. Witness to the breathtaking sunrises over the Golden Isles, yet surrounded by gathering "darkness," and the "evils" of enslavement, 'Usman turns from his captivity on the US east coast to the "Lord" of oriental light. Appealing intimately for morning blessings, voicing a deeply personal "I," 'Usman calls on the God of the dawn. Marooned on "the refuge of the Muses"—Parnassus Plantation—'Usman takes his own "refuge," seeking sanctuary with Allah from his harsh human "masters." Despite all the "evils" encircling him, 'Usman still recognizes the sovereign of the "Daybreak" even as he witnesses the sun rise over the same ocean that had carried him to slavery.

"I take refuge," 'Usman writes, repeating the same declaration expressed by so many others in arriving to the Golden Isles during the decades both before and after his time. In his first-person search for sanctuary, 'Usman pronounces similar sentiments to those uttered by other figures, stretching from Robert Montgomery to Aaron Burr. However, for 'Usman, Georgia's seacoast was no paradisal utopia, no "refuge" from conflict, but a naked coast where he was stripped of everything—or, almost everything. One thing could not be taken from 'Usman: his capacity to inscribe Arabic lines unreadable to his American captors, etching his signature into a strand of US history that has waited until now to come to light.

6

"His name is 'Usman"

This church has given to her country eighty-six ministers of the Gospel and seven foreign missionaries. Midway in St. John's Parish, now Liberty County, was the cradle of revolutionary spirit in Georgia and two of her sons were signers of the Declaration of Independence.

Plaque in front of Midway Church, Georgia[1]

Abiel Holmes was an aspiring historian when he first arrived in Georgia in 1785. As Midway's new minister, however, he was no mere student of history, but a first-person participant. The church that had called Holmes as pastor in 1785 was almost a hundred years old; Holmes was far from the first of the "eighty-six ministers" that Midway had "given to her country." Founded in Dorchester, Massachusetts, in 1695, this Northern church took as its mission the "promotion of religion in the Southern plantations"; migrating first to South Carolina, the church finally arrived to Georgia in 1752.[2] Midway's old church—like its young minister—was a refugee from New England. Of more note than the church's colonial roots, however, was its recent role in the American Revolution. A center of Christian spirituality, this church was also distinguished by a "revolutionary spirit," planted in the heart of Georgia's "Liberty County." A "cradle" of Independence, Midway and its region had even nurtured two "sons" whose signatures would grace Jefferson's "Declaration of Independence"—Lyman Hall and Button Gwinnett—autographing the iconic document drafted by a man from Monticello.

It is apt that Jefferson's landmark document—his 1776 "Declaration"—is memorialized on the façade of the Midway church, not far from Parnassus Plantation where 'Usman penned his Arabic manuscript a dozen years later, in 1788. Jefferson and 'Usman are, of course, an unlikely pair of authors. Jefferson's Declaration, asserting that "all men are created equal," is unrivaled in US historical fame; 'Usman's words, written by an enslaved man suffering brutal inequalities, have remained unknown until now. Nevertheless, the American documents of Jefferson and 'Usman share certain catalysts and characteristics, each surrounded by national struggles, while bearing historic signatures. Midway proudly claims two "sons" who autographed Jefferson's Declaration—a document demanding rights, but also intimating war, overturning the old political order with the stroke of a pen, signaling America's rejection of British rule and monarchal succession. For 'Usman, however, internecine war and crises of succession were nothing new. Arriving to Georgia around 1786, 'Usman reached America immediately after the Revolution—a struggle that represented "America's first Civil War," pitting colonists against their British cousins.[3] Domestic rebellion not only greeted 'Usman in exile, however, but had likely helped deliver him into bondage at home. Reaching US shores recently ravaged by war, it was *jihād* in West Africa that paved the way for 'Usman's enslavement.

Born in eighteenth-century Futa Jallon—"in the interior part of *Guinea*," as Holmes informed Stiles—'Usman was raised in a Muslim region famed for scholarship, but also soldiery, regularly waging war against neighboring states.[4] Despite these conflicts, 'Usman's youth in "*Footah*" was clearly peaceful enough to include education in Islamic traditions. Memorizing Qur'anic chapters, 'Usman was trained not merely to recite this sacred text orally, but to write in elegant lines. Such literary skills would comprise a rare continuity in a life of jarring interruption, linking 'Usman's studies in Africa with his slavery in America. In 1784, however, disaster hit 'Usman's home region with the death of Ibrāhīm ibn Sori—Futa Jallon's leader—a death that further endangered the area's precarious political stability and security. A "century of struggles for power" ensued, engulfing the region in wars that saw many children of Futa Jallon captured and sold into slavery, including the late Ibrāhīm ibn Sori's very own son.[5] Also named Ibrāhīm, Ibn Sori's son would, like 'Usman, arrive to the edges of America, eventually touching the extreme margins too of Thomas Jefferson's own life. If the succession struggle following 1784 proved ruinous for Futa Jallon, this year would also mark a turning point for 'Usman personally, sold very soon after into US slavery. Surviving the Middle Passage horrors crossing the Atlantic, 'Usman was settled near Midway, a West African exile enslaved near an itinerant church, itself a refugee in Georgia. Captive in a foreign land, 'Usman may have recognized, however, an oddly familiar scene. Fresh from sectarian struggles, he witnessed a nation suffering the aftermath of its own break from the "mother country."[6] Transitioning between cultures, each severed by familial strife, 'Usman was surrounded by contending lines of succession, lines that seem to bleed into his own ink, receiving expression from 'Usman's pen.

In February 1788, Abiel Holmes had left 'Usman behind on Parnassus Plantation, carrying away Arabic writings to send north to Ezra Stiles. However, 'Usman did not leave off from his writing, and Holmes would not forget his authorship. An African slave in "Liberty County," 'Usman would elect to become a "signer" himself. By 1790, a different kind of "revolutionary spirit" in early Georgia would pour out onto an Arabic page—a page bearing the signature not of a famous Midway "son," but the autograph of this same parish's hidden Muslim slave.

≈

The year 1790 was a year of anticipation for Abiel Holmes. He was planning his return home for a wedding, not to officiate as a minister, but to be married himself. Departing Georgia, Holmes would trek up to New England in the summer, taking his fiancée's hand, and giving her his name. The year 1790 would also feature another repetition and return for Holmes, however. This same year of his nuptials in New Haven would witness Holmes take away one more written performance by 'Usman, receiving from Parnassus Plantation yet another Arabic document (Figure 4).[7]

This second document recalls the first 'Usman penned for Holmes in 1788. 'Usman starts once more by quoting the Qur'an's first chapter: "The Opener." However, the form of this 1790 document differs from its 1788 predecessor. Instead of a page divided into four small quarters, this second manuscript unfolds in a long continuous column, stretching downward in thirty-one short successive lines.[8] The content of this 1790 document also reflects its cascading form, hinting at a hierarchy linking the world above to our world below. Rather than mere scattered fragments from the Muslim scripture, a catalogue of blessings plunges down 'Usman's page. In row after row, 'Usman honors sacred Muslim names, stretching from angelic figures to historic forerunners. Though not appearing in a precise order from top to bottom, 'Usman's single-page document exalts entities and identities that include the following:

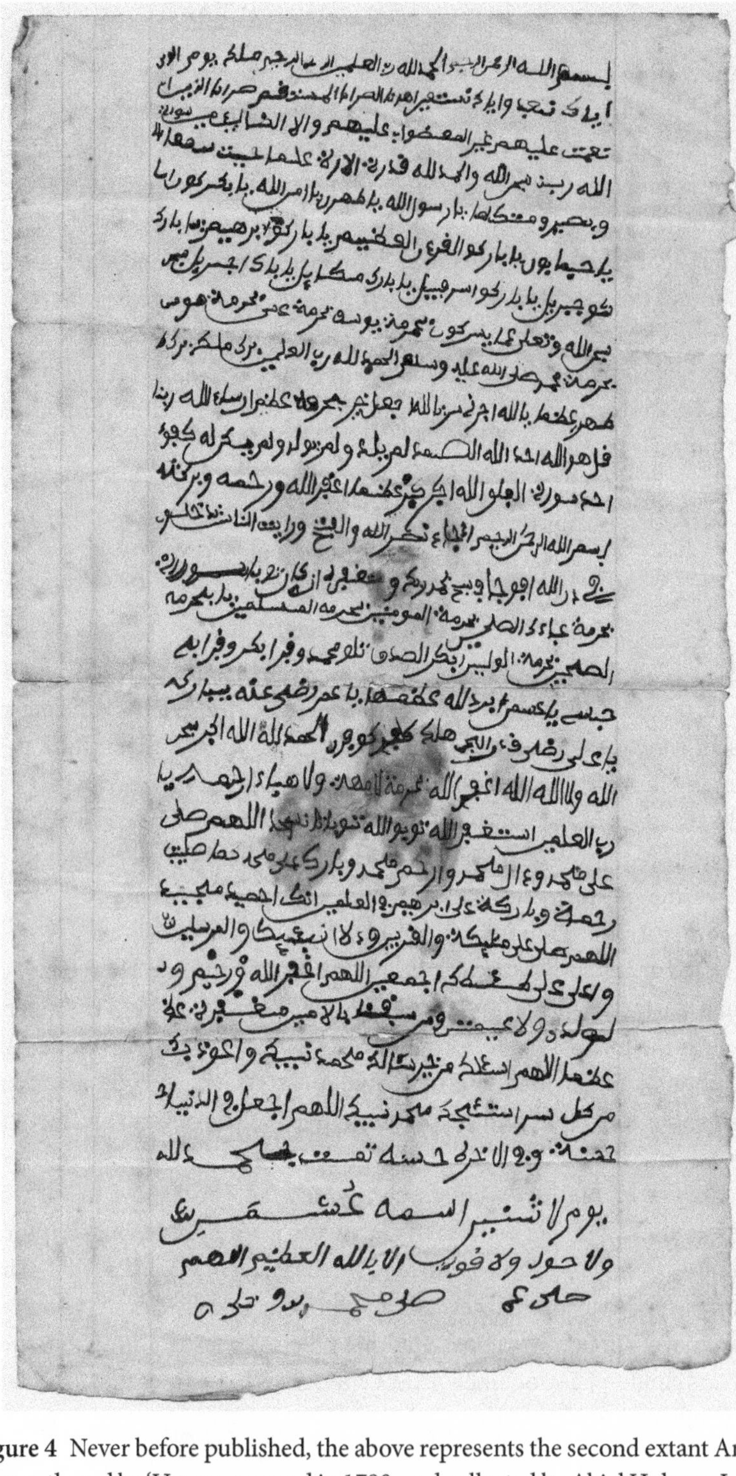

Figure 4 Never before published, the above represents the second extant Arabic page authored by 'Usman, penned in 1790, and collected by Abiel Holmes. Image courtesy of the Massachusetts Historical Society, Boston.

Angels
> Gabriel
>> Israfel
>>> Michael

Prophets
> Abraham
>> Joseph
>>> Jesus
>>>> Muhammad

Caliphs
> Abu Bakr [Muhammad's father-in-law];
>> 'Umar
>>> 'Usman
>>>> 'Ali [Muhammad's son-in-law][9]

Sketching a scattered yet sacred lineage, 'Usman's manuscript implies gene-alogies that synthesize the heavenly and the human. Suffering bondage to a white family at Parnassus Plantation, 'Usman embraces an alternate house-hold in Arabic, outlining a family tree that falls from paradisal heights down to Islam's prophetic roots. A witness to rebellion, living his life amid revolu-tions on both sides of the Atlantic, 'Usman yet invokes a sovereignty that re-mains unshakeable. Despite all upheavals—spanning an African home long lost, and the oppression that forms his American future—'Usman voices a series of blessings, appealing to a stability that endures.

The second document Holmes received from 'Usman in 1790 reflected an Arabic author whose literary skills are clearly undiminished, and whose spirit seems undeterred. Even after suffering five full years of bitter exile and slavery, 'Usman gives vent to no curses; he only affirms, invoking an-gelic forces and the prophetic genealogy that founded his religion. In the year of his own nuptial blessings, Holmes receives these Islamic benedic-tions from an African slave. Acquiring his own in-laws in 1790, Holmes also receives report of a sacred family, with 'Usman invoking not only the Prophet Muhammad, but Muhammad's successors, emphasizing especially his father-in-law, Abu Bakr, known as "the Righteous."[10] In listing these ex-alted authorities, 'Usman's lineage of leaders ironically includes his very own name, with this Muslim slave's identity echoed as he inscribes the name of Islam's third caliph—'Usman.

'Usman's name appears not merely in his list of Muslim leaders, however. To end his 1790 document, 'Usman pens a much more personal signature.

Unlike the first manuscript acquired by Holmes in 1788, this second one closes with 'Usman's own autograph, inscribing these words near its conclusion:

اسمه عسمن ولا حول ولا قوة إلا بالله العظيم
[His name is 'Usman, and there is no might
nor power except with Allah, the Great][11]

Even as he suffers the cruelest of earthly conditions, 'Usman voices his resignation to the divine decree, confessing the exclusive rule of Allah. Amid these Islamic inscriptions, however, 'Usman also inscribes his own identity, writing his name just before his concluding doxology. Amid pious commonplaces, 'Usman pens a few words of deep personal resonance, appending a haunting third- person autograph: "اسمه عسمن"—that is, "His name is 'Usman." In his 1788 letter, Holmes had written to Stiles regarding 'Usman, mentioning this slave's "African name," writing it as "Osamon." In 1790, 'Usman answers back in lines unreadable to Holmes, recording his true name in Arabic. This signature—standing as the sole marker of subjectivity, penned by the first extant Muslim author on US soil—has stayed submerged for more than two centuries. Mere miles from Midway, which mothered "sons [who] were signers of the Declaration of Independence," an orphaned son of West Africa signed his own name, leaving behind a document no less historic, yet entirely forgotten.[12]

'Usman's last known writing—words that spell out his own identity, while consecrating his Islamic heritage—was collected by Holmes in 1790, the same year he trekked home northward to begin his new family. For 'Usman, however, the coming months would witness not familial beginnings, but a loss in the Parnassus household, losing a patriarch of the plantation. Just a year after 'Usman signed his 1790 document, a death was announced—that of Raymond Demere. His death was sudden, and a shock that reverberated beyond the Golden Isles due to Demere's prominence. Not only the son of Georgia's original British colonists, Demere had served George Washington in America's fight against the British, elevated to the rank of major during the Revolution.[13] Demere had returned home as a patriot; although surviving the war, Demere would, however, soon be vanquished by his own property. On May 20, 1791, Raymond Demere was "thrown from his horse" at a plantation near Parnassus. His "neck was broken" and, laying where he landed, Demere "died in about half an hour."[14]

Demere's unexpected death was, of course, most keenly felt by his own family. This loss was especially tragic for Raymond's young wife, Mary. Two months earlier, she had just given birth to their fifth child—also named Raymond Demere—who would grow up never knowing his father, but would eventually be laid to rest on land essential to the entire family, choosing to be buried on Parnassus Plantation itself.[15] For 'Usman, Demere's death in 1791, although sudden, would likely not have seemed extraordinary. 'Usman's life had already witnessed so many lineages cut, so many authorities toppled. Demere was just the latest earthly master brought down to the dust, broken and staring up to heaven from the low-country soil. "Liberty County" would be known as a "cradle" for freedom; its grounds, however, would also be the grave for slave owners.

≈

In the summer of 1790, Holmes arrived back to New Haven for his nuptials, welcomed home by family and friends, including his old professor. Ezra Stiles was especially excited, looking forward to the wedding of his former student, which was to take place on August 29. In a merry mood, two days before the marriage, Stiles sat down to write letters. His cheer was due not exclusively to the upcoming wedding, however, but to the homecoming of another dear friend: Thomas Jefferson. Jefferson had recently arrived from Paris, residing again in America, and "reluctantly" accepting a promotion stateside. At George Washington's urging, Jefferson had agreed to serve as the United States' first secretary of state.[16] Stiles was unable to contain his jubilation on Jefferson's return, not only congratulating his friend on his current appointment, but presciently looking forward to the day that Jefferson would be president. On August 27, Stiles wrote his welcome home, ending his letter to Jefferson with the following words:

> I am rejoyced that the United States are honored with your Counsels and Abilities in the high Department of the Secretary of State. This I say without Adulation, who am a Spectator only and a most cordial Friend to the Liberties and Glory of the American Republic, tho' without the least Efficiency or Influence in its Councils. There are four Characters which I cannot flatter; their Merit is above it. Such are those of a Franklin, an Adams, an Ellsworth, a Jefferson and a Washington. I glory in them all; I rejoice that my Country is happy in their useful Labors. And for yourself I can only wish, that when that best of Men, the present President, shall

be translated to the World of Light, a Jefferson may succede him in the
Presidency of the United States. Forgive me this Effusion of the Sentiments
of sincere Respect and Estimation, and permit me the honor of Subscribing
myself, Dear Sir, Your most affectionate, Obliged, & Hble Servt,

EZRA STILES[17]

In August 1790, Holmes departed the South for New England, leaving behind 'Usman, whose own final writings would trace a lineage of blessed leaders. Arriving in New Haven, Holmes reunited with Stiles in August, even
as Stiles was inscribing the above—his own lineage of leaders—listing not
founders of Islam, but of America. Jefferson himself surfaces in Stiles's catalogue, named as one of the illustrious "Characters," along with "Franklin,"
"Adams," "Ellsworth," and "Washington." And although George Washington
had only recently started his first term, Stiles heralds Jefferson on August 27,
1790, as a potential future president. Stiles cherishes "the present President,"
of course, but his death will inevitably come. And, when Washington "shall
be translated" into heaven, ushered into the "World of Light," Stiles hopes
that "Jefferson may succede him," elevated one step higher, to "the Presidency
of the United States."

For Jefferson, his return from Paris was busy enough without dreaming
of another promotion. Serving in "the high Department of the Secretary
of State" offered sufficient challenges, at least for 1790. Stiles's prophecy on
presidential succession would prove true, of course, but only after years of
turmoil. Jefferson had a difficult decade ahead; his path to the presidency
was neither continuous nor calm. He would rise to the top job finally, only
after surviving the bitter election of 1800—too late for Stiles to witness the
achievement. Washington's death was on Stiles's mind in 1790, but it was
Stiles's own heavenly "translation" that arrived first. Yale's president passed
away in May 1795 at the age of sixty-eight, never to see Jefferson become
president of their beloved new "American Republic."[18]

But on August 27, 1790, it was beginnings, not endings, that Stiles celebrated, writing with unusual emotion and exuberance. In his "effusive" letter
to Jefferson, Stiles begged forgiveness for his "Sentiments," packing his letter's final lines with "rejoyc[ing]" and "happy" feeling. A wedding was upcoming, now that Holmes had arrived in New Haven. But Stiles had another
reason to feel unburdened and joyful. Earlier this same month, August 1790,
Stiles had decided to sign his own name to a pivotal document, autographing a pact with fellow leaders of his state. Together, they were forming the

"Connecticut Society for the Promotion of Freedom." Convinced of slavery's injustice, this "Society" aimed "to support" Connecticut's legislated "gradual emancipation" of all slaves—a cautious forerunner of more committed abolitionists who would enliven New England in the early nineteenth century.[19] Stiles not only helped found this "Freedom" society, but would serve as its first leader. Writing to Jefferson in August 1790, predicting his friend's presidential prospects, it was Stiles himself who had just been elected president of this anti-slavery "Connecticut Society."

Years earlier, as a young clergyman in Newport, Stiles had owned a slave—also named Newport. But by the time Stiles departed for Yale in 1778, he had repented, releasing this lone man from bondage. Stiles's discomfort with US slavery would only turn to collective activism a decade later, however, after receiving "specimens" of Muslim slave authorship in Arabic.[20] Along with "fourteen other men," Stiles "drafted a constitution for the Connecticut Society for the Promotion of Freedom" in August 1790—a beneficent act that punctuated a month of blessings, culminating for Stiles on August 29 with Abiel Holmes's marriage.[21] Two days after joyfully writing to Jefferson on the 27th, Stiles attended the wedding; he was not only a witness, however, but a family member. An old friend of the groom, Stiles was also father of the bride. Abiel Holmes had gifted Ezra Stiles rare Arabic sources, filled with familial names; now, Stiles was giving away his own youngest child, Mary Stiles, offering Holmes his daughter's hand in marriage. Returning from Georgia in 1790—the same year he received 'Usman's sacred family tree and sole signature—Holmes now signed his own marriage contract with Mary. And on the evening of August 29, Mary Stiles would forever change her own signature, known for the rest of her short life as Mrs. Mary Holmes, before dying precisely five years later, on August 29, 1795.[22] Holmes had remotely provided his old professor with historic proof of West African literacy, sending north Arabic documents that dovetailed with Stiles's view of "the unrighteousness of slavery." And, it is this view that moved Stiles to public activism, launching in New Haven an emancipation "Society" in August 1790—the same month that Holmes himself would arrive home to New Haven, returning from Georgia to witness Ezra Stiles become not only an anti-slavery activist, but a very proud father-in-law.

7

"Combinations of Letters"

My last letters will have informed you of the present situation of the business relative to the American captives at Algiers. You will have seen there that nothing has been done, or possible to be done, for their redemption. This I know will not surprize you when you recollect the circumstances attending it. Still I shall leave nothing untried and will write you regularly as you desire respecting it. —Some days ago a person who has resided many years at Algiers, called on me in company with M. Volney whom you know, to speak of a means of procuring peace with that Regency on advantageous terms.

William Short to Jefferson from Paris, July 7, 1790[1]

On August 27, 1790, Ezra Stiles celebrated Jefferson's return from Paris, and his promotion to secretary of state. Even as Stiles's letter arrived to Jefferson, welcoming him home, William Short was also writing to Jefferson, reminding him of the metropolis he had just left behind. Jefferson had bid farewell to liberties awakening in Europe, but slavery in Muslim Africa continued to "haunt" him.[2] Returning to America, Jefferson had been elevated to lead a "high Department." In Algiers, "American captives" faced humiliating service in "workhouses."

William Short had served as Jefferson's private secretary in Paris. It was Short's name that Jefferson had mentioned in the encoded letter to John Adams, which had launched Barclay's mission to Morocco. Now, in 1790, Short was echoing the words of his former boss. Still "nothing has been done" for Algerian "captives," Short notes, recalling Jefferson's earlier complaint to Stiles, on Christmas Eve 1786, that "nothing has been done with Algiers." Before Jefferson had left Paris, however, Short had pledged that "nothing" would be left "untried" in North Africa, no matter how debatable—or dangerous. True to his word, Short reports meeting an unnamed "person" with a covert plan for "procuring peace with that Regency." This "person" is only credible due to the "company" he keeps, arriving at Short's door together with someone very well "known" to Jefferson: "M. Volney."[3]

The Comte de Volney was indeed a figure familiar to Jefferson—and almost his mirror image. A socialite and a linguist, a French aristocrat and an Orientalist, Volney's experiences, and even his expressions, would become Jefferson's own. The two first crossed paths in Paris, reaching the capital from opposite ends of the globe. Jefferson had arrived from the American West in 1784; in 1785, Volney had returned to his French homeland after a tour of the Middle East. A friendship was soon cemented between these two travelers. Sharing recent journeys, both were also preparing to publish their accounts of foreign lands, while struggling at the same time to express themselves in a foreign language. In 1785, Jefferson's French was still clumsy, this "savage from the mountains" struggling with Europe's language of culture; at the very same time, however, Jefferson experienced a communication success, when his first book, *Notes on the State of Virginia*—a cultural and ecological overview of his native land—appeared anonymously in Paris.[4] As for Volney, 1785 saw his return from Arabia to Paris, where he looked forward to publishing his own account of exotic travels and tongues. But, while Jefferson was wrestling with French, Volney was striving to acquaint his fellow Frenchmen with Middle Eastern idioms, working on a grammar of "Oriental languages."[5]

Jefferson and Volney became friends, finally parting in September 1789 when Jefferson left Paris, never to return abroad. Witnessing with enthusiasm the launch of France's revolution, Jefferson would soon grudgingly accept Washington's invitation to assume the "high office" of secretary of state. During his last summer in France, Jefferson had felt first-hand the force of the Bastille's fall, with the prison's "demolition" and its few remaining prisoners released into the streets. One oft-repeated account, though apocryphal, tells of Jefferson drinking with Volney himself when news of the fall of the Bastille arrived to them as they were "conversing in a café."[6] But Jefferson's Paris years would also witness more private failures. He had proved incapable of freeing fellow Americans held captive far away in Algiers—a failure that followed him home, surfacing again in this 1790 message from his former private secretary. Short's letter, invoking secret informants and Muslim slavery, raised matters entirely familiar to Jefferson. Most unsurprising was to find Jefferson's old friend, the Comte de Volney, mixed up in this diplomatic mess, involving an anonymous informant. A veteran of Middle Eastern travel, Volney was also a lover of hidden identities and international intrigue. As Jefferson well knew, it was not only Volney's friend, but Volney himself, whose real name was left out of Short's letter. "Volney" itself was a fiction and a cover, a synthetic pseudonym. Born instead as Constantin François de Chassebœuf, Jefferson's friend had coined his new name by combining "Voltaire" and "Ferney" as an homage to his Enlightenment hero (Voltaire) and the French locale where Voltaire had settled (Ferney).[7]

It was not Volney's name but Jefferson's that would be at stake in the years that followed William Short's 1790 letter. American captivity "at Algiers" was a Middle Eastern dilemma that stayed with Jefferson despite his departure from France. Returning to America, Jefferson would also arrive home with other Middle Eastern materials from Paris—some originating with Volney himself. In 1790, Volney was offering assistance to free Americans from Muslim captivity; he had already aided his friend for many years, however, publishing scholarship that supplied Jefferson with glimpses of Muslim lands and languages.[8] Jefferson did not know, however, as he opened William Short's letter in 1790, that his debts to Volney would require repayment. In the coming decade, Jefferson would be called on to aid Volney, not only hosting this Frenchman after his own incarceration, but helping him disseminate his Middle Eastern studies. Aiding Volney was not without risk, however. Jefferson would himself have to adopt his own subterfuge, seeking to keep his name unknown.

≈

> This idea of portraying unknown foreign sounds by combinations of letters already known, has been so well opposed and refuted by the Honorable Sir William Jones [...]
>
> Volney, discussing "Arabic Consonants" in Chapter 5 of his
The European Alphabet Applied to Asiatic Languages[9]

Can the sounds of one language be accurately expressed by the letters of another? This was a question that bedeviled the Comte de Volney and his scholarly peers. Even "the Honorable Sir William Jones," a father of Eastern linguistics, had grappled with this problem.[10] Are Arabic's "unknown sounds," for instance, expressible via a Western alphabet? Are its exotic gutturals and glottal stops communicable in Latin characters?

This problem had a long pedigree in the eighteenth century, but it was especially Volney's concern during the days he first met Jefferson in Paris. Returning home after a three-year tour of the Middle East, Volney yearned to share this region's languages with his fellow Frenchmen. However, the intricacies of Arabic, Persian, and Turkish proved difficult to introduce. A "simplified" system was needed, Volney decided, leading him to publish in Paris his *Simplification des Langues Orientales*—a book seeking to make Eastern sounds and scripts easier for Europeans to understand. The project of devising a novel method of expressing exotic languages seemed second nature for Volney, of course; his very name was itself a novelty, a "foreign" identity formed from older sounds "already known."[11]

The accessibility of Middle Eastern letters was on Volney's mind when he met Jefferson, who was trying to keep his own letters on the Middle East inaccessible. Volney wished to simplify foreign languages; Jefferson was instead ciphering his own language, trying to hide from spies his correspondence concerning the Barbary Coast. Jefferson's struggle for secrecy was the inverse of Volney's quest for "simplification." And yet Volney himself would help open up new vistas for Jefferson, offering authentic glimpses of the Middle East. Even as he wrote his secret letters in Paris, Jefferson eagerly read Volney's new book, appearing in the same city, his *Voyage en Syrie et en Egypte*. Published in 1787, Volney printed his *Voyage* with majestic imprimatur—"*Avec Approbation & Privilège du Roi*"—"approved" by the "King," the doomed sovereign Louis XVI himself.[12] This travelogue of Muslim lands quickly caught the attention of America's minister to France. By August 1787, Jefferson had acquired Volney's book; and, by September, he had begun buying it for his friends, sending a copy of *Voyage* to George Wythe, his old teacher back in Virginia.[13]

Volney's *Voyage* gained a global readership; but it was Jefferson's personal relationship with Volney himself that would prove most significant to the future president. The exact date when the two men met in Paris is not known. What is clear, however, is that Jefferson was well prepared for their encounter, fostering an amateur interest in precisely the texts and tradition so beloved by Volney. Even as Volney himself was "returning from Syria to France, in March 1785," Jefferson sought from Paris to purchase volumes back in Virginia, dispatching a book order on March 3, 1785.[14] Hoping to secure items from the small library of his old friend and "expert Orientalist" Samuel Henley, Jefferson wrote specifying his favorites, including a sizeable item he lists as:

> Jones *Poeseos Asiaticae Comment.* 8vo. unbound.[15]

This volume of "Asiatic" verse, ordered by Jefferson in 1785, would take many twists and turns before it finally arrived to him several years later. However, it would be worth the wait. Filled with Arabic and Persian writings, this 500-page collection offered Jefferson a glimpse of Islamic literatures in their original languages. This early acquisition in Arabic and Persian, moreover, was far from Jefferson's last. Ordered from Paris, his purchase of *Poeseos Asiaticae* set a precedent, not only for Jefferson's next years in France, but for his later life in America. The "Jones" who authored this "unbound" volume was the very same scholar that so interested Volney—the same "Honorable Sir William Jones" who was grappling with the problem of "portraying unknown foreign sounds by combinations of letters already known" in the eighteenth century. In Jefferson's purchase of this "foreign" book in Paris, Volney himself was rendered more familiar. Meeting Volney after his 1785 return from the Middle East, Jefferson found a new French friend with whom to share not only scholarly discussions, but polite society, frequenting together the Parisian salon of the celebrated Madame Helvétius.[16] Even as he showed interest in Jones's *Poeseos Asiaticae* in Paris, however, Jefferson could not know that the very same unfamiliar "letters" he was collecting in a foreign capital would eventually return to him, arriving two decades later while he was serving in a capital city much closer to home.

≈

نصر من الله وفتح قريب
[Help is from Allah and conquest is close]

The Arabic words quoted above appear in the middle of page 323 of the 1774 edition of William Jones's *Poeseos Asiaticae* purchased by Jefferson from France. Cited by Jones as a verse from an "Asiatic poem," these words originally derive from the Qur'an, quoted from the scripture's sixty-first chapter. Recording on January 24, 1786, his payment for Jones's octavo volume in Paris, Jefferson began collecting, for the very first time, selections from the Muslim scripture in its original language.[17]

A full two decades earlier, while a student in Williamsburg, Jefferson had picked up a copy of *The Koran*, George Sales's widely available English edition—an edition, however, in which "not a single word in Arabic script appears."[18] It is not until Jefferson's stay in Paris, however, that he would purchase volumes printed with copious Arabic lines, integrating into his personal library Qur'anic quotations such as the above. Considering the career that awaited him in America, it is apt that just quotations, not a complete

Arabic Qur'an, arrived to Jefferson. It was mere strands from the Muslim scripture that were purchased from Paris, interwoven with other "Asiatic" writings. Tallying the cost of Jones's volume at the start of 1786—the same year that ends with the arrival in Paris of an Arabic treaty—Jefferson unwittingly renders payment for Arabic words that proclaim proximate victory. "Conquest is close," this Qur'anic quotation announces, despite reaching Jefferson only after immense delay and distance. Original to Arabia, yet crisscrossing the Atlantic, it is from America that Jefferson orders this slice of the Muslim scripture. In two decades' time, Jefferson would again receive Arabic quotations from the Qur'an from far in the American interior—quotations that ironically echo the very verse above. Although initially purchased as part of Jones's elegant "Asiatic" volume, these same words from the Qur'an would confront Jefferson once again in October 1807, but scribbled on a nearly illegible and singular page carried from the American West.[19]

This Qur'anic quotation in Jones's collection foreshadowed a moment many years later in Jefferson's life. However, Jefferson's purchase in 1785 also predicted much more immediate acquisitions made from Parisian publishers. Although a European capital, Paris had long formed a prime center for Arabic studies, and would offer Jefferson access to rare sources. It was in Paris that the American signed a treaty translated from Arabic; but Paris would also witness Jefferson collecting Arabic treatises as well. Soon after ordering Jones's *Poeseos Asiaticae*, Jefferson's stay in the city brought him into contact with Anthony Vieyra, whose published study of Middle Eastern languages—known to Jefferson as *Specimina Arabica et Persica*—was acquired after its 1789 publication. Paris may also have alerted Jefferson to *Rudimenta linguae Arabicae*, a seventeenth-century grammar by Thomas van Erpe, which came equipped with an appendix in Qur'anic Arabic. Published first in 1620 Leiden, but meriting a Paris edition by 1638, this study would represent the oldest Arabic manual that would ever find its way into Jefferson's library.[20]

It would not be such an early grammar, but the very latest grammar on "Oriental Languages" from Paris, however, that claimed personal links to Jefferson. Volney did not complete his *Simplification des Langues Orientales* until five years after Jefferson left the city, but this work would soon make it onto Monticello shelves after its Paris appearance in 1795. Proposing a "new" means to "understand Arabic Persian and Turkish in European characters," Volney's *Simplification* was published in Paris during an especially complicated time, printed the same year that the Terror's aftermath witnessed the rise of France's new Directory. The republican shift in France's domestic politics is signaled at the very opening to Volney's guide to foreign scripts and sounds. His *Voyage*, so beloved by Jefferson, was published in 1787 by royal decree. The frontispiece of Volney's *Simplification*, however, announces itself as appearing "by imprimatur of the Republic" in "Year III"—that is, 1795, counting from September 22, 1792, the French Republic's "first day."[21] Volney's grammar substituted "European characters" for Middle Eastern script; his own European nation had undergone a substitution, however, with the long-reigning "*Roi*" decapitated, displaced by an ascendant "*République*." Even as Volney was revolutionizing Oriental learning, seeking to open Middle Eastern languages for Western understanding, the West itself was being revolutionized, with unpredictable results.

Even before his *Simplification* appeared, the Revolution's uncertainties had begun to impact Volney himself. A French count endowed with Islamic learning, Volney was fruitful in his contradictions, a scholarly aristocrat who was yet sympathetic to proletarian freedoms. Volney even recruited his "Oriental" expertise to promote France's political evolution, publishing his 1791 *The Ruins, or Meditations upon the Revolutions of Empires* two years after the fall of the Bastille.[22] A fictional history of imperial rise and fall, Volney set his "meditations" in the Middle East, narrating the hope of human progress from the perspective of a wanderer in Muslim lands. Recounting the overturning of ancient orders, Volney soon found himself in a precarious position amid the upheavals that continued to unsettle Paris. News of these challenges facing Volney reached Jefferson after he had returned to America in 1790. In another letter from William Short, Jefferson learned that Volney had suffered a "severe shock," accused of accepting a cushy "appointment" in Corsica. Eventually, Volney was publicly denounced and even detained, imprisoned for "10 months" and nearly put to death.[23]

Surviving his Paris incarceration, yet still facing "injustice and persecution," Volney decided to depart France yet again. "Sorrowful at the past" and "anxious for the future," Volney searched for "a peaceful asylum of which Europe no longer offered him the hope."[24] The Middle East was a region already experienced by Volney; the West, however, seemed a place of fresh promise and liberty. Providentially, this scholar of Muslim lands and languages had old friends in the New World, and could expect an especially warm welcome at the top of a "little mountain" in Virginia.

≈

Standing at the summit of Monticello, side-by-side with Thomas Jefferson, Volney thought he could see Egypt. It was June 1796, and Volney had just arrived to Charlottesville, leaving France's tumult far behind, trekking instead through the quiet woods of Albemarle county. As he stood with Jefferson gazing south over the lush green landscape, Volney saw not the American South, however, but North Africa. Opposite to Jefferson's hilltop house, the two men gazed at a small peak—"Willis's Mountain"—which reminded Volney, he insisted, of the great Pyramid of Giza.[25]

Volney's conflation of the view from Jefferson's Virginian home with Egyptian vistas seems fanciful. However, it was Jefferson himself who had first invited such an analogy. Learning that his friend had arrived from France at the end of 1795, Jefferson urged Volney to head for Monticello in December.[26] Renewing his invitation to his Arabist friend the following spring, Jefferson sought to entice Volney's visit with Arabian allusions, writing on April 10:

My house, which had never been more than half finished, had during a war of 8. years and my subsequent absence of 10. years gone into almost total decay. I am now engaged in the repairing altering and finishing it. The noise, confusion and discomfort of the scene will require all your philosophy and patience. However your journey thro' the country from George town to this place will have prepared you in some degree for less comfortable lodgings than I shall be able to give you in your next year's visit. And for the present one you will endeavor to find comfort in a comparison of our covering with that of an Arabian tent, and in what Arabia and it's adust sands cannot shew, groves of poplars, towering mountains, rocks and rivers, blue skies balsamic air yet pure and healthy; and count for something, the affectionate welcome of Dear Sir Your friend & servt

TH: JEFFERSON[27]

Opening with a lifelong concern—Monticello's perpetual renovations—Jefferson laments that his time in public service has slowed private construction. Now returned from Paris, and relieved of his duties as secretary of state, Jefferson directs his energies to endless work on his own home, always "repairing," "altering," and "finishing." In writing Volney, however, Jefferson marries this architectural passion with Volney's profession, framing Monticello as a Middle Eastern lodging. Arriving in June, Volney would glimpse an Egyptian pyramid from this Virginian hill. But, already in April,

Jefferson had first linked East and West, even as he stressed natural contrasts. America's "groves of poplars" are, of course, unlike Arabia's "adust sands." And yet, Jefferson's most personal structure—his private home—does indeed mirror the Middle East. An iconic home in the national imagination, now pictured on the reverse of the US nickel, Monticello is invoked by Jefferson as "an Arabian tent"—a "covering" whose "comfort" would be entirely familiar to an Oriental traveler.[28]

Jefferson's playful Arabian allusion offered a fit invitation to his friend, anticipating the views enjoyed by Volney in America. Stopping at Monticello in the summer, and spotting a Middle Eastern site in the near distance, Volney would push further into the West, traveling to Tennessee and Kentucky through the autumn of 1796. In the wilds of the New World, however, Volney oddly found familiar sights, glimpsed not merely in mountains, but in men. Recording his favorable impressions with highly bigoted phrases, Volney insisted that "the American savages resemble the Bedoween Arabs of Asia and Africa"—an ethnic synthesis that implied verbal overlaps for Volney as well.[29] In Native American idioms, Volney surprisingly heard distinct Arabian accents, even suggesting specific Middle East roots for individual "Indian" words. Later published in his *View of the Climate and Soil of the United States of America*, Volney proposed parallels, for example, between Miami and Arabic, these languages linked in their shared word for the conjunction "with":

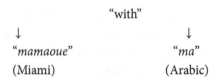

In the 1780s, Jefferson had theorized to Ezra Stiles that "Asia [was] peopled from America." After visiting Jefferson in the 1790s, Volney forged linguistic links between Asia and America, discovering even the simplest word— "with"—conjoining Arabic and American tongues.[30]

Echoing Jefferson, who had equated his own home with "an Arabian tent," Volney would publish in his later works the Arabic overtones he heard whispered by Native Americans. However, there was another verbal bridge between East and West that Volney made in America, but which he forever kept secret. Searching America for Eastern analogues, Volney was hoping also to secure an American translator for his own Eastern "meditations"—his

1791 *The Ruins, or Meditations upon the Revolutions of Empires.* Already rendered once into English without his approval, Volney's *Ruins* had appeared in "cheap" Parisian "editions" flawed by "inaccuracies"—editions that Volney hoped to replace, canvassing for help in producing a new English translation.[31] Volney's wishes were fulfilled in America, but he could not trumpet his good fortune. The translator he had secured had imposed one condition: anonymity. His role in rendering this Middle Eastern fiction must be kept quiet. Ensuring secrecy seemed difficult, however, as Volney's translator was rising ever more in prominence, and would soon become his nation's president. Even before departing for the far West, Volney had met with the future translator of his Middle Eastern fiction—the lone American who dwelt under an Arabian "covering" at the top of a "little mountain" in Virginia.

8

"Go to Mecca; and God will Render you Victorious"

When Volney had arrived to Virginia for his three-week stay in the summer of 1796, it was the sorry state of Jefferson's house that was on his mind. As stressed in his April invitation, Monticello was in disrepair. The ongoing renovations did not discourage Volney's visit, however. Monticello may have been in ruins, but Volney had brought along his own *Ruins* to America, requiring help to render this French text to better fit English audiences. And it would be Jefferson, despite his own domestic renovations, who accepted this task, agreeing to fashion a refurbished English edition of Volney's Middle Eastern "meditations."[1]

Beyond the irony of translating the *Ruins* amid the ruins of Monticello, the timing for Jefferson to take up such a task is also curious. Volney's work was overtly political, championing radical ideas and revolutionary impulses that Jefferson shared. However, in 1796, both men were also, to differing degrees, political fugitives, fleeing the grasp of their respective republics. Volney was evading the dizzying aftermath of the French Revolution, as his homeland spiraled down toward a new era of despotic rule. For Jefferson, it was dreams of pastoral leisure that prompted him to flee Washington. Exhausted by national service, he was eager to return to domestic routines in Virginia. When Volney arrived in June 1796, Jefferson was enjoying one of the few spans of respite from office afforded during his career's four decades. He had renounced his post as secretary of state as 1794 began. By the end of 1796, however, Jefferson would again become a "reluctant candidate," agreeing to stand for America's highest office at the urging of Madison especially. Falling three votes short, Jefferson was instead sworn in as John Adams's vice president on March 4, 1797.[2]

Despite the brevity of his vacation from government, Jefferson yet agreed to translate anew Volney's highly charged political text. But, perhaps anticipating a return to public office, Jefferson also wisely insisted on silence regarding his role in translating Volney's controversial source. The *Ruins* formed not only a revolutionary work, after all, but also a critique of divine revelation, offering a "lesson of religion's tyranny"—a "lesson" Volney set in Muslim lands.[3] A fanciful meditation on the imperial past, and the promises of human progress, Volney's *Ruins* opens with an unnamed traveler, who narrates his arrival to Palmyra, in modern-day Syria, where he marvels at the ancient debris of this Middle Eastern city. In the English rendition that Jefferson would fashion, this work's initial chapter—entitled simply "Voyage"—begins with its narrator's passage eastward, traversing exotic places: "I was travelling in the Ottoman dominions, and through those provinces which were anciently the kingdoms of Egypt and Syria."[4] Giving new life to a fugitive in Muslim lands, Jefferson becomes a linguistic pilgrim via translation, his first-person English carrying forward this Middle Eastern narrative.

Started as a journey, the *Ruins* soon turns to a survey of global religions— a survey that would prompt Jefferson himself to express Muslim views in his own English voice. In Chapter 12, Volney's French unsympathetically dramatizes a debate involving "Imams" and "Santons"—Muslim "saints"— which Jefferson renders as follows:

> And the Imans and the Santons said to the people; it is in chastisement of your sins: you eat pork; you drink wine; you touch unclean things: God hath punished you. Do penance therefore; purify, repeat the profession of faith*; fast from the rising to the setting sun, give the tenth of your goods to the mosques; go to Mecca; and God will render you victorious. And the people, recovering courage, uttered loud cries: There is but one God, said they (transported with fury) and Mahomet is his prophet; accursed be he who believeth not! . . .
> *There is but one God, and Mahomet is his prophet.[5]

Fashioning a version of this fiery sermon, while voicing too the "furious" response from the Muslim faithful, Jefferson translates into his own terms several tenets central to Islam. Refraining from eating pork, regular prayer, and pilgrimage to Mecca all are offered in Jefferson's English. Most foundational to Islam, however, is the declaration that Jefferson renders at page bottom, via a starred footnote—a declaration known as the "*shahāda*," Islam's foundational act of "witnessing" that "There is but one God, and Mahomet is his prophet." On the margins of his English page, Jefferson reproduces the core profession of the Muslim faith, with this same statement also repeated by "the people," who echo these very words. Original to the Qur'an, this sentence is not only Islam's creed, but its formula of conversion. If spoken with intent, in the presence of two witnesses, these words are the very same that usher into Islam those seeking admission. Expressed in his own English, Jefferson translates, twice on a single page, the exact syllables by which a speaker, who wishes conversion, is rendered a Muslim.[6]

Voicing this sacred formula via his version of Volney's French, Jefferson renders an act of Islamic "witnessing," even while ensuring there were no witnesses to his own act of translation. In contrast to the "loud cries" of the "people," Jefferson kept very quiet his transforming of Volney's Middle Eastern fiction into American prose. Inscribed at his Virginian refuge, sur-rounded by enslaved Africans, Jefferson's English version will later reach readerships worldwide. Published in a popular Paris edition, this English rendition of Volney's *Ruins* finally appeared in 1802, but with no translator named.[7] When Anglophone audiences encountered this edition, and its echoes of the Qur'an, they read not only the words of Allah, but unwittingly also the words of an American founder, confronting statements revealed at Mecca, but restructured by the master of Monticello.

The passage above, featuring the Muslim profession rendered by Jefferson, formed part of the *Ruins*'s Chapter 12—a chapter that itself marks a break in Jefferson's manuscript translation, divided from the remaining seven chapters that he would ultimately undertake, finally reaching the end of Chapter 19 sometime before the late summer of 1799.[8] Five long chapters still were left to translate from the twenty-four chapters of Volney's French *Ruins*; and yet, Jefferson would here halt his secret rendition, even as he neared elevation to his nation's highest public office. Before he could finish Volney's work on imperial fall, Jefferson rose to lead the world's newest re-public, itself an "Empire of Liberty."[9] Like his beloved home, Monticello, Jefferson's translation was interrupted during its final stages of construc-tion, as Jefferson himself approached his own elevation to the President's House. A collaborator would be needed to patch up this American ver-sion of Volney's *Ruins*. It should be someone with literary sensibilities; and, ideally, someone familiar with the Middle East. Most essential, Jefferson's co-translator must be discreet, as his own name could never be linked to Volney's incendiary book. Beyond all luck, such a person was found. Jefferson's ally in translating Volney's *Ruins* proved to be an American poet with extensive North African experience, who himself was producing a translation of an Arabic treaty even as Jefferson pursued his translation of Volney's Middle Eastern fiction. Best of all, this American collaborator was personally known to Jefferson, the two men having met years before in Paris, introduced by none other than that other New England Arabist, Ezra Stiles.

≈

Mr. Barlow, Author of the Vission of Columbus, will present you with this. I need say nothing further to commend him to your Civilities and Benevolence, than that he is an American of an ingenious and worthy Character.

Ezra Stiles to Jefferson
April 30, 1788[10]

Joel Barlow arrived to Paris with this letter of introduction from Ezra Stiles—a letter that presented Barlow to Jefferson first and foremost as an "Author." Although commended for his "worthy Character," Barlow's creativity is stressed first, Stiles citing his epic poem on America's founding, Barlow's ambitious 1787 "Vission of Columbus."[11] Sent by Stiles from New Haven, this letter of introduction was written just a month after Yale's president opened Abiel Holmes's letter from Georgia, with its historic Arabic enclosure. Having recently received 'Usman's 1788 writings, Stiles dispatches this personal recommendation, presenting Joel Barlow—a writer who would prove essential not only to Jefferson's translation efforts, but to an act of Arabic translation pivotal to American history.

Stiles's springtime letter did not reach Jefferson until the summer of 1788. "Mr. Barlow of Connecticut arrived here," Jefferson finally noted in Paris on July 8.[12] And yet, despite the delay, it did not take long for these two "ingenious" Americans to exchange "Civilities." For Barlow, Jefferson was an epic figure—literally. In his "Vission of Columbus," Barlow had even honored Jefferson with a passing mention.[13] During their short overlap in Paris, however, it was politics, rather than poetry, that linked the two. An ardent American patriot, Barlow harbored revolutionary sympathies suited to the Parisian upheavals that Jefferson was intently watching in 1788. Unlike Jefferson, however, Barlow would remain in Paris through the Revolution, immersing himself in the city's factional politics, even winning French citizenship by 1792.[14] Eventually, however, Barlow's birth nation would call; and, in 1795, he accepted the appointment as America's consul-general to Algiers. Departing from Paris to the Barbary Coast, Barlow pursued the same path as Thomas Barclay a decade earlier, traveling to North Africa to negotiate yet another US treaty. In his efforts, America's new consul-general to Algiers received aid from a former Algerian slave: Richard O'Brien. Finally released from his captivity, O'Brien had commenced his diplomatic career, capitalizing on his being "intimately acquainted" with North African affairs, as Jefferson wrote to John Paul Jones.[15] With O'Brien's support, Barlow achieved hard-won successes. Securing the release of yet more US prisoners, as well as a historic treaty with Tripoli, Barlow finally returned to France once more in 1798, where he would accept Volney's invitation to complete the translation that Jefferson had left unfinished.[16]

To Jefferson, Joel Barlow seemed an inspired choice as a co-translator for the *Ruins*. A "better hand you could not have found," Jefferson would later write approvingly to Volney.[17] Beyond all probability, Volney had "found" an American successor to Jefferson who was familiar with Muslim lands and also a writer of elegance; even more surprisingly, by the time Barlow returned to Paris in 1797, he had already participated in a sensitive act of translation, generating the English version of America's treaty with Tripoli. Back in 1787, Jefferson had signed an English translation of a US treaty with Morocco in Paris, the Arabic "original" of which he could not read. A decade later, Barlow's in-person diplomacy led him to translate a Barbary Coast treaty, despite his own uncertain facilities with Arabic.[18] And predictably, like the Moroccan treaty that Jefferson had signed, Barlow's Tripoli treaty also featured significant discrepancies between its Arabic original and the 1797 English version ratified in America. Most notorious is Article 11 of the treaty, which reads in Barlow's English translation:

> As the government of the United States of America is not in any sense founded on the Christian Religion,—as it has in itself no character of enmity against the laws, religion or tranquility of Musselmen,—and as the said States never have entered into any war or act of hostility against any Mehomitan nation, it is declared by the parties that no pretext arising from religious opinions shall ever produce an interruption of the harmony existing between the two countries.[19]

Denying the "Christian" character of US "founding," this article seems a curious and controversial aside within an international treaty. Oddly polemical, Barlow's strange Article 11 itself has been explained, however, by a startling claim: the above English is without basis in the treaty's Arabic original, but was instead invented by Barlow, who injected his own liberal ideas into this diplomatic document. Mistranslating a "Mehomitan" treaty to express his political bias, Barlow has long been blamed for simply inserting the above sentences, "fraudulently" refashioning American religious history via a Tripolitan treaty.[20] The earliest critic of this treaty's original text—C. S. Hurgronje—testified that "[t]he eleventh article" was missing in Arabic; where this article should have been, Hurgronje found simply a "letter" that seemed "nonsensical," leading him to conclude that the "Barlow translation [of Article 11] has no equivalent whatever in the Arabic."[21] Hunter Miller, the scholarly successor to Hurgronje, strengthened the assertion, claiming starkly that "Article 11 of the Barlow translation [. . .] does not exist at all. There is no Article 11."[22]

These twentieth-century indictments of Barlow's translation are now widely accepted, and regularly cited in twenty-first-century studies. In her most recent treatment of the Tripoli treaty, for instance, Denise Spellberg relies on these previous critics, speculating that Barlow himself "probably never knew that Article 11 never existed" in Arabic.[23] Claims such as these seem reasonable; they build, however, upon false assumptions, and are belied by archival evidence neglected now for over two centuries. Previously unpublished, four Arabic pages survive within Barlow's personal papers at Harvard—pages that form a rough draft of Tripoli's treaty.[24] Labeled in his own handwriting, entitled by Barlow himself as "Treaty with Tripoli in Arabic," the second of the four Arabic pages features a bottom portion that is reproduced as Figure 5.[25] Pictured below for the very first time, Barlow's own Arabic copy of the "Treaty with Tripoli" does indeed clearly include an "Article 11," headed with an unmistakable title designating "the eleventh article (*ash-shart*)". Far from "never existing" in Arabic, the original treaty's Article 11 still endures today.

Barlow's personal copy, reproduced in Figure 5, finally disproves the long-held assumption that "no Article 11" ever appeared in an Arabic original for America's controversial treaty with a Muslim nation. And yet, Barlow's Arabic copy also seems to support the many critics of his treaty, confirming that Barlow's English Article 11 is anything but a literal rendition of the Arabic. When introduced to Jefferson, Barlow's creative "Character" was what Ezra Stiles stressed. And, it is Barlow's creativity that also emerges in his English version. C. S. Hurgronje's early statements on Tripoli's treaty misled contemporary scholars into believing that no "eleventh article" ever existed in Arabic; and yet, back in 1930, Hurgronje himself had viewed, and even

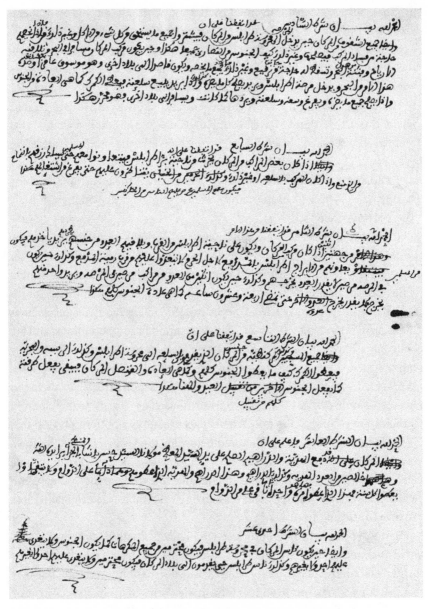

Figure 5 "Treaty with Tripoli in Arabic," MS Am 1448 (698), Houghton Library, Harvard University, housed as part of Houghton's Joel Barlow Papers, 1775–1935. The three Arabic lines at the bottom of this page, opening with the Arabic "الحمد لله" ("praise be Allah"), comprise the Treaty of Tripoli's elusive "Article 11."

rendered, a version of precisely this article, which he mistook as the mere conclusion to a "nonsensical" letter inserted into the treaty.[26] Now, with the identification of the actual Article 11 in Arabic, it is indeed clear that the original treaty implies none of Barlow's contentions regarding Christianity, never suggesting that "the government of the United States of America is not in any sense founded on the Christian Religion." Instead, the treaty's Arabic Article 11 is eager to ensure reciprocal safe passage between the two nations. The Arabic text imaged in Figure 5 first guarantees that "American people" will be "honored" if they are in "Tripoli"; secondly, the article asserts that "the people of Tripoli will likewise be honored if they proceed to the land of the Americans" ("كذلك ناس طرابلس حتى يقدمون الى بلاد المركان فيكون محترمين").[27] Rather than religious history, personal security seems to be the prime imperative of Article 11 in its original Arabic.

The creeds and controversies that infuse Barlow's English are missing from his source; there is no explicit mention of "Christian," or "Musselmen," or "Mehomitan," in the Arabic Article 11. And yet, this does not mean that Barlow's version represents a wholesale fiction, fashioned without recourse to the treaty's original, which I recover for the first time above. In Figure 5, Barlow's copy of the treaty features a clearly labeled "Article 11," which insists in Arabic on the parity between "peoples," legislating mutual goodwill— a reciprocity not unlike Barlow's last words in English stressing "the harmony existing between the two countries." More intriguing are the Islamic overtones of the original Article 11, which again are not inconsistent with Barlow's embrace of "Musselmen" in his English article. As each and every section within Barlow's Arabic source, Article 11's original begins by invoking Allah Himself. Although Barlow's English article has been found curious for its "Mehomitan" sympathies, the original Article 11 begins in Arabic with the most "Mehomitan" words possible: "الحمد لله"— "praise be Allah"—a phrase familiar to all Muslims, especially as it stands at the start of the Qur'an itself.[28]

Opening by praising "Allah," and insisting on the "honor" to be accorded all "peoples," the body of Article 11 also hangs upon an Arabic keyword with spiritual connotations. Neither "Christian" nor "Muslim" is named in the Arabic of Article 11; however, this article does repeat a single term, religious in resonance, as it seeks to define the welfare shared by both Americans in Tripoli, as well as Tripolitans in America. Article 11 in Arabic insists that individuals from each nation should be considered "*muḥtaram*" ("محترم")— a term I translate above as "honored," but which itself has meanings far broader, beyond this basic significance. Typically suggesting simply "esteemed," the Arabic "*muḥtaram*" also has implications of the sanctified; cognate with core terms of Islam, "*muḥtaram*" shares the same Arabic root, for instance, with the honorific applied to Mecca's central mosque, known as "*al-Ḥarām*" ("the Sacred").[29] Labeling Americans and Tripolitans equally as "*muḥtaram*," Article 11 insists on reciprocal security, but also suggests mutual reverence, with both Christians and Muslims made "inviolable" while sojourning "tranquilly" in each other's nations. It is such faint echoes of the sacrosanct in Article 11's Arabic original that may have prompted the wild amplifications of Barlow's version, with his English drowning out all sense of diplomatic "honor" and trumpeting divine "harmony." To what extent Barlow was able to understand Arabic is uncertain, as is the process by which he produced his notorious translation of the Tripoli treaty. What is now clear from the evidence offered by Figure 5, however, is that Barlow did indeed possess a version of Article 11 in Arabic. And, it would seem most likely that this long-lost source did in some way inform Barlow's translation, especially as all of his other English articles are clearly anchored in the Arabic treaty, though often featuring significant discrepancies.[30] Rendering Arabic reciprocity into a parity of religions, the "Christian" critique of Barlow's Article 11 appears to arise from creative extrapolations, not a categorical act of translation "fraud."

A fitting prelude to his next translation project—finalizing Jefferson's rendition of Volney's *Ruins*, which itself is filled with "Mehomitan" phrases—Barlow's curious Article 11, along with the rest of his "Treaty with Tripoli," advanced forward for ratification in 1797. By June 7, 1797, the treaty was given consent in the US Senate, and signed by President John Adams himself on June 10, 1797.[31] Winning public endorsement from the federal government for a treaty advocating "tranquility of Musselmen," Barlow would soon secretly begin to translate the last chapters of a Middle Eastern fiction left unfinished by the man who would next rise to the US presidency. As for Barlow's own Arabic copy of this ratified treaty with Tripoli, that too he would keep secret, stashed among his personal papers, where it has remained lost until now.

≈

Any confidential line I may at any time have the pleasure of receiving from you Shall never by me or my means be made publick. I see the unwarantable and Shamefull attacks at your Charactor from the moment you stepd into office. Such infernal Scoundrels ought to be consign'd to the Algerens or to the——

Last lines of a letter to Jefferson,
written by Thomas Bell, June 12, 1797[32]

Two days after President Adams ratified the Treaty of Tripoli, Thomas Bell closed a letter to Vice President Thomas Jefferson with this postscript, promising to respect any "confidential" communication. Concluding with a curse, Bell abruptly breaks off, leaving his final sentence unfinished. The "infernal Scoundrels" who are attacking Jefferson's "Charactor" should "be consign'd to the Algerens," Bell angrily suggests, or relegated to an even worse fate, left unnamed.

Hinting at his friend's sufferings in the summer of 1797, Bell aptly evokes the specter of America's "infidel" enemies in Muslim lands. Since "the moment" he "stepd into office" as vice president on March 4, Jefferson was not only accused of revolutionary excesses, but also of religious heterodoxy, even associated with "revil[ing] Christianity."[33] Virginia neighbor and friend of the family, Thomas Bell had his own reasons to be sensitive to accusations against Jefferson. During Jefferson's years in Paris, Bell had taken into his household Mary Hemings, the sister of Sally. Unlike Jefferson's rumored relationship, Bell had "openly" embraced Mary Hemings as his "common-law" wife, as well as their "two children."[34] Wishing ill on Jefferson's accusers, hoping that they be captured by African Muslims—"consign'd to the Algerens"—Bell defends his friend's public name. And yet, at his own nearby home, Jefferson was seeking to keep his public name "confidential," ensuring his identity stayed unconnected to his current translation of Volney's Middle Eastern *Ruins*. Bell promises discretion, assuring Jefferson that any lines he might write will "never by me or my means be made publick." At the same time, Jefferson was occupied with writing lines that will indeed be widely published, but never associated with his name until long after he himself was "consign'd" to his own grave at Monticello.

By 1797, Jefferson had reason to be especially glad that he had insisted on anonymity in connection with his work on *The Ruins*. Volney's stay in America had culminated with political controversy, and even accusations of espionage. Having fled the turmoil in France, in America Volney found himself caught up in yet more intrigue. During his stay stateside, Volney was a frequent guest of New York's young senator, a man soon to be associated with

both Jefferson and with scandal—Aaron Burr.[35] It was not Jefferson's future
vice president that caused trouble for Volney, however, but Jefferson's current
superior, President John Adams. Volney was suspected by Adams of "being a
French spy," supposedly on a mission to gather intelligence, in "prepar[ation]
for the reoccupation of Louisiana by France."[36] Although previously asso-
ciating himself with secret plans and personae, Volney was yet shocked to
find himself accused of such a grandiose "conspiracy." How could "I (a lone
Frenchman)," he queried incredulously, "have plotted, in *Kentokey*, to deliver
Louisiana to the Directory?"[37] For Vice President Jefferson, this development
was doubly problematic. Not only did it imperil a friend, but it also helped
engender the Alien and Sedition Acts, signed into law by Adams in 1798—
acts that outraged Jefferson and his Republican allies. As Jefferson noted privately to Madison, Adams's Alien Act was specifically "meant for Volney"
as well as for Victor Collot, another Frenchman suspected of spying on the
American frontier.[38] In Jefferson's view, Volney had become "a Federalist
target."[39] Accused of spying, Volney had supplied Jefferson with a source for
secret translation in 1797. However, Volney also ended up prompting US legislation that would prove unpopular, contributing indirectly to Adams's defeat in the upcoming election, and Jefferson's elevation to the presidency.[40]

Adams's reaction to Volney may have seemed oversensitive, even neurotic.
And yet, his anxieties concerning a western "conspiracy," led by a man with
Middle Eastern interests, proved prophetic. It would not be during Adams's
own presidency, however, but during his successor's two terms, that such an
unrest would arise. But, in 1797, it was Volney who suffered accusations for
covert acts, prompting him to flee America in 1798. Meanwhile, Jefferson
continued his own covert rendition of the *Ruins*, despairing of its comple-
tion finally as the century neared conclusion. By August 1799, Jefferson had
given his work over to William Maclure, who discreetly delivered the English
pages to France, where Barlow was eventually tasked with finishing off
Volney's final chapters.[41] Traversing the ocean, Maclure arrived to Paris carrying Jefferson's rendered pages at the dawn of a new era, with 1799 ticking
over into 1800. More important, by the time his rendition would appear in
Paris, published with Barlow's additions, Jefferson himself had crossed a line.
When the *Ruins* finally appeared for English readers with Volney's approval
in 1802, one of its unnamed translators, voicing this work's Qur'anic echoes,
would himself be the president of the United States.

On March 4, 1801, standing in the recently completed US Senate chamber,
Jefferson took the oath of office. Amid the extraordinary company that

surrounded him, Jefferson's immediate predecessor—and his co-negotiator with a Muslim ambassador fifteen years earlier—was missing. Adams had scurried north, departing home to Quincy, deflated by the protracted campaign and hotly contested election, not decided until February 1801.[42] If Adams was absent, another of Jefferson's rivals stood at his side—Aaron Burr, who had attracted the same number of Electoral College votes, forcing the House of Representatives to decide the election's outcome. Replacing Jefferson himself as vice president, Burr would soon make his own foray into the western interior; unlike Volney, however, Burr would prove a genuine threat. As he took the oath of office in 1801, Jefferson's translation of Volney's Middle Eastern fantasy, which celebrated the end of empires, was quietly advancing toward publication in Paris. At the same time, enemies were also on the move, eager to challenge Jefferson, and to topple his "Empire of Liberty." Despite Barlow's hopes, "hostility" and even "war" with "Mehomitan nations" was on the horizon.

9

"Wr s Unavdble"

On Tuesday, March 17, 1801, Jefferson woke to the fourteenth day of his presidency. Not a significant landmark, of course; but, within just the two weeks that had past, Jefferson had already discovered the public duties of his new office to be many. And yet, it was a private problem that was nagging the American president on that Tuesday in mid-March. Had his translation of Volney's Middle Eastern "meditations" reached Paris safely—and securely? Jefferson had dispatched his English *Ruins* more than a year before, but had never heard of its fate, and had not yet dared to write and ask. Jefferson was now the most recognizable man in America, and had even more reason to ensure that his translation stayed hidden. By the second Tuesday of his presidency, however, Jefferson could no longer abide the uncertainty, and on March 17 he wrote to Volney, but cautiously. "Did you ever recieve the residue of the translation?," the president questioned evasively, cleverly not stipulating *whose* translation of *what*. There was, of course, always the possibility that correspondence could be intercepted, and Jefferson's role discovered.[1]

Volney responded affirmatively: "I received in due time the parcel that you had the kindness to send me by way of Mr. Maclure," adding, "but according to the enclosed note I feared to contradict your wishes even by acknowledging its receipt."[2] Anxious for his American friend's anonymity, Volney had not even sent "acknowledgement," merely forwarding Jefferson's document directly to his Paris publisher, along with Barlow's translation of the final chapters. But not to worry, Volney assured the president. Even the publisher "does not suspect" that Jefferson is the "true source" of the translation. Only one issue remained to be resolved: Volney had kept Jefferson's original manuscript. It is still "in my hands," Volney noted, "I shall await your orders concerning it."[3] A document potentially dangerous to Jefferson's anonymity was sitting on Volney's desk in Paris—a translation of a work imbued with radical politics and Islamic sources, and in the handwriting of the president of the United States. What should be done with it?

Responding to Volney, Jefferson begins not with instructions regarding the fate of this Middle Eastern "meditation" in Paris, but with thanks for a

Middle Eastern gift he had recently received from Volney in Paris—a gift that recalled their time together in 1796 at Monticello:

> I recieved the model of the pyramid, in good order, which you were so kind as to send me, and for which I pray you to accept my grateful thanks. it has corrected the idea I had preconcieved of the form of those masses, which I had not supposed to appear so flat. whenever any good work comes out giving a general view of Egypt, it's inhabitants and antiquities, not too long for one in my situation to have leisure to read, I will thank you to indicate it to me. probably you will know beforehand whether such an one is to be expected.—I am glad you were able to engage so fine a writer of English to translate your work. a better hand you could not have found. when you shall be done with the manuscript you recieved from mr Mc.lure it is desired that it may be burnt.[4]

Spanning ruins and renditions, American and Middle Eastern, Jefferson opens with "grateful thanks," acknowledging the "model of the pyramid" sent along by Volney—the same pyramid that the Frenchman claims he spotted from the top of Monticello. Starting with this miniature copy of Eastern antiquity, Jefferson ends with the modern copy that he himself had manufactured and sent to Paris, alluding to his English version of Volney's own Eastern fantasy. Without naming this work's title or his co-translator's name, Jefferson commends Barlow as a "fine" choice to render the rest of Volney's *Ruins*. But, finally, Jefferson insists that his translated text be burnt, ensuring that it stay silent and indecipherable as hieroglyphics. A born archivist, reproducing even his most minor letters via polygraphs, Jefferson decides to violate his own values.[5] His imperative for secrecy, in this instance, conquered Jefferson's instinct to conserve. The original manuscript of his English translation—featuring Islamic formulae voiced by a US president, and inscribed in Jefferson's own hand—was to "be burnt."

Before his presidency had entered its third week, Jefferson had ordered the destruction of an original manuscript featuring his rendition of a Middle Eastern "meditation." And yet, his presidency had already witnessed the destruction of another Middle Eastern document—one that, like the completed translation of *Ruins*, featured the words of Joel Barlow. In the months leading up to Jefferson's oath of office, belligerence had begun to emanate from Tripoli's leadership once more. The current Bashaw, Yusuf Karamanli, was demanding an increase in US tribute, challenging norms set in 1797 by the same treaty that Barlow had so creatively translated.[6] President Adams had previously rendered payment, but, in response to Tripoli's new exorbitant demands, Jefferson refused. As a result, Bashaw Karamanli declared war on the United States, sending troops to cut down the flagstaff at the American consulate on May 14, 1801. The Treaty of Tripoli, less than four years old, was in ruins.[7]

In the spring of 1801, Jefferson's translation of an "Oriental" fantasy was on its way to press in Paris anonymously, even as his original manuscript was secretly directed to be incinerated. At the same time, in Tripoli, a Middle Eastern treaty was also consigned to the ashes, leading to violence that was anything but a fantasy. In the wake of Tripoli's 1801 declaration, hostilities broke out between US and Muslim forces in the Mediterranean. Continuing until 1805, this conflict would come to be known as the first Barbary War—a war that spanned Jefferson's entire first term, and gave rise to grievances that plagued his presidency until its very end.

≈

SIR

The art of secret writing, or, as it is usually termed, *writing in cypher*, has occasionally engaged the attention both of the states-man & philosopher for many ages; and yet I believe it will be acknowledged, by all who are acquainted with the present state of this art, that it is still far short of perfection.

Robert Patterson to Jefferson, writing from Philadelphia,
December 19, 1801[8]

Just as Jefferson assumed the presidency, war with North Africa broke out—open conflict that would give new impetus for his encoding of correspondence, closing off American letters from outside eyes. Burning manuscripts might ensure secrecy for Jefferson personally; but such an extreme measure could not protect diplomatic letters passing overseas, which always ran the risk of interception. As in Paris many years before, Jefferson's engagements with the Muslim world helped turn his mind toward the "art of secret writing." However, when he exchanged ciphered letters with Adams back in 1785, Jefferson was a lone European minister. Now, as US president, Jefferson had the brightest minds of an entire nation within reach, including one residing not far away in Philadelphia: Robert Patterson.

When Patterson wrote to Jefferson in 1801, he was a professor of mathematics at the University of Pennsylvania. Patterson was, however, no mere academician, but had profound experience solving worldly problems. Indeed, it was practical ingenuity that had pulled Patterson up from obscurity. Irish by birth, Patterson had risked all to immigrate to America as a merchant in the 1770s, only to risk his life once again as an American patriot, fighting against the British in the war reinforced by Jefferson's iconic Declaration. After the Revolution, Patterson settled in Philadelphia, the iconic home of Independence, winning a professorial position that suited his eclectic brilliance. Intrigued not merely by numbers, but "natural philosophy," Patterson made advances in multiple areas essential to the new Republic, devising systems for navigation and manufacturing, while also drafting insignias and stamps, frequently offering his services specifically to Jefferson. In 1803, he would lend "every assistance in [his] power" to the Lewis and Clark mission, "preparing a set of astronomical formulæ" for the team's historic trek to the Pacific, as well as advising Lewis which "chronometer" to carry west.[9] Eventually, in 1805, Jefferson would appoint Patterson to head the National Mint, overseeing America's developing forms of currency.[10]

In 1801, however, Patterson was seeking to solve another sort of problem for Jefferson. He was interested not in how best to circulate money domestically, nor how to propel a trip into the western interior; instead, his concern was keeping American secrets out of circulation, hiding them from foreign eyes, especially in the east. Patterson sent Jefferson the unsolicited note cited above as the first year of his presidency came to a close, even as America's war with Tripoli escalated. Invoking the "philosophic" background to the "art of secret writing," Patterson hints too at this history's deficiencies, not attaining "perfection"—at least not yet. Patterson had a solution, however. He was offering Jefferson a "cypher" that he boasted was unbreakable. Patterson did not merely advertise his encoding strategy; instead, true to his practical character, Patterson was sending an actual sample written in code. After detailing his new ciphering method, Patterson closes his letter with the following challenge:

I shall conclude this paper with a specimen of secret writing, which I may safely defy the united ingenuity of the whole human race to decypher, to the end of time—but which, however, by the help of the key, consisting of not more than eighteen figures, might be read, with the utmost ease, in less than fifteen minutes—[11]

Audaciously "defying" the "whole human race" to crack his code, Patterson presents the president with a task too tantalizing to resist—yet too difficult for Jefferson to accomplish. The "specimen" provided by Patterson amounts to forty lines of text, 2,164 characters in total. The first two lines of this selection read:

> bonirnrsewehaipohiluoeettiseesnhiestctfhuesraeas
> opiacdasthtaleeletubegtneinnfdecwebssssuifemsetnb

Jefferson was confounded by this alphabetic jumble; but this confusion also gave Jefferson clarity, convincing him that Patterson's system could safeguard the nation's secrets. The encoded text that the president held in his hands was indecipherable to him. And yet, this same text hid his very own sentences. Seeking to aid Jefferson as America's latest war unfolded, Patterson had decided to encode a Declaration from America's first war. If Jefferson had succeeded in cracking Patterson's forty lines sent from Philadelphia in 1801, the president would have found iconic words written by himself in Philadelphia a quarter century before, including the sentences that are perhaps most synonymous with the American project:

> We hold these truths to be self-evident, that all men are created equal, that they are endowed by their Creator with certain unalienable Rights, that among these are Life, Liberty and the pursuit of Happiness.[12]

In December 1801, at the close to his inaugural year as American president, Jefferson was unable to read America's own inaugural text, made illiterate by the same freedoms he established. It is the Declaration of Independence that Patterson had encoded, its "self-evident" truths successfully hidden from their author. Not holding the key to decipher his own Declaration, American liberties seemed mere blanks to Jefferson, blinded to the very ideals most intimate to him. In a dangerous time and dealing with a revered document, Patterson yet playfully obscured US Independence, stumping Jefferson with his own sentences. True to Patterson's prediction, Jefferson was never able to solve this cipher. Indeed, the code was not cracked until the twenty-first century, when in 2009 another's "ingenuity" finally prevailed. Rather than "the whole human race," however, it was a single cryptologist who belatedly caught up to Patterson's brilliance, and deciphered his system.[13]

In the same year that Jefferson ordered his secret translation of Middle Eastern *Ruins* be incinerated in Paris, the president found his own original words impossible to translate. Ironically, however, as he struggled to solve Patterson's "cipher," Jefferson engaged with a code that itself echoed the Middle East in its very name. The word "cipher" claims Arabic origins, derived from the term "*ṣifr*" ("صفر"), the same word that gave rise to the English "zero."[14] As Patterson perhaps knew from his mathematical studies, it was Muslims who first brought "zero" to the West, introducing this number, along with its Arabic name—"*ṣifr*"—which became the basis for the two English terms "cipher" and "zero." In staring down at Patterson's "cipher," Jefferson was not only seeking to translate the most American of sentences, but struggling with a code that was etymologically Arabic. In 1801, however, neither Jefferson nor Patterson could possibly know that they would soon be linked again by other indecipherable lines—lines not merely encased in "cypher," but composed in Arabic itself. And these next inscrutable sentences would not be authored by Thomas Jefferson, but would be the very words of Allah Himself.

≈

> I send you a cipher to be used between us, which will give you some trouble to understand, but, once understood, is the easiest to use.
>
> Jefferson to Robert R. Livingston,
> April 18, 1802[15]

Jefferson was convinced: Patterson's cipher should be adopted for sensitive US correspondence. And, on April 18, 1802, Jefferson wrote the words above to his own appointed minister to France, Robert R. Livingston, dispatching Patterson's code and its key for use in Paris.

The problem of safeguarding US secrets in France was, of course, uniquely familiar to Thomas Jefferson, recalling his career's earlier years. And yet, the security problems plaguing Livingston in Paris were on a different scale than those negotiated by Jefferson when he served as minister in the 1780s. During his Parisian sojourn, Jefferson had failed to free Americans in North Africa; Livingston, however, would be tasked with liberating North America itself, wresting control of a huge chunk of the entire continent—the "Louisiana Territory"—from European hands. In April 1802, Louisiana's vast and largely unexplored spaces stretched westward from the Mississippi, reaching halfway to the Pacific. And, for Jefferson, the mysteries still surrounding Louisiana were uppermost on his mind, even as he sent his new "cipher" to Livingston, seeking to keep secret the nation's communications. Concluding his April 18, 1802, letter, Jefferson expressed his anxieties to Livingston directly:

> The cession of Louisiana & the Floridas by Spain to France works most sorely on the US. on this subject the Secretary of state has written to you fully. yet I cannot forbear recurring to it personally, so deep is the impression it makes in my mind.[16]

In April 1802, Jefferson's top concern is "cession," the president made uneasy by the exchange of North American lands between European powers. Spain was preparing to pass "Louisiana" on to France; Napoleon would soon share the same continent with Jefferson's country. Concerned by prospects of America's new and unpredictable neighbor, Jefferson's "personal" worries increasingly became public as the spring of 1802 turned to autumn. By the fall, France's purchase of Louisiana was confirmed, threatening the New World status quo, including trade routes in western territories. This "cession" to France jeopardized US access especially to the essential port of New Orleans. Jefferson's fears would, moreover, soon prove justified. On "October 16, 1802," Americans were outraged to learn that "Juan Ventura Morales, the acting intendant of Louisiana revoked" US "rights" to "deposit" goods at New Orleans.[17] This "suspension" of "our right of deposit," Jefferson wrote in another letter to Livingston, "has thrown this country into such a flame of hostile disposition as can scarcely be described."[18]

In the autumn of 1802, Jefferson found himself increasingly occupied not with secret ciphers, but with open diplomacy, seeking to stave off another war by addressing the international threats on the very threshold of the American continent. This same season, however, Jefferson engaged once more with Robert Patterson, who again proved timely. On the very day that American rights were "revoked" in New Orleans—October 16, 1802—Jefferson wrote to his professor friend for help, asking for another practical application. This time, it was not to improve US intelligence, but orientation, with Jefferson querying Patterson regarding a potential new nautical system, which gauged "Jupiter's satellites at sea." Jefferson soon received a conscientious reply, dispatched by Patterson on November 1, voicing skepticism regarding this potential "improvement" in "navigation."[19]

Patterson's cipher, as Jefferson noted to Livingston in 1802, took considerable "trouble to understand." This trouble was, of course, its virtue. But

Patterson's code ultimately proved too intricate for practical use, preventing the efficient exchange of diplomatic letters. Patterson did not quit, however. Still hoping to help Jefferson settle on a system for national secrecy, Patterson tried again, writing several years later to the president, opening this later letter with the following words:

> Some years ago, I remember to have laid before you a scheme of *secret writing*, which you were pleased to honour with a friendly notice: And relying on your well-tried patience; I would again take the liberty of submitting a few further remarks on the same subject.[20]

After this preface, Patterson moves on to supply Jefferson with yet another method of encoding sensitive correspondence. Explained over the next five pages, Patterson's latest scheme involves multiple steps, first reducing an author's original to shorthand, and then obscuring this shorthand via a "secret alphabet." Furnishing Jefferson with a credible example of a confidential communication to be encoded, Patterson supplies first a full original, with the shorthand to follow:

> The conduct of Spain towards the U.S. must no longer be practised with impunity. War has become unavoidable. Demand your passport, & return as soon as possible.
>
> The cndc of spn/twrds the U.S. mst no lngr b prctsd with impun. Wr s unavdble. Dmnd yr psprt, and rtrn s sn s psbl—.[21]

Patterson had first ciphered the Declaration of Independence, Jefferson's elegant call to resist the British in 1776. As Jefferson's presidency unfolded, Patterson continued to encode threats of conflict, both real and rumored, reflecting the clouds of war that still engulfed the president and his nation. As Patterson seemed to anticipate in this fictional sample, global violence not only seemed "unavoidable" for Jefferson, but also obscure, constantly confronting the embattled president with words difficult to decipher.

≈

To offer the public a new translation of Volney's *Ruins* may require some apology in the view of those who are acquainted with the work only in the

English version which already exists, and which has had a general circulation. But those who are conversant with the book in the author's own language, and have taken pains to compare it with that version, must have been
struck with the errors with which the English performance abounds. They
must have regretted the loss of many original beauties, some of which go far
in composing the essential merits of the work.[22]

Even as Jefferson bore "personal" anxieties regarding Europe, these words—
written to represent Jefferson's own perspective and addressed to a European
"public"—were published in the autumn of 1802. Dated "Paris, November
1, 1802," these sentences launch Joel Barlow's preface to the new English
edition of Volney's *Ruins*, which finally appeared as 1802 neared its end.
On the very day that Patterson replied to Jefferson regarding navigation,
measuring global lines via "Jupiter's satellites," Jefferson's own lines were
conveyed across the globe, introduced by this preface, itself dated the first
day of November 1802. This autumn, Jefferson fretted about the transfer-
ring of North American lands to France; but, at the very same time, his own
American language was transferred to France, with Volney's Middle Eastern
text appearing in Paris in the words of a US president.

Although politely phrased, the "apology" offered by Barlow's preface
is not at all passive, but mounts an attack. Confronting their competitors,
this new edition by the two Americans opens with words of conflict, assail-
ing "the English version which already exists"—the "cheap" version which
Volney so deplored. It is literary "pains" and "loss"—being "struck" and having "regret"—that Barlow invokes, dramatizing the superiority of his and
Jefferson's work over its predecessor. Ostensibly written by "we" the "translators," this introduction was actually the work of Barlow alone; Jefferson
had no hand in introducing their English edition in Paris, avoiding further
contact with this contentious project.[23] And yet, the war of words that prefaces their translation seems to echo issues that plagued Jefferson specifically
during this autumn of 1802. As Barlow drafted his introduction for Volney's
Middle Eastern *Ruins* in France, another letter in translation was on its way
to Jefferson from the Middle East, invoking not a literary conflict, but literal
war. On October 16, 1802, American rights had been revoked at the port of
New Orleans, leading to calls in the United States to take up arms.[24] The very
next day, a letter was written to Jefferson from another port, also raising the
prospect of armed conflict. Written originally in Arabic, the letter would be

supplied to Jefferson in translation—a translation that "salute[d]" the president, offering friendship from an old enemy:

> We Salute and pray for your health and happiness.
> Your Consul OBrien in your name demanded The favour of us to seek and Obtain, The release from Slavery of your Subjects, in the possession of The Pascha of Tripoli. we wrote and Obtained The Same and gave them to your Consul to send to you as a present, and we pray you to receive the same and be assured of our friendship—
> We have been much dissatisfyed to hear That you would think of sending near us The Consul, That you had at Tripoli. whenever he comes we will not receive him. his Character does not Suit us, as we know, wherever he has remained That he has created difficulties and brought On a war And as I will not receive him I am shure it will be well for both nations
> Done in our divan at Algiers with The great Seal of Mustapha Pascha
> Certifyd to be The Substance of The deys
> letter to The Presidt. of the UStates
> [Richard] OBrien[25]

Even as America clashed with its first ally, France, Jefferson received this affectionate letter from Algiers, formerly his main antagonist during his posting in France. Written by the leader of this Barbary Coast nation, Mustapha Pascha, this letter alludes to an issue long familiar to Jefferson: American incarceration in Muslim lands. It is the name invoked at both the very opening and very end to this letter, however, that may have seemed most familiar to Jefferson. Richard O'Brien had counted every day of his captivity in North Africa; even after his 1796 release, he would end his letters by tallying his imprisonment, signing his name as "Richard O'Brien, Who was a captive in Algiers ten years and forty days."[26] Returning to America briefly, O'Brien stayed invested in North African affairs, and was soon sent back to the same Muslim lands where he was once enslaved. Appointed "Consul General at Algiers," O'Brien sought to save men in the very situation he had endured. As Mustapha Pascha wrote to Jefferson, O'Brien was working to secure the "release from Slavery" of American "Subjects" held by his Barbary neighbor, Tripoli. But O'Brien was also helping keep open lines of international communication, "certify[ing]" the "substance" of Mustapha's letter to Jefferson, testifying that the above English accurately reflected the Arabic originally written by the Dey.[27]

In Mustapha Pascha's 1802 update, however, his primary concern seemed not to be O'Brien's release of Americans, but the arrival of another American to North Africa. James Leander Cathcart was once O'Brien's fellow slave in Algiers; by 1802, Cathcart was O'Brien's enemy. The two Americans despised each other, due partly to Cathcart's harsh personality, and partly to O'Brien's soft feelings for Cathcart's "servant girl"—Betsy Robeson—whom O'Brien would court and eventually marry.[28] Cathcart was evidently disliked not merely by his own countrymen, however, but by his Muslim interlocutors. Referring to him merely as "The Consul, That you had at Tripoli," Mustapha Pascha refuses even to receive Cathcart, blaming him for the current conflict on the Barbary Coast, suggesting that Cathcart himself "brought On a war." In this letter from Muslim Africa, a threat of violence seems subtly implied, with American "health and happiness" jeopardized by Jefferson's own consul, who is painted as the potential catalyst for a fresh "war."

This letter was written to Jefferson in the autumn of 1802—a season of war anxieties in Europe, and also the same season that saw Jefferson's translation of a Middle Eastern fantasy advance to press in Paris. At the very time Mustapha Pascha wrote this letter in Arabic, available to the president only by means of the above English translation, Jefferson's own English translation was finally published, rendering Volney's "meditations" arising from his experiences in the Muslim world. Due to his own anonymous efforts, Jefferson was aware in 1802 of the "loss," "pains," and "errors" implied in acts of translation; however, when he eventually received Mustapha Pascha's letter, Jefferson himself would be forced to once again trust translation, unable to read the actual Arabic words inscribed for him in Algiers, which are pictured in Figure 6.[29]

Jefferson's inability to read the original Arabic hid divergences from its English translation, with one weighty word in English wholly absent from the intended Arabic. A more literal translation—as recently offered in the critical edition of Jefferson's papers, with my own very minor adjustments—reads instead as follows:

May this letter of ours arrive among our dear friends, the rulers of America. How are you and how are your circumstances? As for what follows, there are concerns regarding the consul *Wābrīm*, your envoy who has requested that I free the Christians whom the Tripolitans took. I wrote to the sultan of Tripoli who sent them promptly. I placed them in the hands of the consul

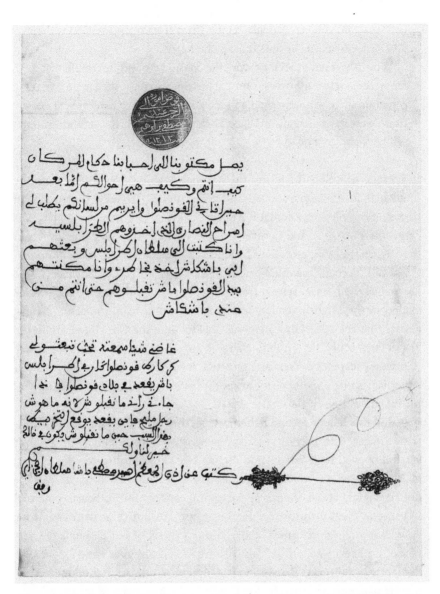

Figure 6 The original October 17, 1802, letter written in Arabic by Mustapha Pascha, whose translation reached Jefferson the following spring. Image courtesy of the Massachusetts Historical Society, Boston.

such that you yourselves might receive them from my possession without delay. I am dismayed by something I have heard.

You wish to send to me *Karkārī*, the consul who was in Tripoli, that he might remain in our land as consul. If he comes to me, I shall in no way receive him since he is not a peaceable man. It is clear that wherever he spends time he creates a great disturbance. For this reason, our not accepting him is for our and your good.[30]

In its tone as well as its terms, the original Arabic subtly differs from the English that Jefferson received and relied upon. Trivially, the American names are spelled in idiomatic Arabic; "O'Brien," for instance, appears as "*Wābrīm*" ("وابريم"), and Cathcart's name—which was edited out entirely in the English translation received by Jefferson—appears in Arabic as "*Karkārī*" ("كركاری"). Perhaps most noticeable in the letter's first half, however, is the absence of the phrase "release from Slavery of your Subjects," which was included in the English version sent to Jefferson; instead, the actual Arabic asserts that the Algerian leader was able to "free the Christians whom the Tripolitans took." In Arabic, there is no mention of "slavery," merely "Christian" captivity. Even as this letter from Africa reaches Jefferson on American shores, the severity of capture is amplified, with Arabic seizure turning into English "slavery."[31]

It is in this letter's second half, however, that the most dramatic substitution surfaces, with a serious escalation emerging in its last lines. The English version opened by Jefferson, and certified by O'Brien, threatens "war"; yet, in Arabic, "war" is omitted altogether. The Dey's Algerian original does indeed complain about "*Karkārī*," expressing concern for Cathcart's potential to cause a "great disturbance." However, the Muslim ruler worries not for "war," but for "righteousness." Only through an act of translation is the irritant of Cathcart weaponized, his "disturbance" framed as violence—a shift that perhaps reflects O'Brien's own hostilities to Cathcart, rather than an authentic danger envisioned by the Dey.[32] In the first years of his presidency, Jefferson had made efforts to maintain silence and secrecy, covering up his own translation of a Middle Eastern "meditation," and disseminating Robert Patterson's codes for ciphering correspondence. In this letter from Algeria, no Arabic cipher is needed to keep meaning hidden. Merely due to slight errors in Arabic translation, the actual import of an Arabic letter stays silent, with "war" and "slavery" offered to the American president, though never stipulated by this letter's Muslim author.

This urgent communiqué from Algiers would arrive long after it was written, delayed by many months before delivered to Jefferson. Dated October 17, 1802, Mustapha's message had to navigate a transatlantic crossing, as well as a process of translation, before Jefferson opened it finally on May 19, 1803.[33] This delay, however, allowed the letter to arrive aptly the very day after another conflict had opened, one that would help to define Jefferson's presidency. The day before Jefferson received the Pascha's letter in translation, with its phantom threats of "war," a very real war broke out between Britain and France, with the former declaring war on May 18, 1803. The Napoleonic wars that ensued would roll on for a decade, finally pressing France into surrender; first, however, this same war between European neighbors would prompt France to relinquish its North American holdings, selling the expansive and expensive "Louisiana Territory."[34] For Jefferson, conflict may have seemed a rare consistency as he endured his tumultuous first term. Triggered by painful acts of translation, and leading to pivotal transfers, war was unpredictable in outcome, but also inevitable in its origin. As Patterson aptly expressed it, "Wr s unavdble."

10

"Mr Jefferson is in Reality a Musselman"

Look at the power given to the President by the provisional government of Louisiana. By one sweeping clause, he is made as despotic
as the Grand Turk. Every officer is appointed by him, holds his commission during his pleasure, and is amenable only to him. He is the
Executive, the Legislature, and the Judicature. What clamor, a few
years ago, lest the President should be vested with too much power,
the department the most dangerous of all to be trusted.[1]

On November 30, 1803, New Orleans witnessed a unique spectacle. In a ceremony of "cession," this port passed from Spain to France, along with the
entire Louisiana Territory. "The Flag of the French Republic" is now "dis-
played" over New Orleans, Jefferson was informed by Andrew Marschalk,
a newsman based in Mississippi, just north in Natchez.[2] For the president,
this European exchange on the American continent was no longer cause for
alarm, however. Spain's surrender of New Orleans itself formed an expected
prelude, anticipating yet another "transfer of sovereignty," from France to
America, just three weeks later on December 20.[3] The sale of Louisiana had
been negotiated successfully in Paris with the assistance of the American
minister, Robert Livingston. One of history's "largest land deals" was
concluded.[4]

The Louisiana Purchase is rightly remembered as not only a vast "land
deal" but also a landmark victory for Jefferson. In 1803, however, this
American acquisition was contentious. Its legitimacy and logistics were
questioned, especially by Jefferson's Federalist foes in Congress. The same
day that New Orleans passed to France—November 30, 1803—Manasseh
Cutler privately wrote the above words, expressing his anxieties to a friend.
A New England minister and congressional representative, Cutler was both-
ered especially by the president's new powers, which seemed to grant him
unlimited sway over all of Louisiana. This vast territory's transfer, for Cutler,

transformed Jefferson into a "Grand Turk"—an Oriental despot reigning over Western domains.

This portrait of the US president as a Muslim ruler is especially ironic as it arises from Jefferson's purchase of American real estate, securing a huge chunk of the continent for national cultivation. Jefferson had long sought to make his name synonymous with New World terrain, promoting his own pastoral image. Even while serving in urbane Paris, Jefferson embraced his persona as "a savage of the mountains." In 1803, he was still proudly laying claim to agrarian roots. Dressed not as a leading politician, but a lowly planter, Jefferson's clothing scandalized the British diplomat Augustus Foster when he was first received at the President's House in 1804. Startled by Jefferson's state of disrepair, Foster afterward described the US president in a letter:

> He is dressed and looks extremely like a very plain farmer, and wears his slippers down to the heels. [. . .] He thrust out his hand to me as he does to everybody and desired me to sit down. Luckily for me I have been in Turkey, and am quite at home in this primeval simplicity of manners.[5]

In 1803, Jefferson seemed a "Grand Turk" to Manasseh Cutler, due to his "sweeping" powers in Louisiana, assuming sole control over "the Executive, the Legislature, and the Judicature." For Augustus Foster, it is not Jefferson's powers, but his "plainness," that turns him into a Turk. Appearing as a "farmer," Jefferson violates decorum in the eyes of this upper-class British diplomat. However, the president's informality also seems familiar to Foster, recalling his prior service in Turkey. Feeling "at home" with the "simplicity of manners" he had experienced in Muslim lands, Foster is reminded of Ottoman environs as he encounters Jefferson in the President's House.

Although planted in US soil, Jefferson is transported to Turkey in the minds of two onlookers, one domestic, one foreign. Rooting America's rural president in Muslim terms, neither Cutler nor Foster could have known how apt their words were, however. On the very same day that America took possession of Louisiana—December 20, 1803—a delivery arrived to Jefferson from Algeria, with the president receiving a present from none other than Richard O'Brien, whose cover letter for his gift read:

> I take The liberty to send your Excellency an Antelope a few Algerine Pigions & doves, a bottle of otto of roses, & a Burnuce or Moorish Ladies

Cloak allso a few of the large breed of Constantine fowls and 2 Measures of Algerine wheat—[6]

On December 20, Jefferson rose to preside over the Louisiana Territory's vast and varied landscapes. On the very same day, Jefferson also obtained flora and fauna from North Africa, receiving not only Algerian "wheat," but even an "Antelope," along with "a few Algerine Pigions."[7] Supplying these ingredients for North African cultivation, clothing was also offered by O'Brien. The US president's "dress" had been deprecated by Foster, who saw Jefferson as "a very plain farmer"; by 1803, Jefferson was equipped not only with seeds for "Moorish" husbandry, but also the means to outfit a Muslim wife, receiving from O'Brien "a Burnuce or Moorish Ladies Cloak," as well as perfume: "a bottle of otto of roses."[8] Cutler had labeled Jefferson the "Grand Turk" ruling over Louisiana; and yet, on the same day the territory came into US possession, Jefferson received O'Brien's gifts from the Muslim world, making Cutler's satiric label seem somewhat less far-fetched.

Jefferson was delighted by these agricultural dispatches from Algeria, and by O'Brien's ability to procure such rare products. "I have recieved from Algiers two pair of beautiful fowls," the president soon announced to his youngest daughter, Mary, in Milton, Virginia. Now, the hens must be housed, her father added, ending his letter with "hopes" that "we shall begin the levelling, and establishment of your hen-house."[9] Only one day after Jefferson joyfully received the caged "fowls" from Algiers, however, a very different act of captivity forced O'Brien to take up his own pen yet again from North Africa; this time, he was giving notice not of a Barbary Coast gift, but of an expensive loss. On December 21, the day after the expansive West had come under US control, O'Brien would write to Edward Preble, Jefferson's Mediterranean commodore, regarding the capture of another US ship. Nearing the end of 1803, O'Brien's letter concerned the USS *Philadelphia*, which in October had become stranded in Tripoli's harbor and subsequently surrendered—the latest casualty in Jefferson's continuing conflict on the Barbary Coast, begun in 1801. Named after a city cherished by Jefferson and O'Brien alike, the *Philadelphia* would cost America dearly, or at least that was Tripoli's design. A sum of "$600" was demanded by Tripoli's Dey for each of the *Philadelphia*'s "278 seamen," O'Brien informed Preble, and a full "$4,000" would be levied for each of the ship's "29 officers."[10]

It was not ransom money, but a military raid, that formed America's reply to the *Philadelphia*'s capture, however. Just two months after O'Brien's letter, "eight marines" led by Stephen Decatur "boarded and burned" the *Philadelphia* in Tripoli's own harbor, destroying the captive ship under the cover of night in February 1804.[11] Bolstering Jefferson's war against the Barbary Coast, the conflict finally culminated, however, with a second covert mission the following year. Departing Alexandria, Egypt, with another "eight Marines," William Eaton would lead a mixed army of "mercenaries" and "bedouin bands" to take the coastal city of Derna—an audacious "five-hundred-mile" march across the desert intended to depose Tripoli's leader, Yusuf Karamanli, replacing him with his much more amenable brother, Hamet.[12] Now synonymous with the storied origins of the American Marines, Eaton's campaign still echoes in the lyric "To the Shores of Tripoli" featured in the Marine Corps hymn—a resonant legacy of Jefferson's military command and early US combat in Muslim Africa.[13]

In 1803, Jefferson was stretched, pulled by opposing polarities, straddling global extremes. Securing Louisianan soil, Jefferson yet suffered losses in Middle Eastern waters. At the same time that the American West was secured, the *Philadelphia* was pirated in the Mediterranean. One continuity crossed the Atlantic, though, as Jefferson fought through his embattled first term. He was increasingly earning the dubious title of "Grand Turk." Satirically labeled a Muslim at home, with jokes inspired both by Jefferson's new frontier "powers" as well as the plainness of his rural dress, the president was also playing sultan in North Africa, secretly fighting for "Executive" control not only of the American frontier, but of coastal cities on Muslim "shores."

≈

In the name of the most merciful God!!!

Praise be ascribed to the most merciful God who inspires his creatures with sentiments worthy of the excellence of his deity, to whom alone adoration is due—

Hamet Ebn Abdul Kadir unto the most Excellent Thomas Jefferson Emir, who commands Emirs, the most distinguish'd among Christians . . . Health

Having enter'd into bonds of the strictest friendship with General Eaton & having render'd him every service in my power during his sojour in these parts, when peace was concluded I presented him with a letter for your Excellency & a beautiful young female Camel (or Dromedary) for your Excellencys own use.[14]

The Algerine wheat and wares received from O'Brien in 1803 would not be the last pastoral gift dispatched to Jefferson from the Barbary Coast. The next present for the president, however, would have to wait until 1805, "when peace was concluded" finally between Tripoli and America. This time, it was not a "Moorish Ladies Cloak," but a "beautiful young female Camel" that was donated to Jefferson. Sent west in the summer of 1805, a "Dromedary" was offered to his "Excellency," intended for the president's own personal transportation.[15]

It is comical to imagine Jefferson perched on a camel, climbing up the slopes of Monticello. However, this letter promising to send Middle Eastern transport to the president seems anything but humorous, earnestly seeking Jefferson's favor. Its serious intent is suggested from its sacred opening. In a formula now familiar to Jefferson, this letter, authored by a certain Hamet Ebn Abdul Kadir, begins with "In the name of the most merciful God!!!"— the first words of the Muslim scripture, and the same words that had opened Richard O'Brien's Algerine diary. Here in 1805, it is not a Qur'anic chapter, however, but a diplomatic gift that this doxology introduces. More original in this letter is another Islamic echo that is personally applied to Jefferson himself. In the words of Abdul Kadir, Jefferson is America's "Emir," an Arabic term that signifies "commander" (أمير), but which has connotations both military and spiritual, a title of sovereignty that was applied to the Muslim Prophet's successors.[16] Endowed with sweeping powers, the president appeared a "Grand Turk" to Manasseh Cutler in 1803; in 1804, Jefferson's disheveled dress seemed Turkish to Augustus Foster as well. Outstripping these Westerners, however, a North African applies Arabic terms to Jefferson, labeling the president in 1805 an "Emir, who commands Emirs." Although "most distinguish'd among Christians," Jefferson receives a Muslim title and a mode of transport from the Middle East, addressed with words from the Qur'an while pledged a camel for his "own use."

This goodwill gift to America was made possible only after "peace" was "concluded" in North Africa. As Abdul Kadir suggests, however, it was an American intermediary that prompted this present—an intermediary who, ironically, was left embittered by the very same peace. William Eaton had spearheaded the sneak attack across the desert to Derna, seeking to supplant Yusuf Karamanli, replacing him with his brother Hamet. Most celebrated among Eaton's party was a native of Fauquier County, Virginia—Presley O'Bannon—the Marine commander and the man who would "hois[t] the first American flag ever flown above a fortress in the Old World."[17]

According to long-standing Marine lore, Hamet Karamanli was so impressed by O'Bannon that he "presented" him with a storied "Mameluke sword"—a sword that inspired a part of Marine officer dress that still persists today.[18] Despite these heroics, the assault led by Eaton and O'Bannon failed to depose Tripoli's leader. Instead, the American capture of Derna prompted Yusuf to come to terms; "recognizing [. . .] a real threat to his regime," Yusuf "signaled Washington of his willingness to negotiate a peaceful conclusion to his war with the United States."[19] A new US treaty was concluded with Tripoli in June, a treaty that was victory enough for Jefferson—but not for Eaton. America had pledged support for Hamet, and yet his brother, Yusuf, still sat in power. To Eaton personally, this was a dishonor; although peace had come, it proved more unsatisfactory than war. With Yusuf ascendant, his brother was left "completely abandonned—(and by a great nation)," as Hamet himself wrote to Jefferson in 1805, citing Eaton's promises specifically. "General Eaton assured me the peace would never be made," Hamet complained to the president, "unless I was placed in my own Seat."[20] Forced to become a Muslim "fugitive living in exile," Hamet sought sanctuary in neighboring North African countries.[21] In 1805, Eaton resented that "Hamet Bashaw" had been "used *solely* as an instrument"—a resentment that would soon return to impact America's "Emir" himself, prompting Eaton to flirt with another aggrieved fugitive whose own aspiring coup involved not Tripoli, but the Louisiana Territory.[22]

As 1805 came to an end, Eaton returned home a hero, but also an advocate for Hamet, lobbying on behalf of his chosen Karamanli brother—a cause he would continue to champion for many years to come.[23] "On entering the ground of war with Hamet Bashaw," Eaton stressed in December, writing to Jefferson's secretary of the navy, "Mr OBannon and myself united in a resolution to perish with him before the walls of Tripoli, or to triumph with him within those walls."[24] Jefferson doubtless saw the justice of Eaton's complaints, but the president knew that any further action from him would invite criticism. Hamet's cause had become a public source of controversy by the time Eaton returned stateside. Charged with "duplicity over the treatment of Hamet," Jefferson also faced potential reproach for sympathy with this Muslim pretender to the throne.[25] In the autumn of 1805, the president's aid for Hamet in exile was debated in the newspapers, leading to a satire published in the pro-Jefferson *Republican Advocate*, and republished in the *National Intelligencer*. Mocking the president's accusers, the newspaper defended Jefferson's "commiseration" for the "Bashaw":

It is reasonably suspected that the overweening commiseration for Hamet's forlorn situation arises from a motive unconnected with humanity: It is suspected to originate in a vehement desire to urge our government into an unwarrantable grant of money to the exiled Bashaw: And should this be done, the very ensuing moment these obstreperous bawlers would cry out shame! Shame! they would bellow, thus to lavish the money of an honest and a Christian people upon a Turk, an Infidel, the enemy of our Holy Faith! Nay, it is extremely questionable, whether a grant of money to Hamet would not be adduced to prove that Mr. Jefferson is in reality a Musselman.[26]

Portrayed as "bawlers" by the *Republican Advocate*, Jefferson's foes emerge as hysterical, "bellowing" against anyone who authentically cares for "Hamet's forlorn situation." Specifically, the president's own sympathy seems "suspect." Jefferson's compassion, his enemies suggest, arises not from "humanity," but from more sinister and unholy affiliations. Calling out Hamet's religious status—as a "Turk" and "Infidel"—critics of Jefferson are said even to "question" the President's "Faith." If Jefferson cares so much for this North African fugitive, perhaps his sympathy extends to Islam itself? Could we not conclude, from such evidence, that "Mr. Jefferson is in reality a Musselman"?

Comic in tone, this attack on Jefferson's own attackers seeks to clear the president's name; however, it also publicly invokes in 1805 the very same Islamic image of Jefferson that had surfaced in personal letters during the previous years. Privately framed as Louisiana's "Grand Turk" and America's "Emir," the president's status as "Musselman" was now satirically queried in the open press. For Jefferson, this situation and these suspicions would soon get a whole lot worse. Ascribed Muslim titles in the months and days leading up to autumn 1805, it was in this same season that Jefferson anticipated welcoming an actual Muslim to the President's House. Supported and surrounded by names long known to Jefferson—Richard O'Brien, William Eaton, Augustus Foster—a North African was coming to dine with the President.

≈

The President was in an undress—Blue coat, red vest, cloth colored small cloths—white hose ragged slippers with his toes out—clean linnen—but his hair dissheiveled.[27]

Congressman Manasseh Cutler had deplored Jefferson's despotic power in a private letter penned at the end of November 1803. Two years later, at the end of November 1805, Senator William Plumer visited the "Grand Turk" himself, and was welcomed by Jefferson at the President's House at 11:00 A.M.[28] Recording their November 29 meeting in his diary, Plumer reports finding Jefferson in a startling state of "undress," echoing Augustus Foster, who had noted Jefferson's slovenly "slippers" a year before. For Senator Plumer, it is again the president's "ragged slippers," as well as his "red," "white," and "blue" outfit, that strikes him as strange. The meeting between Jefferson and Plumer was interrupted, however, by a single sound. A "booming canon" had been fired, signaling the approach of a ship to the nation's capital.[29] Struggling up the Potomac to Washington, yet hindered by "foul weather," this ship navigated difficult final lengths to deliver a North African who would pose great challenges for Jefferson himself. Landing finally on November 30, 1805, Sulaimān Mellimelni, the first Muslim envoy to the United States, had arrived.[30] Sent from Tunis, Mellimelni's mission was to negotiate on behalf of his nation, requesting "indemnification" for Tunisian vessels taken by the US Navy during the last months of the first Barbary War. Aptly, it was an act of American "capture" that had prompted the first Muslim ambassador to step onto US shores.[31]

Announced with an explosion, Mellimelni's mission seemed an eruption in American history, unprecedented in the New World. And yet, his American sojourn, lasting nearly a year, would involve a whole host of familiar US figures. In the coming weeks, it would be William Plumer himself who regularly reported on Mellimelni's movements in Washington. This US senator gained admittance to the Tunisian, however, via recognizable American intermediaries. "I went with Genl Eaton to visit the Tunisian *Ambassador*," Plumer noted in his diary on December 23, first meeting Mellimelni in the company of the disgruntled veteran of the Barbary Coast, William Eaton.[32] A month later, Plumer again visited the Tunisian, taken to Mellimelni by an American even more experienced with North African life. Richard O'Brien, finally returning to stay stateside after his slavery and later service in the Barbary Coast, was home just in time to witness the Tunisian ambassador's reception in Washington. After first meeting Mellimelni in December, Plumer returned with O'Brien in January, recording in his diary that they arrived at an inopportune time, finding Mellimelni "on the carpet prostrate in the act of worshiping his God."[33] Interrupting Arabic prayers, Plumer witnesses a private "act" of Muslim piety likely unfamiliar to him. But, for O'Brien, Mellimelni's prayer was nothing new, of course. By 1805, O'Brien had himself been petitioning Allah's mercy for at least a decade and a half, inscribing prayerful Arabic in his own Algerian diary in 1790.

Plumer was not alone in taking notice of Mellimelni's Muslim practices; the "disheveled" man who stood with Plumer as Mellimelni arrived—Jefferson himself—was also conscious of the ambassador's Muslim faith. Arriving to Washington finally on November 30, Mellimelni was hosted for a "state dinner" at the President's House just ten days later, on December 9, 1805.[34] An evening meal for American dignitaries and visiting diplomats, Jefferson kept in mind especially the month: it was Ramadan, the sacred season of fasting when Muslims refrain from eating until sundown. One of the guests at this meal for Mellimelni noted that it was the Muslim month that dictated the president's scheduling:

> I dined at the President's, in company with the Tunisian Ambassador and his two secretaries. By the invitation, dinner was to have been precisely at sunset—it being in the midst of Ramadan, during which the Turks fast while the sun is above the horizon.[35]

Satirically labeled "a Musselman" in the press just months before, the president now determined his dinner time by the demands of Ramadan. The "Grand Turk" of America, Jefferson eats together with "Turks," playing the role of US "Emir" by refraining from his dinner "while the sun is above the horizon." Remarkable for its content, it is the writer of the above diary entry that is especially apt. Sharing the table with the "Tunisian Ambassador and his two secretaries," the diarist who authored this account was John Quincy Adams.[36] Fifteen years before, the young John Quincy had received word that his mother shared a "Foreign Box" with a "Tripolian," and that his father had met with this same Muslim ambassador, along with Thomas Jefferson. In 1805, as he now shared a dinner during Ramadan with President Jefferson, John Quincy could not possibly know that it was not only his past, but his future, that was implied. Nearly two decades later, John Quincy would himself host on this same spot another African Muslim on a mission to free fellow captives caught in American hands.

≈

I am here in the midst of Africans and Savages. We have an Ambassador from Tunis and his suite in the City, and deputies from eight nations beyond the Mississippi are arrived.[37]

Four days after John Quincy joined Jefferson for dinner on December 9, 1805, Mellimelni was hosted once again by the president—but, this time, he was not the lone exotic guest. Seated at Jefferson's table this time were other travelers, not from a Muslim nation, but from "nations beyond the Mississippi."[38] Soon after Mellimelni's arrival from North Africa, Native American "deputies" had also come to Washington, tribal representatives visiting the president in the wake of the western travels of Lewis and Clark. Quoted above are the words of Augustus Foster—the same British diplomat who had recognized Jefferson's manners as "Turkish" in 1803. Reminiscent of Volney's linguistic synthesis of Far West and Middle East, Foster frames himself as caught in "the midst" of two global extremes: Muslim "Africans" and American "Savages."

It was mere coincidence that emissaries from the Barbary Coast and the American frontier arrived in DC during the same days at the end of 1805. The Washington elite, however, could not resist comparisons between America's indigenous peoples and African Muslims, bridging the Mississippi and the Mediterranean. Invited to a New Year's celebration hosted by the president, his friend the famed socialite Margaret Bayard Smith marveled at perceived similarities between native Africans and Native Americans, noting the

curiosity excited by the appearance of the *Osage-Chiefs* and their attendant *squaws*. And likewise of the Tunisan Minister, Meley Meley, and his splendid and numerous suite. It must be confessed that in their turbaned heads, their bearded faces, their Turkish costume, rich as silk, velvet, cashmere, gold and pearls could make it, attracted more general and marked attention than the more familiar appearance of the European Ministers. These two embassies, one from Africa the other from the wilderness of the Far West, were so unique, so extraordinary, so strangely contrasted, that they were irresistibly attractive to the company at large, though it seems scarcely possible that the President should have been so exclusive in his attention to savage chieftans, as to have neglected proper civilities to the representatives of royalty, however anxious he might have been to court *democratic popularity*, the reason assigned by the writer for his plain dress and plain manners.[39]

Celebrating the dual "embassies" from the exotic "Far West" and North "Africa," Smith finds them "strangely contrasted," and yet similarly "attractive"—and both standing apart from the president, who seems the opposite of exotic, sporting again his "plain dress and plain manners." Smith's language, as she compares "savage chieftans" with "turbaned heads," is thoroughly American in perspective and prejudice, of course. However, according to Smith herself, the "Tunisan Minister" also made the very same connection:

> Meley-Meley expressed a most lively interest about these Osages. He examined their forms countenances and habits and was particularly struck by the mode in which their heads were shaved, leaving only a tuft of hair on the crown. He took off his turban and showed them that his head was shaven after the same fashion, and enquired if their people had always worn it so. "Who then were your fathers? where did your fathers come from? did they come from my country? for in this and other things you do, you are like my people, and our father was Ishmael." Such were some of the observations Meley-Meley made through the medium of their respective interpreters. The Tunisan minister was the lion of the season.[40]

Echoing a theory advanced twenty years earlier by the president himself in a letter to Ezra Stiles—that "Asia" was "peopled from America"—Mellimelni offers speculations on globe migrations conjoining East and West. For the Tunisian, it is cultural similarities that suggest a shared ethnic origin; the "same fashion" of hair hints at a common "father," equating "my people" and "their people." America's "Indians," Mellimelni suggests, were even descended from "Ishmael" himself, progenitor of the Arabs and forefather of the Prophet Muhammad.[41]

At the center of these complex genetic chains stood a single man, of humble dress and simple manners. Jefferson was the unassuming magnet in the midst of the New Year's parties of 1806, pulling together two exotic "embassies" arriving from Muslim Africa and the "Far West wilderness." Still looking like a "very plain farmer," by the first days of 1806 the US president was increasingly also clothed with outlandish titles. By the New Year, he was not only an American "Emir," and the "Grand Turk" of the Louisiana Territory. In Mellimelni's mind at least, Jefferson was also the ruler of a country and a continent whose original inhabitants were "Ishmaelites." For Mellimelni, Jefferson was leading a nation with ancient Middle Eastern roots, occupying land first peopled by the "brethren" of African Muslims.

11

"The Prayer of the Poorest Slave of God"

the public treasure is lavished on Turks and infidels; on singing boys
and dancing girls; to furnish the means of bestiality to an African
barbarian

Representative John Randolph in Congress, March 5, 1806[1]

On his arrival in Washington, Mellimelni was greeted with holiday fanfare.
In December 1805, he was fêted at a dinner at the President's House; by New
Year's Day, 1806, Mellimelni was acclaimed "the lion of the season" by socialite Margaret Bayard Smith. Seasons change, though. Mellimelni's novelty soon wore off, and so did his welcome. As spring neared, the Tunisian
ambassador was still attracting attention—and animal analogies. But rather
than a majestic lion, he was labeled instead "bestial" and "barbarous."

These harsh words were spoken in Congress on March 5, 1806, by John
Randolph, Jefferson's Virginian cousin and, by 1806, a virulent critic.[2] In a
speech soon published in capital newspapers, Randolph swipes at Mellimelni,
but aims obliquely at Jefferson's own administration. The Tunisian, who goes
unnamed, is reviled with epithets both racial and religious. It is the president's
extravagance that seems the real scandal, however, with Jefferson spending
"public treasure" on Mellimelni and his entourage. Randolph's innuendo
plays on the ambassador's rumored fondness for prostitutes—a fondness
that the US government reportedly indulged, James Madison himself supplying Mellimelni with the means to procure "dancing girls" during his stay.[3]
Alluding to Mellimelni's Islamic faith, Randolph classes the Tunisian ambassador and his suite of attendants as mere "Turks and infidels." Most reminiscent for readers in Washington may have been Randolph's last phrase above,
however. Labeling the ambassador an "African barbarian," Randolph seems
to pun on Mellimelni's "Barbary Coast" origins; however, in 1806, this abuse
of a foreigner possessed domestic resonance. Similar words were cruelly

invoked during precisely this period to denigrate enslaved Africans suffering in US captivity.[4]

Even before Randolph's March 5 speech, US attitudes toward Mellimelni had started to sour. Grumbling began in government offices as early as New Year's celebrations. Meeting on January 2, the Senate was surprised to find the African Muslim requesting access to their private conclave. "The Tunisian Ambassador" gave "notice that he wished at 12 OClock to come into the Senate Chamber & pay his respects to them," Senator William Plumer recorded, summarizing in his diary the ensuing debate: should this "African" really be "admitted," granted a "seat in the Chamber"?[5] Samuel L. Mitchill, Republican from New York, stood to declare that Mellimelni had no right to take a seat; indeed, he had no right even to claim the status accorded to him by Jefferson. This "*half-savage*," Mitchill asserted, should not have been granted "the dignified title of *ambassador*." It was a shame, Mitchill added, that Mellimelni had been "received" with "the title of an Ambassador" by both "our Secretary of State" and "the President of the United States." It was a mistake on Jefferson's part to recognize this Muslim African as an authentic diplomatic emissary, Mitchill suggests. Despite discomfort in the Senate, however, Mellimelni would gain entrance, making himself at home in this American body due to the "title" and honors authorized by the president.[6]

It is not surprising to find Mellimelni provoking American bigotry and bias in 1806. This "bestial" view of Mellimelni was not restricted to white Americans; it was shared too by his fellow Muslims. As spring approached, the president increasingly faced public backlash, and was criticized openly in Congress for hosting Mellimelni. In private, however, Jefferson also received grief; he was handed a written protest from a different quarter, a letter of complaint against Mellimelni, inscribed mostly in English, but also signed in Arabic. The Muslim ambassador had arrived in America seeking to negotiate freedom and peace in Tunisia. But it was his arrival that also brought Muslim captivity to American shores, ultimately confronting Jefferson with an imprisoned "Turk" pleading for liberation.

≈

Randolph's speech, with his salvo against the Barbary Coast "Turks," was delivered in Congress on March 5. The very next day, Jefferson had a private talk with the Barbary Coast veteran who was serving as Mellimelni's sometime "interpreter"—William Eaton—who aided the Tunisian, helping to translate his speech during his stay in Washington.[7] However, on March 6, it was not the relaying of a Muslim's expressions, but a private interview with the US president, that was Eaton's concern—and Jefferson likely had little doubt concerning the prospective topic of their conversation. Returning home a military "celebrity" in 1805, by 1806, Eaton was increasingly known as a "complainer."[8] Embittered by the end of the Barbary War, and Jefferson's own reluctance to support Hamet Karamanli, Eaton also had more selfish concerns, claiming too that the US government had failed to compensate him adequately for his services.[9]

Surprisingly, however, on March 6, 1806, it was not Eaton's own past that concerned him, but the president's future. Shadowing Mellimelni around the capital, Eaton had also been approached by another high-profile, yet equally shadowy, figure. Not an exotic Muslim, cutting into political meetings in Washington, Eaton's new contact was an American politician, conspiring to cut the country in two. On March 6, fresh from his service as a Muslim interpreter, Eaton played an informant to the president, warning him of an impending plot.[10] Discontent with Jefferson's dispensing "treasure" on "Turks and infidels" was apparently the least of the president's problems. A plot was formulating to topple the "Grand Turk" himself. Eaton had failed to foment a coup in North Africa; now, he was anxious about insurrection in North America, having heard of a plan to depose not a Muslim Bashaw, but the Master of Monticello.

Eaton's warning was explosive, but it did not come as a complete shock to Jefferson. Similar rumors had rumbled through Washington, and reached Jefferson, in recent months. Following Eaton's visit, Jefferson took little action, seeming to "brus[h] aside" the veteran's advice.[11] Eaton, however, was not a man to be ignored, and he continued to advocate on his own behalf, seeking "public treasure," chasing the back pay owed him from his Barbary War service. By April 9, 1806, Eaton's cause attracted congressional attention, with a "resolution" in the House of Representatives raised to support the veteran's claims.[12] On the evening of that same day, at the President's House, Eaton and his own words were likely on Jefferson's mind. The president was hosting one final dinner, once more honoring the now infamous Tunisian ambassador. Invited to dine alongside the US president and this North African emissary, however, were other dignitaries and diplomats, reflecting the heights of Washington society.[13] As his guests began to arrive on April 9, 1806, Jefferson undoubtedly greeted them with his characteristic serenity and signature calm. But a glaring threat would have also hovered in the president's peripheral vision as dinner began. Eyeing his guests, it was not the Muslim ambassador who had most recently emerged as a menace, but another man that shared the same table. In American newspapers, Mellimelni had been called an African "infidel"; he was a devotee of the "Alcoran" and portrayed as a danger to polite society. But sitting near this North African emissary was an actual killer from New Jersey, and, if Eaton was to be believed, a plotting traitor—even, an aspiring presidential assassin. For Jefferson, the Barbary Powers had posed a perpetual challenge from abroad, confronting him with captivity in Muslim lands since his own ambassadorial years in Paris. And yet, this region's emissary may have seemed mild compared to another of Jefferson's guests on April 9. Even as he honored the "bestial" Mellimelni during dinner, Jefferson could be forgiven if he kept one wary eye fixed on the real "barbarian" in their midst: his own disgraced former vice president, Aaron Burr.

≈

In April 1806, a plot targeting the president was developing, planned by a prior member of Jefferson's innermost circle. At the same time, Mellimelni found himself in a similar situation. A close aide to the Tunisian ambassador—Sulaimān Islāmbūlī—had fallen out with his master. This member of Mellimelni's "Turkish" entourage had proved so insubordinate that he had been consigned to captivity in Washington.[14] Desperate for an advocate, the unfortunate Islāmbūlī needed a higher authority to intervene, but his own national leaders were far away, ruling Muslim lands across the Atlantic. Only one man had power above Mellimelni, and was close at hand: the "Emir" of America himself.

On April 30, 1806, just days after dining with Mellimelni, Jefferson received a plaintive appeal from Sulaimān Islāmbūlī, which opened with the following words:

Sir
Permit me Honble sir to state to you the situation in which I am placed by the arbitrary and unjust turk now Embassador to the US from Tunis. I am a Constantinopolean and have served the limeted time as a slave in Tunis 7 years and have the same discharge as the rest of the turkish retinue, thus situated without one single crime alledged against to be entombed in a prison and in that Country of all others the most free and a country the

people of which I love. I hope you will interfere in my behalf and let me have the parole of honor.[15]

Imprisoned just a short walk away from Jefferson, Islāmbūlī's letter uneasily balances between extremes, spanning contraries of class, culture, and country. Addressed to the President's House from one "entombed in a prison," the author who petitions America's leader identifies himself as a lowly "slave"—a servant of Mellimelni who had arrived as part of his "retinue." Turkish by birth, and Tunisian in service, Islāmbūlī proudly cites his Eastern origins, even as he appeals to the West's premier politician. Although he is a "Constantinopolean," it is Jefferson's own "Country" and its ideals that Islāmbūlī invokes. Highlighting the irony of his "situation," Islāmbūlī finds himself incarcerated in the United States, a Muslim captive in the very nation which he "loves" for its liberties. Not "one single crime" is "alledged against" him, Islāmbūlī insists; nevertheless, he is confined in "that Country of all others the most free."

Drawing a link long familiar to Jefferson, Islāmbūlī ties together unjust incarceration and Islamic identities. Also familiar, however, is his critiques of the Tunisian "Embassador." Held captive after falling out of favor with his master, Islāmbūlī complains of "the arbitrary and unjust turk"—a portrait of Mellimelni that matched the American view so memorably voiced by Randolph. Despite Jefferson's liberal hospitality, hosting dinner after dinner for Mellimelni, the Tunisian continued to make undiplomatic demands. By the spring, Mellimelni had emerged as a serious irritant to Jefferson. James Cathcart, himself a notorious annoyance, recognized Mellimelni as a "political pest of society," as he wrote to James Madison.[16] While his penchant for prostitutes was embarrassing, even more vexing were Mellimelni's inflexible requests for American concessions, as well as his reluctance to return home to North Africa. Mellimelni was evidently enjoying his ambassadorial status, and soon elected to sightsee up the East Coast after his Washington stay, even while cavalierly mistreating his own Tunisian "retinue"—including one of his aggrieved "servants," Sulaimān Islāmbūlī.[17]

By the spring of 1806 Mellimelni's behavior began to pose not merely a political, but a personal problem for Jefferson, with the Tunisian's aide—Islāmbūlī—petitioning the president directly. The urgency of Islāmbūlī's letter rises as it concludes, his final words turning from complaint to plea, asking for Jefferson's immediate "interference":

I hope Honble sir my situation will claim your interference and give me an opportunity of telling my country where real liberty and justice can be found. Allow me once more to impress on your mind that I Am free from the best of discharges from Tunis and am not bound to serve the Bashaw longer than he treats me as a servant ought to be treated. I hope you will not pass me over unnoticed but as a man in distress do what Justice dictates for your Ob[edien]t and very respectful Serv[an]t.[18]

Making more poignant his precarious situation, Islāmbūlī ends with his free conscience, despite his actual incarceration; I am "not bound," Islāmbūlī proclaims emphatically, "I Am free." And although now an imprisoned "slave," Islāmbūlī yet sees himself as a future ambassador. If his release is secured, Islāmbūlī promises the president, he will serve as a cultural advocate for America, taking "an opportunity of telling my country where real liberty and justice can be found." In freeing this fugitive, Jefferson would gain not only the freedom of a single Muslim, but also the means of spreading good report of American freedoms to Muslim lands.

This future political value offered by Islāmbūlī is contingent on the president's personal "interference," of course. And aptly, Islāmbūlī ends by declaring his dependence on Jefferson himself. Closing his letter with a standard valediction, Islāmbūlī informs the president that he is "your Obedient and very respectful Servant"—a conventional sign-off that assumes new significance in light of Islāmbūlī's current "servitude." It is "Servant" that aptly stands as the last word of Islāmbūlī's letter—at least, his letter's last word in English. Consulting the actual manuscript that Jefferson received on April 30, 1806, the final lines of its last page feature an intriguing inscription immediately below Islāmbūlī's "respectful Serv[an]t" (Figure 7).[19]

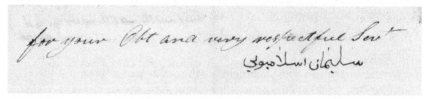

Figure 7 Conclusion to the April 1806 letter, posted from Sulaimān Islāmbūlī to Jefferson in Washington, featuring the former's Arabic autograph. Image courtesy of the Missouri History Museum.

Pledging in abbreviated English to be the President's "Servant," Islāmbūlī ends his letter with a flourish, inscribing his name in authentic Arabic script: "سليمان إسلامبولي" ("*Sulaimān Islāmbūlī*"). At the risk of alienating his audience of one, Islāmbūlī declines to domesticate his own Eastern identity, even as he appeals to an American icon. Despite his vulnerability, desperately imprisoned in Washington, DC, Islāmbūlī elects to autograph his appeal to the US president in the flowing letters of a foreign language. This decision seems even bolder considering the name here inscribed, as "Islāmbūlī" carries a conspicuous religious resonance. Claiming the capital of Turkey as his hometown earlier in his letter—"Constantinople"—Islāmbūlī's own concluding signature recalls yet another name sometimes used for his native city, "Islāmbūl": a name that reflects this historic city's role as the urban heart of "Islām," as well as the center of the Ottoman Empire.[20] Addressed to the pinnacle of American political power, this April 1806 letter from a lowly "servant" ironically ends with an Arabic term that itself suggests a spiritual "submission," the word "Islām" literally signifying "surrender" to God. Hidden within his last Arabic lines, Islāmbūlī traces the very title of the Muslim religion in his signature—"Islām," "إسلام"—with his farewell to the American president implying an alternate object of "obedience." As implied by his own identity, Islāmbūlī pledges service not to Jefferson merely, but also claims in his very name to be a "slave" of Allah.

Little did Sulaimān Islāmbūlī realize, even as he sought asylum from American internment, that he was not the only Muslim captive currently in the United States; in 1806, Islāmbūlī was only one among many devotees of Islam that were striving for release, hoping to return to Africa in freedom. For Jefferson, Islāmbūlī's April letter likely recalled other appeals he had received since his Paris years, pairing Islam with cruel incarceration. However, it was not Jefferson's long past but his immediate future that was traced in these irregular sentences from Islāmbūlī, and especially in the foreign loops of his last line. This petition in April 1806 would not be the last that Jefferson would receive from a Muslim "slave" who was "entombed" in America. In just one year, other appeals from African captives would begin wending their way to the president, featuring not mere Arabic autographs, but written entirely in this language most sacred to Islam.

≈

As to the refractory Tunisians I think we should pay their passage & get rid of them. If they would stipulate to deliver themselves to any Tunisian or other Barbary Agent in England, it would excuse us to the Bey of Tunis.

Jefferson to James Madison
September 16, 1806[21]

No record survives of a reply from Jefferson to Sulaimān Islāmbūlī in April 1806, nor is there evidence of the president's "intervention." It is clear, however, that the fate of Mellimelni's entourage remained on Jefferson's mind through 1806.[22] By autumn, the president finally did intervene, assisting yet more North African aides to the ambassador as they sought to escape their "arbitrary" Muslim master. Writing the above words to his secretary of state, James Madison, on September 16, 1806, Jefferson approved funds for three Muslim fugitives stranded in New York. Willing neither to stay with the ambassador, nor to accompany him home to North Africa, these "Tunisians" had fled Mellimelni's "unjust" treatment, becoming not only escaped Muslims in America, but presenting a diplomatic problem for America's president. With evident irritation, Jefferson directs Madison to "pay their passage," helping these "refractory" North Africans reach England, effectively freeing these underlings from Mellimelni's control.

Spilling even more "public treasure" on his Muslim guests, Jefferson sounds impatient in the autumn of 1806, wishing to deport the Tunisians as quickly as possible—and as quietly. We should just "get rid of them," Jefferson declares in blunt language unusual for America's serene "Grand Turk." Mellimelni's mission to America had proved a scandalous disaster, and the president seemed anxious to avoid additional public attention or intrigue. Equally concerning, as Jefferson hints, is the potential displeasure of his counterpart in Tunis—"the Bey"—whose rage the president hoped not to provoke. Seeking to "excuse" his own "interference" in Tunisian affairs, the US president's fear of the Bey's ire was not without cause. The Tunisian ambassador himself had cited his master's temper as the very reason he was reluctant to leave America. Even while his own servants were fleeing him in fear, Mellimelni informed Jefferson that he too was afraid. According to Mellimelni, if he returned to Tunisia without meeting his goals in America, he would face imprisonment—or much worse. "Failure" could mean "the forfeit of his life."[23]

As his mission neared its end, Mellimelni stressed the potentially fatal consequences of his failure. The ambassador protested especially the ship provided for his trip home—the *Franklin*—the same ship that had been previously captured by his master, and later sold back to the United States. To be gifted the very vessel once taken by Tunisia would seem an insult, Mellimelni explained in a letter to Jefferson, which ends with the following words:

> it is more than my life is worth to return in a vessel that has already belong'd to my Master and was sold to *Christians* by his particular order
>
>   That the immortal *Allah* may have you under his holy protection is the prayer of the poorest Slave of God.[24]

Triangulating his duties among three distinct lords, Mellimelni expresses his fear of his Muslim "Master" in Tunisia, who will take his "life" if he "return[s] in" this same "vessel." Mellimelni then turns to two other sovereigns, one divine and one earthly, figuring himself as a "Slave of God" while also appealing to the US president. Foreshadowing events just one year in the future, Jefferson is situated as the potential savior for a Muslim whose "life" is threatened, with the president petitioned by as a "poor" African "slave." In return for Jefferson's prospective aid Mellimelni can offer only his Islamic prayers, invoking God in Arabic, imploring "the immortal Allah" to keep the US president under His "holy protection."

As the mission from Tunisia came to a close, Jefferson found himself seeking both to save Muslim fugitives from Mellimelni's entourage, and to save Mellimelni himself from the wrath of his own Tunisian "Master." America was unwilling to satisfy conditions demanded by this North African nation for peace, even refusing to offer Mellimelni a replacement ship for the *Franklin*, prompting the ambassador to chart his own transport home to Tunis.[25] But Jefferson had no desire for Mellimelni to lose his liberty, or his life, at home due to this failure to negotiate terms abroad. Despite the irritation he had caused Jefferson, the president ensured that the ambassador did not depart empty-handed; instead, Mellimelni was sent home laden with American goods, aiming to mollify his "Master." These gifts perhaps helped preserve Mellimelni personally, but they also included an instrument designed to preserve Mellimelni's words. Quietly expending yet more "public treasure" on his Muslim sojourner, Jefferson improved Mellimelni's prospects in Tunis by presenting him with "polygraphs" that were "mounted in silver." Procured from his friend, Charles Willson Peale, the president gifted Mellimelni with these mechanisms for literary reproduction—parting presents that not only were made of precious metals, but implied the immense value of manuscripts.[26] Always the archivist, Jefferson sought even to save documents in the Muslim world. With these new polygraphs supplied by the president, leaders on the Barbary Coast could generate copies of their own.[27] For Jefferson, Arabic writings dispatched to him from North Africa had long been lost in translation, with insertions and substitutions shielding their original intent, starting in his Paris years. Now, in 1806, it was Jefferson who worked to ensure that Arabic "originals" in North Africa were retained without alteration.

In the autumn of 1806, as Mellimelni finally departed, Jefferson was unaware that his archival instincts would encourage the preservation of Arabic writings not only abroad, but much closer to home. In one year's time, among Jefferson's small coterie of friends, facsimiles of Arabic originals by African authors would circulate discreetly, reaching not across to the Barbary Coast, but up and down America's Eastern Seaboard.

≈

Mellimelni's diplomatic mission ended with infamy and anxiety in the autumn of 1806. Sailing from Boston, this "poorest Slave of God" returned to North Africa fearing for his future, anticipating fatal consequences for his failure to secure sufficient US concessions. Mellimelni's sojourn abroad was not a total loss, though; at least one of his efforts had succeeded. His prayer to "the immortal Allah" on behalf of Jefferson himself would be answered. In the coming decade, the president proved to be remarkably "protected," despite threats from many sides. And, although Mellimelni's protracted mission had caused headaches, the heart of America's "Grand Turk" was not hardened, seeming to leave Jefferson without lasting bitterness.

Even amid the public furor over Mellimelni's visit, the president himself undertook a private act that reflected sympathy for enslaved Muslims, expressing his compassion through making copies once more. Arriving to America with Mellimelni in 1805, Sulaimān Islāmbūlī would soon make an impassioned plea to the president from prison, this Turkish "slave" begging for release from his own Muslim "master." At the very same time, another petition on behalf of a Muslim slave would surface—a petition Jefferson not only read with interest, but decided to archive, cutting and pasting it into his own scrapbook.[28] Rather than a private plea, it was a published poem that struck Jefferson as special enough to save. Printed in newspapers even as Mellimelni circulated through American society, the following verses on an enslaved African Muslim were preserved by Jefferson in his personal journal:

> THE POOR NEGRO SADI.
> OH! poor Negro, *Sadi*, what sorrow what anguish
> Oppress the lone victim fate dooms for a slave;
> What eye or what heart o'er those sorrows shall languish,
> What finger point out the lone African's grave?
>
> First torn like a wretch from his innocent dwelling,
> And torn from *Abuka*, the wife of his soul;
> Then forc'd, while his heart was indignantly swelling,
> To bow his proud neck to the despot's control,
>
> Think not, Europe, tho' dark his complexion,
> Dark, dark as the hue of the African's fate,
> That his *mind* is devoid of the light of reflection,
> And knows not distinctions of love or of hate.[29]

Lines of woe, weaving together Africa, Islam, and slavery, these memorial lines for a "lone" Muslim were selected by Jefferson, striking him as worthy to remember. Published at the midpoint of his presidency, these verses prompt Jefferson to become a human polygraph, cut out and copied into his own journal. Saving this poem on a "poor" slave, it is an Arabic term that the president preserves in the very first line above: the name "Sadi." Muslim in origin, and Arabic in etymology, "Sadi" signifies "happy" ("سعدي", "*saʿdī*")—a name whose Arabic meaning heightens this poem's tragedy, its felicitous significance entirely at odds with the "anguish" of "Sadi" himself.[30]

Considering Jefferson's experiences during 1805 and 1806, it is unsurprising that these verses published at precisely the same time struck him as significant. Intertwining an "African's fate" with Muslim culture and an Arabic signature, this poem traces the very lines that had encircled Jefferson's life up to 1806—lines that tied him to friends and enemies, from the Comte de Volney to Sulaimān Mellimelni, as well as to more remote figures beyond Jefferson's vision, including a slave named ʿUsman on Georgia's seacoast. Most intriguing in Jefferson's attraction to "The Poor Negro Sadi," however, is the perspective represented in the poem. Rather than merely an account of a Muslim slave, these verses voice partisan advocacy, rejecting "European" bigotry against "the lone victim." Depicting the suffering caused by a "despot's controul," these lines found a sympathetic reader in the same president who was himself labeled a "despot" holding sway over Louisiana. A "Grand Turk" in Washington, with hundreds of enslaved Africans working his Monticello estate, Jefferson's own attention was captured by this single plea on behalf of a Muslim slave. Preserving with his own "fingers" these lines "torn" from published pages, the sorrows of "Sadi" bleed anew in Jefferson's scrapbook, with "Sadi" captured once more in the private journal of America's president.

If poignant, these verses archived by Jefferson would also prove eerily prescient. Even as this poetic eulogy for the fictional "Sadi" appeared in print, the president was only months away from receiving lines from actual Muslim slaves, who would dispatch Arabic verses to Jefferson himself—verses animated by the "light of reflexion," but which had no clear final "fate" in sight, written very much on the run.

12

"The Runners"

This empire is governed by a grand and most puissant bashaw, whom
they dignify with the title of President. He is chosen by persons, who
are chosen by an assembly, elected by the people—hence the mob is
called the sovereign people—and the country, free; the body politic
doubtless resembling a vessel, which is best governed by its tail. The
present bashaw is a very plain old gentleman—something they say
of a humorist, as he amuses himself with impaling butterflies and
pickling tadpoles; he is rather declining in popularity, having given
great offence by wearing red breeches, and tying his horse to a post.
Weekly Wanderer, Randolph, Vermont; April 27, 1807[1]

Exactly one year after Jefferson opened his April 1806 plea from Sulaimān
Islāmbūlī, a letter from another Muslim captive in America appeared in local
newspapers. Signed by "Mustapha Rub-a-Dub Keli Khan," a Tripoli ship cap-
tain "held prisoner in New York," these lines circulated at the very end of
April 1807, published even in rural outlets, like the *Weekly Wanderer* from
Randolph, Vermont. Trapped behind enemy lines, Mustapha spies on the
land of his captivity, writing home to his friend Asem, the "Principal Slave-
Driver" to Tripoli's "Bashaw." Mustapha's concern, however, is America's own
"Bashaw": Thomas Jefferson. Acquiring yet more Muslim titles in Mustapha's
letter, Jefferson is pictured again as a "grand" Sultan who "governs" a New
World "empire"; however, America's "most puissant bashaw" is also lam-
pooned once more for his dress, ridiculed not only for his "plain" style, but
for his "red breeches."

Emphasizing actual elements from Jefferson's life, this letter is, however,
a satiric fake. As his cartoonish name suggests, "Mustapha Rub-a-Dub
Keli Khan" is a fanciful character, created by early America's leading fiction
writer, Washington Irving. First published in his playful New York periodical, *Salmagundi*, Irving produced a whole series of Mustapha letters, which

gained wide circulation in 1807, published also in more conventional news-papers.[2] In syndication, the humor of Mustapha's letters may even have been missed by less sophisticated readers. Irving's letters were facetious, of course; but they capitalized on serious anxieties confronting Jefferson's America. Pictured by Mustapha as a "puissant bashaw," the president's own "Oriental" associations are recognizable to readers in 1807, recalling more earnest portraits of Jefferson as "Emir" and "Grand Turk," originating from both West and East. Interweaving Islam and imprisonment, while sending covert reports of an American president to a "Slave-Driver" in North Africa, Irving's parody cuts rather close to home, even though framed through a Muslim lens.[3]

The timeliness of Irving's satire is evident from his very first Mustapha letter, published in February 1807. Introducing his main character, Irving prefaces Mustapha's words with an editorial note, specifying the original language of his letters to be "Arabic-Greek," now made available to US read-ers via English translation. Mirroring America's actual engagements with Muslim Africa—engagements mediated by dubious acts of rendition—Mustapha speaks only indirectly to his New World audience. His orig-inal phrases, supposedly penned in a foreign tongue, remain hidden from Western view. It is loss of homeland, not language, however, that forms the primary focus of Mustapha's initial letter to Asem, which opens with this lament:

> Thou wilt learn from this letter, most illustrious disciple of Mahomet, that I have for some time resided in New York; the most polished, vast, and mag-nificent city of the United States of America. But what to me are its delights! I wander a captive through its splendid streets, I turn a heavy eye on every rising day that beholds me banished from my country.[4]

In the pages of US newspapers, a Muslim "captive" paints himself as aban-doned and "banished" in the West, even as he gazes daily eastwards to the sunrise. The first ray of dawn, rising above the Atlantic, fails to lighten Mustapha's "heavy eye." Mourning the "immeasurable distance" that divides him from Africa, this Muslim most fears that he will "never again return to his native land." Homeless, isolated, and itinerant, Irving's Mustapha "wan-ders" as an exile in an enemy land. Yearning to share his solitary plight, Mustapha writes to a fellow Muslim and "illustrious disciple of Mahomet" in a language unintelligible to Americans.

First appearing in 1807, Irving's words launched his Mustapha fantasy, but also helped to catalyze his broader career—a career that would lead from this lone Muslim to other isolated "misfits," including the more famous Ichabod Crane and Rip Van Winkle.[5] Irving's satirical letters to Tripoli anticipated his own future American success. They also anticipated other US events much more immediate, however. In early 1807, Irving's Muslim captive wandered through the pages of US newspapers; later that year, actual Muslim captives ran for their lives in US territories. Exiled from African lands, while writing words in their home language, these actual Muslim fugitives, like Irving's fake Mustapha, sought a sympathetic ear. But rather than post messages back to Africa, addressed to a friendly "Slave-Driver," these enslaved Muslims would write words carried instead to a "very plain old gentleman" and a Virginia slave owner: America's own "grand and most puissant bashaw."

≈

ingenuity is foiled in extracting the truth, and credulity is put to the test in its belief

Irving's parody, signed by a Muslim, appeared in the pages of the northern *Weekly Wanderer* on April 27. The very next day, the *Richmond Enquirer*, flagship newspaper of the South, reported an American situation that also "put to the test" its readers' "credulity."[6] This situation was no "Ruba-a-Dub" satire, however, but deadly serious. In the spring of 1807, a sensational crime that was beyond "belief," as well as an upcoming trial, was dominating coverage in the *Richmond Enquirer*. The defendant of this trial was Jefferson's former vice president, Aaron Burr. Seeking to wrest control of territories Jefferson had purchased four years earlier, Burr had been caught in the American West, arrested as he led an improbable insurgency. In his plot, Burr was, according to one prominent witness, even meditating Jefferson's assassination, not only ousting, but eliminating, the "Grand Turk" of Louisiana.

The Burr trial was far from fiction, but it certainly seemed surreal, as the *Enquirer* suggested. Nearing the end of April 1807, "extracting the truth" appeared impossible. Since the opening of the month—when the "misdemeanor" charge against Burr was confirmed by Chief Justice John Marshall— wild rumors and reports of "conspiracy" had run rampant in Richmond's streets.[7] But April proved to be just the beginning. For many more months, this drama unfolded in Richmond, as Burr's trial stretched through the summer of 1807—the very same summer that saw the British bombardment and boarding of the USS *Chesapeake* in Virginia waters. Burr's trial shared the same season with this infamous "Chesapeake Affair"; however, if overlapping in time, these two crises also both claimed connections to Muslim Africa. The *Chesapeake* was just starting on its mission to the Barbary Coast when it was accosted by the British. In Burr's trial, it would be the hero of Jefferson's Barbary Coast war who was first called to testify against the former vice president: William Eaton.

As Eaton took the stand in the summer of 1807, Burr's prosecutors had good reason to be nervous. Eaton was critical to their case, but was increasingly "unsteady." The "first witness for the prosecution," it was Eaton who was also the first military man that Burr had sought to lure to lead his American coup.[8] According to Eaton's testimony, his help had been solicited soon after returning "from the coast of Africa," approached by Burr near the end of 1805. Fresh from his epic trek across this continent's northern edge, Eaton just months earlier was marching on Derne with the Marines, in a bid to depose Tripoli's bashaw. But, in the winter of 1805, Burr needed Eaton's aid to navigate other spaces, seeking to take control of a vast continental territory, supplanting America's own "grand and most puissant bashaw." Burr saw in Eaton a likely ally, due not only to his Barbary daring, but also to his domestic bitterness. Eaton was soured by the failure of his mission, "disgruntled" not with the African Muslims he had fought, but at his own American government. This "resentment," Burr reasoned, could turn Eaton toward treason. The former vice president "seemed desirous of irritating resentment in my breast," Eaton testified in a deposition before the trial in Richmond.[9] Burr harped on "my operations in Barbary" and the "delays of government in adjusting claims for disbursements on that coast during my consular agency at Tunis," Eaton added.[10]

If Eaton seemed a natural target for the vice president's dark ambitions, he was also a significant risk. Eaton had demonstrated bravery in Jefferson's campaigns in Muslim lands, but had proved himself unpredictable. Strong in passions, Eaton always had a weakness for daring acts—and a weakness for drink as well.[11] When news of insurgency began to spread across the country, Burr's foolish efforts to solicit the shaky "General Eaton" seemed almost as surprising as his treason. The former vice president's choice was queried in particular by a former president; from Massachusetts in 1807, John Adams noted that Eaton was a curious accomplice for a conspiracy:

Is Burr So Shallow as Soberly to confide Such a Secret to [Eaton]? But why is he called General Eaton? Our Laws forbid any Commission to be taken under a foreign Power. He had no Commission from the President. He was only appointed by the Ex Bashaw.[12]

Adams was outraged by Burr's grandiose treason, seeking to win the title of America's "Emperor." But Adams also seems irritated by an unearned title accorded to William Eaton. In press accounts of Burr's trial, even in official court proceedings, Eaton was honored as a "General"—a "commission" never granted by Jefferson, Adams stresses. Instead, this rank was awarded to Eaton by Hamet, the pretender to Tripoli's throne.[13] At the very origins to Burr's dubious plot, he had sought to recruit a man whose own military rank was questionable, appointed a "General" only by a Muslim exile and "Ex Bashaw."

Treason may have tempted Eaton, but he was not seduced. This Barbary Coast veteran instead came to America's "Bashaw," seeking to expose the plans of Burr "the Usurper," as Eaton would later label him. But, perhaps finding Eaton's report as questionable as his rank, Jefferson stalled; he "took no action" in response to warnings, even as Burr pursued his plans.[14] By autumn, Eaton was alarmed enough to write to Washington with renewed warning, noting that Burr was now buying up boats in Ohio, preparing to invade the West, first heading to hijack New Orleans.[15] Burr at this time was himself writing down details of his conspiracy; encoding his letters in secret cipher, he sent his plans to another slippery character and co-conspirator, James Wilkinson. Governor of the Louisiana Territory, Wilkinson would ultimately turn on Burr, surrendering his "Cypher[ed]" plans to Jefferson himself, plans that were penned "in the Hieroglyphics of Burr," Wilkinson emphasized.[16] Faced with this familiar mixture—ciphered missives and covert missions, an implausible coup d'état and Barbary Coast veterans—the president was finally alarmed enough to take action. In October, Jefferson met to consider the crisis with his Cabinet, which agreed to commission Stephen Decatur and Edward Preble "to strengthen the naval detachment at New Orleans," enlisting these "heroes" from North Africa to help quash any challenge that Burr might pose to America's vital port city.[17]

By the time consternation had reached this level at Jefferson's Cabinet, however, Burr had arrived to Kentucky, where he was indicted for the first time on November 8, 1806. Accused of "threaten[ing] to open hostilities," and even "high treason," Burr was charged in Frankfort alongside John

Adair, a Kentucky senator and supporter, who had himself "openly advocated" for "western independence."[18] Burr would escape, however, defended in court by "a rising young Kentucky lawyer," Henry Clay. Destined to become, decades later, secretary of state under John Quincy Adams, Clay was seduced by Burr in 1806, even agreeing to act "pro bono" on his behalf, convinced of his famous client's innocence.[19] With Clay's advocacy, Burr was discharged, and by December, he again pursued his plot. As Christmas approached, Burr was finally floating westward on the Cumberland River, bringing to a climax his quixotic insurgency. This river, which snakes across Tennessee and Kentucky, carried Burr on the last leg of his devious quest to gain control of the American West. Departing Nashville on December 22, Burr traveled down the Cumberland, toward its far west mouth, where it meets the Mississippi.[20] By the end of the month, Burr's flotilla "swung into the Mississippi, and the Father of Waters bore them southward."[21] But before they could reach New Orleans and establish a capital for the new "Empire," Burr was betrayed by Wilkinson, who sent a militia to arrest him yet again. On January 16, the disgraced former vice president surrendered just north of Natchez, Mississippi. And there he would stay through the first months of 1807, facing yet another trial, charged once more with treason.[22]

Anticipating Richmond's raucous trial later that same summer, the Natchez proceedings were attended by crowds of curious onlookers. Burr "quickly became a celebrity," and his cause covered the pages of local papers, including the *Mississippi Herald* of Andrew Marschalk—the same newsman who had written to Jefferson in 1803, informing the president of the ceremony that transferred New Orleans to France.[23] To accommodate the number of attendees, Burr's trial was reportedly conducted in the open air, with the vice president examined under still-standing trees, now known as the "Burr Oaks."[24] During the proceedings, Burr was even permitted to stay in comfort on Windy Hill, a nearby plantation, "about five miles from Natchez," owned by the Colonel Benijah Osmun, who also acted as Burr's "bondsman."[25] Dizzyingly familiar, Burr again found sanctuary on a Southern plantation in the wake of high crimes, just as he had three years earlier, in Georgia's Golden Isles. Back in 1804, after killing Alexander Hamilton, Burr had taken refuge on St. Simons Island, a region replete with Muslim slaves, just south of where Abiel Holmes had encountered an African author named 'Usman. In 1807, Osmun was the name of the man who hosted Burr, housing him at his plantation near Natchez. Kept in friendly custody, Burr was lodged only a few miles away from a man destined to become the most celebrated Muslim slave in early America—an Arabic author also held in captivity near Natchez, but who, unlike Burr, was guilty of no crime and who in 1807 had no realistic prospect of release.

For Burr, his Natchez captivity would not last too much longer. In the first week of February, the Mississippi grand jury found no evidence of Burr's guilt. He was, however, still "a wanted man" due to Jefferson's order for his arrest, issued in the autumn. Freed from Natchez but a national fugitive, Burr fled "in disguise", escaping "eastward", running in the direction of the sunrise.[26]

≈

On February 19, 1807, Burr's fugitive run was over. He was taken into custody once more in the Mississippi territory by federal forces, and eventually conveyed to Virginia, where he would face a system of justice more formal than the al fresco proceedings near Natchez. Charged at the circuit court in Richmond on April 1, 1807, Burr's sensational trial attracted the country's attention for months to come, including the president's, despite all the other distractions and dangers that would arise during the spring and summer of 1807.[27] The trial's theatrical character was amplified by the prosecution's first witness—the dissolute "General," William Eaton—who stressed his Barbary service and heroics in Muslim lands from the stand. Eaton's "flair for the dramatic" was not confined to the courtroom, however.[28] His exotic tastes and intoxication spilled out into the streets of Richmond too. High-stakes theater unfolded inside the circuit court; outside, Eaton carried on a low Orientalist comedy. Wearing an "Arab costume" recalling his North African campaigns, Eaton made a drunken spectacle of himself. The "once redoubted Eaton has dwindled down in the eyes of this sarcastic town," Harman Blennerhassett recorded in his diary, describing Eaton as "a ridiculous mountebank, strutting about the streets, under a tremendous hat, with a Turkish sash over colored clothes, when he is not tippling in the taverns."[29] In Richmond barrooms, Eaton sported a "scimitar," topping his "costume" with a "turban." Dallying with local prostitutes, Eaton even ensured that these ladies matched his "Turkish" outfit, reportedly dressing them up in "harem" garb.[30]

Through August 1807, Burr's trial heated up, unfolding in the very same building that Jefferson himself had designed twenty years earlier—Richmond's Capitol Building, whose fame the president had intended to rival the "tomb of Mahomet."[31] Oddly, "Mahomet" also surfaces in the transcripts of the trial at the Capitol, invoked by the prosecution in their efforts to smear Burr and his defense. William Wirt—Jefferson's ally and the government's lead attorney—complained that Burr's legal team were spreading falsehoods; his lawyers, Wirt charged, "are furnishing the joys of a Mahometan paradise to the court as well as to their client."[32] Unrealistically portrayed as an innocent victim struggling against the "savage" government, Burr himself had been sold a "Mahometan paradise," Wirt suggests, with the illusory "joys" of an Islamic afterlife "furnish[ed]" to this man accused of betraying America's own "Grand Turk." Such Eastern touches in Burr's trial further spiced up Richmond's proceedings, prompting a feeding frenzy in the press. Although the former vice president, Burr was now labeled by newspapers a "Grand Imposter," infamous for his "low craft, his innumerable falsehoods, his callous effrontery, his remorseless treachery [. . .] and his strange tricks and manoeuvres." These qualities of "imposture" even earned Burr a new nickname in the summer of 1807, labeled "Mahomet Volpone" in the pages of the *Virginia Argus*.[33] Combining Arabic and Italian, this epithet casts Burr as animalistic, but also Islamic; akin to a sly "fox"—"Volpone"—Burr was first and foremost, the *Virginia Argus* suggests, like the Prophet "Mahomet." A name sacred to Muslims, but far from a compliment in this context, Burr was not only a domestic "Imposter," but framed as a Muslim fugitive from justice in the US press.

True to his repute, Burr would again craftily defy the odds, and evade conviction. After months of legal wrangling, the court proved incapable of upholding the government's charges, and Burr was released. Jefferson may have been a "grand and most puissant bashaw," but he stood powerless as a North African veteran, the drunken "General Eaton," impaired the case against his enemy, "Mahomet Volpone." At the end of September 1807, Burr's improbable dreams of acquittal—likened to a "Mahometan paradise" by the prosecution—were, in fact, realized. He was free once more to flee.

≈

Caught after his staggered quest that had started on the Cumberland River, Burr's trial in Richmond opened in the spring of 1807. It was this same season that the flight of two other fugitives advanced, also on the Cumberland. Taking the very path that Burr had ridden westward, this pair followed the waters of the Cumberland, but pushed in the opposite direction, striving toward the East. Recalling yet reversing Burr's plot, the mission of these two escapees had roots in Muslim Africa; unlike "Mahomet Volpone," however, these Cumberland fugitives were authentic followers of "Mahomet." The most infamous man in America, Burr had acquired a satirical Muslim name during his 1807 trial; at the same time, two other runaways on the same river never revealed their names, but claimed identities that were authentically Muslim. Amid these inversions, a last link connected Burr with two Muslim fugitives who followed the Cumberland's path in the spring of 1807: they shared a single audience, the president of the United States. Jefferson was among many who watched Burr's trial with anxiety; but the president was also one of the very few who would ever learn the tale of two Muslims who were likewise pursuing outlaw hopes in the American West.

It is no coincidence that both Burr and the two Muslim slaves started their opposing journeys on the Cumberland River. A vital east–west waterway, the Cumberland not only offered an essential route across the country, but intersected America's massive north–south thoroughfare—the Mississippi. No records now exist to tell us precisely how two West African Muslims found themselves on the run in rural Kentucky during the spring of 1807. But a clue is offered by their being first caught near Kentucky's far western edges, not far from where the Cumberland connects with the Mississippi. It is the Mississippi that was uniquely capable of delivering men, newly enslaved from Africa, into the very middle of the country. As with so many West Africans—whose stories are hinted in horrifying advertisements published in New Orleans newspapers—the Muslim fugitives caught in Kentucky most likely arrived to America via this essential Louisiana port, the same city that "Mahomet Volpone" had plotted to capture. Traveling north from New Orleans on the Mississippi, unaware of the vast continent that increasingly enveloped them, enslaved Africans could reach the heartland via "America's lifeline to the world."[34] Unlike 'Usman, who suffered captivity on the nation's Atlantic edge, two other African Muslims would be transported to America's interior, where they apparently managed to escape, foraging into the wilds of the New World. Despite being so far inland, this pair evidently saw the wisdom of staying alongside water, keeping close to the Cumberland River, striving in the only direction that held any promise of the familiar, pushing always eastward, toward a far distant home.

The same spring in which Burr's trial began, these two fugitives were reportedly captured near the Cumberland. Unlike "Mahomet Volpone," who had followed this river to establish a selfish empire, these actual Muslims were striving merely for survival. Like Burr, however, their flight was interrupted, stopped after being spotted on the banks of the river, near Kentucky's western edges. According to the only extant record of these two runaways, the Africans "came to a house on Cumberland River," as Ira P. Nash would later tell Jefferson, seemingly "in the month of May."[35] And yet, if they were looking for help, it was not forthcoming. The springtime hospitality of Kentuckians proved icy. Taken from the "house" at which they had arrived, the two men were imprisoned in Hopkinsville, "arrested" and transported "to the Jail of said County" at least twenty miles away, Nash notes.[36] The West Africans whose religious writings in Arabic would eventually reach Thomas Jefferson ironically found themselves incarcerated in a Kentucky county that itself bore a religious name. Captured on the Cumberland, the two Muslim fugitives were jailed at the heart of Kentucky's Christian County.

The unchristian greeting that these fugitives received in 1807 was, of course, to be expected. Despite its name, Christian County was not known for compassion to slaves, populated by at least one family who would later become synonymous with suppressing African liberties. Indeed, the unhappy arrival of escaped Muslims coincided with joyous news delivered to two parents also residing in Christian County. Just ten miles away from where the African pair was jailed in Hopkinsville, Samuel and Jane Davis would learn that their tenth child was on his way. Born the next year, on June 3, 1808, the boy would be christened "Jefferson," the Davises naming their son after the great author of the Declaration of Independence.[37] Jefferson Davis began his life in Christian County, only miles from where two Muslims were first imprisoned, and would eventually rise to become a president himself. Unlike his namesake, Jefferson Davis was destined not to serve as president of the United States, of course, but of the Confederate States, a new country formed in rebellion, headquartered in a familiar statehouse in Richmond, Virginia, and dedicated to the endurance of African slavery.

≈

The suspicion that greeted the two fugitives in Christian County, Kentucky, is no surprise; however, these escaped Africans themselves had a surprise for their captors. Slaves on the run were nothing new in western Kentucky, but these runaways were different.[38] They were immediately remarkable, not merely for their presence, but for something they did not possess—English. As Nash would later report, the fugitive pair could not make themselves understood. Interrogation yielded nothing. Hinting that their time in America had been brief, this linguistic handicap complicated the Africans' situation even further, as they were unable to clarify both from where they had come, as well as point to where they were headed.

Despite their lack of English, one thing was clear to their white captors in Christian County: these "men" were evidently "very desirous to be at liberty." The Kentuckians comprehended only that these two men understood themselves to be no one's property; in their own mind, "they are free People," Nash would note to Jefferson.[39] Although bound in body, the Muslims yet possessed emancipated minds. In yet another irony, this sense of freedom paralleled a law that would very soon come into force. The fugitives captured in Christian County had arrived in 1807, just a year before Jefferson Davis would be born in the same county; they had also arrived, however, during the very last months that the transatlantic slave trade was legal anywhere in the United States—a trade that Jefferson helped to outlaw across America, effective January 1, 1808.[40]

Incapable of imparting their stories, yet making clear the liberty that was their due, the two Africans confronted their Kentucky captors with a final oddity: they *did* have a means to communicate after all, although one that was entirely ineffective. Unable to speak in English, they were able to scribble on paper, writing uninterrupted and alien lines that flowed in narrow rivers of ink, cascading contrary to the expected direction, stretching from right to left. Recalling the first known African writer of Arabic after US Independence—'Usman—twenty years later, two Muslim fugitives were physically imprisoned, but wrote Arabic at their "ease." Unlike the literary production of 'Usman, however, the writings of these two Muslims would not be sent to a mere university president, such as Ezra Stiles, but would make their way instead to the president of the United States.

Mysterious in nation and in name, these captives had seemingly appeared out of nowhere. They spoke nothing intelligible, and what they wrote looked like nonsense. If the authorities in Christian County were literate in Islam's sacred language, however, they may have recognized words that were entirely appropriate to the situation of these two African authors. Signaling that they were "very desirous to be at liberty," these fugitives also wrote eloquent words of speedy flight. Plagued by ellipses and slips in orthography, some of the scattered words that their hands shakily copied implied the following scriptural title:

سورة العاديات
["The Chapter of the Runners"][41]

Like 'Usman before them, the two West African fugitives in Kentucky inscribed selections from their sacred text, tracing terms from Chapter 100 of the Muslim scripture. Quoting the Qur'an in Christian County, the Arabic words written by men on the run reflected their Muslim faith, but also seemed to mirror hopes of flight. A chapter title originally revealed in Mecca, this Middle Eastern phrase now indirectly expressed the predicament of two fugitives stuck in the western wastes of America. In 1807, the Africans had themselves entered a new chapter of their lives, becoming "runners" from pursuit and oppression. And although halted in Christian County, these Muslims still aspired to continue their race toward the sunrise.

But, before they found a chance to travel onward, another traveler would arrive in Kentucky, himself pushing eastward. As if written in a romance by Washington Irving, infused with irony and coincidence, the stranger who arrived in Christian County in 1807 was uniquely prepared to accomplish an unlikely delivery, willing to take the writings by two West Africans to the very highest office of US power. An eccentric who himself emerged from the American wilds, this lone figure would head onward to the Atlantic coast, carrying the case of these two Muslims to the "very plain old gentleman" who was serving as Washington's "present bashaw." The traveler's name was Ira P. Nash.

13

"Conquest is Close"

Ira P. Nash was leading an improbable life in the autumn of 1807—a life typified by such extraordinary moments that his discovery of two Muslim fugitives in western Kentucky may not have seemed entirely out of place.

Ideally suited to the fluid borders of the early frontier, Nash was ingenious and eccentric, and most of all, a misfit. A man on the margins, Nash's life had begun in 1774, the year that marked a margin for America, the last year of British rule before the Revolution's first shots were fired in 1775.[1] Nash's early years had witnessed American shifts in national allegiance; as Nash matured, however, he would welcome more upheaval, striking out for regions whose allegiances were still very much in flux. By his mid-twenties, Nash had already staked a claim in "Upper Louisiana," securing a large land grant in this western territory when it was still under Spanish control. At least three years before Jefferson's famous "purchase" in 1803, Nash already owned a piece of Louisiana.[2] Later lauded as one of "the first Americans ever [to] set foot" in the interior of the modern-day state of Missouri, Nash reportedly forged a path into this expanse even before Lewis and Clark, the president's own "pathfinders."[3]

Settling on the blurry borders of his new nation, Nash's larger-than-life personality was more than sufficient to fill the blank spaces. Fiercely independent, Nash was known for brash acts, infuriating the few neighbors he did come to have. Even on the unregulated edges of America, Nash was labeled an outlaw. The "only man" in Missouri's Boone County ever to be "convicted" of proposing a duel, Nash nearly committed the same crime that would forever be associated with the infamous Aaron Burr.[4] Nash's first wife, Nancy, perhaps driven to despair by her mercurial husband, died tragically, "hanging herself in" their "kitchen."[5] Nash's second marriage also ended unhappily in an acrimonious divorce. This marital split resulted in a court case, *Nash v. Nash*, which formed yet another precedent, qualifying as the very first divorce proceeding in Nash's home county—a court case that saw Ira P. Nash act as his own attorney, of course.[6]

At his death, Nash's fierce autonomy was indelibly inscribed into his legacy. For his internment, Nash stipulated that he should be "buried standing up," planted on top of a hill so he could "look down on his neighbors."[7] Famed for his "countless quarrels," Nash could, however, be surprisingly beneficent, and was also known for his "many a generous deed." Notoriously "pugnacious," Nash set precedents too for liberality. Late in life, he reportedly donated land in Missouri to establish "a seminary of learning"; and, although he had arrived to the territory as a slave owner, Nash would also become "among the very first" in the region to release "certain of his slaves."[8] Likely irritating once again his white neighbors, it is not clear what prompted Nash to liberate the Africans in his charge. Perhaps it was his conscience; perhaps his motives were less pure.[9] What is clear, however, is that Nash stood out among his fellow pioneers, willing to contravene the status quo, even conventions of slavery—a trait that makes Nash seem an especially providential passerby in 1807, encountering two imprisoned Africans on the western edges of Kentucky.

Beyond all hope, this unfortunate pair was discovered by a sympathetic outsider, who had adopted the Louisiana Territory as his home, yet claimed the Atlantic coast as his birthplace. A fellow outlaw and a misfit beyond the understanding of his neighbors, Nash may have been one of the few white men in the region likely to take pity on a pair of escapees. For Nash, these two Africans were not inarticulate slaves merely, but "men"—men whose lives possessed "momentous importance," as he would later write to Jefferson.[10] It was not only his perspective, but Nash's perseverance that made him a fortuitous arrival in 1807 Kentucky. Rarely appreciated by his own neighbors, Nash's flair for the dramatic—stubborn and bold, difficult to daunt or deter—would now be valued. A veteran of long-distance travel, covering immense spaces across the continent, Nash had the fortitude to carry documents all the way back east, to a fellow Virginian living in the US capital. Although a frontier pioneer, Nash was unafraid to make his way to Washington, strolling up Pennsylvania Avenue itself, arriving uninvited to beg an "interview" with the president.

These unusual aspects of Nash's career and character made him an apt conduit—perhaps the only one possible—that could link two Muslims jailed in Kentucky with Thomas Jefferson, wielding power as the president in DC. There was another quirk in Nash's personality, however, that may have prompted him to intervene in this improbable story—a quirk he shared with the president. Among his many oddities was Nash's fascination with encoded identities and words difficult to decipher. Like Jefferson, Ira P. Nash was a devotee of "the secret art of writing," and like the president, Nash was adept too at retaining his own anonymity, enciphering even his own family's name.

≈

The name "Nash" reaches back to Virginia's beginnings. In his paternal line, Ira descended from seventeenth-century figures who first helped settle the "Old Dominion." Colonizing land at the eastern edges of Virginia, the Nash family took root only fifty miles from where America's capital would later be planted.[11] Named for Francis Fauquier—Virginia's colonial governor and mentor to Jefferson—the county where Nash himself began life in 1774 was also the birthplace of Presley O'Bannon, famed for his North African heroics.[12] Two years Nash's junior, O'Bannon was likewise born and raised in Fauquier County before serving with William Eaton overseas. Helping to spearhead America's failed coup in Tripoli, it was O'Bannon who would purportedly receive the "Mamaluke sword" that became a standard symbol of the Marines. Aptly, for both of these natives of Fauquier, Virginia, their birthplace itself offers an unintended Arabic pun. This same Virginia county that fostered both Nash and O'Bannon bears a name that sounds faintly similar to a common Arabic term—"faqīr"—signifying a wandering mystic and mendicant.[13] In the generation following Nash and O'Bannon, another Fauquier County native, Samuel A. Appleton, seems to have capitalized on this overlap, evoking playfully the name of his home county by writing an operetta simply called "The Fakir."[14]

Himself a "fakir" from Fauquier County, Nash led an itinerant life, obeying an urge to push west, just as his forefathers had many years earlier. The seventeenth-century Nashes had crossed from one continent to another, traversing the Atlantic to embrace fresh American prospects. Ira Nash's own restlessness led him instead to cut through a continent, plunging into New World interiors. But, as with his Virginian ancestors, names were also important to Nash. His pioneering forays offered him the chance not only to settle American spaces, but to grant them his own signatures. The most obvious namesake left behind by Nash was his own town, Nashville—not Nashville, Tennessee, but Nashville, Missouri.[15] Much smaller than its more famous counterpart, the Nashville of Missouri's Boone County was founded by Ira, and bore his family name. But like Nash himself, this town's title, and even its precincts, would disappear. In close proximity to the Missouri river,

Nashville was swept away in the very year that Nash died, its waters obliterating his namesake town in 1844.[16]

Although some of Nash's legacies would be literally submerged, other names he coined outlived him. Beyond American places, it was American peoples that Nash named, labeling his children in ways that reflected his own love of esoteric wordplay and exotic identities. For his three daughters, Nash selected names that seem altogether odd: Alpha, Neppy, and Zarada— the last of which carried a distinct Middle Eastern echo. A character name from "Oriental" romances, "Zarada" also recalls the Arabic verb to "strangle," a macabre coincidence considering the tragic manner in which Nash's first wife died.[17] Such eclectic names were also granted to Nash's two sons, who bore monikers that were not only strange, but strangely related. The elder Nash son was christened as "El Man," and the younger as "Man L." Siblings in reciprocal cipher, reversed in syllables, "Man L." and "El Man" shared the same Nash stock, but also the same sounds. Curiously, Nash's experiment with names is again loosely evocative of the East, his "El-Man" faintly reminiscent of Arabic, with "El" similar to this language's definitive article ("al-", meaning "the").[18]

Beyond amusing himself, Nash's playful names seemed to have more earnest intentions—and would lead to more serious consequences. For his sons, Nash devised names that mirrored each other; he used the same strategy, however, to hide his own identity.[19] Staking multiple claims in Missouri, Nash's acquisitions were obscured by his own signature, not always registering land under his regular name—"Ira P. Nash"—but under a seemingly altogether different moniker, namely:

H. Sanari

However, just as Nash mirrored his second son's name with that of his first, this name above is indeed Nash's own, but only when it is read in reverse:

iranaS H.

This pseudonym would, after Nash's death, even become the basis for a legal dispute that made its way all the way to the Missouri Supreme Court. Seeking to prove their ownership of land originally registered to "H. Sanari," Nash's own descendants admitted openly in court proceedings that "H. Sanari" was indeed their forebear's furtive signature.[20]

Nash generated his alter ego by reversing the letters of his name; but this reversal of identity oddly echoed identities on the other side of the world. Claiming plots of land in America, Nash inadvertently created a name reminiscent of a specific African town; helping Nash settle the fresh frontier, "H. Sanari" incidentally recalls a historic center in the Muslim world. In Arabic, "Sanari" or "Sennari" suggests a native of Sennar, a regional capital in Africa's northeast, in modern-day Sudan.[21] Reversing the direction of his own identity, Nash created a new name by writing from right to left, rather than left to right, the very way in which Arabic itself is written; more intriguingly, the pseudonym that Nash generated also faintly overlapped an authentic Arabic name. During the same years that Jefferson was anonymously translating a Middle Eastern fiction, Nash too was translating himself into anonymity, rendering his own identity into a fiction with Middle Eastern echoes. And, while Jefferson had won "Oriental" epithets by acquiring for his nation the far West—satirized as the "Grand Turk" of Louisiana—Nash's own "Oriental" epithet was fashioned to acquire land in the West too, but much more selfishly and secretly. However, by an even more odd coincidence, Nash's embrace of his "Sanari" identity recalled not just any foreign name, but a capital on another continent that had long ago rose to Jefferson's attention, and was even obliquely linked to his dreams of charting the American West. An African city rich in Muslim history, Sennar was essential to the same mapmaker dispatched by Jefferson many years before to Missouri, this Sudanese town invoked by the man whom Jefferson encouraged to survey the very American lands later claimed by "H. Sanari."

≈

With regard to my Voyage, I can only tell you for any certainty that I shall be able to pass as far as the western boundaries of what is called Turkish Nubia, and at a Town called Sennar. You will find this town on any chart. It is on a branch of the Nile: I expect to get there with some surety—but afterwards all is dark before me: my design and wishes are to pass in that parrelel across the Continent. I will write you from Sennar if I can.

John Ledyard writing to Thomas Jefferson
from Cairo, Egypt, September 10, 1788[22]

Nearly twenty years before Nash's journey "across the Continent," carrying Arabic writings to the capital, a letter from another continent was sent to

Thomas Jefferson from Arabic-speaking North Africa. Traveling toward the town of Sennar, this letter was written by John Ledyard, the first man requisitioned by Jefferson to map the American continent.

Jefferson's name will forever be associated with the Lewis and Clark Expedition—the iconic two-year trek commissioned in 1803, which sought to chart a route through the vast American wilderness, stretching from the Mississippi to the Pacific coast.[23] However, Jefferson had been pursuing a similar goal since the beginning of his career. Stationed in Paris during 1786, the same year that he grappled with peace and prisoners in North Africa, Jefferson supported John Ledyard's plans to make a map of the American West. Rather than push to the Pacific from the Atlantic coast, as did Lewis and Clark, Jefferson proposed the opposite route, suggesting Ledyard start from the Pacific coast and proceed eastward. In Jefferson's words, Ledyard would reach America via Russia, "cross[ing] in some of the Russian vessels to Nootka Sound, fall down into the latitude of the Missouri, and penetrate to and through that to the United States."[24] Following this plan supported by Jefferson, Ledyard sought to forge his way across Russia, but was intercepted en route. Suspected of spying for America, Ledyard was arrested, and subsequently "expelled" from Russia on the orders of Catherine the Great.[25]

Frustrated in his attempts to "gain the American Atlantic states" from the west, Ledyard turned his attention to quite another project. "Fearless" in his "courage and enterprise," according to Jefferson's later praise, Ledyard had a fallback plan to map North Africa instead.[26] Abandoning Missouri for Muslim lands, Ledyard proceeded to Egypt, writing to Jefferson in September 1788 from Cairo with an update on his progress, including his hopes of reaching Sennar. "I will write you from Sennar if I can," Ledyard tentatively projected; he would, however, never reach his destination. The words he addressed to Jefferson, quoted above, would be among Ledyard's last, succumbing to illness before he departed for Sennar. "We have lost poor Ledyard," Jefferson heard in 1789 from Thomas Paine, who reported that Ledyard "had agreed with certain Moors to Conduct him to Sennar [but] burst a blood vessel on the operation which carried him off in three days."[27] The first man whom Jefferson had encouraged to map America would fail in the endeavor, only to be buried by Muslims in North Africa.

If Ledyard did not survive to see Sennar, Jefferson himself would glimpse the city, although only in two dimensions. True to Ledyard's prediction in 1788, this North African "town" would appear on "charts" Jefferson secured, acquiring throughout his career the latest maps, local and global. Son of a surveyor and map-maker, Jefferson yearned to fill in blanks, first of all on the American frontier itself, supplying speculative names to western regions. Unlike Ledyard, Jefferson seemed not at all daunted by the "dark before me"; instead, he foraged in his imagination "across the Continent," seeking to illumine dim spaces in the New World with the most ancient of names. Immediately after the Revolution ended, Jefferson started to invent labels for the same western territories that he would not purchase for the United States for nearly twenty years. As early as 1784, Jefferson proposed that the land where "the rivers Wabash, Shawanee, Tanissee, Ohio, Illinois, Missisipi and Missouri" came together "shall be called Polypotamia"—a Greek name signifying the place of "many rivers."[28]

Ledyard died as he strove toward Egypt's Nile. For Jefferson, it was America's rivers that helped sustain his mapping efforts. The charts that eventually emerged as the fruit of Jefferson's dreams were indebted especially to watery routes across the continent. Elevated to the presidency in 1801, Jefferson was finally in a position to muster financial support for a mission to the far West, and in 1803 would secure funds to dispatch Meriwether Lewis and William Clark. This celebrated expedition would, of course, be carried via America's "*potamia*"—the same rivers that had inspired Jefferson in his speculative naming of the interior. The remit of Lewis and Clark, in Jefferson's words, was to find "the most direct & practicable water communication across this continent."[29] Finally accomplished in 1805, it was not until the critical year 1807—the same year that the Cumberland River carried fugitives, both east and west—that Lewis and Clark began to receive due public acclaim. Even poems appeared, published in US newspapers, praising their explorations. Invoking regions and rivers long associated with Jefferson's own life, at the beginning of 1807 an old friend of the president had his verses "On the Discoveries of Captain Lewis" published, emphasizing global waters, bridging North Africa and North America:

> Let the Nile cloak his head in the clouds, and defy
> The researches of science and time;
> Let the Niger escape the keen traveller's eye,
> By plunging or changing his clime.
> Columbus! not so shall thy boundless domain
> Defraud thy brave sons of their right:
> Streams, midlands, and shorelands elude us in vain,
> We shall drag their dark regions to light.[30]

Juxtaposing US "Streams" with the "Nile" and the "Niger," these opening poetic lines contrast successful American exploration with the failure of explorers to crack the code of Africa, the continent that defies both "science and time." "All is dark before me," Ledyard himself had written, as he hoped in vain merely to reach Africa's famous river, the same Nile that is aptly here described as concealing its source, its "head" still hidden "in the clouds." America's own watery regions, however, this poem suggests, could not elude the investigations of Lewis and Clark, with the "dark regions" of "Columbus" inevitably "dragged" into light." This poem of translated spaces, contrasting the mysterious Nile with the West's accessible rivers, was written by the same patriot who a decade earlier had secretly co-translated with the president a Middle Eastern travelogue. Published in Washington's *The National Intelligencer* on January 16, 1807, these lines were authored by none other than Jefferson's "very fine writer of English": Joel Barlow.

≈

Detached from this work, there will be published on a large scale, as soon as a sufficient number of subscribers be obtained to defray the expense, LEWIS & CLARK'S MAP OF NORTH AMERICA.

The Universal Gazette, Washington DC,
September 17, 1807[31]

Barlow's praise for the achievements of Lewis and Clark anticipated a more general interest that grew as 1807 unfolded. Hungry for details, as well as diagrams, the public's desire for actual maps offered an opportunity for publishers. By September 1807, printers were attempting to capitalize on "LEWIS & CLARK" interest with advertisements such as the one above, which appeared in Washington's *The Universal Gazette* on September 17, 1807—precisely the time when Nash was working his way east, leaving behind two Muslim slaves in the far West. As he approached Washington, Nash was departing the precise area of the country that was inspiring so much excitement; unlike Jefferson's two favored explorers, however, Nash was not carrying to the president outlines of American territories, but ink that flowed in more unexpected directions, tracing words of ancient Arabic, from right to left.

On September 17, 1807, Jefferson himself was preparing for a trip, also journeying to Washington. Lacking the enthusiasm of *The Universal Gazette*, and the urgency of Nash's "momentous" mission, Jefferson was reluctant to return to the capital. Extended stays at Monticello were Jefferson's solace, relieving him from some burdens of office, especially as his presidency stretched into the middle of his second term. Wearied by years of service, and looking forward to future retirement, there was little new that Jefferson expected to see as he trekked back to the US capital, and there was no need of a detailed map. The path back to the President's House from Monticello was well worn for Jefferson, with familiar stops at friendly taverns breaking up his journey over four days. Even after a decade of making such round trips, however, the president still made a detailed itinerary, recording with characteristic minuteness the mileage he covered.[32]

Although anticipated to be uneventful, even tedious, Jefferson's trip to Washington that started at the end of September 1807 was punctuated by unpleasant surprises. Not "free from accident as usual," Jefferson suffered a few pitfalls, physical and financial.[33] Leaving on September 30, Jefferson descended from Monticello, in full view of Willis Mountain—the same one Volney had envisioned as an Egyptian pyramid. After this familiar stage, however, Jefferson's trip started to go astray. Passing beyond the aptly named "Meriwether's Gate," Jefferson reached Gordonsville, where he stayed at Gordon's Tavern on the night of September 30, but not before misplacing his "travelling money" sometime that morning. The next day, October 1, Jefferson arrived by evening at another of his accustomed stopping points, Orange Courthouse, before continuing north to Washington. On October 2, attempting to cross the Rapidan River, however, Jefferson encountered additional problems, experiencing more serious property loss. "I was near losing Castor in the Rapidan," Martha was told, Jefferson noting that the horse had decided to lie "down in the river, where waste deep, & being so embarrassed by the shafts of the carriage & harness that he was nearly drowned before the servants, jumping into the water, could lift his head out & cut him loose from the carriage." Pushing back to Washington—where he would struggle to pass his Embargo Act, aimed at Atlantic imports from hostile Britain—Jefferson had nearly failed to negotiate even the narrow waters in front of him. The Rapidan was no Nile, but it sufficed to threaten ruin.[34]

Surviving this upset, Jefferson continued on the next day, October 3. He jotted down the last stages of the journey in his itinerary, including "Fauquier road," the thoroughfare that cut through its namesake county, the birthplace of a man who was also traveling toward Jefferson that same evening. The president finally reached Washington later that morning, summarizing his full trip as having covered "118.424" miles—a precise, even obsessive, estimate of distance. Entering the President's House as noon approached, Jefferson had accomplished his four-day trek, and was greeted by familiar sights, including records of other journeys successfully completed, which hung on his walls in Washington. Adorning Jefferson's residence were "maps, globes [and] charts," reflecting his long-standing geographic interests, as well as his most recent purchases.[35] Especially cherished by the president was a set of the latest maps by Aaron Arrowsmith, including a chart that pictured in minute detail the continent of Africa, which Jefferson had ordered in 1805. Arrowsmith's "large scale" productions—which "were probably among the maps that hung in Jefferson's Cabinet at the President's House," as Susan Stein has argued—extended much further afield than any journey Jefferson had personally undertaken; and yet, these maps featured names with which he had long been familiar.[36]

Satisfying Ledyard's prediction made two decades previously, Jefferson upon his arrival to the President's House on October 3, 1807, was indeed likely able, if he so wished, to "find" on his "chart" the names of many African locales, including "Sennar." But no one could have predicted that on this same day, October 3, Jefferson would be joined in Washington by another traveler, not a map-maker from Sennar, but a man whose secret name was "H. Sanari"—a man who was covertly carrying far different lines for Jefferson, whose latitudes circled the globe, reaching all the way back to Muslim Africa.

≈

Saturday Evn.g. 3 Oct. 1807

Sir

I wish to know whether it would be consistant with the dignity of your Excellency for me to have an interview with you, I am from St. Louis in the Teritory of Louisanna, and have matter of momentous importance to communicate I would be glad to know at what time I may be admitted (if at all) for I shall be readay at any time to wait on your Honour after this Evening.

I am Sir your Obt Hbl Servt
I. Nash[37]

The evening Jefferson arrived home, this letter also arrived to the President's House, addressing its resident deferentially, though with irregular spellings. Invoking the president as "your Excellency," the "St. Louis" author links himself to "the Teritory of Louisanna," an area strongly associated with Jefferson's own "dignity," indeed the very place that had led him to be dubbed a "Grand Turk." Writing in a single run-on sentence, Ira P. Nash sounds breathless, spilling out the desire he has kept bound up in his breast for the hundreds of miles just traveled. Urgently requesting an "interview" with the president, standing "reaxday" to "wait on your Honour after this Evening," Nash seems to have stopped suddenly at Jefferson's door, his imperative mission abruptly ending at the President's House.

Receiving this unexpected note, Jefferson could not possibly have known that Nash's "matter of momentous importance" offered an odd sort of fulfillment of Ledyard's failed mission across the world, twenty years before. Arriving from the far West, Nash was carrying writings native to the East, returning to America's Atlantic coast after an encounter with African Muslims. Far from imaginative speculation, Nash's arrival implied the meeting of global waters, this settler on the Mississippi conveying to Jefferson documents by authors whose homelands were not far from tributaries of the Niger. And, aptly, the very pages Nash was delivering to the president were themselves concerned with bridging differences and distances. Illegible to their American messenger, the Arabic pages carried by Nash seemed entirely exotic; and yet, these same pages traced familiar words, even while promising radical intimacy. Although irregularly inscribed, interrupted by ink blots and obscured by misspellings, the following Arabic words are faintly decipherable among the two pages that Ira P. Nash conveyed from Kentucky:

نصر من الله وفتح قريب
[Help is from Allah and conquest is close][38]

Arising from voyages across vast continents—spanning fakirs from West Africa and a Fauquier County native—the Arabic verses transported by Nash ironically gestured to nearness, proclaiming the proximity of divine victory. These words were, of course, unreadable to Nash. But, to the man Nash wished to see, they should have seemed strangely familiar. The very Arabic line inscribed above had reached Jefferson once before, and could still be found sitting on his shelves at home. Printed in a book he had purchased many years earlier, these Arabic words were the very same that Jefferson had long ago ordered from Paris. A quote from the Qur'an, urging closeness and aspiring for conquest, this citation had reached Jefferson's hands decades before Nash arrived, delivered to him in the pages of a book by Sir William Jones.

The African slaves in Kentucky, despite their desperate conditions, included on their Arabic pages that reached Washington this Qur'anic quotation heralding the nearness of Allah's aid and trust in His triumph. These words were, however, nearing another "Excellency," but one much more human and fallible. The writings of two fugitive Muslim slaves, overcoming vast space and against all odds, had arrived at their improbable destination. And yet, although these Arabic lines were "close" to the center of American power, any "conquest" for their captive authors was still very much in doubt. Victory would depend on the actions of another lonely Virginian, not a misfit who was settling western territories, but the man sitting as US president.

14

"A Word of any Language"

On the morning of October 4, 1807, Jefferson woke up to find himself in his bedroom at the President's House for the first time in two months. Although likely stiff from his eventful journey over four days, Jefferson was not a man given to complaint. And besides, today there was no time for self-pity. Although he had been in Washington for less than a day, a "momentous matter" had already presented itself to the president that could not be postponed. An "interview" had been the sole request of the mysterious traveler whose note arrived the night before—a request that the president had decided to grant.

It was not wholly out of character for Jefferson to agree to meet a man entirely unknown to him; a president of populist ideals, Jefferson was remarkably "accessible" to the American people. But principles were surely not the only reason to meet Ira P. Nash. Jefferson's motivations were likely much more mixed. Self-preservation, not merely public regard, may have seemed at stake. By the beginning of October, Aaron Burr was still on trial for a misdemeanor in Richmond, although acquitted of treason—an acquittal that left Jefferson feeling far from settled. Still eager for evidence against his nemesis, the president also harbored lingering anxieties for "the limits of the law" out West, hearing reports of overzealous recrimination against Burr supporters.[1] The urgency of Nash's note, and his origins in the "Teritory of Louisanna," undoubtedly dovetailed with anxieties that plagued the president at the opening of October 1807. Waiting to speak with Nash directly, Jefferson may have braced for a shock. The frontier had already proved full of surprises. And yet, the president could not have anticipated the curious packet that this traveler had arrived in Washington to deliver. Nash carried no news of western conspiracies; instead, the "matter of momentous importance" he had promised the president turned out to be two manuscripts in a Middle Eastern tongue, written by African authors. If Jefferson was taken aback in the moment, his devotion to historical documentation, and his love of detail, was not long deferred. The day after their meeting, Nash supplied a dutiful summary, providing the president with a written report regarding the two Muslims he had encountered as captives in Kentucky.[2]

It was not Nash's own writings, of course, but the two Arabic pages he transported to Jefferson that proved most precious. The first document was scrawled in large script, its thirteen lines spanning an entire page. The second manuscript was, however, minuscule, its compact script covering an area less than a postcard.[3] Although diminutive, these two documents possessed significance that far outstripped their size, capable of making even an American president feel small. After delivering his documents, Nash surely felt satisfied; not long after his delivery, he departed Washington, heading west once more, home to Louisiana. Jefferson, however, was left confounded on October 4. Despite all his learning—despite his own far travels and foreign acts of translation—the president found himself illiterate as he faced two obscure pages penned on the frontier of the new nation he had helped form. Volumes of rare scholarship lined Jefferson's shelves at home, including books that described the same language in which these two documents were written, even citing some of their very words. And yet, these letters, written by two helpless West Africans, surpassed all of Jefferson's skills. In 1797, Vice President Jefferson had translated a Middle Eastern fiction, Volney's *Ruins*. A decade later, in 1807, manuscripts in Middle Eastern script reached President Jefferson, confronting him with two texts that seemed fantastic, but were tangible facts—texts that transcended not only Jefferson's capacities of rendition, but his reading capabilities too.

If beyond his understanding, the pages that Nash delivered were nevertheless entirely recognizable to Jefferson. The nation's president was one of the few Americans to whom the appearance of Arabic was not at all new. As he gazed at these manuscripts from the American West, Jefferson in 1807 saw the same language of a North African treaty he had authorized twenty years earlier, autographing on the first day of 1787 a compact with Morocco. And, as twenty years before, Jefferson found US freedoms again bound up in Arabic composition. Beyond the specifics of idiom, the issues implied by these documents were also the very same that gave rise to Jefferson's fame. Seemingly foreign to early America, these Arabic documents involved ideas and identities profoundly personal to the president himself. Although illegible, these fluid Middle Eastern lines encircled concrete truths to which Jefferson had dedicated his career. Embodying polarities of race and religion, claiming both Islamic and American origins, these two texts also traced challenges of deciphering and detention, the cracking of codes and unjust captivity. Mirroring his signature issues, these Arabic manuscripts straddled Jefferson's core concerns: literacy and liberty, freedom and speech. Always interwoven in the American enterprise, these strands were tangled up in the Muslim writings delivered by Nash. And now it was the president's task to unravel them.

≈

Their Language is such that the inhabitance have not been able to Learn from where they came or whether they are bound

Ira P. Nash to Jefferson[4]

Nash's follow-up letter, opened by Jefferson on October 5, summarized the problem that the president now faced. Not merely a general overview, however, Nash seems especially sensitive to Jefferson's own interests and ideals. The president had a country to run, of course; and, Nash was surely aware that his own delivery could easily be lost amid the Washington shuffle. But Nash also knew that it was Jefferson—of all US recipients—who might be inclined to acknowledge that this "matter" of two Muslim captives was indeed "momentous." In his follow-up note, Nash succinctly introduces issues aligned with the president's profile, offering sentences such as the above—a sentence that ends with the two Africans being "bound," but begins with "[t]heir Language." The Arabic documents now in Jefferson's hands, Nash suggests, are enveloped by two quandaries: foreign speech and forced captivity.

On the evening of October 3, Jefferson had first heard from the unknown Nash, learning that this traveler had a "matter" of "importance to communicate"; by the next day, Jefferson had learned that Nash's problem concerned communication itself. The incarceration of these two Africans, Nash reported, was inextricably linked to their unintelligibility. Linguistically, these men were doubly suspect; they lacked the oral skills needed to communicate in Kentucky, and yet possessed a literacy that was equally incomprehensible. Failing in their attempts to interrogate the men, the locals instead relied on racial assumptions, "supposing them to be slaves and the property of some person in the United States," as Nash reports. The "people have made general Enquiry and have not been able to assertain anything Satisfactory respecting them," Nash adds in his October follow-up to Jefferson. As a result, they "are still kept in con[fineme]nt."[5] Detained because of their inability to speak in

English, only the men's Arabic writings—now in Jefferson's possession—held out any chance for them to secure their desired "liberty."

As Nash very well knew, Jefferson had dedicated his entire life to the same issues involved in the Africans' plight: freedom and speech. But, unknown to Nash, it was the specific speech inscribed by the captives in Kentucky that made their writings seem personally tailored to the president himself. It was a Middle Eastern dialect that arrived from America's far West—the same dialect that Jefferson had confronted many times before. Lacking the capacity to communicate in English, the two Africans had evidently only lately arrived to this land of their captivity. It was also clear, however, from their facility with Arabic, that these itinerant men originated in an African society with deep Islamic roots. Shaped by this religion's southern progress, the Senegambia had received Arabic alongside Muslim traditions of revelation and rhetoric. A vehicle of liturgy, but also encouraging literacy, Arabic was a marker of high culture in Muslim West Africa; but in America, it was also the only means for two Muslims to communicate across immense distances. An essential aspect of their African heritage—a heritage that, according to American racism in 1807, justified their enslavement—Arabic was both a symptom of this pair's captivity, as well as their only hope for emancipation.

Freedom, language, religion—this triad of human concerns was interwoven in the West African inscriptions that reached Jefferson from Kentucky in 1807. This same triad was central to Jefferson's own most iconic act of authorship. Jefferson's 1776 Declaration of Independence proclaimed freedoms in elegant language, while invoking "Nature's God" as guarantor of human liberties.[6] Ten years later, Jefferson's "Act for Religious Freedom" advanced the same concerns—an "Act" in 1786 that shaped not only Virginia's future, but America's own Bill of Rights, forming the precedent for the Constitution's famed First Amendment. Drafted by Jefferson's friend—James Madison—and infused with Jeffersonian ideals, this 1787 Amendment lists in succession freedoms of faith and expression, its iconic opening clauses reading:

> Congress shall make no law respecting an establishment of religion, or prohibiting the free exercise thereof; or abridging the freedom of speech, or of the press

First formulated in 1787, this amendment to the Constitution ensures freedoms of devotion and diction, inspired by Jefferson's own words.[7] Twenty years later, in 1807, Jefferson would hear of men whose freedoms were very much "abridged," but who were free to author Arabic writings that fused liberties of religion and language. For the two African captives in Kentucky, "freedom of speech" was not at stake; instead, their freedom was itself dependent on effective speech. Rather than the abstract ideals of a public "Act" or "Declaration," Jefferson privately faced inscrutable Arabic lines in 1807—lines that did not theorize potential liberties, but reflected the actual limits of freedom for those considered outside the Republic's religious and linguistic boundaries.

On October 4, 1807, Jefferson held in his hands illegible Arabic lines heavily implicated in American rights—lines that knotted together discrete freedoms, and that were not tied to the president himself. On that Sunday, Jefferson could not know that another American letter was on its way to him, inscribed on this very same day. Also anonymous, and implying freedoms of speech and religion, this other letter on October 4 was, however, much more clear; it was anything but nuanced and indecipherable. Addressed to the US president, this letter—dated October 4, 1807—read in its totality:

> Go to Hell
> you damn'd
> Buggur
> —Go to hell—[8]

Blunt and entirely to the point, this four-line note was sent to the same man that Nash had deferentially called America's "Excellency" on this same weekend. A letter of spiritual license, involving Jefferson's own salvation, it was undoubtedly unpleasant for the president to hear that he was hated—indeed, that he was hell-bound, at least in the mind of his anonymous correspondent. But these same words embodied the very freedoms for which Jefferson had fought. Part of the cost of philosophical ideals was to endure such colloquial curses, apparently. And, at least, in the vulgar English of this American freeman, unlike the sublime Arabic sent by two American slaves, there was no ambiguity, and no need of interpretation.

≈

On October 5, Jefferson received his final letter from Ira P. Nash before this traveler "from St. Louis" began his trek back to "the Teritory of Louisanna." Nash had entered Jefferson's life suddenly, pleading two evenings before for an "interview"; just as suddenly, Nash departed. But, before he left, Nash made a promise. In the final lines that Jefferson opened on October 5, Nash pledges to "write" with an update on the two fugitives, letting the president "know their Situation" when passing through Kentucky again.[9] As Jefferson well knew, however, weeks would likely pass before Nash would reach Christian County, Kentucky, once more, and return a written report. As it turned out, 1807 would end before the president heard from Nash again. In the meantime, the two Arabic manuscripts, and the fate of their Muslim authors, were left in Jefferson's hands.

Jefferson was alone with this quandary, and increasingly felt queasy. It was not his inability to read the delivered Arabic documents that was making Jefferson feel ill, however. The same day he received Nash's final letter in 1807, the president realized that he was "taken with the Influenza," as he reported to Martha. He did not want his family to worry, though. His sickness was not too severe; it was "without either fever or pain." And, a week after Nash had left, the flu had "now nearly passed off," Jefferson assured his daughter.[10] But, during this same time, no progress had been made in another area. As October 1807 entered its second week, it appeared that recovering health was a simpler matter than uncovering the significance of Arabic. Recuperating in the President's House, Jefferson was the sole person in the entire United States grappling with the singular situation that was unfolding hundreds of miles away. And, as days dripped by, Jefferson regained his strength, but did not gain new insights. Contemplating the documents left by Nash, Jefferson realized that their authors were not the only ones who would need help. It was time for the president himself to seek aid.

Jefferson considered the capital first, seeking a translator for these two Arabic manuscripts. As he would record, however, no readers of Arabic were to be found. The two Africans had been caught in Kentucky just one year before the "Act Prohibiting Importation of Slaves" had taken effect. But their writings had arrived one year too late for Jefferson to locate an Arabic translator in Washington. Back in 1806, the capital city seemed rather too full of potential interpreters, packed with Mellimelni and his entourage. By the autumn of 1807, however, the president discovered the US capital devoid of Arabic speakers. For two weeks, Jefferson's search was frustrated, failing even to secure anyone able to decipher the Arabic script. "Here," he would soon write, "we have nobody who understands either the character or language."[11]

After two weeks, Jefferson could easily have given up Nash's "matter" as a lost cause. With no excuse or apology, with no one to answer to, Jefferson could have buried these documents deep in a desk, or even a dustbin, ensuring that they were lost forever and forgotten. If he was tempted, Jefferson yet did no such thing; the Arabic documents did not disappear, and they retained his interest. Indeed, matters of state themselves seemed to conspire to keep Jefferson's mind occupied with issues implied by these Arabic documents, with unrelated national problems faintly paralleling the president's own private struggles. Beyond his office, October was proving an uncertain month for the country, and Jefferson found himself kept in the dark, failing to secure the news he felt he needed. Preoccupied by two American crises, the president was dealing with the aftermath of attacks from both within and without, from both Burr as well as Britain. It is the second of these that Jefferson addressed soon after recovering from his flu, anxiously awaiting England's response to America's grievance regarding the USS *Chesapeake*. "We have no information from England which is decisive of what we are to expect," Jefferson complained just four days after Nash had made his delivery, writing on October 8 to his nephew, John Wayles Eppes.[12] Exasperated by the lack of "information" from overseas, Jefferson suspected that in this case no news was *not* good news, predicting further conflict to come. The "little circumstances which come to us give preponderance rather to the scale of war," Jefferson opined, while acknowledging that any result was yet possible.[13]

Britain was making Jefferson wait. But so was Burr. On the same day that Jefferson wrote to Eppes, he sent a letter to his attorney general, Caesar Augustus Rodney, seeking to assemble all reliable evidence against "the Usurper." Although Burr had recently been acquitted of treason—a "defective" judgment in Jefferson's view—the president still urgently desired "the selection & digestion of the documents respecting Burr's treason," in order to distribute this damning documentation to Congress.[14] Three days later, Jefferson was still without answers. Writing to George Hay on October 11, 1807, the president complained that although "the examination of the witnesses in Burr's case & that of the other persons accused is closed," he had yet to receive "the proceedings & evidence."[15] On October 15, George Hay responded, but only by signaling more deferral. "A copy of the proceedings accompanied by the Judges opinions will be forwarded in a few days," Hay replied, adding that the latter would be "taken from the Gazette, in which they were published by the Editor, who received the original manuscripts from the hands of the Judge."[16] Vexed at his inability to secure first-hand information, Jefferson's irritation, unbeknownst to George Hay, paralleled other issues in the president's care at the opening of October. Jefferson was impatient for "original manuscripts from the hands of the Judge" arising from Burr's trial, of course. But privately, Jefferson also found himself the singular "Judge" over two "original manuscripts" in Arabic, which were solely held by his own "hands."

From October 4 to October 18, no answer arrived from the British, nor did the president receive the desired documentation regarding Burr. As these two weeks passed, equally silent to Jefferson were the two Arabic documents sitting on his desk. Although tangibly available, these texts eluded Jefferson, their lines surrendering "no information," no hint "of what we are to expect." Physically present, but sealed in foreign speech, these Arabic writings were written in a cipher the president simply could not break. Jefferson did, however, have friends who were adept at cracking codes—one friend in particular, who was based in the very same city where Jefferson had first authored American freedoms. Precisely two weeks after Nash's visit, on Sunday, October 18, Jefferson took up his own pen to write an appeal, which he posted to Philadelphia, addressed to Robert Patterson.

≈

Dear Sir

Two men have been taken up in Kentucky and are confined, on suspicion, merely because they cannot make known who they are, not speaking a word of any language understood there.[17]

These are the initial words to survive from the president's pen that make mention of the Arabic documents delivered to him by Ira P. Nash. Sharing this extraordinary story for the first time, Jefferson's opening words are intriguing, not merely for what they imply, but for what they omit. Introducing the African captives only as "two men," Jefferson remarks on neither race nor religion. Passing over ethnicity entirely, the president accents only foreign expression. The conundrum in Kentucky, according to Jefferson's summary in his first sentence, is "merely" due to language, not legality. The cause of their "confin[ment]" is communication failure, Jefferson suggests, casting doubt on the basis for these "two men" being "taken up." While speech and freedom were linked in Nash's last letter to Jefferson, Jefferson's first letter on this same situation two weeks later implies that the *only* reason for this loss of liberty is lack of "language." What Jefferson initially downplays is that these fugitives are incarcerated in Kentucky not due to "suspicion" in general, but to the *specific* suspicion that they are runaway slaves. Arrested not for their English ignorance, these "two men" were, of course, imprisoned due to race, "taken up" for their African origins.

Evasive in his letter's opening, Jefferson knew that his addressee would be able to read between the lines, and would share his sympathy for these enslaved men. Robert Patterson was not only a professor of mathematics and inventor of ciphers, but also an anti-slavery activist. As early as 1797, Patterson had joined the Pennsylvania Society for Promoting the Abolition of Slavery, "the oldest abolitionist society in the country."[18] Founded in 1775, and eventually counting Benjamin Franklin as its leader, the Society was dedicated to "The Relief of Negroes Unlawfully Held in Bondage," and to "Improving the Condition of the African Race." By 1803, Patterson had risen to serve as vice president of this anti-slavery union.[19] However, Jefferson was not writing to Patterson to inspire compassion for these two men "unlawfully held in bondage," but to request assistance. Jefferson needed a translation of his two Arabic documents. It was not only Patterson's compassion for the enslaved, but his passion for encoded words, that the president required.

Jefferson's letter would not only summarize the situation in Kentucky second-hand, but provide Patterson with first-hand proof. Packed with enclosures, the president dispatched to Philadelphia Nash's own letter, as well as the Africans' "original" writings, which Jefferson describes to Patterson on October 18 as follows:

> the inclosed letter from a mr Nash contains all I know of them [the "two men"]: but the writings in Arabic characters are supposed to contain their history, as stated by themselves.[20]

Described to Patterson as penned "in Arabic characters," this passage from Jefferson's letter represents another first—the very first time that the script of these two African manuscripts is identified. Nowhere in Nash's extant notes to Jefferson is the precise idiom of the two documents identified; instead, the president's own familiarity with Islamic sources seems reflected in this accurate identification of Arabic letters. Jefferson not only clarifies the "characters" of these "writings," however, but speculates concerning their "content." Transmitting a "supposition" perhaps gleaned from Nash, Jefferson notes to Patterson that this indecipherable material is self-referential, "contain[ing]" the "history" of the two captives "as stated by themselves."[21] In sharing these enclosures with Patterson, Jefferson expresses his belief that these Arabic documents comprise first-person memoirs. Eluding the notice of all pre-vious biographers of Jefferson, the African writings that he circulated in 1807 were understood by Jefferson himself as acts of Arabic autobiography.

Searching for a translator, Jefferson appeals solely to Patterson, an aca-demic famed for his mathematics, not multilingualism. Although no scholar of languages, Patterson was, however, a lover of codes, and well connected to fellow educators as well as elite merchants in one of the early Republic's premier port cities. Near the end of his letter, Jefferson admits that in Washington "we have nobody who understands either the character or lan-guage" of Arabic, and finally asks for Patterson's help outright:

> is there any one attached to your College, or in your city who can translate these papers? I do not know whether Capt Obrien could do it.[22]

Acknowledging his own failure so far, Jefferson asks Patterson to facilitate the rendition of "these papers," even while offering a tentative suggestion, gesturing to another Philadelphian: Richard O'Brien. America's most cel-ebrated veteran of Muslim prisons, "Capt Obrien" had appealed in vain to Jefferson personally in 1785, receiving little aid as he sought liberation from African "workhouses"; in 1807, O'Brien is named by Jefferson specifically as a potential source to help free two "confined" Muslims from Africa.

It is the conclusion to Jefferson's request on October 18 that seems most interesting, not only raising the stakes for Patterson's task, but also reflecting the president's own commitments. Patterson's capacity to crack the code of these "Arabic characters" could also break these "two men" out of bondage, Jefferson suggests, ending his letter to Patterson as follows:

> you will oblige me by getting it done, if practicable, that I may procure the release of the men if proper. I salute you with affectionate respect.
>
> Th: Jefferson[23]

These final sentiments from the president are couched in conditionals. And yet, despite the semantic deferral, these words still seem audacious. Even with these muted "ifs," Patterson is left with an impression of the president's willingness to "release" two Africans enslaved in America. Slavery divided Jefferson's commitments during his life; and in death, it has tarnished his legacy. In this letter to Patterson, however, Jefferson frames African impris-onment as a problem to be solved. For his whole career, Jefferson argued in the abstract against slavery, even as he continued to profit from the "peculiar institution" personally. Challenging enslavement via universal ideals, Jefferson abided by America's status quo in specifics. During his many decades as a slaveholder, Jefferson rarely intervened to promote the freedom of particular enslaved persons; he released very few of those in his own charge, and even urged his own neighbors *not* to liberate their slaves when they were eager to do so.[24] 1807 seems to mark an exception, however. Faced with two Africans capable of inscribing Arabic, Jefferson voices a readiness to intervene and advocate on their behalf. For these specific captives, Jefferson will make an effort to "procure the release"—a phrase of freedom that surfaces only once in all of Jefferson's letters, arising this single time in 1807 as the president responds to a pair of Muslim prisoners. Jefferson's inclination to secure freedom for these oppressed men finally brought him in line with his high ideals. Although unique in his career, Jefferson's willingness to liberate two Arabic authors is an exception that, at last, conforms to his own rule.

Unlike his 1776 Declaration, which confidently proclaimed national Independence, Jefferson's commitment to liberate African Muslims seems entirely uncertain, dampened by an "if practicable," and an "if proper." The president utters no courageous claims, but is rather doubtful in diction, expressing only possibilities, not promises. Recognizing that freedom always dangles on the smallest particles of language, hanging on indeterminate "ifs," Jefferson was uniquely aware that liberty and captivity are always linguistically conditioned. And yet the president's message—although cautious and concise—is not neutral, but hopefully hints at his authentic intent to act on behalf of two enslaved Muslims. The president was no mere "Judge" of these "original manuscripts"; instead, even with his hesitant apprehensions, Jefferson was an advocate.

≈

Jefferson's October 18 letter to Patterson concluded with his abbreviated autograph, signing off in shorthand as "Th: Jefferson." The president would, however, write additional words on the envelope dispatched to Patterson—final words that likely were the very first that Patterson saw on this historic packet when it arrived in Philadelphia. On the envelope that enclosed the two Arabic manuscripts carried to him from Kentucky, Jefferson wrote simply:

free
Th: Jefferson Pr. US.[25]

Inscribing his abbreviated name again, Jefferson adds his credentials too, entitling himself as "*Pr. US.*" Immediately above this personal identity and presidential authority, however, just a single word is inscribed: "*free.*" By executive prerogative, no postage would be needed; only Jefferson's written word is required for his missive's safe passage. In his letter to Patterson, Jefferson seems friendly and informal; on his envelope, he shifts from affable to official, framing the manuscripts that he enclosed as a matter of state. Posted from the "*Pr. US.*," Jefferson's Muslim manuscripts bear not merely an individual, but a national, impression.

It seems poignant that these Muslim manuscripts, penned in US confinement, traveled to Philadelphia in an envelope inscribed with Jefferson's one-syllable password: "*free.*" Handed this package from the president, filled with historic Arabic writings, Patterson would have first seen a single word signaling "freedom," even as this envelope conveyed texts of captivity. Deprived of their liberty, two Muslim fugitives write documents that newly take flight in 1807, bound gratis for an American city of fraternal love. Inked with a complimentary stamp, Jefferson's signature and insignia proved effective for his envelope's safe arrival to Patterson. Unfortunately for the authors of the Arabic documents enclosed within this official envelope, their own "free" passage would not prove as easy.

15

"Seven of the Arab Dialects"

One last mark is visible on Jefferson's envelope sent to Robert Patterson: a postmark. Still legible at its top left, "October 19" is stamped on this envelope, recording the actual date on which Jefferson's letter was dispatched to Philadelphia, together with its discreet enclosures.[1] The President had penned his note on Sunday, the 18th. But it was not until Monday—the 19th—that his letter made its way out of Washington. This slight delay seems entirely inconsequential, especially considering all the time it had taken Nash to travel from Kentucky, and the two weeks that Jefferson had kept these Arabic writings quietly at the President's House. But this one-day deferral does help reveal the speed with which Robert Patterson tackled Jefferson's task. He responded to the president before the same week was up, replying on Saturday, October 24.[2]

Jefferson's letter was deferred a day; but Patterson refused to allow any deferral whatsoever, despite all else that occupied him. Patterson was a busy man in the autumn of 1807, which was partly Jefferson's fault. Patterson was still serving as professor of mathematics at the University of Pennsylvania. Beyond duties of the fall semester, however, Patterson was also otherwise engaged. Two years earlier, Jefferson had appointed Patterson the head of the US Mint—a sensible choice, in light of Patterson's love of symbols and his skill with numbers.[3] Even with these weighty roles, Patterson treated Jefferson's request as an urgent imperative; the plight of these two Africans was, after all, a presidential directive. The two Arabic manuscripts were in Patterson's possession for only three or four days before he penned his own response. Inventor of secret systems of writing, and adept in shorthand, Patterson sought to crack this new written code for the president as quickly as possible.[4]

Over only a few days in late October 1807, Patterson consulted with three of the most remarkable figures he could find in Philadelphia. Seeking to unravel Jefferson's cryptic writings, Patterson toured this fraternal city, freely circulating Muslim manuscripts penned by Africans imprisoned merely on "suspicion." Consulting diverse contacts, Patterson conferred with a triad that represented diplomacy, trade, and academia. The three men each had his own reaction, reflecting his professional interests and personal experiences, as well as individual prejudices. In October 1807, two manuscripts by Muslim slaves constituted a type of "Rorschach test" for surprised American reviewers. Although visiting these three various men, first in Patterson's mind was the single man whom Jefferson himself had named. In the race against time to translate Arabic writings, Philadelphia was home to an American whose years of experience in Arabic-speaking regions exceeded all others.

≈

Richard O'Brien was back in his adopted hometown after years of captivity and diplomacy in Muslim lands. By the time O'Brien had returned to stay, however, his city had undergone staggering changes, witnessing highs and lows unimaginable in the early 1780s. When O'Brien departed Philadelphia, it was still a colonial port; in the following years, the city would serve as an early US capital, before becoming supplanted by Washington, DC, by 1800. More significant than the vicissitudes of politics, however, was the plague that had struck Philadelphia; the city had been ravaged in the 1790s by yellow fever, losing a sizeable percentage of its population. But, by the beginning of the nineteenth century, Philadelphia was struggling again to rise, with O'Brien finding his home slowly recuperating in the wake of devastating sickness, gaining strength once more in industry and education.[5]

Like his beloved city, O'Brien had seen wild turns of fortune, and the tragedy of death, during his decades overseas. Captured while a ship's captain, O'Brien had first become a slave in Muslim lands; eventually, however, he not only gained emancipation, but rose to a high position, appointed US consul in North Africa.[6] When O'Brien finally arrived back home, he was no longer an unknown merchantman, but a seasoned diplomat, surviving stints as both an imprisoned slave and a professional ambassador. Helping to negotiate peace with Algiers, O'Brien's service in North Africa would, however, end with yet more conflict and a renewed risk of captivity. Swept up in the backlash after America's burning of the *Philadelphia* in February 1804, O'Brien was even suspected of being a spy, accused of duplicity by North African leaders.[7] O'Brien's roller-coaster career did not level out after he returned stateside either. Honored in his homecoming, O'Brien would meet another arrival from North Africa—Mellimelni—during his own ambassadorial visit. However, even as this Muslim mission ended, O'Brien was struck with tragedy once more. In the summer of 1806, O'Brien endured the "loss of one of my Children," as he reported to Jefferson. Departing immediately for Philadelphia, O'Brien later excused his absence to the president. My bereavement "necesiated me to leave washington more Sudden then I had Calculated on," O'Brien apologized, adding that he had missed "[t]he Oppertunity Of personally Thanking you for all your friendship and protection to me dureing my agency in Barbary."[8]

A year after O'Brien's loss, he would be visited by a presidential emissary, Robert Patterson, who carried inscrutable communiqués written in Kentucky. A former captive of Muslims, O'Brien was an obvious candidate to translate these captive Muslim writings. O'Brien was also an apt choice for another reason, however, one that Jefferson could not fully know. The papers the president was circulating in 1807 were authored by Muslim Africans, and filled with quotations from the Qur'an—the same sacred text that O'Brien himself had privately quoted during his own captivity. O'Brien's time in North Africa began in slavery; his stay had ended with intrigue, with accusations of espionage. However, if implicated in intrigues abroad, O'Brien would also bring home some secrets of his own. Departing as a simple son of Philadelphia, Richard had become, by the time he returned, "the Turk O'Brien," as Jefferson was told years later. Given a hero's welcome, O'Brien covertly carried to America echoes of Islam's sacred text within his own private journal.

O'Brien must have seemed a perfect choice to decipher the Arabic writings of African captives, and was certainly the only person Jefferson named in dispatching Patterson on a quest around Philadelphia. But another twist in O'Brien's roller-coaster career lay ahead, long foreshadowed by the precise Arabic usages he had employed in his private journal long ago. When Patterson handed Jefferson's enclosures to O'Brien, the former Algerian slave must have been struck by the uncanny repetition represented by these two Arabic sheets. Twenty-two years before, in 1785, O'Brien had petitioned Jefferson's help to save him from Muslim imprisonment; now, in 1807, Jefferson was petitioning O'Brien to help save two Muslims from American incarceration. In 1785, Jefferson had advised O'Brien to keep quiet and discreet in Muslim lands; now, Jefferson was asking O'Brien to divulge all he could about two documents that were stubbornly refusing to speak. Unfortunately, however, it was not only these details, but also an unhappy outcome, that linked 1785 and 1807. Just as Jefferson had disappointed O'Brien two decades previously, O'Brien would disappoint Jefferson now.

Staring down at the two Arabic papers carried from Kentucky, O'Brien confronted words well known to him. These pages contained Arabic terms whose sounds were familiar to O'Brien due to his North African enslavement, resounding from minarets over "workhouses" and whispered in pious prayers. But there was one problem: O'Brien could not *read* these words. To launch his Algerian journal in the 1790s, O'Brien had penned an Arabic phrase—a phrase, however, that O'Brien had written in English script, not in "Arabic characters." At his diary's beginning, O'Brien inscribed "*Bismillah*"— "in the name of Allah"—a Middle Eastern commonplace expressed in Western letters. From his first moments in Muslim lands, O'Brien's ears were filled with Arabic; and, as his enslavement unfolded, Arabic also proceeded from O'Brien's tongue. But the American seemingly never had the time, or the teacher, to learn Arabic's script. O'Brien's value as an American diplomat on the Barbary Coast had been partly due to his skills of speech—skills that Jefferson had asked him to suppress in 1785, requesting that O'Brien "say nothing to any body." Now, twenty-two years later, Jefferson was asking him to read an alphabet whose forms O'Brien had never studied.[9]

O'Brien must have felt intense frustration as he reviewed these writings in 1807, finding himself unable to assist two fellow prisoners, and two fellow copyists of the Qur'an. If he had been present in Kentucky personally, O'Brien's proximity could have helped, offering him the chance to hear their Arabic enunciated. But, stuck in America's city of freedom, O'Brien's distance ensured that these two captives remained helpless. Patterson reported back O'Brien's failure to Jefferson, writing on October 24 that "Capt. Obrien, though he understands the oral, has no knowledge at all of the written language."[10] And yet, O'Brien had not sent Patterson away entirely empty-handed. O'Brien was a resourceful veteran of North Africa, and his familiarity with Muslim culture could yet be of some use to Jefferson, or so he believed. Unable to translate the papers, O'Brien had a suggestion to help ascertain the identity of these two Africans—an idea sufficiently unorthodox, however, that Patterson seemed reluctant to mention it. Patterson would not disclose the idea until the very end of his report to the president; it was a last option, and would be held in reserve until nothing else remained to pursue.

In the meantime, Patterson had some ideas of his own. Jefferson's suggested translator did indeed have the rare Arabic facility required, but had no Arabic literacy; seemingly so close to success, O'Brien proved in the end a disappointment. Patterson, however, had other streets to tread in Philadelphia— and yet another Richard to try. O'Brien, a former slave in the Middle East, would fail; perhaps a native of the Middle East might prove more useful? In addition to an American captain, Patterson found the means to consult a European cosmopolitan, a man of many cities who, as luck would have it, had recently arrived for the first time to Philadelphia.

≈

Richard Van Lennep had boarded the *Tryal* in 1807, an American schooner bound for Boston. And, in his hands, Richard held at the ready his sketchbook.

Born into a Dutch family residing in Ottoman lands, the twenty-eight-year-old was journeying to America for the first time in 1807, departing his home in Anatolia, sailing from the prominent port city of Smyrna.[11] Richard came from a leading European family of trade; the Van Lenneps had for gen-erations represented Dutch interests on the Aegean Sea, conducting "busi-ness and consular duties at Smyrna for over a century."[12] Although dedicated merchants, the Van Lenneps were also devoted to artistic diversion, painting and writing up their exotic experiences in Asia Minor. After concluding an "exciting hunt" in the Turkish countryside, for instance, the Van Lenneps would together depict their adventures; "one of them would record the inci-dents of the day with his pen, while another would, in the other book, sketch with his pencil the most pictorial scenes of the hunt," as the American dip-lomat S. G. W. Benjamin recalled, who himself had been trained in "the rudi-mentary principles of drawing" by the "Van Lennep brothers."[13]

When Richard Van Lennep departed for America in 1807, his sketchbook helped record his time abroad. Having preserved portraits of his Middle Eastern home, he was now prepared to paint glimpses of the West. And, even before arriving to Boston, Van Lennep would encounter an American scene worthy of depiction. Crossing the Atlantic on the *Tryal*, Richard was struck by "men dancing aboard ship" itself.[14] Preserving this scene in watercolor, he devoted special attention to a single lad, a "black musician" pictured as "playing a homemade fiddle" while stamping his left foot, keeping time as his fellow crewmen danced on deck.[15] Little did Van Lennep know that his impending arrival to America would present quite another scene of African life and US servitude—a scene not of painted music, but of plaintive lines that would stay stubbornly silent.

Not long after reaching Boston, Richard Van Lennep visited Philadelphia, remaining in the city through the end of 1807, not departing until December.[16]

Fortuitously, Richard had arrived to Philadelphia during the precise season that Patterson required help. Searching for someone to sound out Arabic lines, Patterson discovered in his city a painter visiting from Muslim lands. Reflecting his own aesthetic priorities, however, Van Lennep seemed more preoccupied with the visual appearance of Jefferson's pages, rather than their verbal significance. Familiar with Middle Eastern languages, Van Lennep ventured more information than O'Brien had. But, although he was able to read Arabic, Van Lennep was unable to read *this* Arabic, he suggested. "I have shown the papers to a native of Smyrna, Mr. Lennep, now in this city," Patterson informed Jefferson in his October 24 letter, adding:

> He says "they are written in one of seven of the Arab dialects, which one he does not read—He can, however, so far understand them, as to find, that they have been written by very ignorant persons, and in so bad a hand, that it would be very difficult to read even by one who understood the dialect."[17]

Offering the above as a quotation, not merely a paraphrase, Patterson purports to transcribe for the president the precise words spoken by Van Lennep, even while Van Lennep fails to make out one single word in the documents sent by Jefferson. To add insult to injury, Van Lennep's incapacity to read is accompanied by criticism. It is not my fault, Van Lennep asserts, excusing himself by attacking the appearance of these Arabic manuscripts, blaming these men for writing "in so bad a hand." Concerned with African hand-writing, without reference to their captivity in hostile American hands, Van Lennep finds these documents to be "written in one of seven of the Arab dialects"—inconveniently, however, it is the very "one he does not read." Although himself ignorant, unable to translate the contents of the pages, Van Lennep censures the "very ignorant persons" who are their authors. According to Van Lennep, he is able to "so far understand" these writings only enough to assure the president that these writings are impossible to understand. Luckily, Van Lennep would prove wrong.[18]

Offering this pessimistic response to the president in 1807, Van Lennep failed Jefferson—and it would not be the last time. Helping to establish his family's financial interests in the New World, Van Lennep did not return home to the Middle East for fifteen more years. Just before he finally took ship again for Smyrna, in the summer of 1821, Richard decided to make an uninvited pilgrimage to Monticello, hoping to see Jefferson in retirement. In this mission too, Van Lennep would fall short. Writing on June 1, 1821, in a letter addressed to "Thos Jefferson Esqr," Van Lennep excused himself to the former president; unable to reach the top of the "little mountain" due to a storm, he expressed his "regrets at having been obliged to forego the honor" of meeting Jefferson. A "thunderstorm" had surprised Richard and his traveling companion, "compel[ing] them to return to Charlottesville," which was a "great disappointment to them."[19]

Richard was unsuccessful in translating two Arabic manuscripts for Jefferson, citing bad handwriting as his excuse; he would also prove unsuccessful in reaching the top of Jefferson's Monticello due to bad weather. However, Van Lennep's long sojourn in America would end with at least one effective delivery. The year Richard returned to Ottoman soil, a Middle Eastern gift was sent back to Boston, expressing gratitude for the welcome received by the Van Lennep family in America. Aptly, in light of Richard's experiences, this gift, which was procured personally by his older brother Jacob, claimed origins in Muslim African lands, and featured inscriptions, written with letters, sacred and mysterious. This Van Lennep present, posted to Boston, was nothing less than an authentic mummy, recently recovered from Egypt. Reflecting the Egyptomania gripping the West in the nineteenth century, this gift was sent to America during the same year that the Rosetta Stone helped crack the hieroglyphic code, solving Egypt's own ancient cipher.[20] An apt, yet eerie, follow-up to Richard's American visit, the Van Lennep gift dispatched to Boston in 1822 was an African corpse, covered with inscrutable writings. Sailing to America many years earlier, Richard had, on board the *Tryal*, sketched an African crewman, capturing his kinetic recital in watercolor. During his East Coast stay that followed, Van Lennep had stared unsympathetically at writings by "two men"—captured Africans whom he labeled "ignorant," but whose Arabic writings Richard was too ill-informed to read. From lively dancing to living detention, the Van Lennep visit to America also earned an African epilogue, dispatching a dead man across the seas, stolen from this same continent. Richard Van Lennep's American sojourn ends with gifting to the New World an embalmed and entombed carcass, entirely bound and desiccated, sending an African whose language was still on the cusp of inscrutability, marked with sacred Middle Eastern characters dead to American eyes.

≈

Visiting two veterans of Middle East travel, Patterson found no help, despite the promising credentials of these candidates. In consulting O'Brien and Van

Lennep, Patterson spanned a former US slave in Africa and a European aesthete from the Aegean Sea. Perhaps he was searching in the wrong direction? Maybe looking closer at hand would yield more success. Although the order of Patterson's visits is not known, the last of the three figures he mentions to the president in his October 24 summary was a man very close to home, belonging to the first place that Jefferson had himself suggested. Before mentioning either "Capt Obrien" or "your city," Jefferson had queried: "is there any one attached to your College" who could serve as translator?[21]

Samuel Brown Wylie was Patterson's colleague at the University of Pennsylvania. Although much younger, Wylie shared with Patterson not only a place of work, but also personal origins as well. Both men had started life in Ireland, but thirty years apart, with their boyhood homes situated only thirty miles from one another. Born in 1773, Wylie grew up in Moybarg, County Antrim, just north of where Patterson was born in Hillsborough, County Down, in 1743.[22] Following the older man's example, Wylie emigrated from Ireland, and due to his extraordinary talents, garnered interest at the American Ivy League. Both men, however, never forgot their overseas roots, bringing Irish Presbyterian traditions to the New World. For Wylie, these roots gave rise not only to his creed, but to his career. An instructor at the University of Pennsylvania, Wylie was also an ordained pastor. In October 1807, it was not Wylie's piety, but his linguistic proficiency, that drew Patterson to him. Lecturing at the university on ancient languages, Wylie was, like Patterson, fascinated with symbols that were inscrutable to others. But, rather than the mathematical formulas adored by Patterson, it was "jots and tittles" that Wylie loved, teaching Greek to his undergraduates. By a lucky coincidence, however, Wylie had in 1807 just begun to search eastward for further tongues to tackle, settling especially on one language: Arabic. When Patterson arrived to confer with his young friend, carrying with him two foreign pages, it seemed like providence. "Revd. Mr. Wylie," in this very same season, Patterson reported to Jefferson, "had just begun the study of the [Arabic] language."[23]

Wylie was not just intrigued by the documents distributed by the President, he was inspired. Primary materials in Arabic were rare in early America; and it appeared almost miraculous that Wylie should receive manuscripts in the very language that he "had just begun [to] study." Perhaps most surprisingly, this Presbyterian minister's efforts to learn Arabic would be promoted by the penmanship of African Muslims. Unlike Van Lennep, the Arabic papers sent from the president were not only welcomed by Wylie, but sparked his studies; rather than written by "ignorant men," for Wylie these pages were produced by authors capable of teaching even an Ivy League professor. With excited optimism, Wylie told the much older Patterson that these papers sent from the president would offer an impetus to advance his early learning of Arabic. This extraordinary "circumstance," Patterson noted in his October 24 letter to Jefferson, "has given a spur to [Wylie's] exertions."[24] Although unable to make anything out of them just yet—indeed, unable to decipher even a single word—Wylie nevertheless was certain that all would soon be solved. Again opposite to Van Lennep, Wylie not only found value in these writings, but predicted with conviction that these papers could indeed be translated—and quickly. With the untried self-confidence of a young academic, Wylie promised not only Patterson, but the president of the United States himself, that only a few short weeks would be needed for him to read these writings. Wylie "promises in *one month* to give a translation of the papers," Patterson reported to Jefferson.[25]

Nearly twenty years earlier, in 1788, the writings of an enslaved Muslim named 'Usman were opened by an avid Arabist, Ezra Stiles, encouraging his pursuits as Yale's president. In 1807 Muslim manuscripts arrived at the University of Pennsylvania, "spur[ring]" another Ivy League professor to intensify his studies of Arabic. Devoting himself to decoding the curling lines inscribed by two Africans in Kentucky, Samuel B. Wylie even left material proof of his progress, with traces of Arabic studies still evident in his personal library. Gathering sources to support his exploration of Middle Eastern languages, Wylie's advances are suggested by his correction of Arabic print

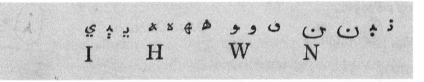

Figure 8 A detail from p. 4 of Wylie's copy of *Pantographia*—a volume listing the letters of the Arabic alphabet. In this left-hand margin of Wylie's copy is a faint, penciled correction, recognizing a slip in the letter at the far right of the image above, offering the accurate "ـﺖ" for the erroneously printed "ـﭑ." Hinting at Wylie's Arabic studies in Philadelphia, this book is still housed at the University of Pennsylvania. Image courtesy of the Kislak Center for Special Collections, Rare Books and Manuscripts, University of Pennsylvania Libraries.

errors in the very volumes he collected, marking typos in the margins of his grammars and guides (Figure 8).[26]

Honing his abilities with Arabic in the wake of October 1807, Wylie developed a precise eye for this language's foreign script, encouraged by the same fugitive manuscripts that Van Lennep labeled as written in so "bad a hand."[27] Useless to Richard Van Lennep, for Wylie these two Arabic documents were of vital interest, stimulating his own Arabic studies at the University of Pennsylvania, which now, two hundred years later, boasts one of the "most prominent" Arabic Studies programs in the United States.[28]

≈

Beyond all odds, it was two Muslim slaves who "spurred" the Arabic "exertions" of Samuel B. Wylie in 1807. And yet, although enthused by their writings, Wylie was unable to aid the Muslim slaves themselves—at least not immediately. Wylie would need time to study before he could decipher their Arabic. Meanwhile, Patterson was left without concrete results. And he was not willing to wait "*one month*" merely on a "promise" from his youthful colleague. The president simply could not be so long postponed.

Instead of hopeful deferral, Patterson chose honest disappointment. Writing to Jefferson before even one week was up, Patterson started his letter on Saturday, October 24 with "regret," opening with the following words:

> Philaa. Octr. 24th. 1807
>
> SIR,
>
> I regret exceedingly that I have not been able to procure a translation of the two little Arabic manuscripts you were pleased to send me for that purpose.[29]

In 1801, Patterson had stumped Jefferson, making the president's own Declaration unrecognizable to him, couched in a private "scheme of *secret writing*." Jefferson's most public words had been so well encased in cipher that Patterson's code defied the "collective ingenuity of mankind" for two centuries. Now, in 1807, Jefferson had stumped Patterson, sending not the Declaration of Independence, but Arabic writings by Muslim authors yearning for liberty.

Although the "collective ingenuity" of Philadelphia was at his own disposal, Patterson had "not been able" to accomplish his task. Jefferson had voiced a readiness to "procure" the release of the Muslim Africans, if warranted. In his reply, Patterson echoed back the president's own words, confessing his inability "to procure a translation." But, without a means to unravel the language of these writings, liberty too was lost for their authors. The president had asked that the manuscripts be translated "if practicable, that I may procure the release of the men if proper"; now, Jefferson's "if practicable" had proved impossible, which meant that his "if proper" would never be tested. Aware of such high stakes, Patterson was not willing to give up so easily, insisting later in his October 24 letter that a chance still remained to solve the puzzle of these Arabic writings and their authors. Summarizing his efforts in Philadelphia, Patterson mentioned his meeting with O'Brien first, and Van Lennep second; finally, Patterson reached Wylie, reporting his friend's "promise" to "give a translation of the papers" in just "*one month*." This audacious pledge seemed doubtful to Patterson, of course; and near the end of his reply to Jefferson, Patterson qualified Wylie's optimism, adding with naked honesty "[i]n this, however, I fear he will be mistaken."[30]

Patterson was right to be skeptical of Wylie's prospects; and yet, realism did not spell defeat. Even as Patterson consulted his three contacts in Philadelphia, receiving their disappointing responses over a few days, he formed his own plan to advance and expand a search for a skillful translator. America's inventor of ciphers, during this short span in October, had not been idle, electing instead to take matters into his own hands—literally.

16

"Humanity certainly Pleads Loud"

On my arrival here on the 3ʳᵈ I found the Stylograph with which
I now write. you have rightly conjectured it's principle. the impression both on the missive & copy retained is from a paper blacked on
both sides, perhaps with coal, as they call it Carbonated paper.
Jefferson to Charles Willson Peale, October 5, 1807[1]

October the 3rd was the day of Jefferson's "arrival" back to Washington—the
Saturday that Jefferson received Ira P. Nash's urgent note in the evening. On
this same Saturday, however, Jefferson enjoyed another surprise. Entering
the President's House after his two months of absence, Jefferson found a novelty waiting for him. Rather than outlandish writings, it was a strange new
writing device: the "Stylograph."[2]

On October 5—the same day that the president received Nash's farewell
summary of the situation in Kentucky—Jefferson wrote the above to Charles
Willson Peale, famed painter and friend, who was working with the president to explore improved technologies for copying. It had been Peale who
had procured for Jefferson the silver-mounted polygraphs that the president
gifted in 1806 to Mellimelni and his Muslim "Master" back in Tunis. Now, in
1807, it was a stylograph that Jefferson himself received—a "newly invented"
device for copying, which the president was eager to try out, reporting his
tests to Peale. Cutting into "Carbonated paper" with "glass brought to a point
like a pencil," this instrument "provided an exact copy of an author's original."
Always interested in practical experiment, Jefferson not only wrote Peale
concerning the stylograph on October 5, however, but utilized the device itself. It is the "Stylograph with which I now write," Jefferson announces to his
friend. Peale was an apt collaborator for Jefferson in searching for the ideal
copying machine. Peale was not just any painter, but a portrait painter—the
very artist responsible for *both* of the iconic images reproduced on the cover
of *Jefferson's Muslim Fugitives*. The book's cover features two Peale portraits,

aptly pairing together Jefferson on the left, and on the right, Yarrow Mamout, a former U.S. Muslim slave. Literate in Arabic, Mamout suffered enslavement in Maryland for over four decades; in 1807 Mamout finally won freedom, and later sat for Peale, who painted his portrait in 1819. Gifting Jefferson copier technology in 1807, Peale would himself preserve the likeness of a West African Muslim who was freed this very same year.[3]

Experimenting with Peale's gift, Jefferson generated literary duplicates by cutting across layers with his new stylograph on October 5—the same day he also started to search for a translator to decipher the layered Arabic documents that had cut their way across the country, carried by Ira P. Nash. Canvassing the capital, Jefferson eventually sent his plea for help to Philadelphia on October 18, even as he experimented with his new stylograph, ensuring that copies of his own letters were preserved. By the time October came to an end, however, Jefferson would discover that he was not alone in reproducing pivotal texts. On Monday, October 26, 1807, Jefferson received Patterson's "regretful" report, penned on October 24, the previous Saturday.[4] As Jefferson opened this letter, it was not Patterson's disappointing news, but a fresh Arabic enclosure, that seemed most remarkable. Patterson was returning the original "two little manuscripts" that Jefferson had originally provided; however, Patterson had also inserted a new lone page for the president's review—a single page whose very existence would eventually offer the only hope for Jefferson's mission to be fulfilled.

≈

I have taken an exact *fac simile* of the manuscripts (of which I have sent you a duplicate) and shall not cease to pursue the enquiry.

Robert Patterson to Jefferson
October 24, 1807[5]

Patterson had started his October 24 letter to Jefferson with "exceeding" apologies, confessing his failure "to procure a translation of the two little Arabic manuscripts." But this same letter of regret ends with words of hope, revealing that these "two" manuscripts have now been multiplied, with Patterson producing an "exact *fac simile*" of these unique documents. Returning the original "Arabic manuscripts" to the president, Patterson also provides "a duplicate" of a copy that he himself has "taken"—an "exact *fac simile*" that will remain with Patterson in Philadelphia, enabling him to pursue Jefferson's mission, even without the originals (Figure 9).[6]

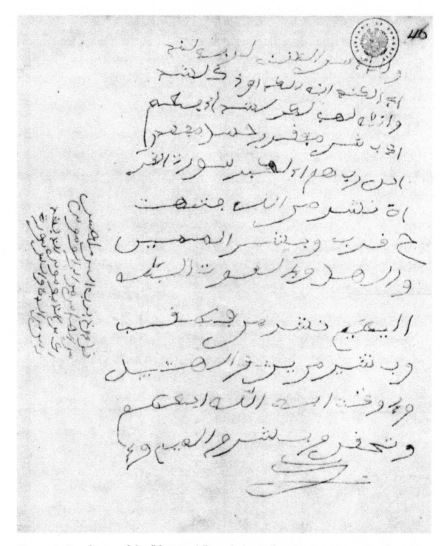

Figure 9 Duplicate of the "*fac simile*" made by Robert Patterson in October 1807 and sent to Jefferson on the 24th from Philadelphia, reproducing on a single page the two Arabic manuscripts penned by Muslim captives in Kentucky. Image courtesy of the Thomas Jefferson Papers, Library of Congress.

After weeks of copying his own English correspondence with his new stylograph, Jefferson himself opened Patterson's letter, finding yet another copy—a "*fac simile*" of Arabic communiqués. When first handed this en-velope on October 26, Jefferson doubtless hoped to find inside the transla-tion he had requested; instead, from Philadelphia, Jefferson received not a rendition, but a reproduction, a "duplicate" of the "two little Arabic manuscripts." As October ended, the president possessed a replica of the Arabic material that he had at the beginning of October. Now, there was two times the text, yet still no translation. In effect, Jefferson had himself been rendered twice as illiterate, finding the Arabic "*fac simile*" from Patterson no more legible than the Arabic documents that he was first handed by Nash.

The purpose of Patterson's "*fac simile*" was not to accent Jefferson's failure, of course, but to hold out a faint possibility for the future success of Jefferson's mission. Patterson needed to keep "duplicates" on the East Coast so as "to pursue the enquiry," seeking to solve the Arabic writings of two hunted men out West. In sympathy with Muslim slaves in Kentucky, Patterson felt unable to renounce his own quest, still hoping to track down a translator with the help of this "*fac simile*" made with his own hands.

Patterson portrays his manufactured page as a "*fac simile*"—"an exact" copy of the material sent to him by Jefferson. And yet, as Patterson correctly notes, Jefferson had sent to Philadelphia "*two* little Arabic manuscripts." Comparing Patterson's "*fac simile*" with the single manuscript that survives in Jefferson's papers, a discrepancy is immediately evident. Despite his claim, Patterson's "*fac simile*" is not "exact." He has merged *both* of the "two little" Arabic manuscripts onto a single page. The one sheet generated by Patterson features two texts, synthesizing plural pages into a single "*fac simile*." To fit this pair onto one page, however, Patterson is not able to put them side-by-side, but turns one of the texts sideways (Figure 10).[7] Rotating the smaller manuscript sent to him from Jefferson, Patterson squeezes this text into the narrow margins at the left of his copied page, with some of the faded lines of his facsimile appearing even less legible now due to their upended slant.

A hybrid document, Patterson's copy fuses together discrete identities; his "*fac simile*" comprises a unique collaboration, merging two Muslim Africans with an Irish Presbyterian. Put to work by captive Arabic authors, an Ivy League professor toils with his own hands, hoping to preserve both of their documents for a future translator. And, in fact, Patterson's "*fac simile*" represents the *only* extant witness to the second and smaller of the two manuscripts sent to Philadelphia by the president. Positioned sideways on Patterson's copied page, the Arabic original for this marginal material is now lost. Only *one* of the two actual manuscripts owned by Jefferson has survived, pictured as Figure 1, at this book's beginning.[8] Today, the only reason that *both* of the two African Muslims are still able to speak is due to Patterson's uncomprehending act of copying. Despite all the literal twists and literary turns involved in this story—despite all its flawed duplications and cross

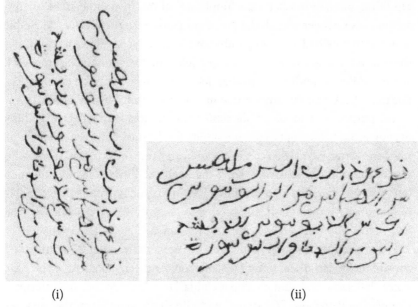

(i)   (ii)

Figure 10 Two details from Robert Patterson "*fac simile*", generated in October 1807. Detail (i) exhibits the Arabic text as erroneously reproduced in Patterson's *fac simile*, oscillated sideways on his copy's page. Detail (ii) displays the Arabic text as it was originally intended by its African author. Images courtesy of the Thomas Jefferson Papers, Library of Congress.

directions—Patterson's slanted text yet survives. Pushed to the margins, this Arabic material is still possible to decipher, even from the improbable edges of a two-century span.

No translator was ever found for these two provocative manuscripts—and for very good reasons. Van Lennep's reaction to the Arabic papers presented by Patterson seemed defensive, dismissing their merit and excusing his own inability to render their contents. However, although perhaps reflecting his own prejudice, Van Lennep's assessment was not entirely incorrect. The Arabic written by the two Kentucky captives is indeed extremely difficult to decipher. Their manuscripts are unevenly inscribed, rife with omissions, made almost illegible due to slips in both spelling and script.[9] After Patterson circulated these Arabic documents in October 1807, the only nineteenth-century reaction to these manuscripts was offered by the first reviewer of Jefferson's own presidential papers during the decade that followed his 1826 death. Published anonymously in 1835, this early assessment reserved a couple of paragraphs to the most startling materials found amid Jefferson's more expected letters—materials written in Arabic, which appeared to the unnamed reviewer in 1835 to be written

> much as if some industrious spider had crawled out of an ink-stand and travelled leisurely over the sheet, dropping grimed spots and trails from his feet.[10]

Painfully ironic, this account of the illegible Arabic in Jefferson's archives emphasizes travel and "trails," framing these writings by escaped Africans in terms of leisure and liberty. No freewheeling "feet" were involved in the inscription of these two Arabic manuscripts, of course. No mere "footnotes" to US history, these manuscripts instead were penned by historic, though forgotten, hands in chains. Rather than a holiday journey, it was a fugitive hunt that lay behind the production of these papers. Purposeful and desperate, they were not written accidentally by an "industrious spider," but by educated men who were not only able to traverse flat pages, but had also forged rivers and forests to survive. Composed under duress in Kentucky, penned in terror and trauma, it seems entirely understandable why such documents would have been clumsily composed.

Despite his many contacts, and his copying efforts, Patterson had failed in October to find an Arabic translator. His inquiries did yield, however, one concrete, if crude, suggestion. Mentioned last of all in Patterson's October 24 letter to Jefferson was a proposition from the first Philadelphian that had come to Jefferson's mind: Richard O'Brien. Unable to read Jefferson's manuscripts, O'Brien lacked the requisite literacy, endowed only with Arabic "orality," as Patterson had noted. O'Brien did, however, have an idea for Jefferson, involving not verbal subtleties, but corporeal substance. Reproducing the writings of these two African Muslims, Patterson had forcefully pushed one manuscript to the edge of his copied page. O'Brien had an even more brazen suggestion, involving not the margins of an authored page, but the margins of the authors' own bodies.

≈

> It was suggested to me by Capt. Obrien, that it may easily be determined, by the sign of circumcision, whether the men be Mahometans or not; though this would not determin the question of their being freemen—yet justice as well as *humanity* certainly pleads loud in their behalf.

I have the honour to be with sentiments of the greatest esteem—Your obedient Servant

R. PATTERSON[11]

This is the close to Patterson's October 24 letter, which Jefferson received on the 26th. Leading with disappointment, Patterson had first summarized his failed attempts in Philadelphia, listing the failures of O'Brien, Van Lennep, and Wylie. Patterson concludes his letter, however, with the above—a bold conclusion, both for the beliefs Patterson espouses, as well as the body parts he intimates. It is no wonder, considering the content of O'Brien's "suggestion," that Patterson left it to the very last. And yet, if these final lines gave Patterson pause, he nevertheless elects to divulge this delicate idea, not wishing to hold anything back. And so, Robert Patterson found himself in October 1807 suggesting that the president of the United States have the genitals of two African captives examined, searching for "the sign of circumcision."

It is O'Brien's intimate experiences in North Africa that underlies this impertinent suggestion. O'Brien's idea seems audacious, considering the organs implied; but its purpose is perhaps even more intriguing. From Patterson, Jefferson again receives advice on reading "signs"—but these signs are no longer spelled on handwritten pages, but on the human anatomy. Although physical, this "sign," however, denotes spirituality, with "circumcision" in the flesh reflecting religious commitments. Writing to Patterson in October, Jefferson had hoped to free these fugitives "if proper," without mentioning either race or religion. Replying to Jefferson, Patterson passes along a rather *im*proper suggestion, with aims of ascertaining whether these two men are "Mahometans." For Jefferson, however, the Muslim identity of these men was likely never in doubt. Over twenty years, the president had directly engaged with many Arabic-speakers from Africa, each professing Islam. As Jefferson himself was first to note, the two African captives in Kentucky sought to communicate in Arabic—the sacred language of the Qur'an, which had migrated to West Africa along with the Muslim faith. There was little reason to question Islamic affiliation; however, what was not clear to Jefferson in 1807 was that the Qur'an itself formed the very content of their Arabic writings. Even while seeking freedoms in America, these men were inscribing lines from Islam's scripture.

At the close of his letter, Patterson freely mentions not only personal body parts, but also the personal freedom that should be accorded to *all* bodies.

Challenging the "justice" of African captivity, Patterson's anti-slavery position is loftier than O'Brien's rather physical "suggestion," but perhaps touched even more tender sensitivities for Jefferson himself. Clearly unsurprised by the prospect of Muslims held in US bondage, Patterson observes that these men's "Mahometan" identities would not, however, be sufficient to secure their liberty. Although "the sign of circumcision" could connote religious confession, "this would not determin the question of their being freemen," Patterson admits.[12] Speaking to Jefferson—himself a slave owner, yet a believer in slavery's abolition—Patterson takes the opportunity offered by these Arabic texts to argue for African freedoms. No neutral mediator himself, Patterson emerges instead as an even more partisan advocate, appealing to commonplace ideals that "plead" for these particular slaves. Transitioning from human flesh to "*humanity*" itself, Patterson emphasizes not physical presence but conscience, arguing for the men's release by gesturing to broad "justice." For Patterson and the president, these Arabic authors were muted, writing words that remained unreadable. And yet, a "loud" voice surfaces on "their behalf," arising not from their own authorship, but from universals shared by all.

Patterson's petition on behalf of the two African authors mirrored their own writings in ways that were impossible for him to fathom. His letter ends by noting that "*humanity*" voices itself "loudly" on behalf of these Muslim captives; however, unbeknownst to Patterson, "humanity" is also explicitly invoked by their Arabic writings. The text that Patterson copied sideways— the same text that survives only due to his 1807 "*fac simile*"—is a "Mahometan" chapter, which is itself simply entitled "Humanity"—in Arabic, "سورة الناس" ("The Chapter of Humanity"). Although immensely difficult to read in Patterson's *fac simile*, close scrutiny reveals the following lines are those most likely implied at the edges of his page, quoted from the very conclusion to the Qur'an:

> Say: I take refuge with the Lord of men,
> the King of men,
> the God of men,
> from the evil of the withdrawing whisperer
> who whispers in the breasts of men
> of jinn and men[13]

The above lines translate the text rotated sideways on Patterson's *fac simile*— an Arabic text that is copied merely on the margins, seemingly offered almost as an afterthought. Comprising the entirety of one of the "two little manu-scripts" written by the two African captives in Kentucky, the material quoted above is, however, no trivial postscript. Instead, it constitutes the critical ep-ilogue to the Qur'an itself. Forming the very final chapter of the scripture—Chapter 114—these words are the climactic sentences of the entire Muslim corpus, which ends with this "Chapter of Humanity." Undiscovered for over two centuries, the final lines inscribed by two African fugitives handed to President Jefferson shakily copy the final lines of Islam's revelation.

When first appealing to Patterson for aid, Jefferson had framed these "writings in Arabic characters" as memoirs. The manuscripts conveyed by Nash are "supposed" to "contain" the Africans' own "history, as stated by themselves," the president observed. However, when the Kentucky cap-tives' words are finally deciphered, as above, they emerge not as individual and original "statements," but as citations from an ancient, universal scrip-ture. And yet, although quoting a communal canon, the specific selections offered by the African fugitives do often read as personally reflective. As with 'Usman two decades earlier, the Qur'anic references written by these Muslims do not form conventional autobiography; they do, however, repre-sent intentional acts of authorship, embodying a deep "history," while also seeming to articulate anxieties particular to their unique situation, reso-nating poignantly with their present enslavement. Opening with Allah—the true source of all sovereignty—the Arabic lines above stress in repetition the "Lord," "King," and "God" of *all* men, with these verses "tak[ing] refuge" in a power that transcends human prejudice. Gesturing to a higher perspective from which all races and regions are viewed impartially, this chapter resists precisely the conditions endured by the two Muslims in America, inverting the hierarchies of social power that have led to their slavery and suffering. Starting with an imperative to "say," the quotation above also ironically commences by commanding the very act that remains impossible for the Kentucky captives. Unable to make themselves understood, these Africans are imprisoned in speech, confronting captors who are ignorant of their lan-guage. Framed as an oral recitation in Arabic, opening with a command to communicate, yet written with words unreadable in America, this Qur'anic chapter also concludes with anxieties of hushed intimations, seeking to flee satanic temptations. Introduced as a "whisperer" who "withdraws," the devil emerges in Chapter 114 as dangerous due to his soft-speaking and covert ap-peal to the interior of mankind. Invoking Allah's mastery, even as they seek to break from captivity, the Africans who copy these lines from the Qur'an request help against the snares of the devil, and yet themselves suffer entirely in human chains, entrapped not by demonic forces, but by the vicious prejudices of "men."

As October neared its end, Jefferson received Patterson's letter of disappointment, but also the "*fac simile*" it enclosed, reproducing on a single page the very same Arabic materials the president had sent north to Philadelphia. For Jefferson, the seduction cautioned by the "Chapter of Humanity" itself stayed silent to him, even as "*humanity*" itself "pleads loud" on "behalf" of the Muslim slaves, in Patterson's words. Receiving notice of his friend's failure in Philadelphia, Jefferson on October 26 was left with words whose whispers remained inaudible to him. Soon, however, all silence would be more than filled by the cacophonous cries of Congress. Jefferson happened to open Patterson's letter on the very day that the Tenth US Congress also opened— the event that the president had returned to Washington to oversee, himself "summon[ing] this special session," preparing to deliver an address to both the House and Senate the very next day. Reconvening Congress early, Jefferson was fully occupied at the end of October. Fear over Burr's domestic insurrection had largely subsided, but Britain's foreign aggression still "seriously threatened the peace of our country," as Jefferson stressed in the opening to his congressional message on October 27.[14]

A busy November soon started in Washington, and for Jefferson, there seemed no clear way to decipher the silent writings penned by two Muslim fugitives. In the far West, the persistent silence that surrounded these fugitives itself started to seem more sinister, however. Unknown to the president, prospects for the Kentucky captives were turning even more grim. Peering down at these documents, inscribed with prayers to "take refuge" from the "whisperer," Jefferson could not have known that whispers were indeed surfacing that would impact the two authors themselves. These African "men" were no longer suspected of mere escape, seeking to "withdraw" from their supposed owners; instead they were thought to harbor "evil" intentions, holding secrets within their own incommunicative "breasts."

17

"Supposed to be Spys"

> Those men, are by some supposed to be Spys. but there is no person
> in these parts can know who they are or what their business.
>
> Ira P. Nash to Jefferson
> November 8, 1807[1]

In October 1807, Jefferson sought a translator, discreetly circulating two Arabic manuscripts on the East coast. Out West, it was not outlandish writings, but strange rumors, that were reportedly circulating. These whispers, unlike the president's search, were unsympathetic. From Washington, the African captives appeared unduly incarcerated, "confined, on suspicion, merely," in Jefferson's words. On the frontier, however, "suspicion" was not so easily dismissed.

Racial prejudice had initially halted the two Muslim fugitives in the spring; by the autumn, it was not bias but apprehensions that seemed to be rising on the Cumberland River. The two Africans, whose "business" remained unknown, appeared to "some" not as escapees, but agents of espionage. Rather than runaway slaves, they seemed to be "spies," infiltrating the interior. Exactly three weeks to the day after Jefferson first wrote to Patterson in Philadelphia for aid, Ira P. Nash penned the above update. Dated November 8, 1807, Nash fulfilled his promise to the president, dispatching an update on the two African authors en route to his home in Missouri. Recounting local distrust, this report of "Spys" represents the very last recorded words that Nash wrote to Thomas Jefferson. News of this odd "supposition" proved to be the final piece of information the president ever received regarding two Muslim runaways in the American West.[2]

Jefferson did not read Nash's ominous words until many weeks after they were written, receiving this last letter only at the very opening of the next year: 1808.[3] Jefferson may, therefore, have been entirely unaware of the suspicions swirling around the two African fugitives in the autumn. And yet, these same suspicions would not be unrelated to the president's attempts to aid these "two men," and especially the failure of his attempts. Jefferson's readiness to "procure" freedom for the African captives was never realized, frustrated most by his incapacity to translate their words. However, the whispers reported by Nash this same autumn likely also played a role in keeping the Muslims confined. Even mistaken suspicions have a strange way of receiving confirmation, especially if believed with sufficient prejudice. Undoubtedly innocent of wild accusations, the Africans would nevertheless resist their unjust treatment, ironically giving false credence to precisely the apprehensions that clouded their horizons.

≈

It is impossible to ascertain how such outlandish rumors began. But, considering the unrests of 1807, and the unexpected arrival of two literate Africans on the American frontier, such suspicions should perhaps not surprise us. It was not unusual for slaves to escape and be recaptured in the early nineteenth century, of course, even in "sparsely settled part[s] of the western frontier" such as Christian County, Kentucky.[4] If not unprecedented, the discovery of two Africans in May 1807, running on the remote west end of the Cumberland River, seemed peculiar, and even more so once they were in custody and questioned. Unable to communicate in English, the strangers could not account for their origins or their destination—or, perhaps, they would not? It may have been when these same men showed themselves literate, albeit writing in foreign lines stretching from right to left, that alarm bells began to ring. Clearly, these Africans were not at all ignorant. In the early Republic, slave literacy of any kind was controversial, often proscribed by law.[5] These particular Africans, however, possessed no mere rudimentary English; instead, they were endowed with linguistic skills beyond the ken of their American captors. Was it possible that Africans could have attained such education at home, in a continent considered by the racist standards of 1807 to be a "dark and benighted region"?[6] This would have been a troubling thought for many Americans, troubling enough to push some to embrace improbable theories. Arriving to the edge of a new nation itself recovering from a coastal war in Muslim North Africa, perhaps these Africans, literate in Arabic, were implicated in America's broader struggles? Could a figure such as Irving's satiric Mustapha, the fictional spy writing in the pages of local papers, have come to life as actual fact?

The American frontier of 1807 offered conditions especially ripe for such far-fetched fears to take shape. These two literate Muslims surfaced in Kentucky just as the state was gripped with conspiracy rumors—rumors that may have helped transmute mere mystery into menace, making two poor slaves seem like sophisticated "spys." Spatially remote, reports in territories were often far from reliable, rumbling with scandals and threats of espionage, foreign and domestic. Most recently, of course, an actual insurrection had been just extinguished, with Burr still on trial during the very days that these two Africans were "taken up" and "confined, on suspicion." Had not Aaron Burr himself sought to enlist William Eaton—hero of North African campaigns—to seize the American West? Perhaps Eaton had recruited his own "Moorish" agents to spy out the land, in advance of Burr's ambitious insurgency. Following Burr's own 1807 capture in Mississippi, the devious James Wilkinson had "spread panic-stricken stories" of a "negro insurrection" that was backing "Burr." Perhaps these two Africans were scattered remnants from such a failed uprising?[7]

During the months in which the two Africans were captive in Kentucky, the messy aftermath of the vice president's plot was still unfolding, with accusations running rampant. Burr was on trial in Virginia during the summer, and the scope of his plans for the West remained vague, with co-conspirators still at large. Few were above suspicion, and possible sympathizers emerged at all levels of society. By October, US papers were publishing trial transcripts that included the claim "that a system of espionage had pervaded the transactions in the Western Country."[8] On October 4, 1807, the very day that Jefferson was discreetly handed the two Arabic manuscripts, a future US president was helping to cover up Burr's intrigue. William Henry Harrison was serving as governor of the Indiana Territory in 1807, and on Sunday, October 4, he wrote a letter to quietly excuse "two men" who had "repented of all the wrong which they have done by following after Traitor Burr."[9] Seeming concerned with backlash and retribution, Harrison also advised that these same men stay silent, never letting "any one know that they were in the Burr conspiracy. If they do in after years they will be accused of being traitors by people not half so worthy as they are."[10]

Of all western states, however, Kentucky had played a critical role in the Burr scandal. Even as Nash journeyed to Jefferson, carrying the Arabic manuscripts penned by two Muslims in the state, Kentucky surfaced in the lingering proceedings against Burr in Virginia. On September 19, "the prosecution began to present testimony to prove [Burr's] overt act within the United States, specifically, at the mouth of the Cumberland River in Kentucky."[11] Some of the state's leading men were also accused of supporting Burr's treason. John Adair, US senator from Kentucky, was not only charged alongside Burr in the autumn of 1806, but was later incarcerated as a co-conspirator by none other than James Wilkinson. In 1807, Adair made an aggrieved appeal published in US newspapers, openly accusing Governor Wilkinson himself of espionage, asserting that:

> in Kentucky the people were more afraid of Wilkinson than Burr; because many of them believe him to be in Spanish pay. A gentleman (pointing to a small man in the room) observed to me, take care what you say, that man is a spy on you from the general, and I would not be surprised if you are confined for that before night; I answered with perhaps some warmth, let him confine me and be G——d, I despise his power. For this I have suffered, for this I have been imprisoned.[12]

Suffering incarceration in the wake of the Burr hysteria, Adair informed fellow Kentuckians that their land had long been replete with "spies"— spies sent not from Burr, but from the government. Perhaps amplifying western resentment of Eastern elites, Adair suggests Washington, not just Wilkinson, is at fault. Jefferson's administration had itself succumbed to the Burr scare, Adair asserts, suspending even the sacred right of "Habeas Corpus," and thus:

> sacrificing the constitution on the altar of oppression and subjecting every citizen in the west to the will of an ambitious unprincipled tyrant. Was this done through the aid of Executive means; or had they just heard the Arabian Nights entertainment of last winter, and shut their doors to keep out Burr and his army, least they might be tied neck and heels and tumbled into the Potomac[?][13]

Invoking Jefferson without naming him, Adair aims his sarcastic query at the US "Executive," suggesting that "every citizen of the west" is potentially oppressed due to actions taken in Washington. The president and his Senate are themselves to blame for overreacting to the fancied plots of Burr the pretender, thereby giving free rein to the tyrannical James Wilkinson. For Adair, "Burr and his army" never posed a real threat. The true injustice instead arose from mere rumors of conspiracy, with Washington succumbing to false reports "last winter" of Burr's rising power, which ultimately amounted to nothing more than spells of an "Arabian Nights entertainment."

Adair was eventually liberated from his incarceration, winning release by the same due process he had accused Jefferson of "sacrificing," even receiving substantial damages from the government for his ordeal.[14] But for two Muslim slaves imprisoned in Adair's home state of Kentucky, such judicial recompense was far out of reach. There was no relief, and no writ of "Habeas Corpus," that could save them. For Africans in America, "the constitution" was already forfeited "on the altar of oppression." As Muslims "in the west," the captives were living anything but a Middle Eastern romance. It was no "Arabian Nights entertainment" that shaped their experiences as they inscribed Arabic to be dispatched to Washington, petitioning the great man on the "Potomac." However, despite their appeals, no help seemed forthcoming, and conditions in Kentucky were insufferable. As Nash had noted to Jefferson in October, the men were not only "kept in confinement" but forced to "labour daily."[15] Although merely presumed to be "the property of some person," these Africans were treated precisely as slaves. And one day, enough was enough. No legislative avenue was open to pursue, and the "Executive" had yet to answer. Denied recourse to humanity's "constitution," there was a more natural route to freedom. All they had to do was once more find the Cumberland River.

≈

وإنه على ذلك لشهيد
[And indeed, He is to that a witness][16]

Carried from Christian County, Kentucky, the larger of the two documents that Nash delivered to Jefferson in the first days of October shakily inscribes these Arabic words. Spanning divine surveillance and human secrets, pairing the Watcher and the watched, the above is another Qur'anic verse—a verse that frames Allah as invisible "witness," invoking God as fully informed of all our thoughts and deeds. Illegible to Nash as he pushed forward to Washington, this line oddly resonated with issues that surrounded the same enslaved men he had left behind. Suspected of espionage, supposed to be secret "witnesses" in the West, the two African authors were thought "by some" to be "spies." Although a paranoid delusion, such accusations of duplicity proved to be self-fulfilling prophecies.

Confronted with grim prospects, the time had come for the two Africans to undertake covert acts. Rather than spying, they instead sought to elude local "witnesses," escaping once more into the wild. The county courthouse where the two Africans had arrived in the spring of 1807 was newly constructed; and the ironically named "Christian jail" where they were most likely held alongside Kentucky's "criminals and debtors" had already proved insecure.[17] In the recent past, other inmates had succeeded in "escaping up [the] chimney." As a result, in May 1806 the Christian County sheriff was requisitioned to "provide a lock and make such other necessary repairs to the doors of the Christian Jail as he thinks necessary for the safe keeping" of those incarcerated.[18] A year later, when a pair of Muslims were arrested, it is unclear if the sheriff had complied with this directive. Whatever additional security measures had been taken, however, proved insufficient. By the fall of 1807, another pair of inmates would escape from Christian County.[19]

It is again Nash's own correspondence that has preserved the only details to survive regarding the route pursued by the two Africans following their Kentucky escape. Fortunately, however, Nash was sufficiently interested in their plight to provide Jefferson a skeletal itinerary, allowing us to piece together an outline of their flight, which was oriented once more toward the sunrise. Traveling again along the Cumberland, which ran south of the "Christian jail," it was east that the pair pushed, following the river, but against its westward flow. Having perhaps learned lessons from their previous experience in the springtime, the two men succeeded for many miles in eluding hostile attention. The stakes were higher now, of course. Increasingly regarded with suspicion, this latest escape would doubtless have confirmed local "suppositions." Unwittingly leaving Kentucky behind, the pair entered the neighboring state of Tennessee, attaining hard-won successes, mile after mile, traveling without aid and avoiding capture. The Africans proved hardy, keeping close to the devious margins of river, as the Cumberland continually wended its way eastward, slowed by regular twists and turns. Finally, as they followed one of the Cumberland's blind bends to the north—where the river rises up into Tennessee's Sumner County—the men were spotted. The pair was "apprehended," as Nash later told Jefferson, and "confined at Gallatin."[20] Against all odds, the escapees had advanced sixty miles. And yet, if exhausted, however, they were not yet finished.

The town where the two Africans were "confined" was named for Albert Gallatin, Jefferson's friend who had just months earlier in 1807 written to the president regarding the "durability of tabby." Winning fame later in life for his study of Native American languages, Gallatin would even be dubbed "the father of American ethnology."[21] In 1807, it was African ethnicity, however, that had forced the two fugitives to halt in Gallatin's namesake town. And yet, this stop would prove to be relatively short for these Muslim men. "[A]fter sometime," Jefferson learned later from Nash, the two Africans once more "escaped from that place also."[22] Again forging along the Cumberland, the fugitive pair was able to cover only half the distance of their first run from Christian County, before being "taken" once more in Tennessee. Advancing thirty-five additional miles, the West Africans reached the middle of the state, where the Cumberland splits in two, its main tributary turning up to the north, and another fork falling down toward the south. Here the Africans made a fatal slip: following the southward route, they were soon stopped once more. On "the Caney Fork" of the Cumberland, the men were captured and conveyed to yet another courthouse, returning to captivity.[23]

A crooked leg at the end of a tortuous trek, there was one last painful irony waiting for the two Africans as they journeyed again to an American jail. Captured on the Caney Fork of the Cumberland, the courthouse to which the men were transported was the seat and center of Smith County—a county named for yet another of Jefferson's friends, a fellow Virginian surveyor and fanatic for maps, Daniel Smith.[24] It was not, however, the name of this county, but the name of the town of their captivity, which seems particularly poignant. The Tennessee town where the two men were taken was named for a famous city from their own home continent, an ancient metropolis on the edge of North Africa. In Tennessee, the two fugitives were "confined" in a small town named Carthage. An African capital whose historic ruins lay in Muslim lands, poised on the Barbary Coast, Carthage was also the US name for a tiny inland settlement where two Muslims found themselves captives in 1807.[25] Languishing in Carthage, there was no confusing Tennessee for Tunisia, however. The two runaways were surrounded by hostile Christian captors, rather than fellow Muslims. And they were still stuck in the American interior, far from any ocean's edges.

Twenty years before, a freshly independent America had been grappling with threats from abroad, confronting especially belligerent North African pirates. In 1786, navigating these national hazards, Jefferson had opened a note from Ezra Stiles, who urged fortitude in the face of Muslim Africa. "*Delenda est Carthago*," Stiles had declared in Latin, quoting the famous exhortation of Cato the Elder: "Carthage must be destroyed!" Now, twenty years later, Jefferson's Muslim fugitives had arrived to Carthage, Tennessee.

And it would be here, in America's own Carthage, that all report of the two Africans, and their aspirations for freedom, would be extinguished.

≈

The same season that witnessed two Muslims once more arrested also saw "Mahomet Volpone" escape yet again. In the autumn of 1807, Aaron Burr had won release in Richmond. And although Chief Justice John Marshall determined "to commit Burr for trial in Ohio," this next proceeding would never take place. He was "bound over for a trial at Chillicothe in January, 1808," but by the winter, the Burr drama had evaporated, with insufficient resolve remaining for his prosecution.[26] The tale of Aaron "the Usurper" was over, but the damage had been done. Rumors of unrest had impacted many lives out West, from governors to senators, and even two African fugitives now trapped in Tennessee. Although Mahomet Volpone had again evaded imprisonment, two innocent "Mahometans" still sat manacled, unjustly "supposed to be Spys."

Acquitted of treason due to lack of evidence, Burr did face consequences, however, but they were societal rather than judicial. A pariah in polite company, Burr's status as an outcast prompted yet another act of flight, departing his homeland altogether. As 1808 dawned, Burr contemplated a period of exile, leaving the United States to live several years in Europe, before returning to relative obscurity in America. Some habits die hard, however, and even as Burr prepared to embark, his flair for the dramatic emerged again.[27] In the days leading up to his overseas trip in 1808, Burr wrote to the person dearest to him, his daughter Theodosia. A letter touching in its intimacy— yet oddly secretive, punctuated with code names and ciphers—Burr ends with a saccharine and melancholy farewell:

> My dear creature, I regret sorely that we cannot meet this evening; but, somehow and somewhere, to-morrow absolutely we will. Perfect arrangements are made for the grand Hegira, and all seems well. Sleep; refresh and strengthen yourself[28]

As histrionic as ever, Burr appeals to a historical reference, casting his impending voyage to Europe as his "grand Hegira." A term of Muslim heritage, "Hegira" is Arabic in origin, signifying the "flight" of none other than the Prophet Muhammad, who fled his enemies in Mecca, seeking refuge in

Medina.[29] Again paralleled to the Muslim Prophet, this time it is Burr himself who adopts an Islamic analogy, even while embracing his impending
identity as an American exile. Invoking Muhammad as his own mirror, Burr
departs his nation cryptically as well as Islamically, with Jefferson's former
vice president now framing himself as a Muslim fugitive.

Burr ends his emotional valediction to Theodosia with a promise of
meeting "somehow and somewhere." After 1808, however, the Burr–
Theodosia relationship would be known for tragic separation. Sailing for
England in June, Burr never saw his beloved daughter again. When her
father finally returned to America in 1812, Theodosia sailed north from
South Carolina for a long-awaited reunion with Burr. But the boat in which
she journeyed—the *Patriot*—was lost at sea, perhaps sunk during a storm.
The *Patriot* was never recovered, however, prompting speculations as to
the cause of its disappearance. Theodosia's fate soon became a matter for
maudlin romance, subjected to the wildest fantasies.[30] Perhaps the most
implausible theory, but one repeated more than once in print, was that
Theodosia's ship was waylaid by Muslim corsairs, and that she herself "was
captured by the Barbary pirates."[31] As the nineteenth century turned to
the twentieth, this absurd "legend" was confidently stated as fact in the US
press. "Theodosia Burr Alston, daughter of Aaron Burr, was doubtless a
later victim of the Barbary pirates," asserted a prominent San Francisco
paper in 1901.[32]

Burr had fancifully aligned himself with Muslim flight, even as he escaped
America, bidding farewell to his dearest Theodosia while launching his
"Hegira" to Europe. Sailing to finally meet her father after his long exile,
however, Burr's own daughter would herself be lost in American waters—a
tragedy that soon submerged Theodosia below the surface of reliable history,
covered over by irrational imaginings of Muslim African violence.

≈

In January 1808, Burr greeted the New Year by planning his escape from
American infamy, accepting an extended exile in Europe. For Jefferson,
January 1808 also heralded exits and endings, but ones more hopeful. The
president had long yearned for retirement, and now his final retreat back to
Monticello was on the horizon. The first days of 1808 signaled the beginning of Jefferson's last full year as president. This upcoming release from office as 1808 began was amplified by another advance toward freedom—an

advance much more earnest and universal. Effective on January 1, 1808, the African slave trade was officially abolished in America. Already outlawed by every state except South Carolina, the American importation of slaves from Africa became a federal crime on New Year's Day.[33] Jefferson was doubtlessly glad for this small step toward emancipation. As he well knew, however, this new law changed little for Africans currently in US bondage. For those already enslaved, this January progress was cold comfort, as it was for the two Muslims who had first surfaced the year before, and whose "release" Jefferson was still hoping "to procure."

Additional pieces of positive news also arrived as the new year began. Apparently, insurrection fever in the West had finally broken during the first winter days of 1808 and health was returning. On January 6, Robert Williams, governor of the Mississippi Territory, wrote to Jefferson from the "town of Washington," Mississippi's territorial capital, near Natchez. Williams had witnessed the Burr "confusion" first-hand, but now reported to Jefferson that "Our Territory is becoming as tranquil as ever it was." "The attempts of the party to throw the Territory into Confusion have intirely failed of success and are render'd harmless," he added.[34] This news from Washington (Mississippi) was entirely welcome in Washington (DC). However, on January 6, 1808, Jefferson was also looking forward to his own domestic "tranquil[ity]." With the start of January, spring would not be far off. Forecasting the season to come with the enthusiasm of a "plain farmer," Jefferson wrote on January 6 to John Taylor, reporting to his Virginian friend regarding an agricultural experiment in the fields of Monticello that he wished to try:

> The African negroes brought over to Georgia a seed which they called Beni, & the botanists Sesamum. I lately recieved a bottle of the oil, which was eaten with sallad by various companies. all agree it is equal to the olive oil. a bushel of seed yields 3. gallons of oil. I propose to cultivate it for my own use at least.[35]

It was the traffic of seeds, not just slaves, that was on Jefferson's mind at the opening to 1808, yearning to "cultivate" at his own home "Beni"—a term African in origin, used by the Gullah peoples of South Carolina and Georgia for "sesame seeds."[36] A culinary legacy from West Africa, Jefferson was hoping to raise this "Low Country" product even further, transplanting it to the top of his little mountain in Virginia. Naming this crop according to its Gullah label—"Beni"—Jefferson would promote the eastward journey of these agricultural roots "brought over to Georgia," cultivating this same seed at Monticello that had long been sown by African Muslims.[37]

On January 6, 1808, amid hopes for tranquility and trade, Jefferson's day was interrupted, and his aspirations were put on hold. Planning the cultivation of an African seed in the soil of his own American home, January 6 would also witness the uprooting of Jefferson's hopes to save two Muslim Africans, whose names he would never know. Jefferson was not only posting his own mail on January 6, 1808, but opening letters, including one dated two months earlier, sent from the far West on November 8, 1807. It carried a signature that Jefferson had first seen at the end of an exhausting day in early October, this letter's initial words reading as follows:

SIR

Those men whose Situation I mentioned to you have made their escape[38]

This was the opening to Ira P. Nash's last surviving letter written to Jefferson, an opening that oddly echoes Jefferson's own first words to Robert Patterson, when the president had written to introduce the Muslim fugitives back in October. Like Jefferson on that occasion, Nash refers only to their humanity, mentioning neither race nor religion. For Nash, these Africans are simply "those men"—men who previously had made trails of illegible ink, and who now had "made their escape," traversing actual trails in the American West. On January 6, even as Jefferson was looking forward to planting African seeds on his own grounds, he would learn that two Africans were no longer on Kentucky soil, breaking their bonds months earlier.

Reading the rest of Nash's final letter, Jefferson learned that the pair had not only fled Christian County, Kentucky, but had been caught and then escaped once more in Gallatin, Tennessee, before finally reaching Carthage via the Cumberland River. It is this letter from Nash that also features his final postscript, revealing a possible reason for the fugitives' urgency: they "are by some supposed to be Spys." Just above this postscript, however, Nash would inscribe a haunting final portrait of the two men, supplying these closing words to his letter's body, written before Nash's own signature:

whither they are there at this moment I am not able to inform myself for I am so far past that place that no person can give me particular information of them—Tis observed that those travellers infalibly steer Eastward when at liberty[39]

Himself in transit, Nash seems still to be pushing home to Missouri even as he posts this letter back to the president in Washington. Although "so far past that place," and moving westward beyond the Mississippi, Nash is yet able to inform Jefferson of the last direction that the fugitive pair had predictably headed: "Eastward." African Muslims, whose lifelong prayers were directed to Mecca, stayed oriented as they "infalibly steered" toward the sunrise. Defined for Nash by acts of daring escape, the two fugitives earn one final title. The last epithet ascribed to these men is not "slaves," nor "negroes," but simply "travellers." For Nash, these men remain in motion, with identities stubbornly itinerant. Perhaps most poignant, however, is Nash's closing word before signing off his last letter to Jefferson. The president would open Nash's letter in the first days of 1808, the same days that saw the African slave trade declared illegal; however, in this letter, the US president also finds that freedom is the last idea associated with this Muslim pair unjustly imprisoned. It is "liberty"—the human right embraced with fraught contradictions throughout Jefferson's entire American career—that concludes his direct contact with two Muslim escapees whose lives were forever after submerged under the silence of incarceration.

18

"His Mountain is made a sort of Mecca"

As 1808 opened, news arrived in Washington that the Muslim fugitives had escaped—again. And, as 1808 unfolded, these fugitives seemed to escape Jefferson's notice as well. The "runners" were on the move, Nash informed the president. Although they had been caught once more in Carthage, Nash could not be sure that these "travellers" had stayed there. "[W]hither they are there at this moment I am not able to inform myself," Nash stressed to Jefferson.[1] On his own return trip, heading toward blurry regions in the far West, Nash was already "so far past that place" that he was unable to offer any further information on the fugitives. In the final months of 1807, Jefferson had failed to find a translator for their Arabic writings; in the first days of 1808, the Arabic authors themselves seemed impossible to find. Their words were too difficult to decipher. Their whereabouts were now uncertain. Perhaps it was just time to let this all go?

But Jefferson did not let it go—at least not entirely. The fugitives had fled eastward into Tennessee, and Nash was too far west to track them. But back in Washington, their Arabic writings stayed secure. The trail of the Muslim authors grew cold during the busy winter of 1808. Yet, the trails of Arabic ink that had arrived to Jefferson in the autumn of 1807 remained entirely tangible, if inexplicable. Through all the upheavals of his later life, these Muslim writings were kept safe, surviving along with countless papers accrued during Jefferson's presidency. Preserved in a single original (Figure 1), as well as in the facsimile duplicate made by Patterson (Figure 9), the Arabic manuscripts stayed with Jefferson as his final full year in office came to an end; and seemingly, they too went into cloistered retirement, even as a new war with Britain was just about to break out in 1812.[2] On August 24, 1814, British forces invaded and incinerated the capital, burning the city's precious books; but Jefferson's own literary encounter with two Muslim slaves' writings would endure, as did his massive collection of personal correspondence and scholarly books sheltered at the top of his "little mountain" deep in the Virginia woods.[3]

The British burning of Washington in 1814—a defining trauma for America during the War of 1812—did not harm Jefferson's Arabic manuscripts. It would, however, come to impact Jefferson's personal library. The nation's "promising congressional library" was a casualty in 1814, its building and its "three-thousand books" reduced to ash.[4] Scandalized by "the destruction of the public library," Jefferson proposed to sell to the capital his own collection—which was double the size—repairing thereby "the Vandalism of our enemy" that had "triumphed at Washington over science as well as the Arts."[5] Rumors of the potential sale evidently spread through the autumn of 1814. Book lovers became pilgrims, making their way to Monticello to view privately the president's legendary library before his books became public property. One such wayfarer was equipped with unusual credentials, carrying a recommendation from Jefferson's old friend and rival John Adams. In a letter dated October 28, 1814, Adams wrote to Jefferson introducing a fellow New Englander:

> Dear Sir
> I have great pleasure in giving this Letter to the Gentleman who requests it. The Revd Edward Everett, the Successor of Mr Buckminster and Thatcher and Cooper in the politest Congregation in Boston, and probably the first litterary Character of his Age and State, is very desirous of Seeing Mr Jefferson. I hope he will arrive before your Library is translated to Washington.[6]

Recently reconciled after years of tense silence, Adams's letter to Jefferson reflects their renewed relationship—a friendship that itself reaches back to US beginnings. Adams's subject, however, is an entirely new connection between the men. Writing to his own presidential "Successor," Adams introduces Jefferson to yet another "Successor": Edward Everett, a rising star of Bostonian intellectual life.

It is no surprise that the young Everett was eager to meet "Mr Jefferson." As Adams well knew, Jefferson and Everett shared many passions, despite their differing ages and regional origins. Partiality to books linked this promising youth from New England to Virginia's patriarch. Journeying south to Monticello, Everett was "very desirous" to "see" not just Jefferson, but his "Library," hoping to arrive before the ex-president's books went north, "translated to Washington." It was not just books in general, however, but "the good Book"—the Bible—that joined Everett to Jefferson. In 1814, Everett was a newly ordained "reverend" preaching Unitarianism, a form of liberal Christianity that had gained ascendency in New England. Confessing divine "unity" while rejecting the Trinity, Everett believed that Jesus was an inspired teacher, not God incarnate—a belief long held by Jefferson, and which he would soon promote by his own innovative act of biblical scholarship. Tied together by private interests, the two men were also linked by public service. Jefferson's illustrious political career was behind him in 1814—a career that the young Bostonian was ambitious to follow. By 1836, Everett would be elected governor of "his State"; by 1852 he had climbed the ranks to become US secretary of state; and, by 1860, Everett would run unsuccessfully for vice president. Everett never attained the very highest offices that Jefferson held. But he did succeed in gaining another presidency not enjoyed by Jefferson; in 1846, Everett was appointed to lead not the United States, but the oldest US college: Harvard.

Such overlaps between the American careers of Everett and Jefferson had parallels far beyond American shores. As Everett embarked for Monticello in 1814, he was considering his own trip overseas, departing the United States after the War of 1812 finally ended in February 1815.[7] Like Jefferson, Everett would visit Europe in the wake of the latest American conflict with Britain— and, like Jefferson, Everett encountered during his post-war travels not only European arts, but also traditions with roots much further east. Thirty years earlier, in 1780s Paris, Jefferson had been invested in Middle Eastern lands and languages, trading covert communiqués and treaties regarding the Muslim world, while acquiring Arabic grammars. Everett would similarly discover overseas the motivations and means to study "Oriental" tongues. In 1814, Jefferson's library was calling Everett to Monticello, with the young reverend hoping to view the collection before it was "translated" to the nation's capital. And yet, Everett would soon encounter in Europe the very same foreign sources that Jefferson had acquired three decades earlier during his own travels abroad.

This foreign link between Jefferson and Everett—with their early sojourns in Europe shaped by Middle Eastern interventions—also returned to America with strange domestic echoes. Everett was a "Successor" to Jefferson in many obvious ways; Everett was his own generation's leading lover of books, a prominent politician, and a European traveler. However, Everett also succeeded Jefferson in a way entirely hidden. While serving as America's third president, Jefferson would encounter Arabic materials penned by US Muslim slaves in Washington; a generation later, again in Washington, Everett would have a strikingly similar experience. In 1807, Jefferson was in-directly handed his "two little Arabic manuscripts" at the President's House;

Everett, twenty years later, would meet an American Muslim at the Capitol Building, welcoming this Arabic author in person at the very center of US legislative power.[8]

In 1814, as Everett departed for Monticello, his meeting with a Muslim slave was entirely unanticipated and still many years in the future. His life, however, would be full of more immediate surprises, the first of which was a looming disappointment: Everett would never make it to the "little mountain." Although "very desirous of Seeing Mr Jefferson," Everett was forced to cut short his travels, recalled to New England by his own congregation, who were apparently "upset" by the young minister's travel plans.[9] Journeying down to meet Jefferson, Everett had reached only as far as Washington, arresting his pilgrimage on the edges of the Potomac.

≈

The most exalted of our young Genius's in Boston have an Ambition to See Montecello, its Library and its Sage. I lately gave a Line of Introduction to Mr Everett, our most celebrated Youth: But his Calls at home, forced him back from Washington.

George Ticknor Esquire who will have the Honour to present this to you, has a reputation here, equal to the Character given him in the enclosed Letter from my Nephew, our Athenæum Man, whom you know.

As you are all *Heluones Librorum* I think you ought to have a Sympathy for each other.[10]

On December 20, 1814, John Adams wrote the above update to Jefferson, apprising his friend that Everett's hopes to reach Monticello had been dashed. But Adams had a substitute. In Everett's place, another young Bostonian was traveling south: George Ticknor—a fellow New Englander on the rise, destined to become Harvard's first professor of modern languages. Everett may have been the "most celebrated Youth" of Boston, but Ticknor was a close second. And unlike Everett, Ticknor had no congregation to complicate his itinerary, arriving at Monticello as planned in January 1815. A fellow "glutton for books"—a "*Heluones Librorum*"—Ticknor shared a literary "Sympathy" with the former president, as Adams predicted. By the time Ticknor reached the little mountain, its elderly master was, however, most worried about his next "literary" meal. Showing off his old library to the young New England scholar, Jefferson also needed help acquiring a new one.

In October 1814, Adams had rightly assumed that Jefferson's "Library" would soon be "translated to Washington." However, when Adams wrote his introduction for Ticknor in December, the purchase of the president's books had not yet been authorized by Congress. Ironically, it was "translation" itself that delayed the library's transfer. Some Washington politicians doubted whether Jefferson's books were suitable for the national library, with many of the former president's volumes unreadable to his fellow Americans, written in a myriad of global dialects, including Middle Eastern tongues. As a nineteenth-century librarian later recalled, "several members of Congress" seemed hesitant to buy Jefferson's library; one of the reasons they balked was that his collection contained "too many books in foreign languages."[11] Nevertheless, on January 26, 1815, Congress finally assented to the purchase, and Jefferson's collection—including his Arabic grammars—was on its way to Washington.[12] Even as the capital was rebuilt, repaired after the British razed its buildings, the Arabic quotations from the Qur'an contained in Jefferson's books would quietly take their place as new blocks in the nation's post-war foundations.

Jefferson's library was authorized for purchase by Congress even as Ticknor climbed the slopes of Monticello, staying with Jefferson for several days near the end of January 1815. As Adams had foreseen, Jefferson enjoyed Ticknor's company, praising the young man extravagantly as "the best bibliograph I have met with."[13] Indulging their appetites, Ticknor first breakfasted with Jefferson on January 21, before these two "gluttons" surveyed his books. In his diary on that day, Ticknor noted that "after breakfast, Mr. Jefferson asked me into his library," a collection "of about seven thousand volumes." Overwhelming in size, Ticknor was inadequate to evaluate the library, finding that "[i]n so short a time I could not, of course, estimate its value, even if I had been competent to do so."[14] Despite his humility, Ticknor's scholarly credentials led Jefferson to solicit his help. Replying to Adams later in 1815, Jefferson informed his old friend that Ticknor:

> very kindly and opportunely offered me the means of reprocuring some part of the literary treasures which I have ceded to Congress to replace the devastations of British Vandalism at Washington. I cannot live without books; but fewer will suffice where amusement, and not use, is the only future object. I am about sending him a catalogue to which less than his critical knolege of books would hardly be adequate.[15]

Oft-quoted, Jefferson's dramatic admission—"I cannot live without books"—emerges in the context of his praise for George Ticknor, grateful for this Bostonian's aid in "reprocur[ing]" his books lately "ceded to Congress."[16] Largely acquired during his early service in Europe, Jefferson's depleted collection would be repaired by Ticknor from his own European travels, the youth acquiring "literary treasures" for the former president, especially sourcing classics for his "amusement."

Ticknor would not set out on his mission alone. On April 16, 1815, he sailed into the Atlantic, and happily, he had company. By his side was seated Edward Everett. The two friends were bound for their first adventure overseas, a sojourn abroad that Everett would regard as an American "pilgrimage."[17] Before reaching Europe, England was the first stop on their itinerary. Seeking to heal "British Vandalism" back at home, Ticknor would arrive in Britain alongside Everett, visiting together the age's most famous English poet, who had himself recently returned from Muslim lands.

≈

The sun, the soil, but not the slave, the same;
Unchanged in all except its foreign lord—
Preserves alike its bounds and boundless fame
That battle-field where Persia's victim-horde
First bowed beneath the brunt of Hellas' sword.

Lord Byron, *Childe Harold's Pilgrimage*,
versifying travels in Ottoman Greece[18]

Lord George Byron in 1815 was a scandalous celebrity—a strange contrast to the two earnest and unknown American youths he encountered in London. Then at the height of his fame, Byron was spending the summer of 1815 publishing installments from his *Turkish Tales*, a series of narrative poems reflecting his recent travels through Ottoman territories, including Albania and Greece—experiences that had also formed the focus of his *Childe Harold's Pilgrimage*, Byron's autobiographical poem, quoted above. Valorizing his voyages in exotic lands, Byron versifies regional stories of Christian slaves taken captive by Muslim rulers, playing up the sensational in poems such as his *The Giour* and *The Corsair*. Byron was himself captivated by his Ottoman sojourn, enthralled especially with Islam. Returning from his travels in 1810, Byron even later purportedly confessed with a dramatic flourish that "I was very near becoming a Mussulman."[19] By the time Everett and Ticknor arrived in London, however, Byron was earnestly opposing Turkish dominion in Europe, championing Greece's independence from Ottoman rule. It was to free Greece from "slavery" that Byron eventually gave his life. Seeking to liberate Hellenic "sun" and "soil" from a "foreign lord," the poet succumbed to sickness in 1824 while advancing Greece's revolutionary campaign against Muslim Turkey, closing his life as "the martyr of Missolonghi."[20]

Britain and Byron were unlikely choices for the beginning of Ticknor and Everett's years abroad. And yet, Byron's wild European engagements would shape the Americans' much more modest plans. Ticknor had left home with a commission from Jefferson, but in Britain the two young Bostonians also accepted a Byronic mission. The US president had asked that Ticknor procure "literary treasures" for him in Europe; but Byron instead required a rather more dangerous treasure be delivered to Muslim Albania. Having met Everett and Ticknor first on June 12, by the end of the month Byron had convinced Ticknor to personally "deliver a pistol" to Ali Pasha—the infamous Vizier of Ioannina.[21] Born in the town of Tepelena, and rising to rule Ottoman territories in the mountainous regions on the Ionian Sea, Ali Pasha was a charismatic and frightening figure, known for both brutal violence and disarming generosity. It was Ali Pasha who had hosted Byron when he arrived to Albania in 1809, during the same tour of Ottoman lands that saw this English infidel reportedly consider conversion.

Sending naïve Bostonians to meet this Muslim governor in 1815, Byron would not learn, for several years, whether his envoys safely arrived. In the end, only one of the Americans would ever meet the mythic Ali Pasha. This time, however, it would not be Ticknor that climbed wooded mountains to pay homage to a national leader. Edward Everett never made it to Monticello; he would, however, be the American that visited Europe's most formidable Muslim.

≈

He expressed great admiration of Lord Byron's poems and thought the *Corsair* the best.

> Edward Everett, in his diary, recording his
> encounter with J. W. Goethe in Weimar, October 1816[22]

Everett and Ticknor left Britain behind in the late summer of 1815. But Byron, or at least his fame, would follow them as they advanced to the Continent. By the beginning of August, the two Americans were in Germany, where they stayed and studied during the better part of the next two years, before traveling on to more exotic areas of Europe. It was in the midst of their German residence, however, that the two New Englanders encountered Europe's most pivotal poet, making a pilgrimage to Weimar, the home of Johann Wolfgang Goethe.

Famed author of the age, it was Goethe's own advanced years that struck the Americans first as they arrived. He had evidently "drank deep of some of the bitterer springs of life," Everett noted in his diary.[23] And yet, the elderly Goethe was still enlivened by poetry and novel projects. As Everett recorded above, Goethe had "great admiration" for one youth in particular. Having traveled to honor Germany's famed author, the Americans heard this homage for a Brit, with Goethe praising Byron and especially his *Corsair*—one of his *Turkish Tales* involving Muslim captivity and piracy.[24] Goethe's partiality for Byron's Oriental dramas, moreover, hinted at his own expanding literary horizons as his old age advanced. "Of late years he has made himself thoroughly acquainted with Persia and Persian literature," Everett remarked in his diary, adding that Goethe:

> Though he does not understand the [Persian] language, he amuses himself with writing the characters.—and has had some of his MSS. illuminated in the Persian manner. He is in general a great admirer of good handwriting, and has a collection of specimens of the writing of great men, in all parts of the world, among the rest, of our Jefferson.[25]

Famed for his *Faust*, the elderly Goethe was reaching beyond Europe to embrace more global interests in 1815, tackling tangible "specimens" from "all parts of the world." Surveying Goethe's latest literary obsessions, Everett notes the German's interest in reading and inscribing Persian—a language written in adapted Arabic script—and even publishing some of his own poetry "in the Persian manner."[26] Although illiterate in Middle Eastern languages, the delicate lines of Persian fascinated Goethe, as does the "good handwriting" of all "great men." Goethe's interest in Islamic "characters" is followed, in Everett's account, by a much more familiar character from America. Cultivating Persian copies, Goethe also collects a presidential original, cherishing an example of handwriting from "our Jefferson." Another national icon privately linked with Middle Eastern letters, Jefferson's own scribbles sit alongside Goethe's Persian illuminations. Completing their pilgrimage in Europe, two Americans found their former president's writings enshrined alongside characters traced in Arabic lines. In 1815, Jefferson's own papers still contained manuscripts in a Middle Eastern language; however, at the same time, his handwriting had won a place "among the rest" in Goethe's "collection," with words written by Monticello's master lying side-by-side with letters from Muslim lands.

≈

Jefferson's handwriting, adjacent to Middle Eastern letters, greeted Everett and Ticknor as they paid homage to Goethe. However, by 1815, Jefferson had already provided Ticknor with his own handwritten guidelines, specifying items he wished to purchase for his personal library—guidelines that themselves included faint Middle Eastern intersections.

Even as he arrived to Germany in the autumn of 1815, Ticknor received Jefferson's thanks for "aid in replacing some of the literary treasures which I furnished to Congress."[27] To better guide Ticknor's efforts, however, Jefferson had enclosed "a catalogue" in his letter, listing classics especially desired. As expected, the former president's list was long on ancient Greek poetry and philosophy; but one item in Jefferson's 1815 wish list may have seemed curious, a book not only much more modern, but also with Middle Eastern margins. Near the bottom of his list of twenty items, Jefferson had included a three-volume work by the prominent English explorer Richard Hakluyt, entitled *The Principal Navigations, Voiages, Traffiques and Discoueries of the English Nation.*[28] Bridging East and West, Hakluyt's *Principal Navigations* spanned opposing ends of the earth, stretching from America to Arabia. Canvassing exotic lands, the second volume of Hakluyt's *Principal Navigations* offers his readers a rare glimpse especially into the "pilgrimage of the Mahumitans, Turkes and Moores unto Mecca"—a Muslim ritual typically concealed from Christian eyes.[29] Describing Islam's sacred city, as well as Mecca's mountainous surroundings, Hakluyt mentions a peak that was said to have offered humanity its very first earthly home:

> Upon the side towards Mecca there are many pipes of water cleare, faire, and fresh, and above all most wholesome, falling down into certaine vessels made of purpose, where the people refresh and wash themselves, and water their cattel. And when Adam and Evah were cast out of paradise by the angel of the Lord, the Mahumetans say, they came to inhabite this litle mountaine of pardons.[30]

Relaying the "Mahumetan" view of "Mecca," Hakluyt surveys the hilly surroundings where "Adam and Evah" started their earthly exile, which is now the same spot where the Muslim faithful wash in "wholesome" waters. An account of sacred pilgrimages, it was this vignette of a "litle mountaine" in Arabia that formed a small part of the order sent from atop Monticello, with Hakluyt's *Principal Navigations* requested by the former president who was safely "inhabit[ing]" his own hilly home in Virginia.

≈

Monticello is a curiosity! artificial to a high degree; in many respects superb. If it had not been called Monticello, I would call it Olympus, and Jove its occupant. In genius, in elevation, in the habits and enjoyments of his life, he is wonderfully lifted up above most mortals. The fog I was told never rises to the level of his mountain[31]

At the very same time that Jefferson's American friends were arriving in Weimar to visit the elderly Goethe, another pilgrimage was underway on the other side of the Atlantic. Richard Rush in October 1816 set out to meet America's retired president, emerging above the "fog" as he climbed the clear peak of this "litle mountaine." Then attorney general of the United States, Rush had first contacted Jefferson four years earlier, presenting the former president with a speech Rush had delivered to "justif[y] the United States declaration of war"—an oration that decried British imprisonment of US sailors, arguing once again that the "impressment of American men [was] even less moral than the enslavement of Africans."[32] Now that the War of 1812 was over, and Jefferson's library had been sold to replace Congress's incinerated collection, Rush would come in person, making a trip to Monticello.

Unlike Goethe, Jefferson appeared undiminished by age in 1816. Indeed, to Rush, the president seemed positively transcendent. Translated into a Greek myth, the president's mountain seemed like "Olympus," and its "occupant"—Jefferson himself—was akin to "Jove." When he spoke with Jefferson, however, another analogy came to Rush's mind. Noting Jefferson's sorrows for his lost books, and his desire to replenish his library from Europe, Rush recalled that:

He lamented to me the loss of his library, and expects an importation of books this fall from Europe. His chief reading is the antient classicks, in the originals. He admitted that they were of no use; but he exclaimed, "they are such a luxury." He reads, he says, no longer for knowledge, but gratification. I need not tell you with what open doors he lives, as you well know that his mountain is made a sort of Mecca.[33]

As part of their own European pilgrimage, Everett and Ticknor had encountered Lord Byron, whose recent Greek travels had inspired his *Turkish Tales*, merging classical antiquity with Muslim modernity. As Rush ascended Monticello, this American slope at first seemed sublimely Greek, "superb[ly]" classical. And yet, Rush would find the master of this "little mountain" to be anything but removed and remote, welcoming strangers with "open doors"— an openness that made Monticello appear closer to a spiritual center. Once the pilgrim had arrived, Jefferson's home no longer seemed a US "Olympus"; instead "his mountain is made a sort of Mecca." It is the most sacred site of Islam that Rush invokes as the analogue for Jefferson's abode—a comparison with ironies that Rush could not possibly have known. On his little mountain, Jefferson was waiting to receive from Ticknor "antient classicks," looking forward to reading these Greek and Latin works once more "in the originals." However, even as Rush heard this "lament" at the "loss" of a library of "classicks," he was unaware that the former president had successfully preserved manuscripts penned by Muslim captives—written relics in Arabic that stayed submerged even as Jefferson dwelt far above the "fog" on top of the "Mecca" that was Monticello.

19

"A Sect by Myself"

In October 1816, Richard Rush climbed Jefferson's mountain and found its occupant "lamenting" the loss of his library. Bereft of its books, Monticello seemed a little airy. Pilgrims kept coming, though, providing company for Jefferson. But without his volumes to read, a vacancy reigned on Jefferson's peak. Miles of shelving needed restocking to make up for the "6,487" books that had migrated north to Washington.[1]

Monticello's shelves were still waiting for American help from abroad. But, by October 1816, all Jefferson could tell Rush was that he was "expect[ing] an importation of books this fall from Europe." Everett and Ticknor had been busy, but they had much more to do than buy books. Unlike the lofty and lonely "genius" in Virginia, the two youths had joined a vibrant community in Lower Saxony. Just a few weeks before Rush arrived at Monticello, Jefferson had received a letter from Ticknor, who raved about his new home at the University of Göttingen—a storied center of European scholarship. Opened by Jefferson in June, Ticknor's letter exults in the joys of college life in Germany, reporting that:

> the principal theologian & most popular professor here (Eichhorn) has written a very learned and eloquent book and delivers to a crowded audience lectures no less learned & eloquent to prove that the New Testament was written in the latter end of the second century—and another professor of much reputation (Schultz) teaches that "a miracle is a natural and a revelation a metaphysical impossibility"—If truth is to be attained by freedom of inquiry, as I doubt not it is, the German professors & literati are certainly in the high road, and have the way quietly open before them.[2]

Intoxicated by Enlightenment free-thinking, young Ticknor celebrates ideals beloved by the elderly Jefferson, including the "freedom of inquiry" on offer at Göttingen. Citing liberal discoveries related to religion and "revelation," Ticknor seems excited by professors who pack lecture halls, even as they tear down traditions. Especially "popular" are scholars such as Johann

Gottfried Eichhorn, who argues that the "New Testament" was "written" long after Jesus's death, not composed until "the latter end of the second century." Biblical mysteries are either myths or mere "natural" events, according to Ticknor's new teachers. Such an empirical approach to the Bible found a sympathetic ear at Monticello, as Ticknor well knew. Ticknor could not know, however, that Jefferson was himself pursuing similar ideas in Virginia. Despite his isolation and lack of a library, Jefferson on his little mountain was treading the same "high road" pursued in Göttingen. While waiting for books from Europe, Jefferson was cutting out both "miracles" and "metaphysics" from his own American bibles; and, at the same time, he was also at work designing a new institution of higher learning.

When Jefferson received Ticknor's letter in June 1816, he was doubtless impressed by its account of Eichhorn, whose rational explanations of religion mirrored Jefferson's own. And yet, Ticknor failed to mention another area of Eichhorn's expertise that might have intrigued Jefferson as well. Not only a biblical critic, Eichhorn was also a linguist, an authority on Middle Eastern languages, and Arabic especially. Dedicated to questioning Christian origins, Eichhorn also helped advance the study of Islamic texts and traditions.[3] Traveling with Everett, Ticknor had journeyed to Europe with a pledge to help replicate Monticello's library. Instead, the American youths would replicate Jefferson's experiences. Back in 1785, during Jefferson's European residence, he was forced to contend with Muslim lands, negotiating war and peace with Arabic-speaking Africans. In 1815, three decades later, arriving to Europe with Jefferson in mind, Ticknor and Everett would find Arabic and Africa once more intertwined.

≈

We commenced this week Abulfedes' *Africa* in Arabick, and find it much easier than I expected.

Edward Everett, diary entry describing his studies
with Eichhorn at Göttingen, December 14, 1815[4]

In June 1816, Jefferson had received his update from Ticknor, hearing of "the high road" open before "German professors & literati." By that time, however, Ticknor and Everett had been studying at Göttingen for many months. First landing in Britain during the summer of 1815, by August the two Americans had departed for the Continent. Byron had requested that his present of a pistol be delivered to the scandalous Ali Pasha in Muslim Albania. But Everett and Ticknor were headed to Germany, where they encountered a rather different celebrity with his own "Oriental" credentials. Eichhorn was the "most popular professor" at Göttingen, teaching biblical criticism to crowds of undergraduates. He also offered, however, Arabic lessons to select students. And, in 1815, it would be a young American who Eichhorn privately tutored in Islam's sacred language: Edward Everett.[5]

Ticknor and Everett had arrived in Göttingen on August 4, 1815. Ticknor was so impressed by the university that he felt "like the pilgrim who had reached the shrine of his faith."[6] It was Everett, however, who seemed most affected by his stay and studies at Göttingen, eventually receiving there his Ph.D., becoming "the first American to be awarded a doctorate at a German university."[7] Although he had traveled abroad to study conventional subjects—Greek literature and the Bible—it was not long before Everett was pursuing Göttingen's most "popular professor" further East, "occupy[ing] himself a good deal with Arabic under Eichhorn," as Ticknor later recalled.[8] By Monday, October 30, 1815, Everett had scheduled "four hours a week for the coming semester" of tutelage "in Arabick with Eichhorn." A couple days later, Everett began to study the alphabet, benefiting from Eichhorn's "Arabick privatissimum" which "was upon the letters." Advancing speedily, Everett eventually began taking an Arabic "lesson of him daily." By mid-December, Eichhorn had assigned Everett his first full Arabic text to read— an assignment that led Everett to record his "easy" success with this Arabic source in his diary, in the entry quoted above, dated December 14, 1815.[9]

Of all books to choose, it was a text entitled "*Africa*" that would stand at the start to Everett's Arabic reading, as he records in his December diary. Written by a medieval Muslim geographer, Abu 'l-Fida, this fourteenth-century survey of Africa would catalyze Everett's Arabic studies in 1815. This specific text was not Everett's choice, yet it was also no coincidence. "Abulfedes' *Africa*" had been a longtime favorite of his Arabic instructor. Eichhorn had dedicated much effort to publishing a modern edition of Abu 'l-Fida's text on Africa in 1791—the same Arabic edition that Everett would much later be prompted to read.[10] Eichhorn's own early work on "*Abulfedes' Africa*" was, as Everett later recorded in his diary, no mere abstraction, but had arisen in the wake of political interests, provoked by the founding of "the African Institution [. . .] in England."[11] Known originally as Britain's Society for the Abolition of the Slave Trade, by 1807 England's "African Institution" was dedicating itself to re-colonizing the continent, securing a new home for freed slaves by working toward "the success and the stability of the Colony of Sierra Leone."[12]

In 1807, Jefferson had been confronted with Arabic writings by two enslaved Africans, and had not only failed to read their documents, but proved incapable of "procur[ing]" their release. It was in this same year— 1807—that "the African Institution" was established, a cause intertwined with Eichhorn's own earlier production of an Arabic edition of *Africa*, which he later taught to the young American, Edward Everett. Traveling with Ticknor, even as his friend secured books for Jefferson, Everett was offered in Europe a linguistic ability that Jefferson had lacked, equipping this New Englander not only to read *Africa* in Arabic, but to read the Arabic writings of Africans—a skill that would come in handy many years later, when Everett himself met a former Muslim slave in Washington, DC. "Abulfedes' *Africa*" was not Everett's selection to start his serious "Arabick" studies, but the personal preference of his professor. And yet, this preference would prove providential for Everett's own life, anticipating an encounter in America that was itself neither "expected," nor at all "easy."

≈

[Virginia] has applied itself to establishments for education, by taking up the plan I proposed to them 40. years ago, which you will see explained in the Notes on Virginia. they have provided for this special object an ample fund, and a growing one. they propose an elementary school in every ward or township, for reading, writing and common arithmetic; a college in every district, suppose of 80. or 100. miles square, for laying the foundations of the sciences in general, to wit, languages geography & the higher branches of Arithmetic; and a single University embracing every science deemed useful in the present state of the world. this last may very possibly be placed near Charlottesville, which you know is under view from Monticello.

Jefferson to George Ticknor,

June 6, 1817[13]

In June 1816, young Ticknor's evangelical fervor for Göttingen education reached Monticello. A year later, Jefferson had his own pedagogical cause to trumpet, sending Ticknor good news from Virginia. The state was adopting a system of education that Jefferson had proposed long ago—a system ascending from "elementary schools" up to "a single University." "Embrac[ing]" both the simplest and most advanced, stretching from "foundations" to the "higher branches," this overhaul of Virginia education was public, but also deeply personal to Jefferson. The state's new schools would conform to "the plan I proposed to them 40. years ago," Jefferson boasts, culminating in a university to lie "under view from Monticello." Offering instruction in "every science deemed useful," this lone university was to be multiple in its disciplines, but also in its dialects, with "Languages" listed by Jefferson as the first of its "sciences." Designing a southern school "to rival Harvard" in New England, Jefferson refused to be excelled by the "high road" Ticknor and Everett had discovered in Göttingen.[14] Instead the University of Virginia would rise on soil just a little lower than Jefferson's own sublime "Olympus."

Jefferson's reply was too late to reach Ticknor in Göttingen. By the time Jefferson's letter was posted in the summer of 1817, Ticknor had moved on, arriving in the European city most cherished by Jefferson himself. Paris in 1785 had witnessed Jefferson's publication of his first book, his 1785 *Notes on Virginia*. In 1817, Ticknor would be in Paris where he received Jefferson's letter, itself suggesting that he consult "Notes on Virginia." Ticknor was in Paris not to read Jefferson's first book, of course, but partly to buy new books for the former president. Writing to a Paris bookseller in advance, Jefferson noted that "I expect mr Ticknor is arriving at Paris about this time," adding that "I pray you to consult him, & consider his advice as absolutely controuling my own choice."[15] Spending his money on books once more in France, Jefferson in 1817 also surrenders his own liberty, deeming Ticknor to be his trustee, allowing this American youth to "controu[l]" his "own choice."

In 1817, Paris would offer two young Americans not only new books, but new experiences. Like Jefferson thirty years earlier, Ticknor—and later Everett, who arrived in the autumn—found France a marvel, dazzled by the city's deep scholarship and its high society. Ticknor was even aided by letters of introduction from Jefferson himself, helping him gain access to exclusive company.[16] If France offered novelties, it also featured continuities. Writing home to Massachusetts by the end of 1817, Everett praised European advances to the current president of Harvard, John Kirkland. Detailing Harvard's Parisian competition, Everett's letter—dated December 3, 1817— even lists the lectures on offer at the "Royale Colleges," noting to President Kirkland that at the Collège de France:

> M. Caussin will unfold the principles of the Arabic grammar & explain select passages of the Coran Mondays, Wednesdays, & Fridays at 8'clock[17]

Tracing a trajectory of Arabic studies stretching from Germany to France, in Paris Everett discovers instruction centered on the same language he had imbibed at Göttingen. Instead of a book on *Africa* by a Muslim geographer, however, it is the Muslim scripture itself that is "select[ively]" explained in Paris, with "the Coran" taught at France's premier "Collège." Invoking Islam's sacred writ as he wrote home to Harvard, Everett's updates were doubtlessly welcomed by President Kirkland. However, Kirkland was anticipating not only news, but Everett's actual return from Europe. Everett's travels were supposed to help him train for a professorship in Classics, hired to lecture on "Greek Literature" at his alma mater.[18] And yet, Everett seemed to be spending his time not only with the *Iliad*, but with Islamic sources, during his European sojourns.

It was not until 1819, as his time abroad was nearing an end, that Everett finally struck out eastward to see Greece itself. However, in the lands of European antiquity, Everett ironically found an outlet for his recent Arabic learning. As Byron had discovered years before, the home of the Athenians was not only under Ottoman control, but also imbued with Islamic culture. By the time Everett returned to Harvard late in 1819, he had visited Greece; but he had learned there not merely how best to teach the niceties of Greek grammar. When he saw President Kirkland once more in New England, Everett's ears had been filled with European lectures, but also with live recitations of the Arabic "Coran" itself.

≈

> From Corfu we passed over in a row boat to the coast of Albania; and pro-
> ceeded to Yanina, its capital, where we were received with great kindness by
> Ali Pacha, to whom I had a letter from Lord Byron
>
> > Edward Everett, recalling his trip
> > toward Greece via Albania in 1819[19]

In the spring of 1819, on his way to Ottoman-controlled Greece, Everett arrived to Albania, where he was hosted with "great kindness" by the notoriously cruel Ali Pasha. Gaining favor with a letter from Lord Byron, Everett was graciously "received," despite having no pistol to offer Ali Pasha as a present.[20] Ticknor was no longer with Everett, having traveled to Spain in 1818; Ticknor too was preparing for his own professorship, invited by President Kirkland to serve as Harvard's new lecturer in French and Spanish.[21] But, even without Byron's gift for Ali Pasha, Everett evidently enjoyed his initial Muslim meeting in Europe—a meeting that would be the first of many.

Advancing overland in March 1819, Everett pushed through Albania, reaching Greece after taking "the road over Mount Parnassus."[22] Thirty years earlier, Abiel Holmes had visited "Parnassus" in America, discovering on that low-lying Georgia plantation a "great literary curiosity" named 'Usman. Everett's climb over the actual mountain of the Muses in Greece surprisingly led to similar Arabic marvels. Reaching Athens, he found in this historic capital not philosophers but Sufis—Muslim mystics known for their sacred chants and ecstatic states. Noting that Greece's "Areopagus" had been "controverted" from a pagan temple into a Turkish mosque, Everett was undeterred, and visited the historic site "to see the performances of a company of Dervises."[23] Detailing the ceremony of this spiritual "sect," Everett jotted down in his diary:

> the Mosque was covered with a straw matted carpet, & sheep skins laid on the floor round the room in a Circle.—The Walls were ornamented with various Arabic phrases in large flourishing characters [. . .] The Service began by the elder Dervish kneeling in the Corner, quite near the Wall, with his face toward it, while 2 more kneeled in the middle of the room, without however responding to the Chant [. . .] which in point of matter seemed monotonous; as the words 'Allah', 'bismillah', 'Mohammed', occurred perpetually[24]

Witnessing a sacred drama of the "Dervishes," Everett accents especially the sensual character of this pious "Service." It is "ornaments" that attract not only his eyes but ears, ranging from the "matted carpet" to the "monotonous" hymn. Unlike most Westerners, however, Everett is able not only to step inside this mosque, but to enter into the very meaning of the "matter." Visually, distinct "Arabic phrases" emerge "in large flourishing characters" on the walls; orally, Everett catches specific "words" in the "Chant." As a result of his recent Arabic studies, Islam's sacred names are available to this Bostonian outsider. Isolating "*Allah*" and "*Mohammed*," Everett also spells out an entire phrase "*bismillah*"—"in the name of Allah"—the very same phrase that an Algerian captive, Richard O'Brien, had inscribed in his own diary almost three decades before.

Everett's travels through Muslim lands would also faintly recall O'Brien's own, involving dangers of "piracy" and shipwreck. Unlike O'Brien, however,

Everett would not be cast into prison, but offered protection by his Muslim contacts. Sailing in the Aegean sea during his 1819 trip, Everett's ship was grounded on a reef, and he was forced to "qui[t] the sinking vessel," as he later recalled. Coming ashore "on the uninhabited side of the isle of Lemnos," it became "necessary that a portion of [his] party should cross the island—a wild, mountain region."[25] Everett braved this upland hike, accompanied only by a single Muslim guide, named Mustapha:

> I crossed the mountain with honest Mustapha, carrying with me, as he well knew, a considerable sum of money, without which the vessel could not have been hired. The inhabitants of the port bore, at that time, a very indifferent reputation; piracy was hardly considered a crime under the law of nations as understood in the Grecian islands. If Mustapha had taken my life in the desolate passes of Lemnos, and made his way with his plunder to the town, there would have been none to inquire into the event, or to quarrel with it if it had come to light. But I felt [s]ecure beneath the protection of his stalwart arm[26]

Washington Irving had invoked the name "Mustapha" unsympathetically and satirically. But, for Everett, Mustapha would signify a savior. Rather than a fictional Muslim spy in the United States, this actual Mustapha in the "Grecian islands" proved to be a "stalwart arm," protecting an American menaced in Eastern lands. Refusing the supposed seductions of "plunder," the servant Mustapha is a source of "protection" despite Everett's vulnerability.

Kept safe by Muslim hands, Everett ended his trip by marveling at Muslim handwriting. Stopping not at Greece merely, Everett drove even further east, moving from territories under Turkish control to Turkey's capital itself. Reaching Istanbul in May 1819, Everett would recall his stay in this city as affording him "an opportunity of seeing the Imperial Mosques," offering a rare glimpse not only of grand architecture, but of "gilded" Arabic:

> Between the tapers is the *Misabah*, or sacred stand on wh[ich] the Koran is opened. Around the walls are sentences from the Koran, gilded & engraved like our sign boards: Of four of them the characters were traced by the present Sultan,—who writes in fine Writing[27]

Training to be a professor of sacred literature, it is scriptural letters that Everett most carefully observes in the above. Unlike his fellow Americans,

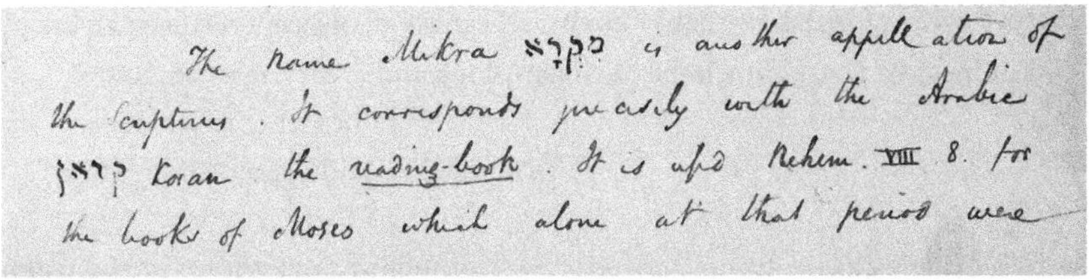
The name Mikra מִקְרָא is another appellation of the Scriptures. It corresponds precisely with the Arabic קראן Koran the reading-book. It is used Nehem. VIII 8. for the books of Moses which alone at that period were

Figure 11 Excerpted from Everett's own manuscript notes on "The Old Testament," the second-to-last line features his inscription of the word "Koran" in Hebrew characters ("קראן"). This title for Islam's scripture— which Everett reproduces in Hebrew, and also renders into English as "the *reading- book*"— is evidently invoked as a comparison for parallel labels from the Bible. Image courtesy of the Massachusetts Historical Society.

Everett is able to size up the "fine Writing" in Arabic that adorns this historic mosque. Capable of discerning "sentences from the Koran" inscribed on its walls, Everett is particularly impressed by "the characters" reportedly "traced by the present Sultan," finding political authority and elegant calligraphy united in this holy space.

Scrutinizing these Qur'anic tracings by the Sultan, Everett would soon return to New England, leaving for home as autumn 1819 neared. The Muslim scripture would follow Everett back to Massachusetts, however. Although Harvard's new professor of Greek, Everett found outlets for his ancient Middle Eastern interests, appealing to Islamic sources in the same scholarly notes that supported his Ivy League teaching, as witnessed in Figure 11.[28]

Two years before he stood in Turkey's capital, Everett had visited Weimar, where he viewed Goethe's collection of Islamic calligraphy placed alongside the "good handwriting" of an American president. During his final excursion to Istanbul, even as his overseas sojourn neared an end, Everett would witness the inscriptions of another national leader, finding phrases from the Qur'an adorning the "walls" of a mosque. Having witnessed this second instance of "fine Writing" in 1819, Everett was ready to return stateside. Little did he know, however, that even as he departed for home and for Harvard, America's own "Grand Turk" was engaged in his own act of sacred inscription, while also seeking to adorn "walls" very near to him with the "Koran."

≈

> As I again approach my native country, I cannot choose but recollect all the
> kindness you have shown me during my long and dreary absence from it
>
> Ticknor's letter to Jefferson
> written while sailing home, May 1819[29]

As George Ticknor "approach[ed]" his homeland once more, in the wake of his "long" absence, it was America's "first citizen" who was first on his mind. This May 1819 letter was written by Ticknor aboard ship, with still no land in sight, and now no friend at his side. Everett was continuing to tour Turkey even as Ticknor departed Europe, feeling rather "dreary" despite his previous enthusiasm. This disappointed tone was perhaps partly put on for Jefferson's benefit, as it was the former president who was let down by Ticknor. Although recruited to help Jefferson secure desired books in ancient languages from Europe, Ticknor refused Jefferson's invitation to become professor of modern languages at the University of Virginia. You have "informed me, how deeply you are interested in the extensive plan for the improvement of Education in Virginia," Ticknor wrote in his May 1819 letter, but added that he simply could not join Jefferson's cause. Instead, Ticknor was returning to Harvard, the same university Jefferson hoped to rival. Coming home, Ticknor's letter to the former president reads like a farewell, his return to the United States signaling a refusal to join Jefferson.

With Ticknor's homecoming to Harvard, Jefferson was left not only without a professor of languages for his fledgling university, but without his traveling book-buyer abroad. Jefferson had other options for acquiring books, however, some of which he desired—others not as much. At the same time Ticknor was penning his letter of apology in the summer of 1819, Jefferson also received an unsolicited package from another young Ivy Leaguer, whose name was strikingly familiar. This package came from Philadelphia, dispatched by a Presbyterian minister, who enclosed his recently published book as a gift—a minister named Ezra Stiles Ely. Christened after Jefferson's old friend—Ezra Stiles—Ely was a Yale graduate and a staunch Calvinist. And, in his 1819 letter to Jefferson, it was his religious commitments that Ely stressed, despite knowing them to differ drastically from the president's Unitarianism.[30] Jefferson responded cordially to Ezra Stiles Ely, but without concession. I have received "the book you were so kind as to forward to me," Jefferson noted in his June 1819 reply, but also clarified his own religious position:

we probably differ on that which relates to the dogmas of theology, the foundation of all sectarianism, and on which no two sects dream alike; for if they did they would then be of the same. you say you are a Calvinist. I am not. I am of a sect by myself, as far as I know.[31]

Musing further on spiritual matters, Jefferson emphasizes his dislike of religious "dogmas" altogether, framing Jesus with the following words:

the benevolent and sublime reformer of that religion has told us only that [God] is good and perfect, but has not defined him. I am therefore of his theology, believing that we have neither words nor ideas adequate to that definition. and if we could all, after his example, leave the subject as undefinable, we should all be of one sect, doers of good & eschewers of evil. no doctrines of his lead to schism. it is the speculations of crazy theologists which have made a Babel of a religion the most moral and sublime ever preached to man, and calculated to heal, and not to create differences.[32]

Acknowledging first Ely's "kind" gift, Jefferson goes on to harshly criticize religious "speculations" and "crazy theologists"—an oblique swipe at Ezra Stiles Ely himself, whose Calvinism had contributed, in Jefferson's view, to making a "Babel" of "religion." Espousing a simple belief in a single God as taught by a merely human Jesus, Jefferson believes that "neither words nor ideas" are "adequate" to express the Absolute. "[W]e should all be of one sect," Jefferson opines, even while ironically defining himself as the ultimate sectarian, his own religious party numbering just one, himself. In the 1780s, Ezra Stiles had exchanged letters with Jefferson, while scrutinizing Arabic writings from Georgia, reading 'Usman's Islamic confession of one "good and perfect" God. Thirty years later, it is Ezra Stiles's namesake—Ezra Stiles Ely—to whom Jefferson sends his own monotheistic confession, espousing a Unitarianism that recalls Islam's rejection of a complex godhead, figuring Jesus as merely a man, though highly "moral and sublime."

The book and beliefs that Ezra Stiles Ely sent in 1819 were very little to Jefferson's liking. But, as this year advanced, Jefferson would set about making his own book reflecting his religious views, generating "*The Life and Morals of Jesus of Nazareth*." Now known widely as "The Jefferson Bible," this homemade book was an abridgement of the gospels, produced by literally slicing out selections from multiple editions and pasting them together to form a refined canon. At the same time that cutting-edge Göttingen professors were criticizing biblical miracles, Jefferson manually cuts out these supernatural elements, "extracting" from the gospels everything indicating divine intervention.[33] Retaining only passages reflecting Jesus's humanity, Jefferson's revised gospel ends without a resurrection, concluding merely with the morbid words "There laid they Jesus: and rolled a great stone to the door of the sepulchre, and departed."[34] Hiring a bookbinder to formalize this self-fashioned volume, Jefferson encased his "Life" of Jesus in hard covers, even as the text itself encloses the original Christian "reformer" within a stony tomb.

Aptly final, "The Jefferson Bible"—with its "sepulchral" ending—helped round out the library that the former president collected during the last years of his own life, becoming one more volume for Monticello's shelves. However, even after 1819, Jefferson continued to contribute to another library. As part of his "extensive plan for the improvement of Education in Virginia," Jefferson spent some of his last years ordering books for the University of Virginia, ensuring that the school's undergraduates had access to the latest advances in all sciences, including religion. Jefferson would keep his *The Life and Morals of Jesus of Nazareth*" for himself; but, for his cherished university, Jefferson acquired other sacred texts, with their own religious risks. Buying some of the same books that his young American friends had read at Göttingen, Jefferson purchased for his University of Virginia dozens of volumes published by none other than Johann Gottfried Eichhorn—Europe's prolific biblical critic, as well as Everett's personal teacher of Arabic.[35]

In one of his last orders for the university library, Jefferson sought to secure not just studies authored by a European Arabist, however, but the Arabic scripture itself. Conferring with Madison concerning their wish list for the "Theological Catalogue for the Library of the University," Jefferson stipulated an item echoing moments from his earlier career. Listed among the volumes to be acquired for his Virginian institution, the former president specifically requested a copy of:

The Koran.[36]

As their peers in France and Germany, American students too, Jefferson believed, should have access to the Muslim scripture. When an undergraduate in eighteenth-century Virginia, Jefferson had privately acquired his own copy of *The Koran.* For Virginia undergraduates in the nineteenth century, Jefferson sought to make available the Qur'an free of charge, bequeathing Islam's foundational text to the same institution he had helped to found.

Jefferson's homemade bible would remain his personal property, alongside Arabic manuscripts acquired many years before, written by Muslims who had chosen their own scriptural passages to inscribe. Although preserving privately such select items, Jefferson ordered for his public "seminary" at least one source that portrayed Jesus as a mortal prophet, with the former president seeking to keep "the Koran" close at hand for those studying under Monticello's gaze.[37]

20

"Slave of the Most Merciful"

In the opening days of 1819, Jefferson witnessed his life's last major achievement. After years of preparation, the University of Virginia was approved, its charter passed by the state's General Assembly on January 25.[1]

Officially instituted, Jefferson's university yet still seemed somewhat aspirational in 1819. Much remained to do down below in Charlottesville. It would take time to attract sufficient students, and the construction of adequate buildings would extend through 1826, the same year that Jefferson died.[2] Overseeing the school's staggered start, Jefferson ensured that the end of his life also helped to advertise his fledgling university. His memorial, planted on Monticello's own grounds, would proudly commemorate the college. Of the three achievements celebrated on Jefferson's epitaph, the first two frame him as an "Author"; he was the writer of the "Declaration of American Independence" and "the Statute of Virginia for religious freedom." The final legacy claimed by Jefferson, however, shifts from his pen to his paternity. On his grave, Jefferson is lastly labeled "Father of the University of Virginia." For Jefferson, this institution was the child of his old age; it was fathered, not merely founded. Although the future alma mater of countless Virginians, the university begins by making a pater once more of Thomas Jefferson.[3]

1819 started with this paternal success for Jefferson, but this year also marked a troubling time for Jefferson's surrogate son. In his youth, John Quincy Adams had "appeared [. . .] to be almost as much" Jefferson's "boy as mine," as his actual father, John Adams, acknowledged.[4] By 1819, however, John Quincy was no longer a carefree "boy," but an anxious politician grappling with Jefferson's own legacy. This year, the same that witnessed Jefferson's last achievement, John Quincy was questioning the first achievement later inscribed on Jefferson's epitaph: his Declaration of Independence. During the decade and a half that had followed their dinner together during Ramadan in 1805, the younger Adams had steadily risen. Appointed a professor at Harvard in 1805, John Quincy returned to politics in 1808, and was eventually appointed secretary of state in 1817.[5] By 1819, he was only six years away from attaining even higher office. Following in the footsteps of both of his "fathers," John Quincy would be elected president in 1825, entering a White House rebuilt after being burnt by the British a decade earlier.

This promising political future was not on John Quincy's mind as 1819 came to a close. Instead, he was preoccupied with the perilous future of the same Republic his fathers had founded. It was the "Missouri Question" that dominated the national debate in December, with the territory's proposed admission to the Union enflaming sentiments, North and South, sparking debates regarding slavery's expansion. Would Missouri be admitted as a free state, or a slave state? Even Jefferson returned to the fray from retired seclusion; "the Missouri question aroused and filled me with alarm," Jefferson wrote to his old personal secretary and friend, William Short, expressing his worries regarding the "Union" and its "duration."[6] For John Quincy, it was not the elderly Jefferson's current anxieties, but his early authorship, that seemed central to the debate. The crux of America's problem could be seen in its former president's contradictions, which in December 1819 seemed to forecast even more ominous conflicts to come. With chilling prescience, John Quincy in the dying days of 1819 wrote the following entry in his diary, dated December 27:

> Jefferson is one of the great men whom this country has produced, one of the men who has contributed largely to the formation of our national character—to much that is good and to not a little that is evil in our sentiments and manners. His Declaration of Independence is an abridged Alcoran of political doctrine, laying open the first foundations of civil society; but he does not appear to have been aware that it also laid open a precipice into which the slave-holding planters of his country sooner or later must fall. With the Declaration of Independence on their lips, and the merciless scourge of slavery in their hands, a more flagrant image of human inconsistency can scarcely be conceived than one of our Southern slave-holding republicans. Jefferson has been himself all his life a slave-holder, but he has published opinions so blasting to the very existence of slavery, that, however creditable they may be to his candor and humanity, they speak not much for his prudence or his forecast as a Virginian planter. The seeds of the Declaration of Independence are yet maturing. The harvest will be what West, the painter, calls the terrible sublime.[7]

A paragon of the "national character" for John Quincy, Jefferson is an ambivalent founding father, both a plantation "slave-holder" and an author whose ideals will "blast" the "very existence of slavery." Embodying "much that is good," as well as "not a little that is evil," Jefferson seems a sower of "seeds," literal and literary. He is "a Virginian planter" whose own fields are worked by African captives; and yet Jefferson has also planted freedom for all peoples in the "maturing" liberties of his "Declaration of Independence." The "human inconsistency" of the South, typified by Jefferson himself, portends a frightful reckoning, John Quincy suggests. The "harvest" of Jefferson's high principles will be a bloody abyss, the nation falling over a "precipice" while also ascending to witness its "terrible sublime."

Adams's diary entry—dated December 27, 1819—not only predicted America's coming conflict, but was penned exactly forty-one years before this national tragedy was sparked. It would be on December 27, 1860, that South Carolina launched the "first overt act of the Civil War," seizing Castle Pinckney, a federal fort, which eventually became a prison for captured Union soldiers.[8] Uncannily far-sighted, John Quincy's prediction of America's future ironically finds him appealing to Islamic prophecy. Jefferson's "Declaration of Independence" is itself aligned with Muslim scripture; for John Quincy, the best description of Jefferson's founding document is "an abridged Alcoran of political doctrine." Like the Qur'an, Jefferson's "Declaration" is authoritative and original, establishing a new civil society, while accruing sacred status. This private comment by John Quincy seems especially intriguing considering its date—1819—the same year in which Jefferson was himself "abridging" another scripture, cutting up the Christian gospels, denying Jesus's divinity, offering a Unitarian message that overlaps Islam. In crediting Jefferson with authoring his own Qur'an of American liberties, however, John Quincy was also unaware, of course, that Jefferson had himself confronted passages from the actual "Alcoran" in Arabic a decade earlier, inscribed by two Muslim slaves striving for their own liberties in America.

In the weeks after John Quincy penned his prophetic remarks, the "Missouri Question" was settled. Congress had come to its notorious "compromise," which purportedly maintained a precarious "balance of power" in the United States. Missouri and Maine would be admitted to the Union together, the first as a "slave state," the second as a "free state."[9] This 1820 tradeoff sought to prevent, but would only postpone, the horrible "harvest" John Quincy had foreseen. If delaying the Civil War, the "Missouri Compromise" also represented another step toward America's "terrible sublime" sparked forty years in the future. A shameful landmark for the nation, expanding slavery westward, the "Missouri Compromise" was a "turning point" for John Quincy personally. Regarded as an immoral capitulation to Southern "planters," Missouri's admission to the Union and its pro-slavery constitution galvanized John Quincy's political resolve, even as he soon rose to accept America's highest political office, winning the presidency by the middle of the decade.[10]

In 1825, John Quincy entered the White House, taking the oath of office on March 4. A second generation of US politicians was now ascendant, with original patriots beginning to fade. Of all the founders, Jefferson, however, was neither easy to replace nor easy to forget. Jefferson would witness John Quincy enter their country's highest office in 1825, and would still have one more year to live. The epitaph of this "Author" and "Father" was not to be laid until 1826. With enduring relevance, Jefferson's "abridged Alcoran" of 1776 remained essential to American debates, of course; however, Jefferson's living oracles were also still coveted in 1826. Mere mortals, living in the lands overlooked by his "sort of Mecca," continued to seek Jefferson's opinions from on high, soliciting "sublime" pronouncements from Monticello.

≈

on the question of the lawfulness of slavery, that is, of the right of one man to appropriate to himself the faculties of another without his consent, I certainly retain my early opinions. on that however of third persons to interfere between the parties, and the effect of conventional modifications of that pretension, we are probably nearer together.

Jefferson to Edward Everett,
April 8, 1826[11]

These sentences are among the very last that Jefferson ever wrote on the subject that has most tarnished his legacy. Specifically, this is the final time that the word "slavery" surfaces in the extant correspondence of America's third president. And, of all the people in Jefferson's life, it is to Edward Everett that these words were addressed.[12]

Written in April 1826, a full year into John Quincy Adams's presidency, these final sentences on "slavery" seem to justify the ambivalent portrait of Jefferson sketched by his dear "boy." Jefferson's words are replete with the "human inconsistency" that so concerned the younger Adams in 1819. Jefferson had celebrated his very last birthday five days before, having turned seventy-three on April 13, 1826. Even as he entered his final weeks of life, however, Jefferson informed Everett that he still "retain[s]" his "early opinions" on slavery. I reject the "right of one man to appropriate to himself the faculties of another without his consent," Jefferson proclaims. And yet, still a lawyer to the end, Jefferson undercuts this bold assertion with juridical reservations. Although opposed to slavery in the abstract, Jefferson sees no legal basis for "third persons to interfere between the parties" in this immoral institution. In 1825, American law for Jefferson ensured the status quo, keeping Africans enslaved—including hundreds of his own.[13] Writing as if with objective disinterest, Jefferson keeps one fact from Edward Everett. Two decades earlier, the president had not stayed so neutral. At the beginning of October 1807, Jefferson had received Arabic manuscripts that moved him to play the role of a "third person"; seemingly ready to "interfere," the president had taken steps, although preliminary and conditional, toward securing the freedom of two African escapees in Kentucky. At least once in his life, Jefferson had expressed willingness to obtain liberty for enslaved men in America whose "faculties" were "appropriated" without "consent." This particular moment of contradiction is left unmentioned to Everett, even as Jefferson addresses his career's greatest contradiction—"slavery"—for the very last time. However, it is precisely this contradiction that would have been especially meaningful to Jefferson's addressee. Edward Everett would soon encounter a situation with odd echoes of Jefferson's own.

Jefferson's last views on slavery were not volunteered unsolicited. Everett had prompted these opinions by sending Jefferson yet another publication— not a book from Europe, but a speech authored by Everett himself. Sworn into office the same year as John Quincy Adams, Everett had been elected as a Massachusetts congressman in 1825. Only a year into his term, however, Everett's constituents were taken aback by a speech he delivered in Congress, voicing a surprising stance on slavery. It is this speech that Everett had sent to the ex-president from Washington on March 29, 1826, his cover letter beginning:

> Dear Sir,
> I beg leave to ask Your acceptance of a speech lately delivered by me, on a motion to Amend the Constitution.—Some of the doctrines, I fear, will not meet your approbation, particularly those on the subject of slavery: which, while my Countrymen in New England are severely attacking them, are

also at Variance with those, so powerfully expressed in Your Notes on Virginia.[14]

Everett had first come to Jefferson's attention in 1815, when he was endorsed by John Adams as the "first litterary Character of his Age and State." A decade later, however, Everett was disappointing many of his "Countrymen in New England." The primary aim of Everett's speech had been to argue against "Amend[ing] the Constitution"—an issue that arose in the aftermath of John Quincy's 1824 election, which was closely contested. No candidate had received sufficient votes to claim victory, and the election was turned over to Congress to arbitrate. Adams was acclaimed president in a "backroom bargain" facilitated by none other than Henry Clay, the Kentuckian who had once secured Aaron Burr's freedom.[15] John Quincy's foes called for a constitutional amendment to prevent Congress from deciding such close contests in the future. Everett argued against this amendment. And yet, in a concession to John Quincy's opponents, many of whom were Southerners, Everett also noted that the Constitution protected their region's "rights" as well. Setting himself against Northern "radicalism," especially recent enthusiasm in New England to recolonize Africa with released American slaves, Everett argued against the North's "interference" in slave-holding states. Such a position made Everett seem not only more conservative than fellow Bostonians, but more sympathetic to the South than his old friend from Virginia.[16] Jefferson himself had "powerfully expressed" support for African colonization in the very volume Everett here invokes as "Your Notes on Virginia," namely the 1785 *Notes on the State of Virginia*. This cause was, however, much more recently linked to Jefferson, with the retired president helping to inspire the American Colonization Society, even earning him dubious repute as "a founding father of colonization."[17]

Everett was a Bostonian who had never owned another human being. And yet, in seeking compromise to avoid national catastrophe, Everett found himself cast as a defender of Southern "rights" against Jefferson, a "Virginian Planter" and slave owner. Jefferson replied with a gentle rebuke on April 8, 1826, offering his final explicit statements on "slavery," suggesting that no one has the "right" to "appropriate [. . .] the faculties of another."[18] His letter also ended with an invitation, however, welcoming Everett to complete the trip to Monticello he had begun years before. "In some of the letters you have been kind enough to write me," Jefferson concludes, "I have been made to hope the favor of a visit from Washington. it would be recieved with sincere welcome."[19] Everett responded one last time on April 16, 1826, defending his speech against Northern "interference" as motivated by the "impracticable" character of "Emancipation":

> On the subject of Slavery, I do not mean to maintain that in the Abstract, One man has a right "to appropriate to himself the faculties of Another with-out his Consent."—But it is Another question, whether, taking things as they Are, the kind and Merciful Master, who feeds & clothes and from birth till death supports his Slave, has not a right to his obedience, in a State of Society, where a general Emancipation is allowed to be impracticable. [...]
>
> I feel much indebted to You for your kindness in inviting me to Monticello. Mrs Everett and our two little children Are With me this Winter, & the inconvenience of travelling En famille, As well as our General impatience to get home after the long session, will prevent my availing my-self of Your kind invitation this Year. Another session I may have it in my power.[20]

Quoting Jefferson's own words back to him, Everett also mirrors the president's contradictions. Like Jefferson, Everett finds slavery repugnant in the "Abstract," but this institution's abolition seems "impracticable" in the current climate. Assuaging his own conscience with an empty hypothetical, Everett imagines the situation of a supposedly "kind and Merciful Master," while positing America as a static "State of Society" with little or no potential for "a general Emancipation."

A disappointment to his Northern neighbors, Everett ends his letter by promising to fulfill his pilgrimage down south to Monticello. This last promise would too be broken, however. But, this time, it was not Everett's travels abroad, but Jefferson's own final departure that forever prevented the visit. "Another session" for the aging Jefferson would never come. Everett's letter arrived just months before Monticello's "Jove" would vanish. And, it was Everett's own family—including his "two little children"—that forestalled any late plans to visit. Everett was *En famille,* which restricted his travel, he noted to Jefferson. Fatherhood, at least in Everett's mind, would prevent his ever meeting the nation's own father in the flesh.

≈

In 1826, Jefferson wrote to Everett, citing for the last time African "slavery," while neglecting to mention his "intervention" long ago on behalf of two enslaved Muslims. 1826 would also witness the first letter written by yet another Muslim enslaved in America—a Muslim who would soon come face-to-face with Edward Everett. This African was no mere "Abstraction," but he did in at least one sense match Everett's ideals, defining himself as a "slave" of a "Merciful Master." The Arabic name of this enslaved man precisely echoed Everett's own phrase. He was Ibrāhīm 'Abd ar-Raḥmān—"Abraham, the Slave of the Most Merciful."[21]

'Abd ar-Raḥmān had already endured four decades of American slavery when he wrote his first recorded Arabic letter on October 3, 1826—an act of authorship that would result in his rising to become the most celebrated Muslim slave in the United States.[22] A native of Futa Jallon, and son of its late Emir, 'Abd ar-Raḥmān was also a compatriot of the enslaved Muslim encountered by Abiel Holmes on Parnassus Plantation: 'Usman. Taken from the same African homeland, the American destinations reached by 'Abd ar-Raḥmān and 'Usman in the 1780s differed starkly. While 'Usman was made captive on the East coast, 'Abd ar-Raḥmān was enslaved in western Mississippi, which was still in Spanish hands.[23] It would be Jefferson's successors who eventually met 'Abd ar-Raḥmān; but it was Jefferson who helped negotiate the national borders that shaped this enslaved man's life. Prompted by American interests in trafficking on the Mississippi, Jefferson would be "unremitting in his efforts" to secure rights around the river—efforts that would bear fruit finally in 1795, during Jefferson's brief hiatus from public service, with the Treaty of San Lorenzo.[24] In this transfer of Natchez's surroundings to US control, 'Abd ar-Raḥmān now found himself enslaved in an ever-expanding republic, full of mighty rivers, which was first envisioned by the master of Monticello.

Made to work a plantation north of New Orleans, 'Abd ar-Raḥmān was enslaved near Natchez, Mississippi—the same town from which Andrew Marschalk had reported to Jefferson of yet another territorial handover, with Louisiana passing from Spain to France in 1803, leading up to its final US acquisition. Marschalk had been in Natchez four years later, to cover the controversies swirling around "Mahomet Volpone" as Burr arrived in Mississippi. Finally, two decades later, Natchez events would prompt Marschalk to make another report, this time in reaction to an actual "Mahometan" slave. Traveling to Thomas Foster's plantation in 1826, Marschalk witnessed 'Abd ar-Raḥmān write a "letter in Arabic" at "Natchez on October 3"—a letter that was penned "in my presence," Marschalk proudly reported, employing precisely the same phrase used by Abiel Holmes in 1788 when marveling at 'Usman's Arabic writing in Georgia.[25] Sending north this news of a slave's literacy, Marschalk's 1826 report from Natchez made its way to Washington, with 'Abd ar-Raḥmān's Arabic writings eventually handed to none other than Henry Clay, serving as secretary of state under John Quincy Adams.[26] No longer concerned with massive territorial transfer, as was his 1803 update to Jefferson, Marschalk's communications with the capital now concerned the repatriation of a single Muslim. And unlike the sly Mahomet Volpone, once liberated by Clay, this authentic "Mahometan" from Africa deserved to be freed from his Natchez confinement. We should be "sending him home," Clay would conclude, convinced by Marschalk's letter.[27]

Penned on October 3, 1826, 'Abd ar-Rahmān's Arabic letter dispatched to Washington shared sacred content with the "two little Arabic manuscripts" carried to Jefferson in the same city two decades earlier—and was also written for the very same purpose. 'Abd ar-Rahmān's letter reportedly "was made up of quotations from the Koran so pieced together as to constitute a plea for help," with this act of copying the Muslim scripture once again reflecting an American slave's desire to be released.[28] This Arabic letter would ultimately yield success, however, not the failure experienced by the fugitives who had copied the Qur'an in pages conveyed to Jefferson; but this 1826 letter's success was partly due, however, to groundwork established by Jefferson's own earliest engagements with the Muslim world. In December 1786, Jefferson had received the first US treaty with Morocco, signing this compact on the New Year's Day that followed; four decades later, in 1826, the United States now had a consul in Morocco, where 'Abd ar-Raḥmān's letter was sent under the misapprehension that this Muslim slave must be North African in origin.[29] Eventually, Morocco's own Sultan himself would petition for 'Abd ar-Raḥmān's release, a petition that prompted John Quincy Adams himself to act, hoping to make "favorable impressions in behalf of the United States," as Henry Clay would inform Marschalk.[30] Unlike Jefferson's initial entanglements with Islam and captivity—marked by the failure to secure O'Brien's release from Algiers—Jefferson's "own boy," John Quincy Adams, managed to help secure release of a Muslim African enslaved in America. Twenty years after Jefferson's receipt of two mysterious Arabic manuscripts, American diplomacy in the Muslim world was itself advanced by means of the penmanship of an enslaved West African.

Arabic writings in Washington had finally helped release an enslaved Muslim. And, in Washington, 'Abd ar-Raḥmān would receive a personal welcome. Although now free, 'Abd ar-Raḥmān elected to lengthen his unhappy stay in America for the sake of his extended family. During his decades of enslavement, he had not only married, but fathered children and grandchildren whose liberty he needed to secure before leaving US shores. Petitioning to purchase his family's freedom, 'Abd ar-Raḥmān embarked on an east-coast "fund-raising tour," supported by none other than the American Colonization Society.[31] To attract attention and financial aid, 'Abd ar-Raḥmān even played the part of a Moroccan "Prince," wearing "Oriental" garb, a getup that included a scimitar and turban as he traveled north.[32] Recalling William Eaton at Burr's trial, 'Abd ar-Raḥmān donned stereotypical trappings of the Muslim world, seeking to win notice. Unlike Eaton and his self-centered concerns—courting fame and womanizing with a "harem"—'Abd ar-Raḥmān's Oriental act aimed to save the woman and children he loved.

With such flourishes, 'Abd ar-Raḥmān finally reached Washington in the May of 1828, two decades after news of two other Muslim fugitives had reached this same city much more quietly. A curiosity to congressmen, and a wonder at the White House, 'Abd ar-Raḥmān would himself, however, meet with an oddity in America's high halls of power. At the US Capitol itself, 'Abd ar-Raḥmān encountered an American for whom Arabic writings were not at all strange, but uncannily familiar.

≈

The African Prince called to see us. I gave him 5$. His story is exceedingly curious.

Edward Everett entered this terse record in his diary on May 25, 1828, recording 'Abd ar-Raḥmān's Sunday visit to the US Congress.[33] In very few words, Everett describes his meeting with this freed Muslim slave, contributing also only a few dollars to his cause. A modest tribute for an African "Prince," Everett's "5$" and his brief entry seem economical, but his encounter with 'Abd ar-Raḥmān would prove immensely valuable, its impact deepening through time.[34] Contributing little to the collection of this "African Prince," Everett yet notes that 'Abd ar-Raḥmān's "story is exceedingly curious"—a "story" that stayed fresh in his mind, with Everett able to recall decades later his first encounter in vivid detail:

I saw this remarkable person, who was then probably about sixty-five years of age. He was rather tall and spare, but quite erect. His hair was white, but he had apparently none of the infirmities of age. He spoke the English language and without accent. His complexion was quite black, but his features not of the common African type. He had an ease and dignity of manner which I have never seen surpassed, and which, considering the life he had led, were truly wonderful. His deportment would have been thought that of a gentleman in any company, however refined. He was evidently one of nature's nobility. Besides his knowledge of the literal Arabic, he was acquainted with several of the living dialects of Western Africa.[35]

Playing on this freed slave's princely profile, Everett frames 'Abd ar-Raḥmān as "nature's nobility" even as he accents "features" of ethnicity, emphasizing "complexion" and color. It is not 'Abd ar-Raḥmān's skin but his culture, however, that seems most "[un]common" to Everett, who sees not genetics, but a "gentleman," in this African Muslim. 'Abd ar-Raḥmān is a sophisticated scholar, his linguistic capacities exceptional, even among this "company" of congressmen. Speaking "the English language and without accent," 'Abd ar-Raḥmān's verbal skills also bridge the "literal" and the "living." Not only is he "acquainted" with "dialects of Western Africa," he is endowed with "knowledge" of "Arabic."

It was his literacy in Arabic, of course, that had gained 'Abd ar-Raḥmān his liberty, and it also kept him locked in Everett's memory. Marveling at his "ease and dignity of manner," 'Abd ar-Raḥmān's "manner" was "never [. . .] surpassed" for Everett. It was not merely "wonder," however, that Everett took away from their meeting, but material proof of 'Abd ar-Raḥmān's "extraordinary attainment"—proof that Everett privately retained, secluded among his papers. In encountering 'Abd ar-Raḥmān, Everett was not the only one to give a gift in 1828, receiving a note from the Muslim slave worth much more than "5$." As Jefferson in Washington two decades before, Everett would be handed Arabic lines authored by an African Muslim in search of American emancipation. And, just like Jefferson's "two little manuscripts," this document penned by 'Abd ar-Raḥmān would stay hidden until now, reproduced here for the first time as Figure 12.[36]

> His name is 'Abd ar-Raḥmān in the land of Futa Jall(on)
> [son of] our Imām Ibrāhīm in the land of [. . .]
> [may God bless] Muḥammad, His prophet, /

and his people, and his companions, and grant him peace entire.
The Shaikh, the jurist, the Mecca[n] and Medina[n], Adam, said:
"O Allah, and in Allah, and from Allah" [. . .]

Not content to leave America's orator empty-handed, 'Abd ar-Raḥmān authors his own literary performance for Edward Everett—a single page of Arabic that epitomizes "[h]is story," filled with names, both African and Islamic, spanning the personal, the familial, and the spiritual. An act of introduction, this page aptly starts with the author himself—"his name is 'Abd ar-Raḥmān," he declares, writing in the third person as did his compatriot, 'Usman, when introducing himself in Georgia nearly three decades before.[37] It is the name at the end of this single page, however, that 'Abd ar-Raḥmān offers most insistently, concluding with: "O Allah, and in Allah, and from Allah." Repeating Islam's most exalted divine name—an Arabic term unreadable to most American congressman in 1828—this pious repetition was, however, entirely familiar to Everett. He had heard a similar "monotonous" chant in Ottoman-controlled Athens, sitting with Sufis as they "perpetually"

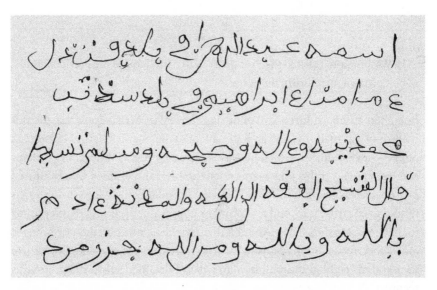

Figure 12 The first five lines of the Arabic document authored by 'Abd ar-Raḥmān, retained in the papers of Edward Everett, with my English translation above. Never before published, this image is reproduced from the original held by the Department of Special Collections of the Hesburgh Libraries of Notre Dame.

uttered the "word Allah." Now, far from Greece's own ancient capital, Everett would receive this repeating Islamic formula, even as he held a position at the US Capitol—a formula that 'Abd ar-Raḥmān himself quotes from his own "Shaikh," who is associated with Arabia's sacred capitals, "Mecca" and "Medina."[38]

In light of 'Abd ar-Raḥmān's own mission in 1828, it is understandable that not heaven, but his own homeland, is also emphasized in this page preserved by Everett. Immediately after his own name, 'Abd ar-Raḥmān spells out his place of origin—"Futa Jallon"—as well as his father's name, the late emir, "Imām Ibrāhīm." Unsurprisingly, both his own father and motherland were foremost in 'Abd ar-Raḥmān's mind as he sought to return home in 1828, hoping to secure funds to repatriate not only himself, but his entire family. Seeking to redeem his own sons from slavery, 'Abd ar-Raḥmān visited the House of Representatives, where he met Everett; however, 'Abd ar-Raḥmān had already visited another house, encountering there a fellow son of a former national leader. As a freed Muslim slave, 'Abd ar-Raḥmān made his way to the White House on May 22, 1828, where he found Jefferson's own surrogate "boy" serving as US president.

≈

In Washington, I visited the President's house, but I found the President the best piece of furniture in the house[39]

In a letter to his children still enduring slavery in Mississippi, this memorable quip was made by 'Abd ar-Raḥmān following his visit to the "President's house"—a visit during which he was received by both John Quincy Adams and Henry Clay. If this joke seems uncharitable, John Quincy would himself prove even less generous on May 22. In the president's own diary, he notes his refusal to contribute to 'Abd ar-Raḥmān's collection, declining to offer funds to this freed Muslim slave. "Abdul Rahaman the emancipated moor brought me a subscription book to raise a fund for purchasing the freedom of his five sons and his eight grand-children, to which I declined subscribing," Adams recorded.[40]

Even as Adams Jr. received 'Abd ar-Raḥmān in Washington, it was likely that the president's own parents, natural and adoptive, were on his mind. John Quincy had first heard of a Muslim diplomat—also named 'Abd ar-Raḥmān—from his mother. This diplomat, the "Minister from Tripoli," had attracted the eyes of Abigail Adams in London, while also raising the ire of her husband, John Adams Sr. Years later, John Quincy broke bread with yet another Muslim envoy—Mellimelni—at a dinner hosted by Jefferson, which was delayed to coincide with the end of the day's Ramadan fast. In 1828, John Quincy had helped secure 'Abd ar-Raḥmān's own release; however, he now refused to take further political risk, or personal exposure, by expending money to help free this Muslim's enslaved family. Looking for protection, 'Abd ar-Raḥmān—a supposed "emancipated moor"—found merely a "piece of furniture," but no funds, at "the President's house."[41]

After his flippant remark, 'Abd ar-Raḥmān's own letter to his children shifts in tone, turning from cutting irony to familial tenderness. Addressing his sons specifically, 'Abd ar-Raḥmān concludes his note with a plea, added as a poignant postscript:

> My dear boys, Simeon and Prince, for God's sake dont let Lee get a wife until you hear from me[42]

In the same letter that he had mocked a famous son, President Adams Jr., 'Abd ar-Raḥmān tells his own "boys" to ensure that the family grows no further, requesting that his youngest son be kept from taking a "wife." Repeating the sacred Arabic name of Allah in his page to Everett, 'Abd ar-Raḥmān's English is rather less pious, imploring his sons "for God's sake" to stop family expansion. 'Abd ar-Raḥmān was, of course, experiencing enough troubles trying to save his existing "five sons" and "eight grand-children."

In 1826, it was family burdens that had prevented Edward Everett from making his pilgrimage from Washington to Monticello. As 'Abd ar-Raḥmān arrived to Washington two years later, it was his own "travelling *En famille*" that formed a much more serious concern as he sought to flee America and reach African shores once more. 'Abd ar-Raḥmān's anxieties, expressed in his postscript to his sons, turned out to be more than justified. The size of his family would soon lead to a tragic split. On February 7, 1829, sailing from Jefferson's home state of Virginia, 'Abd ar-Raḥmān, together with his wife Isabella, departed their land of bondage, bound for Liberia.[43] Although sufficient funds had not yet been secured, they still had hopes that their children and grandchildren would be redeemed and reunite with them in Africa. For 'Abd ar-Raḥmān, however, these hopes would prove futile. He would never see his sons or daughters again.

21

"Their Eulogy will be Uttered
in other Languages"

The contemporary and successive generations of men will disappear, and in the long lapse of ages, the races of America, like those of
Greece and Rome, may pass away. The fabric of American freedom,
like all things human, however firm and fair, may crumble into dust.
But the cause in which these our fathers shone is immortal. They
did that to which no age, no people of civilized men, can be indif-
ferent. Their eulogy will be uttered in other languages, when those
we speak, like us who speak them, shall be all forgotten. And when
the great account of humanity shall be closed, in the bright list of
those who have best adorned and served it, shall be found the names
of our Adams and our Jefferson![1]

In the summer of 1826, 'Abd ar-Raḥmān was on the cusp of a new life,
summoning the will to write his first Arabic document in many decades.
Authored in the "presence" of Andrew Marschalk, this letter would lead to
'Abd ar-Raḥmān's freedom, eventually ushering him into the presence of a US
president, where he petitioned for his children's freedom. For John Quincy
Adams, however, the summer of 1826 was not a time of presence, but absence. This US president was doubly orphaned in 1826, experiencing the loss
of two fathers in July. On the very same day, at opposite ends of the country,
Thomas Jefferson and John Adams both died on July 4, 1826. The deaths of
these two founders coincided not only with each other, but also with the half-
century anniversary of Jefferson's Declaration of Independence, which had
been ratified exactly fifty years before on July 4, 1776.

Countless eulogies were delivered in the days following July 4, 1826,
marveling at this fateful and fatal coincidence.[2] Even in death, however,
Jefferson threatened to eclipse John Adams. Jefferson had died hours before

his friend, and in the ensuing days, public mourning for Jefferson conspicuously surpassed that for Adams, at least in some quarters.[3] One eulogy
that sought balance is quoted above—a eulogy delivered on August 1 by
none other than Edward Everett.[4] Linking the two men in whose correspondence he had featured, Everett offers a lament reaching beyond these
outsized figures, foreseeing the death of the very republic they founded.
Although patriotic, Everett's confidence in US prospects seems shaky, eulogizing not only the "pass[ing]" of Jefferson and Adams, but of "American
freedom" itself. Everett envisions an ominous future where "the races of
America, like those of Greece and Rome, may pass away"; and yet, even
after the nation's death, the fame of Jefferson and Adams will remain alive
in translation, carried forward in dialects unknown. "[T]heir eulogy will be
uttered in other languages, when those we speak, like us who speak them,
shall be all forgotten," Everett insists. Years earlier, Everett had himself witnessed the cultural evolution of "Greece," hearing first-hand Arabic chants
of Allah emanating from temples anciently built for pagan deities. Soon, he
would encounter again the Arabic name of Allah repeated, not intoned, but
inscribed, in an American manuscript. For Everett, the day that American
eulogies might "be uttered in other languages" was perhaps not difficult to
imagine.

At the end to the above elegiac passage, Everett shifts from human migration to heavenly merit, framing Jefferson and Adams in apocalyptic
terms. The "names of our Adams and our Jefferson" will still be "found"
at the end of the world, Everett insists, inscribed in a "bright list" of celestial heroes, even when the "great account of humanity shall be closed."
Enshrined as American saints, the two founders were cast in sacred terms
by Everett, but not by him alone, of course. Other religious memorials
emerged, but were not always meant so earnestly. Inverting the sancti-
mony of Everett, Jefferson's critics ridiculed his canonization. Six years
after Jefferson's death, John Randolph, his Monticello neighbor and nemesis, was still voicing complaints against his late cousin, remarking in
1832 that:

> I cannot live in this miserable, undone country, where as the Turks follow
> their sacred standard, which is a pair of Mahomet's green breeches, we are
> governed by the old red breeches of that prince of projectors, St. Thomas
> of *Canting*bury; and surely Becket himself never had more pilgrims at his
> shrine, than the saint of Monticello.[5]

Complaining of "pilgrims" to Monticello, Randolph sneers at the pious traffic climbing the mountain path to pay respects to "St. Thomas." As with Everett, Randolph sees America's end in Jefferson's passing; but, for Randolph, America has not been "undone" due to Jefferson's death, but due to those who memorialize him, making a shrine of Monticello. In death, as in life, Jefferson attracts American company; but, in Randolph's satire, Jefferson also again invites Islamic comparisons. Drawn to Jefferson's home after his death, tourists to the little mountain are like "Turks," with the former president himself labeled both an American "prince" and the Arabian Prophet, critiqued as the "Mahomet" of Monticello. The young Jefferson had designed Virginia's statehouse to rival "the tomb of Mahomet"; posthumously, Jefferson's own Virginia tomb is likened to a Muslim "shrine," with Randolph adding one final jab at poor Thomas's "old red breeches."

Randolph's bitter requiem was, of course, a minority view, overshadowed by glowing eulogies like the one delivered by Everett—a performance that helped Everett win recognition as the nation's foremost orator, dubbed the "American Cicero."[6] The 1826 deaths of Jefferson and Adams offered an occasion for Everett to find his elegiac voice; but the decade was not yet over. In 1826, Monticello's "sublime" peak became sacred ground, attracting earnest pilgrims to Jefferson's "sort of Mecca," as well as bitter satire, with Randolph ridiculing the late president as an American "Mahomet." 1826 also saw the beginning of a different pilgrimage, which would soon end with the death of an actual "Mahometan"—a Muslim with sufficient reason to wish no longer to "live in this miserable, undone country." Striving to return home to "utter" his thoughts once more in "other languages," this African's death would again inspire America's orator into elegiac speech. As the 1820s came to an end, Everett would be presented with yet another subject to eulogize.

≈

... he embarked with his wife for Liberia in company with one hundred and sixty emigrants. He died shortly after his return to the coast of Africa. This melancholy event is briefly recorded in the thirteenth annual report of the Colonization Society, and no further account is given of his restoration to his native land and to his kindred. We are left to conjecture, as to the position in which he was placed when his feet pressed again the soil of Africa, and he found himself restored to his father's house. It is probable that he was disappointed in his hopes of happiness to be enjoyed on the return to his native land.

Edward Everett, memorializing
Ibrāhīm 'Abd ar-Raḥmān[7]

1829 marked twenty-two years since two Africans dispatched their Arabic writings to Jefferson, perhaps hoping for prospects to return home. In 1829, this dream of African return was realized, not by Jefferson's Muslim fugitives, however, but by a fellow Arabic author enslaved in America. Ibrāhīm 'Abd ar-Raḥmān, imbued with a "native nobility" in Everett's words, finally reached his "native" land once more. According to Everett's account of this homecoming, however, 'Abd ar-Raḥmān's earthly "restoration" in 1829 was soon followed by his eternal rest. "He died shortly after his return to the coast of Africa," Everett poignantly notes in his memorial, delivered decades after 'Abd ar-Raḥmān's passing. Released from American bondage, this African stood on home "soil," but was "shortly" released from the bonds of life, his hopes of liberty ending with the ultimate "disappointment" of death.[8]

Possessing few details on this "melancholy event," Everett finds himself forced into "conjecture." A single rumor did, however, reach Everett regarding the last days of 'Abd ar-Raḥmān. During his American tour, 'Abd ar-Raḥmān had convinced benefactors that he had converted to Christianity. But, immediately upon reaching Africa, 'Abd ar-Raḥmān "restored" himself to his home spirituality: Islam. Reportedly "embrac[ing] the religion of the Koran" once more after arriving to "African soil," 'Abd ar-Raḥmān's religious "return" offers an especially resonant subject for Everett's memorial:

On his return to his native land, his new-born [Christian] faith had to undergo a formidable trial. With the rush of thoughts that came back upon his mind,—country regained, home revisited, the surviving friends of his youth restored to his embrace, the minaret from which, in his childhood, he had, heard the muezzin call the hour of prayer, again presented to his eyes,—with all these faded ideas starting into fresh life, was it strange if his faith in the new religion should be shaken? Was it strange if the thought occurred to him, that the Bible might be the book of the white man, and the Koran the book of the dark races? [. . .] I think we should feel charitably toward an African prince, who, having become a Christian while held in Christian bondage, returns to the religion in which he was brought up, when restored to his native land. But I repeat, I have only a dim recollection that such was the case with Abdul.[9]

In his elegy for the "fathers" of America, Jefferson and Adams, Everett had made an imaginative leap, envisioning their fame from the perspective of heaven. Eulogizing 'Abd ar-Raḥmān, Everett again engages his imagination, but adopts a new spiritual outlook—an outlook sympathetic to Islamic re-conversion. Defending his subject's religious defection, Everett sympathizes with 'Abd ar-Raḥmān's return to the faith of his fathers. Circumstances are unclear, Everett admits; and yet, "dim recollection" does not prevent Everett from vividly projecting himself into the place of 'Abd ar-Raḥmān. Drawing on his own memories of Muslim lands, Everett muses especially on "the minaret," from which the freed Muslim slave would have "heard the muezzin call the hour of prayer." Blending American oration with fancied African experience, Everett seems to savor Islamic sights and sounds, sug-gesting that cruel "Christian bondage" justified 'Abd ar-Raḥmān's return to "the Koran."

A Muslim "prince" to the end, 'Abd ar-Raḥmān dies, in Everett's account, believing in one God and a human Jesus—beliefs also endorsed by Everett's other elegiac subject, Thomas Jefferson, who in Randolph's satire was him-self made into a Mahometan "prince" at his death. But while Jefferson's own "name" will resound forever, echoing in the heavens, 'Abd ar-Raḥmān's name is truncated by Everett. In the above, he is referred to only as "Abdul"—an Arabic abbreviation, as Everett knew, meaning simply "Slave of the."[10] Eliding the start and end to this name, Everett sheds the Arabic for both "Abraham" and "Most Merciful," leaving only the middle term of "Abdul." An informal nickname, Everett's shortened label for this African "prince" also unbinds 'Abd ar-Raḥman from any one master. Still named a "slave," Everett denudes "Abdul" from the subjects of possession, this nominal term appear-ing without any proprietor, disconnected from all owners, human or divine.

If eager to drop the name "Abraham" as he eulogized this African "slave," this same name, however, would forcefully shape the future of Everett's el-egiac career, as well as his evolving engagements with US slavery. Another Abraham would soon rise to lead Everett's nation as it faced its greatest test—a crisis shaped by the suffering of Africans, and sparking a conflict entirely devoid of "mercy."

≈

Some one has observed, that it is no less pleasing than instructive to behold "a great mind in *déshabillé*." In few cases could the delight or instruction be greater than in that of Jefferson. Usefulness to his race, and the untiring pursuit of knowledge, seem to have been his prominent desire and aim.[11]

With national fanfare, Jefferson's body was entombed at Monticello in 1826. But his literary "corpus" would also come to attract public notice. Jefferson's eulogists, like Everett, eventually exhausted their efforts; but, in the decade that followed Jefferson's death, his archivists were just starting to uncover the riches buried in his personal papers. The above words stand at the opening to the second article in a two-part series in 1835, surveying the former president's private collection, published in the New York periodical *The Knickerbocker*—a series entitled simply "Jefferson Papers."[12] Known during his life for his informal dress, Jefferson appears entirely undressed in these posthumous articles, or so the above introduction promises. Jefferson's naked psyche is to be glimpsed in his private letters and manuscripts, his "great mind" unclothed, standing starkly in "*déshabillé*." This article offers an intimate view of Jefferson, beginning with this over-familiar language; more important, however, this anonymous article may have been written by a familiar name—Everett—but not Edward Everett. This two-part article series, like all contributions to *The Knickerbocker*, was published without naming its author. There is circumstantial evidence, however, to suggest that this 1835 assessment of Jefferson's papers may have been penned by one of the people most dear to Edward Everett—his older brother, Alexander.

Recently US minister to Spain, Alexander Hill Everett was, like his younger brother, a leading New England *literatus*, and, at least once, also a correspondent of Jefferson's.[13] After the president's passing, however, Alexander would be a leading proponent of Jefferson's fame, writing articles to assess his influence and legacy. Yet another Everett eulogizing the former president, Alexander delivered on the tenth anniversary of Jefferson's death a lengthy "Defence of the Character and Principles of Mr. Jefferson" in 1836; already a year earlier, however, he had published in 1835 an essay simply entitled "Character of Jefferson" for the *North American Review*. And, in this same year, it may have been Alexander who also authored the two anonymous *Knickerbocker* articles "Jefferson Papers"—articles that not only reveal Jefferson's literary remains, but, uniquely, hint at his specific Islamic engagements.[14] Sifting through holdings of national significance, "Jefferson Papers" also touches on texts more international in flavor. Commenting on Jefferson's letters that have eluded notice until now, this two-part series in 1835 ends with a haunting assessment of an Arabic manuscript surprisingly found in the president's possession. Marveling at Jefferson's 1807 letter to Robert Patterson, requesting help to secure a translation, *The Knickerbocker* article reveals that this letter held an Arabic enclosure, which:

> is marked with strange characters; but we believe that no one was ever found who could "make known the interpretation thereof;" nor do any of our venerable acquaintances remember what disposition was made of the poor Arabians. We are ourselves excessively familiar with the Arabian tongue, and should be strongly tempted to translate the document spoken of, were it not that we are just now rather busily engaged in other matters. The paper looks much as if some industrious spider had crawled out of an ink-stand and travelled leisurely over the sheet, dropping grimed spots and trails from his feet,
>
> —"as fast as the Arabian trees
> Their medicinal gum."[15]

Twenty-five years after Jefferson's own frustrated quest to solve the mystery of two Muslim fugitives, the confused hunt continues, this 1835 article briefly puzzling over their Arabic writings after the president's own death. Echoing Jefferson—who had failed to find a translator—this article not only quotes the president's words a quarter century later, but repeats his inability to "make known the interpretation thereof." With humor characteristic of *The Knickerbocker*, however, its author sarcastically boasts of Arabic literacy, claiming with tongue in cheek to be "excessively familiar with the Arabian tongue." Comic in tone, serious overlaps yet emerge in this *Knickerbocker* article. Like 'Abd ar-Raḥmān himself, the Arabic authors from 1807 are ethnically reframed, identified not as West Africans but as "poor Arabians." Concluding the above, this 1835 article pivots away from comedy and toward tragedy, ending with a final quotation from *Othello*. For the *Knickerbocker* reviewer, the "Arabian" lines that "drip" across Jefferson's illegible page recall Shakespeare's own classic drama, whose protagonist, the "Moor" Othello, tells his own backstory of being "sold to slavery."[16]

Lending a tragic frame to Arabic writings subsequently concealed for two centuries, "Jefferson Papers" aptly closes inconclusively, offering no final "interpretation." Again failing to resolve the same issues more seriously explored by Jefferson himself, this article echoes his "pursuit of knowledge," which years earlier had fallen short. Claiming to be unable to locate anyone who "remember[s] what disposition was made of the poor Arabians," this very first memorial to expose Jefferson's private letters gestures to the elusiveness of human recall, even as it ties an iconic founding father to a Muslim enigma. In this initial study of Jefferson as a subject for archivists, his literary corpus is linked to bodily loss, intertwined with the disappearance of two men whose "strange" Arabic "characters" would forever inhabit the papers of an American president.

≈

> You, Mr. President, well remember that twenty-one years ago, you and I saw in one of the committee rooms of yonder Capitol, a native African, who had been 40 years a field slave in the West Indies and in this country, and wrote at the age of 70 the Arabic character, with the fluency and the elegance of a scribe.[17]

On January 18, 1853, Edward Everett offered these words, not in memory of a dead president, but seeking to inspire a living president, prompting him to "remember" the past. The "Mr. President" addressed by Everett was not Jefferson, of course, nor any US president, but the president of the American Colonization Society (ACS). This same society had divided Everett from Jefferson just before the latter's death, with Everett rejecting African repatriation. Now, the ACS was his audience, and Everett had come around to endorse this cause. It is not Jefferson whom Everett cites for changing his views, however, but an African Muslim. Ibrāhīm 'Abd ar-Raḥmān had been dead for twenty-five years in 1853, but he was still on Everett's mind, helping to liberate the Bostonian from his own abstract acceptance of slavery in the South.

A quarter century after 'Abd ar-Raḥmān's passing, Everett still vividly recalls the vitality of the Muslim he met in Washington. It is not his "complexion," however, but his "Arabic characters" that Everett especially remembers—not 'Abd ar-Raḥmān's "natural air" merely, but his "fluency" and scribal "elegance." Addressing the ACS and its president in 1853, Everett's praise for Arabic penmanship may have seemed more authoritative due to his own recent stint as a president; standing to speak to the ACS, Everett was currently serving as the US secretary of state, but he was also the most recent leader of his alma mater, completing in 1849 his term as president of Harvard. Lending intellectual weight to his survey of 'Abd ar-Raḥmān's literacy accomplishments, Everett was among America's premier educators by 1853. Unknown to his ACS audience, however, Everett's tutelage of his own family was even more relevant to his appreciation of 'Abd ar-Raḥmān, training his children in traditions not unrelated to this Muslim slave. Everett's older brother, Alexander, may possibly have been the *Knickerbocker* archivist who first took notice of Jefferson's "Arabian" papers; Everett's youngest son, William, however, would actually study Arabian writings, encouraged by his father. Keeping a diary of his son's progress during the late 1840s, Everett marveled at little William's increasing literacy, even gaining familiarity with Islamic sources, noting that the boy:

> goes over a book again and again, till he is master of almost every idea, & often has possessed himself of the exact words of long passages. When we had got home, I requested him to bring the first volume of the Arabian Nights, & read me the passage about "sacred books" to which he had alluded in our walk. He got the book & read the Paragraph, beginning the "Moosulmans" are taught in the Koraun & c. toward the beginning of the section on the "Mahummedan Religion."[18]

Memorizing "long passages," young William Everett discusses "sacred books" with his father as they pleasantly "walk" together. Growing into a little "master" of sources, including "Mahummedan" ones, Everett's son reads aloud a passage that treats "the Koraun" itself, the same text that had been memorized by a former Muslim slave who years before had written out Arabic "words" for Everett himself. Proud father and president of Harvard when he wrote this entry, Everett had been prevented years earlier from making a pilgrimage to Monticello. Due to family duties, Everett never made the trek to the "little Mecca" in Virginia, where a former US president "possessed" Qur'anic inscriptions authored by other Muslim fugitives. In the coming decades, however, Everett's own family would help remind him of "the Koraun," strolling Harvard Yard with his son as they surveyed together the "Mahummedan Religion." Unlike 'Abd ar-Raḥmān, who died far from his own children, Everett had the privilege of staying close with his son, watching William follow in his father's footsteps. Eventually graduating from Harvard, William would even win a lectureship at the university. An instructor at his father's alma mater, William was also granted housing where, ironically, historic Arabic slave writings had likely been stored many years before. Assuming his Harvard post, William Everett lived in the "Holmes House," named for none other than Abiel Holmes and his family—the same house to which Holmes had moved after his return from Georgia. Fresh from collecting 'Usman's writings at Parnassus, Holmes would publicly minister in Cambridge during the following four decades, living in the same "gambrel-roofed old house" later occupied by William Everett, whose own father had also collected Arabic writings by another US Muslim slave.[19]

Such overlaps of family tradition and Arabic transmissions, with precious Muslim documents passing between New England parents and children, were likely not on Everett's mind as he memorialized 'Abd ar-Raḥmān in 1853. And yet, as his address to the ACS unfolded, Everett did stress continuities of "blood" and ethnic comparisons. For Everett, 'Abd ar-Raḥmān embodied an African ideal, one unsurpassed by Western peers:

> And how few Americans or Europeans, after forty years' bondage, would have come out like Abdul, unbroken in body and mind! Let us all learn by this example to respect the African race, as one whose best specimens will not suffer in comparison with our own, and remember, that there are races in Europe, which fall far below the boasted standard of Caucasian blood. [. . .] we see in the instance of Abdul, (and no doubt the annals of the slave trade could furnish hundreds of similar cases,) that Africans born and bred to high fortune, and educated in all the learning of the Mahometan countries, are liable to be subjected to all the horrors of the middle passage, and all the woes of hopeless bondage. If we could read these dark annals, I fear we should find that for one case like Abdul of a person of this description, able to bear up under this heavy and dispiriting load, hundreds sink down broken-hearted, and bury their sorrows in the only refuge which never fails the children of misery, the grave.[20]

Reflecting a disturbing racial discourse that plagued his era, Everett's account implies essentializing categories, contrasting types, "Caucasian" and "African." And yet, Everett seeks to invert "standard" hierarchies of his day. In 'Abd ar-Raḥmān, Everett glimpses the fallacy of privileging "European" heritage. A Muslim marvel—an African slave who is yet literate in Arabic—'Abd ar-Raḥmān is capable of overturning broader, bigoted assumptions of "Americans or Europeans." Although exemplary, 'Abd ar-Raḥmān is also an "example" for Everett, his seemingly unique case yet implying "hundreds of similar cases." Singular in fortitude, 'Abd ar-Raḥmān's story hints at other captive Africans "educated in all the learning of the Mahometan countries," but who are yet kept silent in the "annals" of US history.

Raised with "Koranic" knowledge, like his own son William, Everett views the enslaved Muslim sons and daughters of Africa as "children of misery." Granted no access to Harvard paths, their Arabic papers are quietly collected by Ivy League professors; capable of stunning composition, these literate Muslim slaves are yet suppressed in captivity, "sink[ing] down broken-hearted." Ending his elegy on 'Abd ar-Raḥmān with the grim silence of death, Everett concludes that the "only refuge" for most Muslim slaves is "the grave," with their "Mahometan" learning and literacy consigned to American soil.

≈

A decade later, fresh graves stretched out in front of Edward Everett as he rose to deliver another address. In 1853, Everett had spoken before the president of the American Colonization Society; in 1863, a more powerful president was a part of Everett's audience. Ascending the stage to speak as "America's Orator," Everett surveyed a field of recent American slaughter in Gettysburg, Pennsylvania. It was November 19, 1863, and Everett was preparing to deliver the longest eulogy of his life, even as another Abraham listened with his characteristic stoic patience. Speaking first, Everett's Gettysburg Address lasted more than two hours; President Lincoln followed, reportedly delivering his own Gettysburg Address in just "two minutes."[21]

The North and South were locked in their death struggle, the US Civil War. America's "terrible sublime" had come. Its "harvest" was blood, sowed into the autumn soil upon which Everett stood together with Abraham Lincoln in 1863. Turning pastoral grounds into battlefield graves, Gettysburg's violence had been faintly foreseen by John Quincy's prophesy back in 1819—a prophecy that warned of the contradictory seeds cultivated by a single "Virginian planter," Thomas Jefferson, whose "abridged Alcoran of political doctrine" promised freedoms that would crack the Union. Invited to eulogize the slain US soldiers and their sacrifice, Everett began his Gettysburg Address not with the dead on this domestic field, however, but with his own remembered life on foreign shores. Touring Muslim lands in his youth, Everett had encountered cultural conflict that was centuries old, anticipating America's own ongoing struggle. Recounting his arrival in Ottoman Greece, Everett told his Gettysburg audience of Grecian ruins that still survive from ancient battles between East and West, with these remnants offering a precedent for the present violence between North and South. Greece's wars with ancient Persia, Everett proclaimed, testify to a valor like that exemplified at Gettysburg:

> although the columns, beneath the hand of time and barbaric violence, have long since disappeared, the venerable mound still marks the spot where they fought and fell,—
>> "That battle-field where Persia's victim-horde
>> First bowed beneath the brunt of Hellas' sword."
>
> And shall I, fellow-citizens, who, after an interval of twenty-three centuries, a youthful pilgrim from the world unknown to ancient Greece, have wandered over that illustrious plain, ready to put off the shoes from off my feet, as one that stands on holy ground,—who have gazed with respectful emotion on the mound which still protects the dust of those who rolled back the tide of Persian invasion, and rescued the land of popular liberty, of letters, and of arts, from the ruthless foe,—stand unmoved over the graves of our dear brethren, who so lately, on three of those all-important days which decide a nation's history,—days on whose issue it depended whether this august republican Union, founded by some of the wisest statesmen that ever lived, cemented with the blood of some of the purest patriots that ever died, should perish or endure,—rolled back the tide of an invasion, not less unprovoked, not less ruthless, than that which came to plant the dark banner of Asiatic despotism and slavery on the free soil of Greece? Heaven forbid![22]

Remembering his own past as "a youthful pilgrim," while memorializing the young men who will forever stay buried under this American field, Everett lauds the North, which seems to him like "the free soil of Greece," fending off the South's "Asiatic despotism and slavery." Reminding his audience of Old World "columns" in the midst of New World carnage, Everett traces repetitions of history, even while repeating the very words of another historic pilgrim, citing in the above two familiar lines from a famous poet:

> That battle-field where Persia's victim-horde
> First bowed beneath the brunt of Hellas' sword[23]

Quoting verses from Byron's elegy to Greece—a Western nation that long ago contended with Persia, but was now controlled by Turkey—Everett slips these uncredited verses into his Gettysburg Address, even as he publicly invokes his own sojourn in Muslim lands. Linking America's domestic struggle to foreign layers of Greece's own "civil" strife—strife with ancient Persians and modern Ottomans—Everett invoked global analogies that may have appeared rather stretched to his audience. But America's Orator knew better. Traveling to Europe with Ticknor, who purchased Greek books for a former president at Monticello, Everett's early pilgrimage had introduced him to Sufi chants and Islamicate languages. More important, like Monticello's master, Everett was aware that Muslims were themselves enslaved in the United States, and had stakes in the same Civil War that prompted his present eulogy. From the vantage of this freshly sacred soil, Gettysburg seemed to Everett like Greece, a site of resistance to Oriental despotism and "Asiatic" slavery. Yet, as Everett well knew, America's war was itself partially fought for the freedom of men and women shaped by Middle Eastern traditions. Even as he stood in front of Lincoln to deliver the first Gettysburg Address, Everett possessed a fragment of original Arabic writings, penned in 1828 by a freed slave—a slave whose own Muslim compatriots were still captive in 1860s America, their continued bondage a contributing cause for the nation's bloody struggle.

Leaving unnamed the British poet responsible for his quoted verses, Everett also leaves unnamed the political authors of his own nation, insisting merely that America was "founded by some of the wisest statesmen that ever lived." Lincoln, however, had a more specific "statesman" in mind. As the US president rose after Everett to deliver his own iconic eulogy, memorized by successive American generations, Lincoln recalled words written by another president, invoking Jefferson while gazing out over the "terrible sublime" of Gettysburg. It was Jefferson, after all, who like Lincoln had heralded universal freedoms. Unlike Lincoln, however, Jefferson had not wished to risk American peace to secure liberty for all, refusing to "intervene" to emancipate Africans, except in one specific case that would long stay secret. Where Jefferson had failed, Lincoln would succeed, or so he hoped, issuing his Emancipation Proclamation at the start of 1863, on New Year's Day. And yet, as 1863 unfolded, Lincoln's Proclamation was followed merely by more death. As he opened his own Gettysburg Address on November 19, Lincoln decided to invoke not his recent Proclamation, but a historic Declaration:

> Four score and seven years ago our fathers brought forth on this continent, a new nation, conceived in Liberty, and dedicated to the proposition that all men are created equal.[24]

Taking this "proposition" from the Declaration of Independence, Lincoln—like Everett just before him—inserts an unattributed quotation into his Address, but one entirely familiar to his hearers, echoing Jefferson's most famous phrase that "all men are created equal." Jefferson was an unsurprising source for Lincoln to quote in 1863; for reasons entirely unknown to Lincoln, however, Jefferson also haunted the citation chosen by Everett, Lincoln's fellow speaker. Byron's verses lionizing Greece, supporting that nation's struggles against Muslim rule, were quoted by Everett even as he championed Union efforts to emancipate American slaves, many of whom were Muslim. Everett is then followed by Lincoln, who himself recalls Jefferson—the US president who was the covert recipient of Arabic writings by US Muslim slaves, and the US president most likely to recognize the aptness of Everett's own Oriental comparisons.

With no recourse to modern microphones, Lincoln's "ten complicated sentences" delivered in two minutes can hardly have been heard by many on November 19, 1863.[25] Lincoln's words have, however, been amplified in the American mind during the century and a half following 1863, even while other historic words, inscribed at the margins of America's civil struggle, have remained inaudible. Proclaiming "a new birth of freedom" in an expansive graveyard, expressing hope that democracy "shall not perish from the earth" while standing on ground recently covered with the slain, Lincoln knew the audacity of his speech, as well as its ironies. And yet, a few ironies stayed hidden from Lincoln on November 19. Distilling Jefferson's Declaration down to its most memorable words, Lincoln was himself abridging the same text that President John Quincy Adams had previously aligned with the Muslim scripture. Invoked at this turning point in America's tragic struggle over slavery, it is Jefferson's own "abridged Alcoran of political doctrine" that Lincoln quotes at Gettysburg. Citing these words of the master of Monticello, Lincoln recalled the man who had authored America's "abridged Alcoran," but also the same man that kept secret and silent actual Qur'anic inscriptions, authored by enslaved Muslims whose own "eulogies" have now waited over two centuries to be "uttered."

22

"A Barely Discernible Horizon"

Two hundred years ago this summer, at the sunrise of America's first full century, veterans of the American Revolution came here and founded Smith County. In their minds' eye, the very idea of what America could become was still then a barely discernible horizon. Yet they moved toward it, convinced of its fineness, certain the distance would yield a place better than they had ever known. Each of us has our own sense of the next, finer horizon.[1]

On June 16, 1999, Albert Gore Jr. delivered these words, standing on the steps of the Smith County courthouse, in Carthage, Tennessee. Gore was beginning his run for president, reaching for new horizons after enduring two embattled terms as Bill Clinton's number two. Carthage's own "native son," Gore was warmly welcomed by old friends and family in the Tennessee town where as a boy he had worked on his father's farm. Applauding him in the afternoon sunshine, smiling faces greeted Al Gore on June 16; however, he was also joined by a more ethereal presence. Standing on the courthouse steps, Gore sensed the soul of his own father, Albert Gore Sr., who had passed away just a year before. "I miss my dad," Gore Jr. told the Carthage crowd, "but I know he's here in spirit."[2]

The Smith County courthouse was well chosen as the stage for announcing his candidacy, and for memorializing his father. This small-town center was an ideal backdrop, Gore calculated, to accent his rural roots and heartland values. Although vice president of the United States, Gore stood in Carthage as a "hometown boy" made good.[3] And yet, as he addressed his lively audience on June 16, Gore was unaware that his selected stage was also shared by other ghostly figures—fugitive "spirits" entirely unknown to modern-day Carthage. Shrouded in mystery, an African pair had once climbed these same courthouse steps, standing in the very place where Gore was launching his presidential campaign nearly "[t]wo hundred years" later. These men were not "veterans of the American Revolution" pushing into the interior from the East Coast, but Muslim slaves arriving to Carthage from even farther in the American West. They had "moved toward" this town in Tennessee, seeking a "finer horizon" of freedom. And yet, "what America could become" had proved to be full of horrors, not hope. Forging difficult "distances," they nevertheless pushed eastward, with little confidence that this "would yield a place better." As they approached Carthage in 1807, these two Muslims must have yearned for the same comforts that Al Gore enjoyed on June 16, 1999: sympathetic faces, the solace of family and friends, the security of home. On the cusp of the twenty-first century, Al Gore looked forward from the steps of the Smith County courthouse, reaching for even higher national stature. On these same courthouse steps, at the start of the nineteenth century, two men only desired retreat, hoping to return across an ocean and reach Africa, the same continent where ancient Carthage lay in ruins.

Carthage, Tennessee—despite Gore's soaring rhetoric—has proved to be a place of compelling gravity, grounding high ambitions, and eclipsing hopes of escape. It was in Carthage that Jefferson's Muslim fugitives were locked up in 1807, but also where they became entirely obstructed from the view of history. Not only "barely discernible," at the Smith County courthouse in 1807 two Africans became invisible. These "travelers" had continually pushed "Eastward when at liberty," as Nash reported to Jefferson, steering toward the "sunrise."[4] But, after their capture in Smith County, they faded wholly from view, disappearing on the very steps where Al Gore would clamor for attention in 1999. Entirely unknown to the aspiring president who stood in Carthage at the end of the twentieth century, the plight of these two men was known only to the president whose two terms had started the nineteenth century. In 1807, Jefferson was told that the "sunrise" had pulled two African escapees toward Carthage. It was in Carthage, however, that dusk fell, and their fate was henceforth shrouded in darkness. Below history's "horizon," their story was submerged in this Tennessee town, seemingly refusing to rise "ever" to be "known" again.[5]

In 1999, Al Gore stood on the steps of the Carthage courthouse meditating on the promise of America's future, hazily projecting the next millennium. Despite his forward gaze, however, Gore begins his announcement speech with a backward glance, celebrating an old anniversary, with 1999 marking "two hundred years" since "veterans of the American Revolution" had first come out to Tennessee's "Smith County." Recalling the summer of 1799, Gore harked back to the very year that another vice president was nearing his own bitter election battle, to be fought in 1800. Like Vice President Gore in 1999, Vice President Jefferson in 1799 was approaching an acrimonious struggle for the presidency; unlike Gore, however, Jefferson was not then loudly announcing his political intentions, but anonymously fashioning a political text. "Two hundred years ago this summer," Gore's vice presidential predecessor was preparing to send to press his translation of Volney's *Ruins*. Enlivening this Oriental fantasy with his own English, Jefferson was traversing in 1799 not physical spaces in the American West, but instead spanning linguistic "distances" that crossed the Middle East, newly expressing the Qur'anic echoes of Volney's French *Ruins* for American readers.

On the cusp of close elections, Jefferson and Gore engaged in inverse efforts. More obviously, the two men would experience inverse outcomes. The votes of both 1800 and 2000 were closely contested—so closely that arbitration was required for each. 1800 saw an exact tie emerge between Jefferson and Aaron Burr in the Electoral College, forcing Congress to decide the "deadlock" in Jefferson's favor.[6] In 2000, another close result in the Electoral College led to mediation in Washington. This time, however, the presidency hung in the balance not at Congress, but at the Supreme Court. And, where Jefferson succeeded, arbitration would hand Gore defeat. Carthage's "native son" failed to reach that "next, finer horizon" in his political career.[7] This loss would have consequences reaching far beyond Gore's personal ambitions, of course, with implications for history worldwide. In the first year of the twenty-first century, only months after Gore's failed bid to become commander-in-chief, the United States came under attack. Gore's idealistic Carthage speech, spoken on the brink of a new millennium, entirely missed the ominous future that fast approached. Looming on America's "next horizon" in 1999 were "barely discernible" threats—threats that would materialize in American skies one clear September morning in the very year that followed Al Gore's loss. The closely contested election of 1800 was awarded to Jefferson, and so it was Jefferson who held office when America faced its first war with Muslim pirates in 1801. It would be Jefferson, not Burr, who prosecuted this war and settled peace in Muslim Africa, holding firm against the Barbary powers while seeking diplomatic resolutions. In 2000, however, the election would slip from Gore's grasp. And so, it would not be Gore, but another son and namesake who occupied the Oval Office when America faced the horrors of September 11, 2001. Instead of Al Gore Jr., it was George Bush Jr., who was president on 9/11 and presided over the conflicts that followed. It was Bush, not Gore, who held office for the first two presidential terms of the new century, years characterized by unceasing hostilities in Middle Eastern countries where lasting peace seems still beyond our horizons.

Standing on the steps of the Carthage courthouse, Gore looked up into the noon sunshine, welcoming the twenty-first century on a cloudless day. And yet it was not the limitless sky over Carthage, but the brick building that formed Gore's stage that prophesied the immediate American future. Enthusiastically launched in Carthage, Gore's campaign would end with ac-rimony and exhaustion on the steps of the Supreme Court, which decided *Bush v. Gore* in favor of the former, certifying the Republican candidate's win in Florida.[8] The Carthage courthouse chosen by Gore for his announcement was not just a place of justice, however, but a former jail—the last known prison for two Muslim fugitives. Launching his bid to become president, which was destined to fail, Gore was standing in the same spot where a pair of Arabic authors had failed to win their own freedoms, despite the Qur'anic appeals dispatched to the sitting president in 1807. On the courthouse steps once climbed by these two captives, Gore welcomed an American millennium that was soon to be haunted by scandals of Muslim incarcera-tion. Gazing into the unsearchable future, Gore stood where two forgotten "Mahometans" had been jailed in 1807, even as he greeted a century that would open with outrage over Guantanamo Bay and Abu Ghraib.[9]

≈

Halfway through this century, when my father saw that thousands of his fellow Tennesseans were forced to obey Jim Crow laws, he knew America could do better. He saw a horizon in which his black and white constit-uents shared the same hopes in the same world. He fought against the Southern Manifesto and for voting rights. His last election was lost—but his conscience won.

Surging with optimism, Gore's announcement continued with these words, tracking expansion of US freedoms for both "black and white." Leaving behind "the American Revolution," Gore critiques the "Jim Crow laws," which leads him forward to the fight against "the Southern Manifesto"—the pro-segregation policy formulated "halfway" through the twentieth cen-tury.[10] Although spanning historical periods, a single "spirit" still infuses Gore's speech—that of his own father, Al Gore Sr.—who surfaces again as his Carthage announcement unfolds. An inspiration to his son, Al Gore Sr.

emerges as a champion of progressive causes. His final candidacy failed and he lost his Senate seat in 1970, but his father's "conscience" won, Gore insists, a sentiment that seems prophetic of Jr.'s fate as well.[11] Straddling political loss and the persistence of ideals, Al Gore the son, like his father, was destined to lose his own "last election."

In 1999, Al Gore Jr. launched his doomed campaign by invoking his father's loss. Today, twenty years later, Democratic dreams seem even more remote in Carthage, Tennessee. A Republican stronghold, Smith County voted for Donald Trump by more than 70 percent in 2016.[12] And yet the Gore family name still survives in ruby-red Carthage, faintly visible on faded signs around this small Tennessee town, vestiges of an era long past. Other identities, even more alien and historic than Al Gore in Trump country, have disappeared altogether from Carthage, absent from both its posted signs and its public registers. Bearing the most generic of English names, "Smith County" is also where two foreign names became unrecoverable. Still standing at the heart of Carthage, the archives at the Smith County courthouse retain handwritten records from its earliest years, reaching back to the building's construction in 1805. And yet, the Muslim names of two West Africans who arrived there in 1807 are absent from its recorded court proceedings, seemingly not meriting a single mention. The "hopes" and trials of Smith County's earliest "white constituents" are transcribed with care, but the courthouse's 1807 records offer no trace of two "black" fugitives. Outside the brick courthouse in 1999, Carthage's "native son" Al Gore Jr. announced his presidential campaign, proudly bearing the name of his own father as he invoked the fathers of the nation. Inside this same courthouse, two anonymous fugitives—Muslim sons of West Africa—were held captive in Carthage, but left no hint of their names, nor their ultimate fate.

This erasure of names has helped keep silent the story that *Jefferson's Muslim Fugitives* tells for the first time. It is not only the names of these West African fugitives that have been lost to history, but the name of another Western "traveler"—the man that trekked to Washington from the "Teritory of Louisanna" conveying Arabic writings to a US president. Ira P. Nash was an American misfit; but he is also the one who fit this story together, playing an essential role in these improbable events. It was Nash who carried to Jefferson the "matter of momentous importance" inscribed in Arabic letters at the beginning of October 1807, and it was Nash who later sent his report to the president, revealing that these fugitives had once more fled, naming Carthage as their last known location. Without Nash's intervention, there would be no story to recover; and without him, the story would not have survived to be told. His letters offer the very few details that we now have respecting these two African escapees. It is Nash's own name, however, that too has become lost, hidden in plain sight. A lover of wordplay, Nash fashioned aliases for himself, as well as odd names for his own family; making foreign the most familiar of identities, Nash even inverted his own name as "H. Sanari," endowing it with faint Eastern overtones. Although Nash tried to disguise his identity during his own lifetime, errors after his death have also helped keep his name obscure, and conceal his connection to Jefferson specifically. Despite the pivotal letters Nash sent to the president in 1807, the name "Ira P. Nash" has yet to appear in print catalogues of Jefferson's correspondence, nor in published studies of Jefferson's life and labors. This omission is not due to Nash's use of an "Oriental" alias, but to a tiny embellishment he adds to his English signature, rendering his autographed initials easy to misconstrue. As a result, Ira's 1807 letters to Jefferson—the very letters concerning two Muslim fugitives in Kentucky—have often been erroneously catalogued, filed under alternate names, such as "J. Nash" or even "Frank Nash."[13] Ira P. Nash transported illegible Arabic letters to Washington in 1807; Nash's own letters, mostly deposited in Washington, have also suffered from illegibility, helping to prevent historians from piecing together the story told by *Jefferson's Muslim Fugitives*.

Like the two authors whose indecipherable documents he delivered, Nash's own name has remained hidden from Jefferson scholars. And yet, with careful examination, and knowledge of context, Nash's name becomes clear. The same cannot be said for the two Muslims whose manuscripts Nash carried eastward in 1807. These men are never named by Nash himself, despite his love for foreign words and alien identities. Just as the court records still held in Carthage, the names of these two Arabic authors in Kentucky never surface in Nash's letters. The very title of the current book reflects this loss, surrendering to the irretrievability of these names. *Jefferson's Muslim Fugitives* is a work of historical recovery, unearthing for the first time the story of two African "travelers." And yet, this book must itself end without knowing the most basic words assigned to these Muslim fugitives at the very beginning of their lives: their names.

For Al Gore, Carthage signaled the endurance of ideals and identities amid electoral defeat. Despite political losses, Carthage sustained Gore's family name, while witnessing too the victory of his father's "conscience." However, for two anonymous Africans at the opening of the nineteenth century, the "same world" that Gore celebrates at the end of the twentieth would come much too late. For these Muslim fugitives, Carthage was not only their "last" recorded place, but where their personal identities were forever "lost."

≈

> Here, at the center of my hometown, in the heart of America, in the midst of the people I love, that is the new horizon I see. I need you for this journey, so together let us vow in these first long days of summer that we'll work through the night so that our children may make a clean start from the right place, a higher place, in a fresh century.
> (APPLAUSE)
> Thank you, and may God bless you.
> And God bless America.

These were the final words delivered by Albert Gore Jr. on June 16, 1999, as he confidently launched his doomed campaign. Gore's presidential bid would fail, of course. But so did his predictions for America. From the vantage of 2019, Gore's words, delivered during the "long days of summer" in 1999, may seem naïve, heedless of the autumnal conflicts to come. The two decades that have followed his June speech have held countless surprises, but the "fresh century" and "clean start" heralded by Gore have yet to arrive in America.

Forecasting millennial expectations, Gore "founded" his future optimism on the final year of another century, gesturing back to 1799, the year that Smith County was founded. However, in 1799 Gore's predecessor as vice president was preoccupied not with American promises, but with Middle Eastern *Ruins*. Two hundred years before Gore scanned the limitless skies over Carthage, Thomas Jefferson was peering downwards, engrossed in deep layers of language and culture, secretly translating Volney's text that recounted "the fall of empires." Jefferson was acclaimed by his peers as America's "first Citizen," but he himself was uniquely mindful that modern achievements rose from buried histories. The nation he helped found was no "clean start," but was built from a messy past, from hidden precedents and peoples. One of the "veterans of the American Revolution," Jefferson was no mere witness to the origins of the nation. Instead, he was America's own "Author," composing the most original of US documents, the Declaration of Independence. And yet, despite his priority among the founding fathers, Jefferson was not charmed by a simple idea of pure beginnings, but rather sought to stave off the ravages of time. He preserved his own writings, while reviving ancient models, transplanting them to American soil. Jefferson's nation was not merely a "higher place," but also a place with rich and tangled roots, nourished by complex global currents and international exchange.

Designing a Capitol building for his native Virginia, Jefferson would copy an ancient European temple, erecting in Richmond a statehouse projected to rival "the tomb of Mahomet." Writing to Stiles from Paris, Jefferson speculated that "Asia" was "peopled from America." Later, at Monticello, Jefferson hosted Volney, whose subsequent sojourn in the New World unearthed supposed Middle Eastern accents in Native American languages. As he was inaugurated president, Jefferson battled Barbary Muslims abroad, on the same coast where ancient Carthage lay in rubble. And, as his presidency approached its end, Jefferson was handed Arabic writings authored by two Africans, whose last known prison was a newly built courthouse in Carthage, Tennessee. In 1999, Carthage was where Gore looked hopefully to the horizons, dreaming of an America that was "fresh." For President Jefferson, Carthage was a name that signaled not newness but historical repetition, while recalling challenges that punctuated his entire career, a name that spanned Islam and Africa, Arabic communiqués and American captivity. "*Delenda est Carthago*," Stiles had once declared to Jefferson, "Carthage must be destroyed!" But, as Jefferson well knew, Carthage would not stay subdued. Lying conquered on an African coast in the Muslim world, Carthage would return in America, its name erected again in Tennessee, rising up from antique ruins to impact "New World" futures.

On June 16, 1999, Al Gore was the focus of public attention, as he stood at the very "heart of America." At the Smith County courthouse, the vice president occupied "the center of [his] hometown," surrounded by both immediate family and a vast nation that extended from sea to sea. He was a man "in the midst," intersecting domestic circles and America's coastal extremes. The town of Carthage had not always been at the "center," however. For Jefferson's peers at the end of the eighteenth century—for the "veterans of the American Revolution" who had arrived in Smith County "two hundred years" before—Carthage represented the utmost margins. Like its African namesake, perched on another continent's coastline, Carthage, Tennessee, was a peripheral place, on the edge of the early nation. Even as these pioneers reached Carthage in the summer of 1799, however, America's vice president was preparing to burst open his country's parameters. Soon to win the presidency, Thomas Jefferson was only four years away from making a purchase of land that radically remapped America, shifting Tennessee from the frontier to the heartland. It was America's vice president in 1799, Thomas Jefferson, who was most responsible for transforming the "hometown" of a later vice president, Al Gore, into "the heart of America" in 1999. After the Louisiana Purchase, Carthage was no longer on the borders of the United States, but instead sat "in the midst" of a nation that Jefferson helped to integrate across the continent.

Two centuries ago, Jefferson shifted Carthage from distant edges toward the nation's interior. Today, his surviving papers have the power to perform a similar task. The story of two Muslim authors, whose tracks end in Carthage, has occupied the very edges of American memory, sitting beyond even the peripheral vision of historians. However, due to Jefferson's agency— his intervention on behalf of these Muslim fugitives, and his retention of their writings—this story that concludes in Carthage is at least partially recoverable. Refusing to blithely idealize "the fresh," but instead preserving evidence even of his own failures, Jefferson safely stored illegible papers authored by Muslim men whose fugitive run had led them to Carthage. It is this fugitive run, forgotten in the nineteenth century, that now seems of renewed relevance to "the heart of America," merging racial, religious, and regional identities that demand attention in the nation's twenty-first century. Looking to the horizons in 1999, Gore could not see that America's "travels" would soon include war in Muslim lands. A beloved center in his own life, Carthage was also the stage where Gore announced his "heartland" campaign. Unbeknownst to him, the nation was itself not far from tragedy, soon to be wounded to the heart, and face the gulf of Ground Zero. However, in 1999, Gore was also unable to see that the very steps upon which he stood in Carthage had already formed the epicenter of a Muslim story vital to "the heart of America"—a story of injustice and violence, but also of American endurance and Arabic communications, a story that speaks with special urgency in 2019.

Jefferson's own readiness to retain even what he could not read, to preserve letters that were strangely familiar but much too foreign to decipher, is what makes it now possible to recover this story that ends at Carthage, shifting the issues and identities it implies toward the center of our own "conscience." Always the map-maker, Jefferson would have appreciated his posthumous ability to draw parameters anew, revisioning America's historical "horizons," with new centers of meaning allowed to emerge. Although Jefferson did not claim the categorical "freshness" celebrated by Gore in Carthage—a freshness that would soon expire in the days that followed June 1999—Jefferson did foster more contingent hopes, believing always in human potential and possibilities of the nation. Jefferson had inserted a double conditional into his subtle command to Robert Patterson in 1807. Soliciting a translation of the two Arabic manuscripts penned by Muslim fugitives in Kentucky, Jefferson wrote to Philadelphia with a complex imperative, writing that "you will oblige me by getting it done, if practicable, that I may procure the release of the men if proper." Both of Jefferson's conditionals went unsatisfied during his lifetime, but after two centuries, promises still lurk in his pair of "ifs." Jefferson would himself never receive a rendition of the two Arabic pages he held in his hands in 1807. Neither is there any evidence that the two men who were held in the American West ever gained lasting "release." However, the president's commission, with its lingering contingencies, seems now ready to receive a response, no matter how partial and belated. In *Jefferson's Muslim Fugitives*, it has at last become "practicable" to decipher the difficult writings of these two West Africans, piecing together for the first time also their story from the scant materials that have survived. And yet, in undertaking this task, seeking to satisfy Jefferson's first conditional, it is his second "if" that now seems even more urgent. The two Muslims who were prospectively to be freed in 1807 died long ago, as did the American president who was willing, but only "if proper," to free them. And yet, despite time's "distance" and the death of generations, Jefferson's conditionals continue to resonate. His polite imperatives still seem to demand responses, tasking their readers to work for a "release"—a "release" from haunting injustice as well as historical illusions, seeking not to make a "clean start," but to read the past anew with all its conditional promises, interrogating the "ifs" upon which has always depended "the very idea of what America could become."

Notes

Prologue

1. Letters authored by Thomas Jefferson—as well as by fellow founders, John Adams, James Madison, and George Washington—are quoted from the digital editions of the National Historical Publications and Records Commission (NHPRC) and cited according to their acronyms (e.g., the *Papers of Thomas Jefferson Digital Edition* as *PTJDE*). The *PTJDE* features items not yet published as part of *The Papers of Thomas Jefferson*, eds. Julian P. Boyd et al., 43 vols. to date (Princeton: Princeton University Press, 1950–2018), which I do, however, cite subsequently for its invaluable annotations. In citing *PTJDE* letters, I abbreviate Jefferson's name as "TJ"; the above derives from TJ to John Benson, March 5, 1809, *PTJDE*.

2. For the "three wagons" that "transported the belongings of a retiring president from the national capital to Monticello," see Lucia Stanton's *Free Some Day: The African-American Families of Monticello* (Charlottesville: Thomas Jefferson Foundation, 2000), 63. Stanton records the enslaved wagoner, David Hern, as helping to organize this caravan, which also carried enslaved women and children, namely "a pregnant Fanny Hern and Edith Fossett and her two children" (63). See also Kevin Hayes's superlative *The Road to Monticello: The Life and Mind of Thomas Jefferson* (Oxford: Oxford University Press, 2008), for Jefferson's "[a]nticipating his retirement by more than a year" by earlier dispatching "much of his presidential library back to Monticello" (515). The "three wagons" sent to Monticello as part of the final move planned in March 1809, were, Hayes notes, "partly filled" not merely with "books" but also Jefferson's "papers" (515).

3. Entitled "American Literature to 1830: Faith, Reason, Imagination," this graduate course at Northern Illinois University (ENGL 676) met on Thursday evenings in the spring 2009 semester. The course's readings for its Thursday, March 5, session featured letters by Jefferson; readings for the Thursday, March 19, session included the writings of Ibrāhīm ʿAbd ar-Raḥmān ibn Sori and ʿUmar ibn Sayyid. No meeting for the intervening Thursday—March 12—was scheduled due to spring recess.

4. This initiative, supported by an NEH Teaching Development Fellowship, included my translation of previously unpublished Arabic materials by the enslaved West African Muslim ʿUmar ibn Sayyid—materials published on my initiative's website with permissions graciously granted by Spartanburg County Historical Association and the E. H. Little Library at Davidson College (see www.niu.edu/arabicslavewritings).

5. An early pioneer of the field, and an author who also sought to make the Muslim slave experience accessible to broader audiences, is Terry Alford, whose biography of Ibrāhīm ʿAbd ar-Raḥmān ibn Sori—*Prince among Slaves*—originally appeared

in 1977 and was republished by Oxford University Press in 1986. Most essential to the early scholarship on Muslim slave writings, in particular, however, was the work of Allan D. Austin, especially his *African Muslims in Antebellum America: A Sourcebook* (New York: Garland Publishing, 1984), and the successor study, his *African Muslims in Antebellum America: Transatlantic Stories and Spiritual Struggles* (New York: Routledge, 1997). In addition to my indebtedness to his scholarship, I also acknowledge the generous encouragement I received from Allan in correspondence during my work's earliest stages in 2011.

Chapter 1

1. Ira P. Nash to TJ, October 3, 1807, *PTJDE*; the original manuscript of Nash's letter is housed as part of the William K. Bixby Collection, Missouri Historical Society.

2. For Sangster's keeping of a "Fairfax County ordinary [. . .] located five miles from Bull Run, probably somewhere to the southeast of present Clifton," see James A. Bear and Lucia Stanton, eds., *Jefferson's Memorandum Books: Accounts, with Legal Records and Miscellany, 1767–1826* (Princeton: Princeton University Press, 1997), 1150–1151. Jefferson regularly refers to this inn as "Songster's tavern," or more simply as "Songster's" (see, for instance, TJ to George Washington, July 30, 1792, *PTJDE* and TJ to Henry Rose, November 4, 1801, *PTJDE*).

3. For these details of Jefferson's return trip from Monticello, see TJ to Martha Jefferson Randolph, October 12, 1807, *PTJDE*.

4. Jefferson's arrival in Washington on the morning of October 3 is suggested by a letter to Thomas Mann Randolph dated October 4, in which Jefferson notes that he "arrived here yesterday morning" (*PTJDE*). This arrival date is also consistent with Jefferson's own travel itinerary (TJ, Table of Mileages, September 30, 1807, *PTJDE*).

5. In an undated follow-up letter to Jefferson, but which the president marks as receiving on Monday, October 5, Nash mentions meeting the president "yesterday" (i.e., Sunday, October 4)—a meeting at which Nash "presented" Jefferson with "the piece" of Arabic writing. Nash's initial note, petitioning for "an interview" with Jefferson, was not penned until late in the day on Saturday, October 3; Nash himself dates this initial letter as "Saturday Evening" and mentions that he would be available to meet Jefferson "any time [. . .] *after* this Evening" (my italics; Ira P. Nash to TJ, October 3, 1807, *PTJDE*). Hence Nash's meeting with the president must have taken place sometime on October 4 (i.e., the day *after* the evening of October 3 and the day *before* Nash's follow-up letter, which Jefferson marks as receiving on October 5, and which refers to their meeting as taking place "yesterday").

6. Details on this affair are offered by Robert J. Allison, *Stephen Decatur: American Naval Hero, 1779–1820* (Amherst: University of Massachusetts Press, 2005), 84.

7. For this letter from John Adams to Benjamin Rush, September 1, 1807, see *The Papers of John Adams, Digital Edition* (*PJADE*); the "y" of "ever" in square brackets appears to be missing or obscured from the original, but is provided by the *PJADE*. For prior quotation of this letter, and its relation to the impressment crisis, see Roger

G. Kennedy, *Burr, Hamilton, and Jefferson: A Study in Character* (New York: Oxford University Press, 2002), 312.

8. These "acts of aggression" are treated by William R. Nester, *The Jeffersonian Vision, 1801–1815: The Art of American Power during the Early Republic* (Washington, DC: Potomac Books, 2013), 93.

9. Garry Wills, *Henry Adams and the Making of America* (Boston: Houghton Mifflin, 2007), 223.

10. TJ to Robert Patterson, October 18, 1807, *PTJDE*.

11. For the *Chesapeake*'s Mediterranean destination, and the intersection between the impressment crisis and the aftermath of Jefferson's Barbary campaign, see Robert J. Allison, *The Crescent Obscured: The United States and the Muslim World, 1776–1815* (New York: Oxford University Press, 1995), 207.

12. For the *Chesapeake*'s "ill-starred monthlong journey," see Michael R. Beschloss, *Presidents of War* (New York: Crown, 2018), 10.

13. For these quotations, see Ira P. Nash to TJ, October 5, 1807, *PTJDE*. See Chapter 12, note 35, for this tentative designation of "the month of May."

14. As explored further below, the only times Jefferson's Arabic materials penned by fugitive Africans have received even passing mention in print is as part of two discrete efforts to catalogue Jefferson's papers, one in the nineteenth century, and one in the twentieth. See respectively "Jefferson Papers: Number Two," *Knickerbocker Magazine* 6 (1835): 537–540, and "Islamic Manuscripts in North American Collections, pt. 4," *MELA Notes, the Journal of the Middle East Librarians Association* 35 (1985): 6–10. Both of these cataloguing efforts were published anonymously, and mistake the origins of these Arabic papers due to being unaware of their contexts. Neither of these brief mentions, for instance, recognizes that the Arabic material owned by Jefferson was penned by enslaved Africans. The brief twentieth-century mention of the Arabic document in Jefferson's papers even suggests that the manuscript seems to be written "in a rather large, crude Western hand, possibly that of Thomas Jefferson," which is wholly incorrect (see "Islamic Manuscripts in North American Collections, pt. 4," 7). Also, it is clear that both of these cataloguing efforts had access merely to *one*, not both, of the two Arabic manuscripts Jefferson originally received from Ira P. Nash on October 4, 1807.

15. William Dalzell to TJ, February 10, 1809, *PTJDE*.

16. John B. Boles, *Jefferson: Architect of American Liberty* (Boulder, CO: Basic Books, 2017), 596.

17. Jefferson's relationship with Sally Hemings has generated an entire subfield of critical speculation and apologetics in Jefferson studies spanning two centuries. Most recently, Monticello itself has shifted its presentation of this subject; see Farah Stockman, "Monticello Is Done Avoiding Jefferson's Relationship with Sally Hemings," *New York Times*, June 16, 2018 (www.nytimes.com/2018/06/16/us/sally-hemings-exhibit-monticello.html). During my own recent visit in 2017, the contrary view was still on offer at the Monticello bookstore, which included among its titles William G. Hyland's *In Defense of Thomas Jefferson: The Sally Hemings Sex Scandal* (New York: Thomas Dunne Books, 2009)—a study that queries the DNA evidence

now customarily cited to prove a sexual relationship between Jefferson and Sally Hemings (17 and ff.).

18. For Jefferson's October 5, 1765, purchase, see Paul P. Hoffman, ed., *Virginia Gazette Daybooks, 1750–1752 and 1764–1766* (Charlottesville: University of Virginia Microfilm Publications, 1967), segment 2, folio 202; and Kevin J. Hayes, "How Thomas Jefferson Read the Qur'an," *Early American Literature* 39, no. 2 (2004): 247–261 (247, 259).

19. For the controversy sparked by Ellison's choice, see John Nichols, "Keith Ellison and the Jefferson Koran," *The Nation* (January 3, 2007), which emphasizes that criticism leveled against Ellison by "Virginia Congressman Virgil Goode" also "[p]redictably [. . .] found a forum on Fox News" (www.thenation.com/article/keith-ellison-and-jefferson-koran). For coverage in the *Washington Post*, see Frederic J. Frommer, "Ellison Uses Thomas Jefferson's Quran," January 5, 2007 (www.washingtonpost. com/wp-dyn/content/article/2007/01/05/AR2007010500512.html). George Sale's translation—the same purchased by Jefferson—has "persisted as the longest lasting, most popular, and influential English translation, having gone through at least 123 editions in both Britain and the United States up to 1975" (Bruce B. Lawrence, *The Koran in English: A Biography* [Princeton: Princeton University Press, 2017], 38).

20. Denise A. Spellberg, *Thomas Jefferson's Qur'an: Islam and the Founders* (New York: Alfred A. Knopf, 2013); for Ellison as a foreground to Spellberg's own study, see x–xi.

21. Michael Gomez, "Muslims in Early America," *The Journal of Southern History* 60, no. 4 (1994): 671–710 (682). For the "tens of thousands" figure, see also Spellberg, *Thomas Jefferson's Qur'an*, 7.

22. Patrick Bowen, *A History of Conversion to Islam in the United States: 1920–1975* (Leiden: Brill, 2017), 20.

23. For Futa Jallon's role as a "famous centre of Islamic learning" in eighteenth-century West Africa, see Elizabeth Isichei, *A History of African Societies to 1870* (Cambridge: Cambridge University Press, 1997), 301.

24. Spellberg, *Thomas Jefferson's Qur'an*, 123. Spellberg does, however, devote significant attention to Muslim slaves in the context of early American engagements with Islam, emphasizing especially the story of Ibrāhīm 'Abd ar-Raḥmān, which I also address in this book (for the first mention of Muslim slaves in Spellberg's study, see p. 10).

25. Several African Muslims authored Arabic in North America well before US Independence. Especially well known is Job Ben Solomon, a Muslim slave who first "wrote [and] pronounced the words 'Allah' and 'Muhammad'" in Arabic in 1731 Maryland; see Austin, *African Muslims*, 56.

Chapter 2

1. TJ to Charles Bellini, September 30, 1785, *PTJDE*. Jefferson's self-description as a "savage of the mountains of America" is oft-quoted; see, for instance, Kariann Yokota, *Unbecoming British: How Revolutionary America Became a Postcolonial Nation*

(New York: Oxford University Press, 2010), which recognizes Jefferson's phrase to be offered "only partly in jest" (8).

2. A year earlier, when Jefferson first arrived to France with his elder daughter, Martha, she noted in a letter that "at our arrival [. . .] papa spoke very little french and me not a word" (*Thomas Jefferson Travels: Collected Travel Writing, 1765–1826*, ed. Anthony Brandt [Washington: National Geographic Society, 2006], 6). However, by the summer of 1786, Jefferson was still bemoaning his French inadequacies. Writing to St. John de Crèvecoeur on July 11, 1786, Jefferson opens by noting that his incapacity "to write in French so as to be sure of conveying my true meaning, or perhaps any meaning at all" (*PTJDE*).

3. Richard O'Brien to TJ, August 24, 1785, *PTJDE*. O'Brien's name is spelled variously in late eighteenth- and early nineteenth-century sources, including in his very own letters (e.g., "O'Bryen" and "Obryan"; see, for instance, TJ to John Jay, December 31, 1786, *PTJDE*). For the sake of clarity, I have standardized the name to read "O'Brien" in my citations.

4. See Lawrence A. Peskin, *Captives and Countrymen: Barbary Slavery and the American Public, 1785–1816* (Baltimore: Johns Hopkins University Press, 2009), which opens by describing the arrest of O'Brien's ship ("the Dauphin of Philadelphia"), noting that his vessel was just one of two taken, captured along with "the Maria of Boston" (1). Although these two vessels were themselves American, the nationality of their crews has been disputed. Peskin suggests that it was "twenty-one Americans" who were taken "hostage," including "Captain Richard O'Brien of the Dauphin and James L. Cathcart" (*Captives and Countrymen*, 1). This same episode is treated in Francis D. Cogliano, *Emperor of Liberty: Thomas Jefferson's Foreign Policy* (New Haven: Yale University Press, 2014), who similarly notes that "[i]n the two incidents the Algerians had captured twenty-one Americans" (42). But see Priscilla H. Roberts and Richard S. Roberts, *Thomas Barclay (1728–1793): Consul in France, Diplomat in Barbary* (Bethlehem, PA: Lehigh University Press, 2008), which emphasizes that "[o]f the twenty-one crew members held in Algiers eight only were American" (333). This reckoning of "eight" Americans is derived from contemporary records kept by one of the enslaved men in Algiers, P. R. Randall (see his Enclosure I: P. R. Randall to his Father, April 2, 1786, *PTJDE*).

5. These details surface in an 1805 letter written by Richard O'Brien to Jefferson's close confidant, and sometime private secretary, William Armistead Burwell (July 12, 1805, *PTJDE*).

6. For accusations of Jefferson's supposed "abandonment" of Richmond, see the editorial annotations to the *PTJDE*'s I. Diary of Arnold's Invasion and Notes on Subsequent Events in 1781: Versions of 1796?, 1805, and 1816. For this quotation, paraphrasing Jefferson critic Thomas Turner—that is, "Jefferson timidly abandoned the seat of government during Arnold's invasion"—see Dumas Malone, *Jefferson and His Time*, 6 vols. (Boston: Little, Brown and Company, 1948–1981), II:15. These words—"continu[ing] upon the spot during the whole Scene"—are the last in Richard O'Brien's letter to Burwell cited immediately above. Although the occasion of O'Brien's letter is not explicitly stipulated, he likely wrote to aid Burwell's

advocacy as he "led Jefferson's defense in 1805 against the accusations of the journalist James Callender" (Susan Stein, *The Worlds of Thomas Jefferson at Monticello* [New York: Thomas Jefferson Memorial Foundation, 1993], 206).

7. See Henry Wiencek, *Master of the Mountain: Thomas Jefferson and His Slaves* (New York: Farrar, Straus and Giroux, 2013), 27–28, for Jefferson's critique of the slave trade in his authoring of *Summary View* as well as the Declaration of Independence.

8. For this preamble's attribution to Gouverneur Morris, see James J. Kirschke, *Gouverneur Morris: Author, Statesman, and Man of the World* (New York: T. Dunne, 2005), 170. As Kirschke notes, Morris also "emerged as the most vociferous opponent of slavery" at the "Constitutional Convention" (176).

9. This reckoning is offered by Jesse Holland in his *The Invisibles: The Untold Story of African American Slaves in the White House* (Guilford, CT: Rowman & Littlefield, 2016), 82. See also Boles, *Jefferson: Architect of American Liberty*, who notes that "[w]hile the other children inherited young slaves, Peter gave Thomas his trusted slave valet, Sawney, who was roughly Peter's age" (14).

10. William H. Adams, *The Paris Years of Thomas Jefferson* (New Haven: Yale University Press, 2000), 137.

11. The landmark study of Jefferson's relationship with Sally Hemings is Annette Gordon-Reed, *Thomas Jefferson and Sally Hemings: An American Controversy* (Charlottesville: University of Virginia Press, 1997). See also Catherine Kerrison's recent *Jefferson's Daughters: Three Sisters, White and Black, in a Young America* (New York: Ballantine Books, 2018), which notes that "[h]ow and when their relationship changed during Hemings's two years in Paris have been the subject of much controversy" (94).

12. TJ to James Madison, September 1, 1785, *PTJDE*.

13. For in-depth treatment of Jefferson's architectural efforts, see Jack McLaughlin, *Jefferson and Monticello: The Biography of a Builder* (New York: H. Holt, 1988); it is McLaughlin who connects Jefferson to his father via their shared surveying work, noting that "Jefferson apparently learned to do architectural drawings at an early age" (58). Jefferson also "officially held the post of Albemarle County surveyor," although "[t]here is no evidence indicated that he was actively engaged in surveying," as Joel Kovarsky recognizes in his *The True Geography of Our Country: Jefferson's Cartographic Vision* (Charlottesville: University of Virginia Press, 2014), 10–11.

14. For Jefferson's additions to the President's House, see Patrick Phillips-Schrock, *The White House: An Illustrated Architectural History* (Jefferson, NC: McFarland & Co., 2013), 33.

15. TJ to James Madison, February 8, 1786, *PTJDE*.

16. For this quote, see Michael C. Hardy, *The Capitals of the Confederacy: A History* (Charleston: The History Press, 2015), 32. Maison Carrée as Jefferson's model is treated by Ralph G. Giordano, *The Architectural Ideology of Thomas Jefferson* (Jefferson, NC: McFarland & Co., 2012), 101.

17. Evidence of slave labor on Virginia's Capitol has very recently come to light. See Mark Holmberg, "18th-century Vouchers Show Slaves Helped Build Virginia Capitol," *Richmond Times-Dispatch*, July 29, 2016 (www.richmond.com/news/

holmberg-th-century-vouchers-show-slaves-helped-build-virginia-capitol/article_
c1034222-b23c-55e9-93cd-e3e1ce41e54a.html).

18. Jefferson's role in designing Richmond's Capitol—later the center of the Confederacy—occasionally surfaces within studies of the Civil War itself; see Nelson Lankford, *Richmond Burning: The Last Days of the Confederate Capital* (New York: Penguin Books, 2003), 13.

19. TJ to Richard O'Brien, September 29, 1785, *PTJDE*.

20. See TJ to Richard O'Brien, November 4, 1785. In this letter, Jefferson notes that "Mr. Adams [. . .] and myself have agreed to authorise the bearer hereof Mr. Lamb to treat for your redemption," but also adds the caution that "if [freedom] can be obtained for sums within our power, we shall have the money paid. But in this we act without instruction from Congress." Recent treatment of John Lamb's mission is offered by Peskin, *Captives and Countrymen*, 31. For Jefferson's understanding that "22. of our citizens [are] in slavery," see TJ to Francis Eppes, December 11, 1785, *PTJDE*. As suggested above, the typical count is not "22" but "twenty-one," and the nationality of the crew in captivity has been disputed.

21. Especially fatal to the Algerian prisoners was a 1794 plague, which killed at least seven of the captives according to James L. Cathcart's own account (see his *The Captives: Eleven Years a Prisoner in Algiers*, ed. Jane B. Newkirk [La Porte: Herald Print, 1899], 274).

22. See Peskin, *Captives and Countrymen*, who notes that "Captives began writing home as soon as possible after landing in Algiers" and that "[w]hile O'Brien took the lead, other prisoners, too, were able to send off letters to friends, family, and government officials" (19). My research into Richard O'Brien, and his 1790 diary in particular, was graciously aided by librarians at the Historical Society of Pennsylvania, and especially David Haugaard, director of research services.

23. Reports of O'Brien "conform[ing] outwardly to the Mohammedan religion" made their way even into posthumous remembrances; for this precise phrase, see *Appletons' Cyclopaedia of American Biography, Volume 4*, eds. James Grant Wilson and John Fiske (New York: D. Appleton and Co., 1888), 551. For reference to "the Turk O'Brien," see William Thornton to TJ, August 30, 1809, *PTJDE*. Between O'Brien's enslavement and his consular service in North Africa, he returned stateside in 1796, "over[seeing] the construction of three cruisers commissioned by" the Algerian Dey, as Allison has noted (*The Crescent Obscured*, 154). For contemporary record of O'Brien's return to serve in the United States, see George Washington to Dey Hassan Bashaw, June 13, 1796, *PGWDE*—a letter that Washington begins by noting "the late arrival of Captain O'Brien from Lisbon."

24. For Jefferson being "haunted" by the "plight of the men aboard the *Maria* and the *Dauphin*," see Brian Kilmeade and Don Yaeger, *Thomas Jefferson and the Tripoli Pirates: The Forgotten War That Changed American History* (New York: Sentinel, 2015), 8. To bolster this claim, however, this same page in Kilmeade and Yaeger's study erroneously synthesizes discrete letters, fusing together quotations from TJ to Francis Eppes, August 30, 1785, and TJ to Francis Eppes, December 11, 1785, as if they derived from a single letter.

25. For this quotation, see *Founding the Republic: A Documentary History*, ed. John J. Patrick (Westport, CT: Greenwood Press, 1995), 94.

26. This quotation, and its relation to Jefferson specifically, is addressed by Daniel L. Dreisbach, *Thomas Jefferson and the Wall of Separation between Church and State* (New York: New York University Press, 2003), 1.

27. This passage derives from Jefferson's own autobiography, and is quoted from the *PTJDE* (*Autobiography*, January 6, 1821, entry). This passage is, unsurprisingly, frequently treated; see, for instance, Mark A. Beliles and Jerry Newcombe, *Doubting Thomas?: The Religious Life and Legacy of Thomas Jefferson* (New York: Morgan James Publishing, 2014), 222.

28. Jefferson's grave with this epitaph is still viewable by visitors to Monticello's grounds. For previous print quotation, however, see Frederick D. Nichols and Ralph E. Griswold, *Thomas Jefferson, Landscape Architect* (Charlottesville: University of Virginia Press, 1981), 178.

Chapter 3

1. Richard Brown notes that Patrick Henry initially resisted Jefferson's "Religious Freedom Act," considering it "neither necessary nor desirable to treat all religious beliefs equally" (*Self-Evident Truths: Contesting Equal Rights from the Revolution to the Civil War* [New Haven: Yale University Press, 2017], 41). According to Jon Kukla, however, Henry soon embraced his state's achievement, "celebrat[ing] Jefferson's statute as the highest and best expression of Virginia's commitment to religious freedom" (*Patrick Henry: Champion of Liberty* [New York: Simon & Schuster, 2018], 282).

2. Although dated January 16, 1786, Barclay's letter—a duplicate of an original to be dispatched to Patrick Henry via another "packet"—oddly seems to have come into Jefferson's hands two days earlier (see Thomas Barclay to TJ, January 14, 1786, *PTJDE*). For Barclay's letter as indeed dated January 16, 1786, see William Palmer et al., eds. *Calendar of Virginia State Papers and Other Manuscripts*, 11 vols. (Richmond: Virginia State Library, 1875–1893), IV:81.

3. Although "the exact date of [Barclay's] departure is unclear [. . .] it was around January 24," notes Roberts and Roberts, *Thomas Barclay*, 335.

4. For recent invocation, as well as interrogation, of Morocco's traditional title as "America's oldest ally," see Jacob Mundy, "The Geopolitical Functions of the Western Sahara Conflict: US Hegemony, Moroccan Stability, and Sahrawi Strategies of Resistance," in *Global, Regional, and Local Dimensions of Western Sahara's Protracted Decolonization: When a Conflict Gets Old*, ed. García Ojeda (New York: Palgrave Macmillan, 2017), 53–78 (56).

5. Previously unpublished in its ciphered original, I quote this letter—Thomas Jefferson to John Adams, August 17, 1785, Adams Family Papers, Massachusetts Historical Society—courtesy of the MHS. This August 17, 1786, letter is included in the *PTJDE*, but the digital edition does not include Jefferson's original ciphered material quoted above, replacing the letter's encoded lines with English equivalents.

6. These glosses for Jefferson's cipher, supplied by Adams, are quoted from TJ to John Adams, August 17, 1785, *PTJDE*. In the weeks leading up to this letter, Jefferson had

already discussed, and even utilized, their mutual cipher (see TJ to John Adams, July 31, 1785, *PTJDE*).

7. In his response to Jefferson, Adams notes that "[i]f Mr Barclay will undertake the Voyage, I am for looking no farther. We cannot find a Steadier, or more prudent Man" (John Adams to TJ, August 23, 1785, *PTJDE*).

8. During the early months of 1783, before the Treaty of Paris was signed, Jefferson was already ciphering correspondence; see TJ to James Madison, January 31, 1783, as well as TJ to James Madison, February 7, 1783, *PTJDE*.

9. For this letter see *Adams Family Correspondence, January 1786—February 1787*, eds. Margaret Hogan et al. (Cambridge, MA: Belknap Press, 2005), 35, as well as Abigail Adams 2d to John Quincy Adams, September 24, 1785, *PJADE*.

10. Abigail Adams's initial, negative impressions of Paris are highlighted by Woody Holton, *Abigail Adams* (New York: Free Press, 2009), 204. However, Adams's reluctance to leave Paris and bid Jefferson farewell are also evident in a 1785 letter, in which she regrets leaving the city in "Spring" as well as "the loss of Mr. Jeffersons Society" (Abigail Adams to Cotton Tufts, April 26, 1785, *PJADE*).

11. A common Muslim name, the second term of 'Abd ar-Raḥmān recalls the Qur'an, which regularly refers to God as "*ar-Raḥmān*" ("the Merciful" or "the Most Merciful"; see, for example, the very title of the scripture's Chapter 55, "*Sūrat ar-Raḥmān*"). 'Abd ar-Raḥmān Aga—the "Minister from Tripoli"—is often ascribed additional honorifics, including "Haggi" (i.e., the Arabic *ḥājjī*, "pilgrim"); see, for instance, Roberts and Roberts, *Thomas Barclay*, 182–184.

12. For Jefferson's stay in London, see Malone, *Jefferson and His Time*, II:28–29. As Jefferson would inform John Jay on March 12—the day after his arrival—he traveled to England to treat with the "minister from Tripoli," but was also there to conclude a treaty with "the minister of Portugal" (TJ to John Jay, March 12, 1786, *PTJDE*).

13. The American Peace Commissioners to John Jay, March 28, 1786, *PTJDE*.

14. The American Peace Commissioners to John Jay, March 28, 1786, *PTJDE*. Beyond the detailed discussion of this letter offered by Spellberg in her *Thomas Jefferson's Qur'an*, 149 (cited further below), this letter has also risen to widespread notice due to its quotation in prominent venues. See, for instance, this letter as cited by Christopher Hitchens in his "Jefferson Versus the Muslim Pirates," in *Arguably: Essays* (New York: Twelve, 2012), 12–20 (14).

15. See Spellberg, *Thomas Jefferson's Qur'an*, 139.

16. Thomas Barclay to the American Peace Commissioners, October 2, 1786, *PTJDE*. Barclay's letter continues on to list a full "11" items, featuring additional translations and contextual documents for the "original Treaty."

17. Barclay's travel "itinerary"—departing Paris in January and arriving to Morocco in June—is tracked by Roberts and Roberts, *Thomas Barclay*, 175.

18. Jefferson would observe to Joseph Priestley that "to read the Latin & Greek authors in their original is a sublime luxury" (TJ to Joseph Priestley, January 27, 1800, *PTJDE*). For Jefferson's own multilingual book collection see Chapter 18, note 11.

19. The first printing of this passage is offered in *Laws of the United States of America* (Philadelphia: Andrew Brown, 1791), 392. For a more recent printing, see *Treaties and*

Other International Agreements of the United States of America: 1776–1949, Volume 9, ed. Charles I. Bevans (Washington, DC: US Government Printing Office, 1972), 1287.

20. For this definition of "Moor," and the term's problematic racial history, see Kenneth Addison, *"We Hold These Truths to Be Self-Evident . . .": An Interdisciplinary Analysis of the Roots of Racism and Slavery in America* (Lanham, MD: University Press of America, 2009), 171.

21. This Arabic original is quoted from *Treaties and Other International Acts of the United States of America,* ed. Hunter Miller, 8 vols. (Washington, DC: United States Government Printing Office, 1931–1948), II:192. The English translation that follows is my own, but benefits from my consulting the slightly different rendition offered by Christiaan Snouck Hurgronje in this same edition (II:221). Immediately previous to this Arabic quotation, Article 6 introduces the above with the phrase "الشرط السادس أنه" ("Clause Six is that [. . .]").

22. Despite such significant discrepancies between this treaty's Arabic source and its English translation, the "original" compact with Morocco invariably goes unanalyzed, not only in Jefferson studies, but in all recent accounts that address this historic treaty between the United States and a Muslim power. I render "سيد" as "Master" as this term here refers to the Moroccan Sultan, but this same Arabic word is regularly invoked in specifically religious settings (where "lord," or "liege lord," better conveys its significance).

23. TJ to Thomas Barclay, December 27, 1786, *PTJDE.*

24. These are the words of Congressman Philip Miller Crane, delivered in the House of Representatives on July 22, 2004; see *Congressional Record, Proceedings and Debates of the 108th Congress, Vol. 150, Part 13* (Washington, DC: US Government Printing Office, 2004), 17268.

Chapter 4

1. TJ to Ezra Stiles, December 24, 1786, *PTJDE.*

2. Besides Jefferson's letter to Stiles, two other letters are extant—one to Maria Cosway, and one to James Maury—authored on December 24, 1786.

3. For Jefferson's arrival to New Haven on June 8, 1784, see the entry in his own Memorandum Books, 1784, *PTJDE,* in which Jefferson notes tersely that "Pd. at Newhaven for 2. oz. bark 6." Stiles's own record for this same day is much more detailed, as quoted below. Stiles's relationship with Jefferson has increasingly received attention, mentioned especially in studies of early American "Natural History" (e.g., Keith Thomson, *Jefferson's Shadow: The Story of His Science* [New Haven: Yale University Press, 2014], 59).

4. Ezra Stiles, *The Literary Diary of Ezra Stiles,* ed. Franklin Bowditch Dexter, 3 vols. (New York: C. Scribner's Sons, 1901), III:125.

5. For recent sustained treatment of Stiles's Arabic interests, see my *The Islamic Lineage of American Literary Culture: Muslim Sources from the Revolution to Reconstruction* (New York: Oxford University Press, 2016), 1–32.

6. For "*Hebrew, Chaldee* and *Arabic,*" see Stiles, *Diary,* III:278, and Einboden, *Islamic Lineage,* 31, which treats Stiles's commencement address in the context of his reading Muslim

sources, including the Qur'an (19–20). "Ivy League" is a twentieth-century category, arising from collegiate athletics. However, as this phrase has come to imply more broadly America's early, elite institutions of higher learning, it is invoked below for this purpose, designating colleges including Harvard, Yale, and the University of Pennsylvania.

7. TJ to Ezra Stiles, July 17, 1785, *PTJDE*. The material in the square brackets is my own, provided for the sake of clarity.

8. For Jefferson's sustained aspirations for Greece—both political and linguistic—see his letter to George Wythe (September 16, 1787, *PTJDE*), in which Jefferson confesses that "I cannot help looking forward to the reestablishment of the Greeks as a people, and the language of Homer becoming again a living language as among possible events."

9. Ezra Stiles to TJ, September 14, 1786, *PTJDE*.

10. Yale's doctorate was not the only Ivy League honor Jefferson would receive. Also in 1786, Harvard awarded Jefferson the same degree, although notice was not sent to Paris until a year later. See Joseph Willard to TJ, September 24, 1788, *PTJDE*, in which Willard, president of Harvard, sends Jefferson: "a Diploma for a Doctorate of Laws, which was conferred by Harvard University, in this place, more than a year ago, and which various circumstances have prevented my conveying before."

11. William H. Adams, *The Paris Years of Thomas Jefferson* (New Haven: Yale University Press, 2000), 96. Such early recognition by Stiles of Jefferson's authorship of the Declaration is noted previously by Hayes, *The Road to Monticello*, 271.

12. Ezra Stiles to TJ, September 14, 1786, *PTJDE*. In the *PTJDE*, several word endings are provided merely in square brackets ("Barb[ary]," "sub[d]u[ed]," and "subsi[dize]").

13. For previous treatment of this Latin quotation, see Allison, *The Crescent Obscured*, 10. Jefferson himself had previously invoked, and even adapted, Cato's formula; see Michael Kranish, *Flight from Monticello: Thomas Jefferson at War* (Oxford: Oxford University Press, 2011), 68.

14. Stiles's receipt of Jefferson's letter on August 17, 1787, is recorded in *Diary*, III:276.

15. For the "Tornadoes and Hurricanes" plaguing New England in August 1787, see Stiles, *Diary*, III:278.

16. I thank Yale University's Beinecke Library for hosting my research over several years, permitting my recovery of quotations from Stiles's original manuscript diary; this selection derives from Ezra Stiles, Literary Diary, vol. 13, pp. 62–63, held as part of the Beinecke's MS Vault Stiles.

17. The above quotation from Stiles's diary represents the very first time it has been published in full, featuring Stiles's Arabic inscription. In the only printed version available, Stiles's entry does appear, but is redacted, with its Arabic materials cut (see Stiles, *Diary*, III:276). This edition, published by Franklin Bowditch Dexter, regularly suppresses the Arabic featured in Stiles's manuscript diary (for other instances, see Einboden, *Islamic Lineage*, 27–28).

18. As explored further below, Jefferson's interests in generating facsimiles spanned his entire career. For Jefferson's own engagement with copying technology in Paris specifically, see Howard C. Rice, *Thomas Jefferson's Paris* (Princeton: Princeton University Press, 2015), 83.

19. Jefferson's speculations regarding links between Asiatic peoples and the Native North Americans—here expressed to Stiles in a private letter—was articulated

earlier in print, featured as part of his 1785 *Notes on the State of Virginia*, in which Jefferson opines that "[t]he resemblance between the Indians of America and the eastern inhabitants of Asia, would induce us to conjecture, that the former are the descendants of the latter, or the latter of the former." These views received wider distribution due to subsequent quotation in nineteenth-century studies. This precise selection, for instance, is featured in John McIntosh's influential *The Origin of the North American Indians: With a Faithful Description of Their Manners and Customs* (New York: Cornish, Lamport & Company, 1858), 86.

20. In Stiles's Arabic transcription, the "*ī*" is missing from "*raḥīm*," which I here supply (altering Stiles's incorrect "الرحم" to read instead "الرحيم"). It is unclear whether this omission is attributable to Stiles's own faulty transcription, or due to an error in the source he copies.

21. This quotation represents the King James Version of Proverbs 16:25.

Chapter 5

1. Never before published, this quotation derives from page 1 of Abiel Holmes to Ezra Stiles, February 22, 1788, Quincy, Wendell, Holmes, and Upham Family Papers, Massachusetts Historical Society. The italics included in my transcription reflect Holmes's own underlining of these specific terms (e.g., "Clio or Urania").

2. Listed among the nine muses, Clio and Urania are often "coupled" together; see, for instance, E. R. Gregory, *Milton and the Muses* (Tuscaloosa: University of Alabama Press, 1989), 112, 115.

3. The Arabic name "*Uthmān*" has historically varied in pronunciation, differing across regions of Persianate, Turkish, and West African cultural influence. For example, the initial "*th*" of this name is frequently sounded instead as "*s*," yielding "*Usmān*" or "*Osman*." For the Caliph 'Uthmān's reign in "647," which coincided with the initial Muslim "maritime expeditions against Crete, Cyprus and Rhodes," see Alexander Gillespie, *The Causes of War. Volume 1: 3000 BCE to 1000 CE* (Oxford: Hart Publishing, 2013), 230.

4. Rarely mentioned in accounts of early coastal Georgia, the site of Parnassus Plantation is still locatable in Bryan County, although its historic buildings are now entirely gone. In addition to visiting this site several times, I have greatly benefited from the scholarship and encouragement of Buddy Sullivan. The early history of Parnassus Plantation, and its connections to the Demere family in particular, is traced by Sullivan in his *From Beautiful Zion to Red Bird Creek: A History of Bryan County, Georgia* (Darien, GA: McIntosh County Board of Commissioners, 2000), 107–108.

5. Holmes's role as Midway's minister is most comprehensively addressed in early overviews of this historic Georgia church. See, for instance, John B. Mallard, *A Short Account of the Congregational Church at Midway, Georgia* (Savannah: Thomas Purse, 1840), 26–28. My reference to "tidewater" recalls the title of Buddy Sullivan's own *Early Days on the Georgia Tidewater: The Story of Mcintosh County & Sapelo* (Darien, GA: McIntosh County Board of Commissioners, 2001)—a book that offers

a vivid overview of the region's rice plantation culture in the early Republic (see, e.g., 220–225).

6. Abiel Holmes, *American Annals, Or, a Chronological History of America, from Its Discovery in 1492 to 1806* (Cambridge, MA: W. Hilliard, 1805).

7. As mentioned above, the landmark studies of US Muslim slave writings were produced by Austin (1984 and 1997), which record ample evidence of literate African Muslims in America well before the Revolution. 'Usman's inscriptions, however—witnessed by Abiel Holmes initially in 1788, and recorded once more in 1790—mark the first extant acts of Arabic authorship by an enslaved Muslim after US Independence in 1783. I have been unable to find any mention of 'Usman in any previous source.

8. For these lines, see Sylvanus Urban, "An Address to James Oglethorpe, Esq; on his settling the Colony in Georgia," *Gentleman's Magazine: or, Monthly Intelligencer* (April 1733): 209. Although not receiving significant prior treatment, this poem has been reproduced in Hennig Cohen, "Two Colonial Poems on the Settling of Georgia," *The Georgia Historical Quarterly* 37, no. 2 (1953): 129–136.

9. This phrase derives from the very title of Robert Montgomery and John Barnwell, *The Most Delightful Golden Islands. Being a Proposal for the Establishment of a Colony in the Country to the South of Carolina* (London, 1717). For Montgomery's featuring these specific islands in his utopian vision—that is, "St. Symon" as well as "Sapella or Sapola"—see Louis De Vorsey Jr., "Oglethorpe and the Earliest Maps of Georgia," in *Oglethorpe in Perspective: Georgia's Founder after Two Hundred Years*, eds. Phinizy Spalding and Harvey H. Jackson (Tuscaloosa: University of Alabama Press, 2006), 22–43 (27).

10. Albert Berry Saye, *A Constitutional History of Georgia, 1732–1945* (Athens: University of Georgia Press, 2010), links Montgomery's utopian vision to the "Genesis of Georgia" (3). Kenneth Coleman, in his "The Southern Frontier: Georgia's Founding and the Expansion of South Carolina," *The Georgia Historical Quarterly*, 56, no. 2 (1972): 163–174, notes that Montgomery's dream was to establish "a settlement between the Savannah and Altamaha river"—the precise area where Georgia's Bryan County, including Parnassus Plantation, is now situated (166).

11. For Oglethorpe's contribution to this contra-Ottoman campaign, see Rodney Baine and Mary Williams, "James Oglethorpe in Europe: Recent Findings of His Military Life," in *Oglethorpe in Perspective*, 112–121 (especially 113–115).

12. For "Gibraltar" as a "latinized" form of "*Jabal Ṭāriq*," and its origins with Ṭāriq ibn Ziyād, see Christina Civantos, *The Afterlife of Al-Andalus: Muslim Iberia in Contemporary Arab and Hispanic Narratives* (Albany: State University of New York Press, 2017), 114.

13. See June Hall McCash, *Jekyll Island's Early Years: From Prehistory through Reconstruction* (Athens: University of Georgia Press, 2005), 72. For early recognition of Oglethorpe's troops serving in Gibraltar before Georgia, see Robert Wright, *A Memoir of General James Oglethorpe* (London: Chapman and Hall, 1867), 191.

14. This quote derives from Jonathan Bryan, *Journal of a Visit to the Georgia Islands of St. Catharines, Green, Ossabaw, Sapelo, St. Simons, Jekyll, and Cumberland*, eds. Virginia Wood and Mary Bullard (Macon, GA: Mercer University Press, 1996), 75. Raymond

Demere (d. 1791) was named for his uncle (Raymond Demere, d. 1766) and was the son of Paul Demere (d. 1760), who served with his brother in Gibraltar. See Daniel Tortora, *Carolina in Crisis: Cherokees, Colonists, and Slaves in the American Southeast, 1756–1763* (Chapel Hill: University of North Carolina Press, 2015), 38. For the original Demere brothers, and their Gibraltar background, see also Edward J. Cashin, *William Bartram and the American Revolution on the Southern Frontier* (Columbia: University of South Carolina Press, 2006), 85.

15. Reflecting especially the concentration of enslaved West African Muslims in America's coastal Southeast, and particularly in Georgia's Golden Isles, Gullah culture is overviewed by William Pollitzer in his *The Gullah People and Their African Heritage* (Athens: University of Georgia Press, 1999); see p. 6, which touches on the same stretch of Georgia's seacoast where 'Usman himself was enslaved.

16. See *Sapelo Voices: Historical Anthropology and the Oral Traditions of Gullah-Geechee Communities on Sapelo Island, Georgia*, eds. Ray Crook, Cornelia Bailey, Norma Harris, and Karen Smith (Carrollton: State University of West Georgia Press, 2003), 207. For this endurance of "Islamic prayer" in the region, see also Spellberg, *Thomas Jefferson's Qur'an*, 273.

17. *The Origins, History, and Future of the Federal Reserve: A Return to Jekyll Island*, eds. Michael Bordo and William Roberds (New York: Cambridge University Press, 2013), a book that arose from a 2010 conference marking the centenary of the 1910 Jekyll Island meeting that ultimately led to the Federal Reserve's establishment in 1913 (1). For Jekyll Island as "a mecca for vacationers," see Susan K. Wood, "Millionaire's Village," *Outdoors in Georgia 7*, no. 7 (1977): 3–8 (3).

18. The origins of the lighthouse on St. Simons Island, as well as its cycles of building and rebuilding, are treated by Kevin McCarthy, *Georgia's Lighthouses and Historic Coastal Sites* (Sarasota: Pineapple Press, 1998), 90 and ff.

19. The enslavement of Bilali on John Couper's plantation is highlighted by John Otto in his *Cannon's Point Plantation, 1794–1860: Living Conditions and Status Patterns in the Old South* (New York: Academic Press, 1984), 36.

20. This etymology is noted by Garland Cannon, *The Arabic Contributions to the English Language: An Historical Dictionary* (Wiesbaden: Harrassowitz, 1994), 315. The Arabic etymology of "tabby" was early recognized by Mitford Mathews, *Some Sources of Southernisms* (Birmingham: University of Alabama Press, 1948), 128–129, which notes that "our friends in Georgia who use this word tabby are in reality speaking Arabic without perhaps suspecting it" (129). See also the historical marker dedicated to "Tabby" erected at the Horton House site on Jekyll Island that asserts that "[t]he word tabby is African in origin, with an Arabic background." Interestingly, the Horton House, constructed from tabby, itself has deep roots in the Demere family; see June McCash, *Jekyll Island's Early Years: From Prehistory through Reconstruction* (Athens: University of Georgia Press, 2005), 77.

21. Albert Gallatin to TJ, May 25, 1807, *PTJDE*.

22. For the building of St. Simons lighthouse in 1808, see Elinor De Wire, *Lighthouses of the South* (Stillwater, MN: Voyageur Press, 2004), 109.

23. For Jefferson serving as a conduit between Lafayette and Nathanael Greene, see especially editorial annotations to TJ to Nathanael Greene, January 12, 1786, *PTJDE*.

24. T. Reed Ferguson treats the olives on Couper's plantation, as well as Jefferson's role in procuring them, in his *John Couper Family at Cannon's Point* (Macon, GA: Mercer University Press, 1995), 151–152. Ferguson's study even features an image of an "invoice for shipment of olive plants [. . .] to John Couper" in 1825 (151), and quotes a March 1806 letter authored by Jefferson to "M. Cathalan, the American Consul at Marseille" to "get the admirable olive of your canton transferred to my own country" as "Mr. John Couper of St. Simons Island in Georgia, now proposes to undertake [the cultivation of olives]" (152)—a letter that intriguingly is not featured in the otherwise comprehensive *PTJDE*.

25. David O. Stewart, *American Emperor: Aaron Burr's Challenge to Jefferson's America* (New York: Simon & Schuster, 2014), 26.

26. Ferguson, *John Couper*, 142.

27. Buckner F. Melton Jr., *Aaron Burr: Conspiracy to Treason* (New York: Wiley, 2002), 60–61.

28. See Thomas Sumter Sr. to TJ, September 17, 1804, *PTJDE*, which informs the president of Burr's residence in the Golden Isles, noting that "Probably you have heard, the V—Pt—. is at St. Simons Island."

29. Writing from Cambridge, Massachusetts, in 1804, Holmes would inform Jefferson that "I have, for several years, been collecting and arranging materials for a Chronological History of America, and have, at length, ventured to offer Proposals for publishing a work, under the title of American Annals" (Abiel Holmes to TJ, October 18, 1804, *PTJDE*).

30. For these quotations, see TJ to Abiel Holmes, December 7, 1804, *PTJDE*.

31. Holmes eventually published his meticulous recordings of daily temperatures in 1809, which appeared as "Account of Meteorological Observations, Made in Georgia and South Carolina," *Memoirs of the American Academy of Arts and Sciences* 3, no. 1 (1809): 107–112. In his article, Holmes notes "Thermometer broken" on p. 108. I offer my thanks to Timothy Salls, Manager of Manuscript Collections, New England Historic Genealogical Society, for facilitating my review of the original manuscript that seems to have served as Abiel Holmes's source for his published material—that is, "Thermometrical register" (1784, 1787–1794)—archived at the NEHGS as Mss. A 2003.

32. Quoted from p. 1 of Holmes to Stiles, February 22, 1788 (MHS; cited in full, note 1, above).

33. Quoted from p. 2 of Holmes to Stiles (MHS; cited in full, note 1, above). Immediately after this passage, Holmes notes his attempts to use Middle Eastern languages to communicate with 'Usman, which Holmes doubtlessly acquired as an undergraduate at Yale, studying under Stiles himself. Holmes notes that "He [i.e., 'Usman] pronounces some of the letters also just as the Hebrew are pronounced; particularly *Auleph, Caph,* and *Vau.* He does not, however, understand the Hebrew. I tried him with that passage (which I take to be *Syriac) Eloi, Eloi, lama sabactani*; and he plainly signified to me that he understood it, though he had not sufficient knowledge of the *English* to explain it to me."

34. I first uncovered this 1788 manuscript—"Transcription of Qur'anic quotations and Islamic prayers written by a West African slave at a plantation near Sunbury, Georgia," Quincy, Wendell, Holmes, and Upham Family Papers, Massachusetts Historical Society—in 2013, and am grateful especially to Anna Clutterbuck-Cook at the MHS for her aid at that time, and over many years subsequent. A single sheet, with its recto entirely inscribed with Arabic, this manuscript is divided into four discrete quarters, progressing from the top right and concluding on the bottom left (consistent with Arabic's inscription from right to left). The document is dated on its reverse by Holmes, who testifies that "This Manuscript was written in my presence Feb.ʸ 21. 1788 by a Negro lately imported from Africa." Holmes's verso affidavit also comes with a clarification, appending a paratext to parse the place of his "presence." Explicitly locating himself with 'Usman on "Parnassus" Plantation in his letter to Stiles, Holmes describes this same location on the recto of his manuscript as "At Mrs [or Mr.?] Miller's Plantation, near Sunbury Georgia." This twofold description of his location—namely, at Parnassus Plantation and at "Miller's Plantation"—is likely due to the merger of the Demere and Miller families in a 1784 marriage, which is discussed further in Chapter 6, note 15.

35. For the "three fifths" clause, and its relation to Thomas Jefferson in particular, see Garry Wills, *Negro President: Jefferson and the Slave Power* (Boston: Houghton Mifflin, 2005), 1 and ff.

36. These Arabic verses—representing the very opening to the *Fātiḥah*—occupy almost the entirety of the first line in the initial quarter of 'Usman's 1788 document (i.e., the top right quarter; one further word is included on this line, i.e., "مالك," "King"). The remainder of the *Fātiḥah* continues through the first three lines of this document, with its last words appearing at the beginning of line four. In 'Usman's Arabic, however, diacritic marks appear irregularly and the script is occasionally unclear. This English translation of the opening to the Qur'an is adapted from A. J. Arberry's version, offered in his *The Koran Interpreted* (London, Allen & Unwin, 1955), the translation quoted or consulted throughout the present study, especially in my provision of English equivalents for Arabic quotations from the Qur'an.

37. Chapter 103 is inscribed by 'Usman within the upper left-hand quarter of his Arabic document, beginning in the middle of this quarter's seventh line—a quarter that also opens with scattered Arabic quotations from Chapters 106 and 107 of the Qur'an.

38. Chapters 113 and 114—the penultimate and last chapters of the Qur'an—are inscribed by 'Usman at the very bottom to his 1788 manuscript's first quarter (i.e., its top left-hand quarter). The provided English translation from the Qur'an's Chapter 113 is again quoted from A. J. Arberry's edition.

Chapter 6

1. For this quotation, see the plaque that adorns Midway's Congregational Church, which is quoted also by George Williams, *First Light: The Formation of Harvard College in 1636 and Evolution of a Republic of Letters in Cambridge* (Göttingen: Vandenhoeck & Ruprecht, 2014), 7.

2. For this quotation, see Mallard, *A Short Account*, 4.

3. The Revolution is termed as "America's first Civil War" in the very title to Thomas Allen's *Tories: Fighting for the King in America's First Civil War* (New York: Harper, 2010).

4. For "*Footah*" as 'Usman's homeland, located "in the interior part of *Guinea*," see p. 1 of Holmes's February 22, 1788, letter, first cited earlier in Chapter 5, note 32. Although "*Footah*" could presumably describe *either* Futa Jallon or Futa Toro, Holmes's designation of 'Usman's home region as "the interior part of *Guinea*" strongly suggests the former (Futa Jallon indeed formed the center of "*Guinea*," while Futa Toro was located north in Senegal). For Futa Jallon's role in shaping African Muslim history, see John Voll, *Islam, Continuity, and Change in the Modern World* (Syracuse: Syracuse University Press, 1994), 76.

5. The "century of struggles for power" that arose after Ibrāhīm ibn Sori's death is treated by G. T. Stride and Caroline Ifeka, *Peoples and Empires of West Africa: West Africa in History 1000–1800* (Walton-on-Thames, UK: Nelson, 1982), 149. For Futa Jallon's challenges during Ibrāhīm ibn Sori's reign, as well as his 1784 death, see Lamin Sanneh, *The Jakhanke: The History of an Islamic Clerical People of the Senegambia* (London: International African Institute, 1979), 94.

6. A commonplace in early America, Britain's characterization as the "mother country" also surfaces in Jefferson's letters (e.g., TJ to Abigail Adams, July 7, 1785, *PTJDE*).

7. This Arabic document—entitled at the MHS as "Transcription of Qur'anic quotations and Islamic prayers written by a West African slave at a plantation near Sunbury, Georgia, with Arabic signature, [1790]"—shares the same folder as the 1788 manuscript penned by 'Usman, also housed as part of the Massachusetts Historical Society's Quincy, Wendell, Holmes, and Upham Family Papers. According to this manuscript's verso, this Arabic document was inscribed by 'Usman in 1790; however, additional details—including a more precise date, as well as the means by which Holmes acquired this second document—are not recorded, unlike the verso to 'Usman's 1788 Arabic document (see Chapter 5, note 34).

8. Again unlike his 1788 Arabic manuscript, which was folded in four discrete quarters, 'Usman's 1790 Arabic document comprises a single, broad page. Distinctive in its numerous blessed names, this 1790 document does include Qur'anic quotations familiar from 1788, however, not only opening with the *Fātiḥah*, but also featuring chapters such as Chapter 112 (beginning in line 11 of the manuscript) and Chapter 110 (beginning in its line 13).

9. For these figures in 'Usman's 1790 document, see line 7, which names in order Gabriel ("جبريل"), Israfel ("إسرافيل"), and Michael ("مخائيل"). For Abraham ("إبراهيم") see line 6, and for Joseph and Jesus ("يوسف" and "عيسى"), see line 8. The Prophet is mentioned both by name (line 9, "محمد," as well as line 26, "محمد نبيك," i.e., "Muḥammad, thy Prophet"), as well by customary titles (line 5, "رسول الله," "Messenger of *Allāh*"). For the Caliphs—Abu Bakr, 'Umar, 'Usman, and 'Ali—and their role as prophetic successors, see lines 16–18.

10. Abu Bakr—the father of Muḥammad's wife, 'Ā'ishah—is designated by 'Usman not once, but twice in line 16, although the first element of the Caliph's name ("أبو," i.e., *'Abū*) is somewhat unclear. The second part of this name is, however, entirely

patent—i.e., "بكر" (*Bakr*)—and 'Usman also offers a characteristic honorific, i.e., "*aṣ-ṣiddīq*" ("الصديق"; "the righteous," although without the *yā'* visible), which helps to make certain that he is referring to Abu Bakr.

11. These Arabic phrases appear in the very last lines of 'Usman's 1790 document. The doxology that is inscribed immediately after 'Usman's name, that is, "ولا حول ولا قوة إلا بالله العظيم" ("and there is no might nor power except with Allah, the Great"), is a traditional expression of piety, known as the "*Ḥawqala*." For this doxology, see Fallou Ngom, *Muslims Beyond the Arab World: The Odyssey of 'Ajamī and the Murīdiyya* (New York: Oxford University Press, 2016), 148.

12. Unlike his 1790 manuscript, 'Usman's 1788 Arabic document evidences no sign of his signature. It does, however, conclude with a similar doxology, blessing the Prophet Muḥammad (see the bottom left-hand quarter of this 1788 document, concluding with the term, "تمت," i.e., "*fini*").

13. Raymond Demere occasionally surfaces in George Washington's Revolutionary-era letters. See, for example, Brigadier General Lachlan McIntosh to George Washington, April 13, 1777, *Papers of George Washington Digital Edition* (*PGWDE*), in which McIntosh mentions to Washington a "Raymond Demeré Esqr," who is described as "act[ing] a short time as my Brigade Major."

14. For these quoted details regarding Demere's death, see Margaret Shannon, "One Georgia Family: 1776–1976," *The Atlanta Constitution* (July 4, 1976), 156, 159–162 (160).

15. For Demere's marriage to Mary (née Miller) on Thursday, December 23, 1784, see "Marriages and Deaths in Georgia Colony, 1763–1800," *The Genealogical Quarterly Magazine* 4, no. 3 (1903): 161–168 (162). Mary's father—Samuel Miller—had recently died in 1784, and it is possible that Mary's mother, "Mrs. Miller," had come to live with Raymond and Mary on Parnassus Plantation after their 1784 marriage (accounting thereby for Abiel Holmes's verso ascription of Demere's Parnassus to the "Miller" family in 1788). The Demere family's early links to Parnassus are established by Sullivan (*From Beautiful Zion to Red Bird Creek*, 107–108); these links are also evident in nineteenth-century print sources. See, for instance, an 1834 notice in the *Daily Savannah Republican* concerning the death of the "youngest son of Raymond P. Demere" who passed away at "Parnassus, Bryan county" (October 11, 1834; p. 2).

16. For Jefferson's "reluctance" to accept the secretary of state post, see, for instance, Conor C. O'Brien, *The Long Affair: Thomas Jefferson and the French Revolution, 1785–1800* (Chicago: University of Chicago Press, 1998), 69.

17. Ezra Stiles to TJ, August 27, 1790, *PTJDE*. Although Stiles mentions that there are "four Characters" who are above "flatter[y]," he lists five figures in his next sentence, including Jefferson.

18. For Stiles's death, see Einboden, *Islamic Lineage*, 33.

19. Although the activities of "The Connecticut Society for the Promotion of Freedom" pale in comparison to anti-slavery activism undertaken during later decades in New England, Stiles's inaugural address as president of this society nevertheless served as a precedent for abolitionists leading up to the Civil War. Stiles's address is cited, for

instance, by Amos Phelps in his *Lectures on Slavery, and Its Remedy* (Boston: New-England Anti-Slavery Society, 1834), 272.

20. See Stiles, *Diary*, II:271, for his June 9, 1778, entry, in which Stiles records that "I freed or liberated my Negro Man Newport, about aet. 30. Settled all my Affairs, & myself & seven children set out in two Carriages for New Haven."

21. This quotation is from Craig Wilder, *Ebony and Ivy: Race, Slavery, and the Troubled History of America's Universities* (New York: Bloomsbury Press, 2014), 244.

22. The marriage between Holmes and Stiles's daughter is recorded in Stiles, *Diary*, III:401, where he notes that "Rev. Abiel Holmes & my Daughter Polly published: and in the Even^g they were married by Dr Wales." For the death of Mary—or Polly, as Stiles fondly referred to his daughter—on August 29, 1795, see *The Life of Ezra Stiles* (Boston: Thomas & Andrews, 1798), 375, the first biography of Stiles, which was written by none other than Abiel Holmes himself.

Chapter 7

1. William Short to TJ, July 7, 1790, *PTJDE*.

2. See Chapter 2, note 24.

3. For the most comprehensive overview of Jefferson's initial encounter with Volney in Paris, and for the first extant written exchange between the two men, see Volney to TJ, November 16, 1793, *PTJDE*, and its attendant annotations.

4. Not published in Paris until 1785, but begun many years earlier, *Notes on the State of Virginia* is often referred to as Jefferson's "only book" (see, for instance, James Golden and Alan Golden, *Thomas Jefferson and the Rhetoric of Virtue* [Lanham, MD: Rowman & Littlefield, 2002], 322). I designate Jefferson's *Notes* instead as his *first* book, due to the pivotal role he would play in producing another book, as discussed later.

5. This phrase—"Oriental languages"—derives from the title of Volney's 1795 grammar, but also reflects a widespread eighteenth-century usage, covering multiple languages, including Turkish, Persian, and Arabic. For Volney's "Oriental languages" grammar, see Richard Lepsius, *Standard Alphabet for Reducing Unwritten Languages and Foreign Graphic Systems to a Uniform Orthography in European Letters* (Amsterdam: Benjamins, 1981), 19.

6. This quotation is taken from the most recent retelling of this oft-repeated account, included by Jonathan Israel in his *Expanding Blaze: How the American Revolution Ignited the World, 1775–1848* (Princeton: Princeton University Press, 2017), 266. For this account as deriving from *Mémoires de François-Yves Besnard* (Paris: H. Champion 1880), and being "fanciful," see *The Papers of Thomas Jefferson*, XV:xxxiii. Jefferson himself does, however, testify to the ongoing "demolition of the Bastille" in TJ to John Jay, July 19, 1789, *PTJDE*.

7. This origin to Volney's name is offered by Colin Kidd, *The World of Mr. Casaubon: Britain's Wars of Mythography, 1700–1870* (Cambridge: Cambridge University Press, 2017), 141.

8. For Jefferson's ownership of books authored by Volney, including his grammar of "Oriental Languages," see notes 20 and 21.

9. This work was originally published as Constantin-François de Chasseboeuf Volney, *L'Alfabet européen appliqué aux langues asiatiques* (Paris: Firmin Didot, 1818). The French original of this quotation is to be found in Volney, *Oeuvres complètes de Volney*, 8 vols. (Paris: Bossange Frères, 1821), VIII:56.

10. For this era's philological debates regarding transliteration, and engagements between Volney and Jones in particular, see Michael MacMahon, "Orthography and the Early History of Phonetics," in *The Oxford Handbook of the History of Linguistics*, ed. Keith Allan (Oxford: Oxford University Press, 2013), 105–122 (120).

11. See Volney, *Simplification des langues orientales, ou Méthode nouvelle et facile d'apprendre les langues arabe, persane et turque, avec des caractères européens* (Paris: an III [1795]).

12. Volney, *Voyage en Syrie et en Égypte pendant les années 1783, 1784, et 1785*, 2 vols. (Paris: Desenne and Volland, 1787). This phrase—"*Avec Approbation & Privilège du Roi*"—appears on the unpaginated frontispiece of the first volume to Volney's 1787 *Voyage*.

13. TJ to George Wythe, with enclosure, September 16, 1787, *PTJDE*.

14. This book order is offered in TJ to Samuel Henley, March 3, 1785, *PTJDE*. For Volney "returning from Syria to France, in March 1785," see his own *Travels through Egypt and Syria, in the Years 1783, 1784, and 1785*, 2 vols. (New York: J. Tiebout, 1798), I:123.

15. I capitalize the abbreviated Latin title of Jones's volume for the sake of clarity, which Jefferson lists as "*Poeseos asiaticae comment.*" This edition acquired by Jefferson— totaling 542 pages with appendices—is William Jones, *Poeseos asiaticæ commentariorum libri sex cum appendice* (Londini, e Typographeo Richardsoniano, veneunt apud T. Cadell, 1774). For previous recognition of Jefferson's purchase of *Poeseos Asiaticae*, see Hayes, *The Road to Monticello*, 200–201, who also describes Henley as an "expert Orientalist" (Hayes, "How Thomas Jefferson Read the Qur'an," 258). Jefferson's own initial order in 1785 did not arrive to Henley, and was eventually resent by Jefferson in the autumn (see TJ to Samuel Henley, October 14, 1785, *PTJDE*). Although meeting Jefferson in 1770s Virginia, Henley was a loyalist who returned to England after the Revolution, leaving behind many of his valuable books, from which Jefferson later purchased multiple items, including Jones's 1774 *Poeseos Asiaticae* (hence, Jefferson's 1785 letter in October was sent to Henley in England, addressed to "Rendlesham near Melton and Ipswich in Suffolk"). Without specifying particular items, Jefferson had, however, offered to purchase books from Henley as early as 1778 (see TJ to Samuel Henley, June 9, 1778, *PTJDE*). Although receiving mention in the pioneering scholarship of Kevin Hayes, Jefferson's purchase of Jones's *Poeseos Asiaticae* has not received adequate attention, especially considering this volume's inclusion of authentic echoes of the Qur'an in Arabic, as treated below. Spellberg mentions *Poeseos Asiaticae* in passing, but does not engage with the work's contents; her *Thomas Jefferson's Qur'an* describes "William Jones's *Poesesos* [sic] *Asiaticae commentaria*" as "an eight-volume collection" (360), thereby mistakenly reading Jefferson's "8vo." to indicate a number of volumes ("8vo." does not signify "eight-volume," however, but rather "octavo").

16. Some sources even surmise that Volney and Jefferson "had met" at Madame Helvétius's salon; see, for instance, Jared Hickman, *Black Prometheus: Race and*

Radicalism in the Age of Atlantic Slavery (New York: Oxford University Press, 2017), 176. Letters exchanged between Volney and Jefferson make clear at the very least that Helvétius was a shared link between the two men; see Volney to TJ, June 24, 1801, *PTJDE*. For Jefferson's frequenting of Helvétius's salon, see also Pierre Jean Georges Cabanis to TJ, October 20, 1802, *PTJDE*.

17. This Arabic line—"نصر من الله وفتح قريب"—is quoted from Jones, *Poeseos asiaticæ commentariorum*, 323, appearing as part of his selections from *al-Maqāmāt al-Harīriyah*. Jefferson's payment to Henley for the books purchased from his library back in Virginia was a drawn-out affair, unfolding over 1785, culminating with Henley acknowledging to Jefferson that "I am perfectly satisfied with the value set upon [the books] and [. . .] have directed a friend to draw upon you on my account for the sum mentioned" (Samuel Henley to TJ, November 16, 1785, *PTJDE*). It was not until January 24, 1786, however, that Jefferson signaled the conclusion of the transaction (see his entry in Memorandum Books, 1786, *PTJDE*, in which Jefferson records that "[a]ccepted Jos. Johnson's bill of exchange [. . .] this was to pay S. Henley for the books of his which I bought of the Revd. Jas. Madison"). The purchase of Henley's books has understandably confused some previous critics, who assume that, due to Henley's residence in England by 1785, that Jefferson needed to acquire the books "from Britain"; instead, Henley's books stayed in Virginia when he departed, remaining in the care of "Revd Jas. Madison" back in Virginia, as Jefferson notes (see, for instance, Spellberg's *Thomas Jefferson's Qur'an*, 360 which suggests that "[t]he books from his friend Samuel Henley did not arrive in Virginia from Britain until 1785").

18. It is Alexander Bevilacqua who has recently recognized that "not a single word in Arabic script appears" in Sale's *Koran*; see *The Republic of Arabic Letters: Islam and the European Enlightenment* (Cambridge, MA: The Belknap Press of Harvard University Press, 2018), 71.

19. Rather than Vieyra's profuse Latin title—*Brevis, clara, facilis ac jocunda non solum Arabicam Linguam, sed etiam hodiernam Persicam*—Jefferson refers to this work more concisely as *Specimina Arabica et Persica*; see Duff Green, *Catalogue of the Library of Congress: December, 1830* (Washington, DC: Duff Green, 1830), 250. Vieyra's attempt to meet Jefferson in Paris is suggested by TJ to Anthony Vieyra, January 28, 1787, *PTJDE*.

20. For Jefferson's ownership of the 1628 edition of *Rudimenta linguae Arabicae*—an edition published not in Paris, but in Leiden—see Green, *Catalogue of the Library of Congress*, 248. It is unclear when Jefferson acquired this Arabic grammar; however, this edition includes a full reproduction of the Qur'an's Chapter 64 in Arabic, with an interlinear Latin translation, commencing on its p. 174 (which is, however, unpaginated in Jefferson's 1628 edition).

21. It is the unpaginated frontispiece to Volney, *Simplification des langues orientales*, 1795, that records these details, characterizing this work as appearing "*De L'Imprimerie de la République*" and "*An III.*" Volney's *Simplification* has received little attention from Jefferson scholars, regularly overlooked or inaccurately described (see, e.g., the single-volume *Simplification* designated as an "eight-volume" text in Spellberg, *Thomas Jefferson's Qur'an*, 360).

22. Volney's original French *Ruins* was published as *Les ruines ou Méditations sur les révolutions des empires*, with its frontispiece specifying the date of its appearance as August 1791. The political contexts for this work are unmistakable from its frontispiece, which characterizes Volney himself as *"Député à l'Assemblée Nationale de 1789."*

23. William Short to TJ, January 28, 1790, *PTJDE*. Volney's imprisonment and near-execution is treated by Wessel Krul, "Volney, Frankenstein, and the Lessons of History," in *Revolutionary Histories: Cultural Crossings, 1775–1875*, ed. Wil Verhoeven (Basingstoke: Palgrave, 2001), 26–47, which notes in particular that "Volney spent 10 months in prison, and most probably was only saved from the guillotine by the downfall of Robespierre" (32).

24. These are Volney's own words, taken from the autobiographical introduction to his *View of the Climate and Soil of the United States of America, Etc. Few Ms. Notes* (London: J. Johnson, 1804), iv.

25. For this exchange between Volney and Jefferson, see Karl Lehmann, *Thomas Jefferson: American Humanist* (Charlottesville: University of Virginia Press, 1991), 24.

26. See TJ to Volney, December 9, 1795, *PTJDE*, a letter in which Jefferson notes to Volney that "[i]t will be peculiarly gratifying to me to possess you here, and to be your Mentor for whatever may regard this state."

27. TJ to Volney, April 10, 1796, *PTJDE*.

28. For Jefferson's description of his home renovations, see McLaughlin, *Jefferson and Monticello*, 259–260. McLaughlin suggests that it was the "remov[al]" of "part of [Monticello's] roof," and its "replace[ment]" by a "temporary canvass," that inspired Jefferson's "Arabian tent" reference.

29. Volney, *View of the Climate*, 445.

30. This supposed link between the Miami and Arabic languages—comparing their ostensibly similar words for "with"—is made by Volney in his *View of the Climate*, 501. For Volney's study of the Miami language in Philadelphia, see Anthony Wallace, *Jefferson and the Indians: The Tragic Fate of the First Americans* (Cambridge, MA: Belknap Press, 1999), 117–118.

31. These unauthorized "cheap editions" of *The Ruins*, which Volney regarded as marred by "inaccuracies," are treated in *The Oxford History of Literary Translation in English: Volume 4: 1790–1900*, eds. Peter France and Kenneth Haynes (Oxford: Oxford University Press, 2006), 499.

Chapter 8

1. It is unclear when precisely Jefferson agreed to undertake his English translation of Volney's *Ruins*, although it is often assumed, and occasionally even asserted, that he agreed to do so during their weeks together at Monticello in June 1796. See, for instance, Sidney Blumenthal, *A Self-Made Man: The Political Life of Abraham Lincoln, Volume I, 1809–1849* (New York: Simon & Schuster, 2016), 65, which claims that it was at "Monticello, where" Volney "began a literary project with Jefferson." The two men

did, however, stay connected during Volney's subsequent years in America, with Volney "elected to membership in the American Philosophical Society in January 1797, no doubt on Jefferson's recommendation," as Wallace notes (*Jefferson and the Indians*, 116).

2. Jefferson is portrayed as a "reluctant candidate" for president in 1796 by James Sharp, *American Politics in the Early Republic: The New Nation in Crisis* (New Haven: Yale University Press, 1993), 228. For this "three vote" differential, see David McCullough, *John Adams* (New York: Simon & Schuster, 2001), 489.

3. Volney's *Ruins* as a "lesson of religion's tyranny" is emphasized by Mary Harper, "Narratives for a Liminal Age. Ballanche, Custine, Nerval," in *Home and Its Dislocations in Nineteenth-Century France*, ed. Suzanne Nash (Albany: State University of New York Press, 1993), 65–84 (80).

4. Volney, *A New Translation of Volney's Ruins: Or Meditations on the Revolution of Empires*, trans. Joel Barlow and Thomas Jefferson, 2 vols. (Paris: Levrault, quai Malaquais, 1802), I:1–2. This above quotation represents the end of the first long sentence of Jefferson's translation within Volney's first chapter. However, this same sentence, as rendered by Jefferson, also begins by accenting the narrator's "travel-ling," and incorporates several Muslim-specific references, featuring not only "a mussulman prince," but also specifying "the Hegira" in a footnote. Even before its Chapter 1—entitled "The Voyage"—Jefferson's English *Ruins* also begins with a trans-lated "Invocation" (I:ix–xii), as well as an unpaginated plate immediately before page xi, which pictures a turbaned figure in "Oriental" garb overlooking a desert landscape dotted with ruins.

5. Volney, *A New Translation*, I:98–99.

6. This significant paratext in his translation is not original to Jefferson, but renders a footnote within Volney's French text; see p. 82 of Volney's original *Les ruines ou Méditations sur les révolutions des empires* (Paris, 1791).

7. See the unpaginated frontispiece of this edition translated by Jefferson and Barlow. Although not including a name, the cover of *A New Translation* does advertise this edition as being "Made Under the Inspection of the Author."

8. The *PTJDE* annotations to TJ to Volney, March 17, 1801, supply the most detailed account of Jefferson's manuscript translation of *Ruins* and its provenance. Most im-portant, the *PTJDE* editors here emphasize that Chapters 1 through 12 of Jefferson's translation became separated from his Chapters 13 through 19.

9. Jefferson's oft-quoted phrase—"Empire of Liberty"—derives from a 1780 letter, namely, TJ to George Rogers Clark, December 25, 1780, *PTJDE*. This phrase has subsequently supplied the title to studies including Robert Tucker and David Hendrickson's *Empire of Liberty: The Statecraft of Thomas Jefferson* (New York: Oxford University Press, 1992).

10. Ezra Stiles to TJ, April 30, 1788, *PTJDE*.

11. See Joel Barlow, *The Vision of Columbus; a Poem* (London: C. Dilly & J. Stockdale, 1787), a poem that would later be developed into Barlow's 1807 *The Columbiad*.

12. TJ to John Brown Cutting, July 8, 1788, *PTJDE*.

13. See Barlow, *The Vision of Columbus*, which lauds "Nash, Rutledge, Jefferson, in council great, / And Jay and Laurens oped the rolls of fate" (164).

14. Richard Buel, *Joel Barlow: American Citizen in a Revolutionary World* (Baltimore: Johns Hopkins University Press, 2011), 164.

15. See TJ to John Paul Jones, June 1, 1792, *PTJDE*. For Jefferson's recommendation of O'Brien, see also Christine Sears, "Slavery as Social Mobility? Western Slaves in Late-Eighteenth Century Algiers," in *Rough Waters: American Involvement with the Mediterranean in the Eighteenth and Nineteenth Centuries*, eds. Silvia Marzagalli, James Sofka, and John McCusker (St. John's: International Maritime Economic History Association, 2010), 207–220 (219).

16. For Barlow "single-handedly liberat[ing] 101 of his countrymen" in North Africa, see Peter P. Hill's *Joel Barlow: American Diplomat and Nation Builder* (Washington, DC: Potomac Books, 2012), 61. Barlow's agreement to translate the remainder of Volney's *Ruins* is treated by Buel, *Joel Barlow*, 260.

17. TJ to Volney, April 20, 1802, *PTJDE*.

18. Despite Barlow's extended service in North Africa and his role in producing the English version of a pivotal Arabic treaty—as addressed below—his facility with this Middle Eastern language, or lack thereof, regularly goes entirely untreated. See, for example, Arabic's absence from recent biographies of Barlow, including Buel (2011) and Hill (2012).

19. *Treaties and Other International Agreements of the United States of America, 1776–1949, Volume 11*, ed. Charles I. Bevans (Washington, DC: US Government Printing Office, 1968), 1072.

20. For the "Tripoli Treaty" supposedly "uncovered" as a "fraud," see Morton Borden, *Jews, Turks, and Infidels* (Chapel Hill: University of North Carolina Press, 2011), 76.

21. *Treaties, Volume 11*, ed. Bevans, 1077.

22. *Treaties, Volume 11*, ed. Bevans, 1070.

23. Spellberg, *Thomas Jefferson's Qur'an*, 212.

24. I have found no previous treatment, or even published mention, of Barlow's personal Arabic copy of the Tripoli treaty, despite the copious critical attention previously paid to this controversial agreement. I designate this Harvard manuscript in Barlow's papers as a rough draft of the treaty, as there are many emendations to the Arabic text throughout (and especially to articles such as the fourth), clearly suggesting a slightly earlier version of the agreement than the "official" copy printed in *Treaties*, ed. Miller, II:350–363.

25. I am thankful to Mary Haegert at Harvard's Houghton Library for her aid in securing this image from MS Am 1448 (698). Barlow's own handwritten title is inked on "sequence five" of the manuscript, with editorial annotations below his title in pencil reading "The above in English is by Joel Barlow."

26. The "nonsensical" letter that Hurgronje located within the Treaty of Tripoli, supposedly inserted in place of Article 11, is reproduced in *Treaties*, ed. Miller, II:360. For the actual Arabic Article 11 on this page (which Hurgronje assumes is a conclusion to the erroneously inserted, foregoing letter on this same page), see the last three lines of *Treaties*, ed. Miller, II:360. Hurgronje's translation of this Arabic material (II:360) appears in *Treaties*, ed. Miller, II:371–372.

27. This represents my transcription of the Arabic from the final line of p. 2 of "Treaty with Tripoli in Arabic," MS Am 1448 (698), Houghton Library, Harvard University, pictured as Figure 5. The translation I offer nearly matches the one supplied by Hurgronje, who was rendering parallel material from the official Arabic copy of the treaty to which he had access (parallel material he mistakenly identifies, however, as comprising merely the conclusion to the erroneously-inserted "letter"). For Hurgronje's translation—namely "and likewise people from Tripoli, if they proceed to the country of the Americans, they shall be honored [. . .]"—see *Treaties*, ed. Miller, II:372.

28. In Barlow's manuscript—that is, "Treaty with Tripoli in Arabic"—the phrase "الحمد لله" ("praise be Allah") appears at the opening to each of the treaty's twelve articles, as well as the treaty's preamble (MS Am 1448 [698], Houghton Library, Harvard University). This phrase is a common expression of piety in Islam, and comprises the very first words of the Qur'an after its opening doxology (i.e., the *basmala*, "In the name of Allah, the most Merciful, the most Compassionate").

29. The Arabic root from which "*muḥtaram*" derives—that is, *Ḥ-R-M*—is also the source of words such as "*ḥarām*" ("forbidden," "taboo," "sacred"), which comprises the second term in *al-Masjid al-Ḥarām*, that is, Mecca's "Sacred Mosque."

30. Although Barlow's Article 11 has rightly generated much comment and controversy, his English translation of Tripoli's treaty features numerous divergences from the original Arabic source that have gone unnoticed, including the one emphasized in note 28 above (whether this original Arabic source is considered either as the "official" version as that featured as *Treaties*, ed. Miller, II:350–363, or his own "Treaty with Tripoli in Arabic," which is quoted for this first time as Figure 5). However, Spellberg's speculation that Barlow "probably never knew that Article 11 never existed" (*Thomas Jefferson's Qur'an*, 212) is incorrect not only due to the fact that Article 11 *did* exist in Arabic, but also due to the demarcated sections of above MS Am 1448 (698); in this Arabic original that Barlow not only possessed, but which he entitled, the treaty's twelve articles are clearly distinguished.

31. *Treaties, Volume 11*, ed. Bevans, 1070.

32. Thomas Bell to TJ, June 12, 1797, *PTJDE*.

33. Most notoriously, in 1796, William Loughton Smith published his *The Pretensions of Thomas Jefferson to the Presidency Examined; and the Charges against John Adams Refuted*, which attacked Jefferson's religious views (Philadelphia, 1796; see especially 36 and ff.). It is on p. 38 in Smith's *Pretensions* that Jefferson is associated with the *National Gazette*, and this newspaper's supposed commitment "*to revile Christianity.*" For Smith's *Pretensions of Thomas Jefferson* as giving rise to the "hue and cry about Mr. Jefferson's religion," in the words of DeWitt Clinton, see Dreisbach, *Thomas Jefferson and the Wall of Separation*, 168. For recent treatment of Jefferson's supposed "infidelity," see Stephen Vicchio, *Jefferson's Religion* (Eugene, OR: Wipf & Stock Publishing, 2007), esp. 9 ff.; see also Spellberg, *Thomas Jefferson's Qur'an*, 212–213.

34. For these quotations, and the relationship between Thomas Bell and Mary Hemings, see Marie Schwartz, *Ties That Bound: Founding First Ladies and Slaves* (Chicago: University of Chicago Press, 2017), 174.

35. Volney is identified as Burr's guest in Kennedy, *Burr, Hamilton, and Jefferson*, 106, as well as Nancy Isenberg, *Fallen Founder: The Life of Aaron Burr* (New York: Penguin Books, 2008), 159.

36. Jonathan Daniels, *Ordeal of Ambition: Jefferson, Hamilton, Burr* (Garden City, NY: Doubleday, 1970), 393.

37. This quotation appears in François Furstenberg, *When the United States Spoke French: Five Refugees Who Shaped a Nation* (New York: Penguin Press, 2015), 371. For the French original of Volney's quote, including his idiomatic spelling of "*Kentokey*," see Volney, *Tableau du climat et du sol des Etats-Unis d'Amérique* (Paris: Courcier, 1803), iii.

38. For Jefferson's belief that these controversial acts were "meant for Volney & Collot," see TJ to James Madison, April 26, 1798, *PTJDE*. Unlike with Volney, the charges against Victor Collot seem to have been much more credible; for Collot's "journey" in the far West as a "wholly French espionage affair," see David Narrett, *Adventurism and Empire: The Struggle for Mastery in the Louisiana-Florida Borderlands, 1762–1803* (Chapel Hill: University of North Carolina Press, 2015), 235.

39. Terri Diane Halperin, *The Alien and Sedition Acts of 1798: Testing the Constitution* (Baltimore: Johns Hopkins University Press, 2016), 36.

40. Edward J. Larson notes that the "Naturalization, Alien, and Sedition Acts" initially "proved popular" but soon appeared to the public as "authoritarian" and "set" the "stage" for "the election of 1800" (*A Magnificent Catastrophe: The Tumultuous Election of 1800, America's First Presidential Campaign* [New York: Free Press, 2008], 3–36).

41. For Maclure's role in conveying Jefferson's translation to Volney, see the *PTJDE* annotations supplied as part of TJ to Volney, March 17, 1801.

42. In his first extant letter written after Jefferson's inauguration, Adams notes that he departed Washington on that very same day: March 4, 1801. See John Adams to Samuel Dexter, March 23, 1801, *PJADE*.

Chapter 9

1. TJ to Volney, March 17, 1801, *PTJDE*.

2. Volney to TJ, June 24, 1801, *PTJDE*. Volney's original is in French; this quoted English constitutes the translation offered by editors of the *PTJDE*.

3. Volney to TJ, June 24, 1801, *PTJDE*.

4. TJ from Volney, [June 25, 1801], *PTJDE*.

5. David Weir even speculates that Jefferson's instruction to Volney "raises questions about Jefferson's attitude toward the material he translated" (*American Orient: Imagining the East from the Colonial Era through the Twentieth Century* [Amherst: University of Massachusetts Press, 2011], 26).

6. Frank Lambert, *The Barbary Wars: American Independence in the Atlantic World* (New York: Hill and Wang, 2007), 124.

7. For this date, see *White Slaves, African Masters: An Anthology of American Barbary Captivity Narratives*, ed. Paul M. Baepler (Chicago: University of Chicago Press, 1999), 159, as well as Lambert, *The Barbary Wars*, 101.

8. Robert Patterson to TJ, December 19, 1801, *PTJDE*.

9. For these quotations, see Robert Patterson to TJ, March 15, 1803, *PTJDE*. Although not frequently accorded a prominent role in Jefferson biographies, Patterson does merit regular mention in studies of the Lewis and Clark mission. See, for instance, Stephen E. Ambrose, *Undaunted Courage: Meriwether Lewis, Thomas Jefferson, and the Opening of the American West* (New York: Simon & Schuster, 2014), which emphasizes Patterson's role in selecting Meriwether Lewis's chronometer (87).

10. For Jefferson's appointment of Patterson as director of the Mint, see TJ to Robert Patterson, April 27, 1805, *PTJDE*.

11. Robert Patterson to TJ, December 19, 1801, *PTJDE*.

12. This selection from the Declaration is quoted from the *PTJDE*, that is, The Declaration of Independence as Adopted by Congress, 11 June–4 July 1776. Patterson's encoded lines include these sentences from the Declaration, but begin even earlier, starting with "In Congress, July Fourth, one thousand seven hundred and seventy six"; see Rachel Emma Silverman, "Two Centuries On, a Cryptologist Cracks a Presidential Code," *Wall Street Journal*, July 2, 2009.

13. It was Lawren Smithline, "a mathematician at [Princeton's] Center for Communications Research," who solved Patterson's cipher in 2009. In addition to Silverman's article cited above, for Smithline see Craig Lambert, "Coded to the Last: Jefferson's Conundrum," *Harvard Magazine*, July–August 2009.

14. For the Arabic etymology of the English term "cipher," see Leila Avrin, *Scribes, Script, and Books: The Book Arts from Antiquity to the Renaissance* (Chicago: American Library Association, 2010), 268.

15. TJ to Robert R. Livingston, April 18, 1802, *PTJDE*.

16. TJ to Robert R. Livingston, April 18, 1802, *PTJDE*.

17. Thomas Paine, *The Complete Writings of Thomas Paine*, 2 vols. (New York: Citadel Press, 1945), I:1431.

18. TJ to Robert R. Livingston, February 3, 1803, *PTJDE*. For partial quotation of this letter and its political contexts, see Paul A. Gilje, *Free Trade and Sailors' Rights in the War of 1812* (New York: Cambridge University Press, 2013), 131.

19. For Jefferson's query and Patterson's reply, see respectively TJ to Robert Patterson, October 16, 1802, *PTJDE*, and Robert Patterson to TJ, November 1, 1802, *PTJDE*.

20. Robert Patterson to TJ, December 30, 1805, *PTJDE*.

21. Robert Patterson to TJ, December 30, 1805, *PTJDE*.

22. Volney, *A New Translation*, v–vi.

23. The full title of this introduction reads "Preface of the Translator" (Volney, *A New Translation*, v); throughout the preface, it is a first-person plural voice that is utilized ("we"). No evidence exists, however, that Jefferson contributed to writing this preface (a single letter authored by Jefferson to Barlow survives from the spring of 1802—TJ to Joel Barlow, May 3, 1802, *PTJDE*—but this letter makes no mention of Volney or his *Ruins*).

24. The date of the revocation of US rights is given variably as October 16, 1802, or as October 18. For the latter, see George C. Daughan, *If by Sea: The Forging of the American Navy—from the American Revolution to the War of 1812* (New York: Basic

Books, 2011), which notes that "on October 18, 1802, in direct violation of the Pinckney Treaty of 1795, the Spanish intendant in New Orleans, Juan Ventura Morales, had withdrawn the right of deposit" (361). However, although Morales's "announce[ment] that the port of New Orleans is shut against foreign commerce, and also the American deposit" was not relayed to US officials until October 18, this announcement was made on October 16, 1802 (for these documents, and this quotation, see *State Papers and Correspondence Bearing Upon the Purchase of the Territory of Louisiana* [Washington: Government Printing Office, 1903], 54–55).

25. Mustafa Baba, Dey of Algiers, to TJ, October 17, 1802, *PTJDE*.

26. A letter by Richard O'Brien, dated October 12, 1785, addressed to the governor of Massachusetts, Samuel Adams, features precisely this signature—that is, "Richard O'Brien, Who was a captive in Algiers ten years and forty days." This letter was published on p. 3 of the January 14, 1796, issue of *The Maryland Gazette*.

27. As the *PTJDE* annotations specify, it is "at foot of" this same letter's text that O'Brien added "Certifyd to be The Substance of The deys letter to The Presidt. of the UStates Obrien." More important, this English version of the Dey's Arabic letter is "in O'Brien's hand," although his role in personally translating the letter is not explicitly asserted (see Mustafa Baba, Dey of Algiers, to TJ, October 17, 1802, *PTJDE*).

28. For the spat between Cathcart and O'Brien over Betsy Robeson, see Peter D. Eicher, *Raising the Flag: America's First Envoys in Faraway Lands* (Lincoln, NE: Potomac Books, 2018), 51, as well as Michael L. S. Kitzen, *Tripoli and the United States at War: A History of American Relations with the Barbary States, 1785–1805* (Jefferson, NC: McFarland, 1993), 27 and ff.

29. Mustafa Baba, the Dey of Algiers, to the American Government, October 17, 1802, Coolidge Collection of Thomas Jefferson Manuscripts, Massachusetts Historical Society. Appearing courtesy of the MHS, this image has also previously appeared in the Princeton University Press print edition of Jefferson's Papers, namely *The Papers of Thomas Jefferson*, XXVIII (the image of this letter appears between pp. 314 and 315).

30. I quote, and slightly adapt, the English version of this letter offered in the *PTJDE*'s editorial annotations to Mustafa Baba, Dey of Algiers, to TJ, October 17, 1802. My adaptations are minimal, supplying slightly more precise transliterations to the Arabic names included in the Dey's Arabic original, as well as altering two phrases, which I address immediately below.

31. Rather than the rendition offered by *PTJDE* editors—which reads "the Christians whom the Tripolitans seized"—I offer the more muted English "the Christians whom the Tripolitans took" (the verb in Arabic is generic, i.e. "اخذوهم," "[they] took them"). I also substitute my "not a peaceable man" for the *PTJDE* editors' rendition of "not a good man," seeking better to express the conciliatory implications of the Arabic adjective used by the Dey ("صلح").

32. O'Brien's own personal objection to Cathcart's appointment as Consul—which seemingly bleeds into the English rendition of the Dey's letter—was also directly expressed to James Madison (see Richard O'Brien to James Madison, October 11, 1802 [Abstract], *PJMDE*, including its annotations).

33. For Jefferson recording his receipt of this letter on May 19, 1803, see the annotations to Mustafa Baba, Dey of Algiers, to TJ, October 17, 1802, *PTJDE*.

34. For Britain's May 18, 1803, declaration of war on France as anticipating the Louisiana Purchase, see Robert Donald Bush, *The Louisiana Purchase: A Global Context* (New York: Routledge, 2014), 47.

Chapter 10

1. Manasseh Cutler, *Life, Journals and Correspondence of Rev. Manasseh Cutler, LL.D*, eds. Julia Perkins Cutler et al. (Cincinnati: R. Clarke & Co., 1888), 148.

2. Andrew Marschalk to TJ, December 8, 1803, *PTJDE*.

3. Henry Beers, *French and Spanish Records of Louisiana: A Bibliographical Guide to Archive and Manuscript Sources* (Baton Rouge: Louisiana State University Press, 1989), 80.

4. For the "Louisiana Purchase" as "one of the largest land deals in history," see William Martel, *Grand Strategy in Theory and Practice: The Need for an Effective American Foreign Policy* (Cambridge: Cambridge University Press, 2015), 179.

5. This letter first appeared in print as part of Vere Foster, ed., *The Two Duchesses: Georgiana, Duchess of Devonshire, Elizabeth, Duchess of Devonshire* (London: Blackie, 1898), 198.

6. Richard O'Brien to TJ, October 8, 1803, *PTJDE*. For Jefferson's "20 Dec" receipt, see the *PTJDE* annotations to this letter.

7. O'Brien's letter, dated October 8, 1803, makes it clear that he shipped these gifts to Jefferson on board the *Betsy Walk*—a ship captained by Miles Reddick regularly used to transport goods between North Africa and America. For the *Betsy Walk*'s service, see, for instance, Richard O'Brien to James Madison, October 3, 1803, *PJMDE*, as well as *Naval Documents Related to the United States Wars with the Barbary Powers*, ed. Dudley W. Knox, 7 vols. (Washington: US Government Printing Office, 1939–1945), II, 437, which records *Betsy Walk* transporting "the timber and plank [. . .] for Algiers."

8. A "burnuce"— in Arabic, "برنس" ("*burnus*")— is a "cloak" designed either for men or women. From O'Brien's description, it appears that the "burnuce" he gifted to Jefferson was specifically tailored for "Ladies."

9. See TJ to Mary Jefferson Eppes, January 29, 1804, for the president's boast that "I have recieved (*sic*) from Algiers two pair of beautiful fowls," which he notes are "something larger than our common fowls with fine aigrettes." Jefferson's receipt of the "fowls" from Algiers, and his projected "hen-house," is treated also in Malone, *Jefferson and His Time*, IV, 412.

10. See Richard O'Brien to Edward Preble, December 21, 1803, *PJMDE*. A portrait of the *Philadelphia*'s stranding is offered in Joshua London's *Victory in Tripoli: How America's War with the Barbary Pirates Established the U.S. Navy and Built a Nation* (Hoboken: Wiley Publishing, 2005), 135.

11. For the *Philadelphia* being "boarded and burned", see Kenneth Hagan, *This People's Navy: The Making of American Sea Power* (New York: Free Press, 1992), 60. For the role

of the "eight marines" led by Stephen Decatur, see George Clark, *Battle History of the United States Marine Corps: 1775-1945* (Jefferson, NC: McFarland & Co., 2010), 28, as well as Spencer Tucker, *Stephen Decatur: A Life Most Bold and Daring* (Annapolis: Naval Institute Press, 2004), 48.

12. For the "eight marines" who contributed to Eaton's force, which also included "mercenaries" and "bedouin bands," see Allan Millett, *Semper Fidelis: The History of the United States Marine Corps* (New York: Free Press, 1991), 44. For the "five-hundred-mile march across the desert to Derna," see Robert J. Allison, ed., *Narratives of Barbary Captivity: Recollections of James Leander Cathcart, Jonathan Cowdery, and William Ray* (Chicago: R.R. Donnelley & Sons, 2007), lxvi.

13. For the Marine Corps hymn echoing Eaton's mission—although "in fact, [Eaton's company] reached only Darna," and not "To the Shores of Tripoli"—see Michael Oren, *Power, Faith and Fantasy: America in the Middle East, 1776 to the Present* (New York: Norton, 2008), 77.

14. Hamet Ebn Abdul Kadir to TJ, August 18, 1805, *PTJDE*.

15. Independent of this 1805 letter authored by Hamet Ebn Abdul Kadir, I have not uncovered evidence of a delivery of this "Dromedary" to Jefferson. The letter itself, however, stayed on Jefferson's mind, still a concern during the first weeks of 1806. See James Leander Cathcart to TJ, January 24, 1806, *PTJDE*, which reflects Jefferson's search for an English translation of Abdul Kadir's original Arabic letter. In particular, Cathcart records presenting this letter to "the Tunisian Ambassador"—who is discussed further below—and learning that this Arabic letter seems to concern "a beautiful young female Dromedary." It would appear that Abdul Kadir's letter was soon thereafter translated into English, perhaps with aid from the Tunisian Ambassador himself.

16. For Islam's early caliphs adopting the title of "*amīr*"—and specifically "commander (*amīr*) of the believers"—see Patricia Crone and Martin Hinds, *God's Caliph: Religious Authority in the First Centuries of Islam* (Cambridge: Cambridge University Press, 2003), 11.

17. Frank E. Evans, "The Sword of the Corps," *Marine Corps Gazette*, 1:3 (September, 1916): 269–278 (273).

18. Sources differ regarding the historicity of this "Mameluke sword" tradition. Evans, cited immediately above, asserts that O'Bannon "undoubtedly brought back with him" a Mameluke sword "as a memento of his service" ("The Sword of the Corps," 272). Additionally, Clark, *Battle History*, suggests that a sword was indeed given to O'Bannon from Hamet, but was subsequently lost (31). John Selby, *United States Marine Corps* (Oxford: Osprey Publishing, 2002) also reports this "Mameluke sword" tradition without skepticism (5). Alternatively, see Andrew Oliver, *American Travelers on the Nile: Early U.S. Visitors to Egypt, 1774–1839* (London: I.B. Tauris, 2015), which suggests that "[t]he story that Hamet presented one to Presley O'Bannon at Derna in gratitude for his services is the one that has become current but is not actually true" (48).

19. See John Carter, *Covert Operations as a Tool of Presidential Foreign Policy in American History from 1800 to 1920: Foreign Policy in the Shadows* (Lewiston: Edwin Mellen Press, 2000), 24.

20. Ahmad Qaramanli to TJ, August 5, 1805, *PTJDE*.

21. For Hamet as "a fugitive living in exile in Tunis," see Charles Chaillé-Long, "The American Soldier Abroad," *Frank Leslie's Popular Monthly* 24:4 (1887): 387–395 (390).

22. For Eaton's 1805 letter expressing resentment at the "instrumental" use of Hamet, see Charles Prentiss, *The Life of the Late Gen. William Eaton* (Brookfield, MA: E. Merriam & Co., 1813), 344.

23. Eaton persisted in his advocacy for Hamet for several years; see, for instance, William Eaton to TJ, February 12, 1808, *PTJDE*, in which Eaton passes along to the president a letter from Hamet, while framing America's treatment of him as a "sacrifice of national dignity."

24. *Naval Documents*, V, 315.

25. It is Sears, "Slavery as Social Mobility?", 182 which mentions that Jefferson faced "charges of duplicity over the treatment of Hamet." Controversy also arose from the affair due to the fact that Eaton's daring trek, attempting to "place" Hamet "on the throne" of Tripoli, was not directly ordered by the President, but reflected Eaton's own initiative. And yet, despite Eaton "exceed[ing] the limits of [his] discretionary powers," Jefferson nevertheless "did try to protect Eaton from blame" (Jeremy Bailey, *Thomas Jefferson and Executive Power* [New York: Cambridge University Press, 2010], 234).

26. This quotation is from p. 1 of the October 25, 1805, edition of *The National Intelligencer and Washington Advertiser*; however, this article itself cites an antecedent source, namely the *Republican Advocate*, a newspaper based in Fredericktown, Maryland (1802–1808).

27. William Plumer, *William Plumer's Memorandum of Proceedings in the United States Senate (1803–1807)*, ed. Everett Somerville Brown (New York: Macmillan, 1923), 333, cited subsequently as *Memorandum*. Plumer's observation on Jefferson's dress is often quoted; see, for instance, Simon Newman, *Parades and the Politics of the Street: Festive Culture in the Early American Republic* (Philadelphia: University of Pennsylvania Press, 1997), 79. Plumer's meeting with Jefferson as the setting for Mellimelni's arrival was first emphasized by Julia Macleod and Louis Wright's "Mellimelli: A Problem for President Jefferson in North African Diplomacy," *The Virginia Quarterly Review* 20:4 (1944), which also offers the above quotation (555–565). Plumer's visit is detailed more recently by Spellberg, who includes a partial quotation of this entry in her *Thomas Jefferson's Qur'an*, 220.

28. For the time of Plumer's visit to Jefferson as "11 OClock AM," see *Memorandum*, 333.

29. This quotation derives from Macleod and Wright, "Mellimelli," 556.

30. For the "foul weather" that delayed Mellimelni's ship—the "frigate *Congress*"— see Macleod and Wright, "Mellimelli: A Problem," 556. The name of the Tunisian ambassador is variously spelled in both nineteenth-century and contemporary sources, appearing as "Melimelli," "Mellimelli," "Melli Melli," and occasionally, "Mellimelni." It is the latter spelling that I adopt throughout *Jefferson's Muslim Fugitives*, on the basis of a manuscript letter I uncovered at the Phillips Library that offers a contemporary, authoritative source on the ambassador's name in Arabic. Samuel Harris, Jr. (d. 1810), a young prodigy of Middle Eastern languages, records his meeting of the

Tunisian ambassador in the fall of 1806 in Boston, and spells out of his name, speci-fying that it reads in Arabic as "ململني" (i.e., with an "ni" at the very end of the name). This letter from Samuel Harris, dated "Boston October 28, 1806," is archived in Box 1, folder 6 of MH 36 William Bentley Papers, Phillips Library, Peabody Essex Museum, Salem. Harris's Arabic clarification regarding Mellimelni's name appears on p. 2 of this letter.

31. For these terms of Mellimelni's visit, see Timothy Marr's superlative *The Cultural Roots of American Islamicism* (New York: Cambridge University Press, 2010), 66.

32. *Memorandum*, 358.

33. *Memorandum*, 382.

34. This dinner has attracted much academic attention, and has even sparked political controversy. The circumstances of the dinner are helpfully summarized by Spellberg, *Thomas Jefferson's Qur'an*, 220, as well as by Marr, *Cultural Roots*, 66. Debate was sparked especially by President Obama's statement on August 10, 2012—at the White House's Iftar dinner—that "Thomas Jefferson once held a sunset dinner here with an envoy from Tunisia, perhaps the first Iftar at the White House, more than 200 years ago"; see Omid Safi and Juliane Hammer, "Introduction: American Islam, Muslim Americans, and the American Experiment," in *The Cambridge Companion to American Islam*, eds. Omid Safi and Juliane Hammer (Cambridge: Cambridge University Press, 2013), 1–14 (4).

35. John Quincy Adams, *The Diary of John Quincy Adams: 1794–1845*, ed. Allan Nevins (New York: Scribner, 1951), 38. See also Spellberg, *Thomas Jefferson's Qur'an*, 221, for a more extended quotation of this diary entry.

36. Adams, *Diary*, 38. See also Cynthia Kierner, *Martha Jefferson Randolph, Daughter of Monticello: Her Life and Times* (Chapel Hill: University of North Carolina Press, 2014), 131.

37. *The Two Duchesses*, 257.

38. *The Two Duchesses*, 257.

39. Margaret B. Smith, *The First Forty Years of Washington Society*, ed. Gaillard Hunt (New York: Scribner, 1906), 400–401.

40. Smith, *First Forty Years*, 403.

41. This fascinating quotation from Margaret Bayard Smith is rarely noticed; how-ever, its language is echoed in Ethel Lewis's *The White House: An Informal History of Its Architecture, Interiors and Gardens* (New York: Dodd, Mead & Co., 1937), 54. Although not quoting the above, Spellberg also mentions Mellimelni's link between "Native Americans" and "Arabs" (*Thomas Jefferson's Qur'an*, 221).

Chapter 11

1. John Randolph, *The Speech of the Hon. J. Randolph, Representative for the State of Virginia, in the General Congress of America* (London: J. Butterworth, 1806), 23.

2. For the complex relationship between these cousins—Thomas Jefferson and John Randolph—see Alf Mapp, *Thomas Jefferson: Passionate Pilgrim* (Lanham, MD: Rowman & Littlefield, 2008), 42–43.

3. See Irving Brant, *James Madison; Secretary of State, 1800–1809* (Indianapolis: Bobbs-Merrill, 1953), who notes Madison's description of funds reserved for "Georgia a Greek" as "appropriations for foreign intercourse" (306). This characterization is also addressed in Isenberg, *Fallen Founder*, 234.

4. For this vicious rhetoric, see, for example, Samuel Cartwright's assertion that "plantation laws" were effective in "gradually and silently converting the African barbarian"— a statement cited in Horace Gray and John Lowell, *A Legal Review of the Case of Dred Scott, as Decided by the Supreme Court of the United States* (Boston: Crosby, Nichols, and Company, 1857), 48.

5. *Memorandum*, 364. For treatment of this episode, including Mellimelni's bid to gain access to the US Senate, and the denigration of him as an "African barbarian," see Macleod and Wright, "Mellimelli: A Problem," 560.

6. *Memorandum*, 364–365.

7. During their meeting with Mellimelni, "Eaton was the interpreter," Plumer himself states directly; however, it was Mellimelni's "Italian" that Eaton was rendering, as Plumer also records (*Memorandum*, 358). It is possible, however, that Eaton also relied on his Arabic skills that he had acquired during his Barbary Coast service. Cassandra Vivian, *Americans in Egypt, 1770–1915: Explorers, Consuls, Travelers, Soldiers, Missionaries, Writers, and Scientists* (Jefferson, NC: McFarland, 2012), quotes a contemporary witness who described Eaton "speaking fluent Arabic" while in North Africa (49). However, Vivian also questions this report, noting that Eaton himself "used an interpreter" in Arabic-speaking lands.

8. The first Barbary War "created a number of celebrities for the new republic, including Edward Preble, Stephen Decatur, William Eaton, and Presley O'Bannon, all of whom returned home to a hero's welcome," as Gary Ohls has recently noted (*American Amphibious Warfare: The Roots of Tradition to 1865* [Annapolis: Naval Institute Press, 2017], 83). For Eaton as "a complainer," or even "a perennial complainer," see respectively Boles, *Jefferson*, 400, and Wills, *Henry Adams*, 206.

9. Eaton's frustrations, especially with Jefferson, are stressed in Oren, *Power, Faith, and Fantasy*, which even asserts that "Eaton would never forgive what he regarded as [. . .] Jefferson's double cross" (65). See also Louis Wright and Julia Macleod, "William Eaton's Relations with Aaron Burr," *Mississippi Valley Historical Review* 31, no. 4 (1945): 523–536, which notes that "Eaton had spent considerable sums out of his own pocket while consul in Barbary, and he had had a claim for reimbursement before Congress since the session of 1803–1804" (530). Eaton's funding requests, and his outstanding accounts, had long concerned Jefferson specifically, with documents in the president's own hand related to Eaton's claims written as early as 1803. See *PTJDE*'s I. Draft Notes on Eaton's Accounts, July 2, 1803, as well as II. Notes on Eaton's Accounts, on or after July 2, 1803.

10. For Eaton's meeting with Jefferson on "March 6, 1806" to warn the president of Burr's plot, see Wills, *Henry Adams*, 206. Ronald Zellar also notes that "[t]he first time Eaton discussed Burr's activities with President Jefferson [was] around March, 1806"; however, Zellar suggests that during this meeting Eaton "failed to mention the outrageous plans of Burr that he would later allege" (*A Brave Man Stands Firm: The*

Historic Battles between Chief Justice John Marshall and President Thomas Jefferson [New York: Algora Publishing, 2011], 177).

11. Stewart's *American Emperor* notes that "Jefferson brushed aside" Eaton, and specifically his "advice" that Jefferson "ge[t] Burr out of the country by appointing him to an important diplomatic post" (125). Stewart also recognizes, however, that Jefferson had heard of such rumors of Western conspiracies much earlier, including "[i]n early December [1805]" when "President Jefferson received two anonymous letters warning him against Burr" (29).

12. See *American State Papers: Documents, Legislative and Executive, of the Congress of the United States in Relation to the Public Lands [. . .] March 4, 1789 to June 15, 1834*, ed. Walter Lowrie (Washington, DC: Gales and Seaton, 1834) for "John Cotton Smith, from the Committee of Claims" making a "report," leading ultimately to the resolution "[t]hat the proper accounting officers be authorized and directed to liquidate and settle the accounts subsisting between the United States and William Eaton" (323).

13. See Lucia Goodwin's sixteen-page "Barbarians and Savages in the President's House" (Charlottesville: Thomas Jefferson Memorial Foundation, 1983), which formed a "Keepsake to the Anniversary Dinner at Monticello, April 12, 1983." Goodwin offers a list of the diners at this April 9, 1806, dinner, noting that on this evening, "Tunisian Ambassador Mellimelli has a last dinner at the President's House, in company with Aaron Burr, most of the heads of department, French minister Turreau, and James Leander Cathcart" (14–15).

14. Although intersecting issues of urgent relevance to the president—Islam and Arabic, captivity and diplomacy—Sulaimān Islāmbūlī and his 1806 letter have never before been treated in studies of Jefferson.

15. Sulayman Islambuli to TJ, April 29, 1806, *PTJDE*. In citing this letter, I provide the *PTJDE*'s preferred usage—"Sulayman Islambuli"—rather than my more standard transliteration of his Arabic name ("Sulaimān Islāmbūlī").

16. For Cathcart's aspiration "to deliver the United States from this political pest of society," see *Naval Documents*, VI:476. Cathcart's characterization is often cited; see, for instance, Marr, *Cultural Roots*, 66.

17. For Mellimelni's "journey up the eastern seaboard to Baltimore, Philadelphia, New York, and Boston," undertaken "[b]etween May and September" of 1806, see Marr, *Cultural Roots*, 66.

18. Sulayman Islambuli to TJ, April 29, 1806, *PTJDE*.

19. The Arabic signature imaged in Figure 7 is not transcribed in the *PTJDE*'s Sulayman Islambuli to TJ, April 29, 1806; however, this signature is suggested by editorial annotation, which notes "*[signature in Arabic script]*." Reproduced as Figure 7, Mellimelni's Arabic autograph derives from p. 3 of the original manuscript of his 1806 letter, now housed at the Missouri History Museum (MHM). Catalogued as "Letter signed Suleiman Islamboli (signature in Arabic) to Thomas Jefferson, April 29, 1806," this four-page item forms a part of the Missouri History Museum's Thomas Jefferson Collection, c. 1773–1961 (bulk 1779–1826). As noted in the MHM catalogue, Jefferson himself characterizes Islāmbūlī as "one of the suite of the [Tunisian] embassy" on this letter's fourth page.

20. See Ibrāhīm Naṣr Allāh, *Lanterns of the King of Galilee: A Novel of 18th-Century Palestine*, trans. Nancy N. Roberts (Cairo: American University in Cairo Press, 2015) for "Islambul, meaning 'city of Islam'" as a name for "Istanbul"—a name which "appeared shortly after the Ottoman conquest of the city in 1453" (174).

21. James Madison to TJ, September 16, 1806, *PTJDE*.

22. Madison kept Jefferson apprised of the situation involving Mellimelni's "refractory" servants. See James Madison to TJ, July 25, 1806, *PTJDE* in which Madison speaks of the "Tunisians," and encloses a letter concerning this topic arising from his own correspondence with New York mayor DeWitt Clinton. In this letter—James Madison to DeWitt Clinton, July 25, 1806—Madison mentions specifically "Mahomet Choux, an Officer of the suite, Mustapha the Cook, and Soliman the Barber," this final name perhaps referring to the same Sulaimān Islāmbūlī who had contacted Jefferson in April 1806.

23. *Memorandum*, 487.

24. Sulayman Melmelli to TJ, July 26, 1806, *PTJDE*.

25. See Joseph Wheelan's *Jefferson's War: America's First War on Terror, 1801–1805* (New York: Carroll & Graf Publishers, 2003), which describes "Melli Melli hunt[ing] for a merchantman to take him back to Tunis," and his eventual "charter[ing] the *Two Brothers*" (320).

26. For Jefferson initiating the process to secure polygraphs for Tripolian gifts, see TJ to Charles Willson Peale, January 1, 1806, *PTJDE*, in which the president notes that "[w]e have to make up some presents for Tripoli, & [. . .] I propose to make the Polygraph an article. we want three of them, one for the Bey, one for his Secretary of state, & one for the Ambassador here. but they must be entirely mounted in silver." See also Jefferson's follow-up letter to Peale (TJ to Charles Willson Peale, February 18 1806, *PTJDE*), as well as Charles Willson Peale to James Madison, March 19, 1806, *PJMDE*, which mentions that the "three Polygraphs intended as presents for Tripoli are finished."

27. Little attention has been dedicated to these "three Polygraphs"; however, they are treated by Martha Elena Rojas in her "Negotiating Gifts: Jefferson's Diplomatic Presents," in *Old World, New World: America and Europe in the Age of Jefferson*, eds. Leonard Sadosky et al. (Charlottesville: University of Virginia Press, 2010), 179–199 (195–197); in particular, Rojas raises the question of the polygraph's suitability for Arabic, querying, "[w]as it amenable to Arabic calligraphy?" (197).

28. For this quotation see Jonathan Gross, ed., *Thomas Jefferson's Scrapbooks: Poems of Nation, Family, & Romantic Love Collected by America's Third President* (Hanover, NH: Steerforth Press, 2006), 347. Selected by Jefferson from a "London Paper," and ascribed to "Rosa Matilda"—the pen name of Charlotte Byrne, also known as Charlotte Dacre—this poem was first published a year earlier in her *Hours of Solitude*, 2 vols. (London: Hughes and Ridgeway, 1805), I:117–122. In addition to British papers, "The Poor Negro Sadi" was appearing in US papers even as Mellimelni was on his way to America; see, for instance, the poem's appearance on p. 4 of the September 23, 1805, issue of *The Vermont Gazette*.

29. For the significance of the name "*sa'dī*," and its role within early American receptions of Islamicate culture and poetry specifically, see Einboden, *Islamic Lineage*, 152–158.

30. This poem on "Sadi" was only one of many Muslim-themed pieces Jefferson preserved in his scrapbooks; indeed, this poem is not even the only one that involves a figure named "Sadi." Jefferson also excerpted, for instance, the following items (paginations provided as per Gross's *Thomas Jefferson's Scrapbooks*): "Sadi the Moor" (359); "A Persian Gazel" (361–362); "A Persian Song. Of Hafiz" (363–364); "Osmam and Zorida" (434–435); and "An Ode from Hafiz" (458–459).

Chapter 12

1. [Washington Irving], "A Letter from Mustapha Rub-a-Dub Keli Khan, Captain of a Ketch," *Weekly Wanderer*, Randolph, Vermont (April 27, 1807), 2. The *Weekly Wanderer* does not attribute this "letter" to an author; however, Irving's authorship is made clear by editions of his collected works, which appeared later in his lifetime. For the selection quoted above, for instance, see Washington Irving, *The Beauties of Washington Irving* (Glasgow: Griffin, 1830), 3.

2. This particular letter appeared first in *Salmagundi* on Friday, February 13, 1807. See Washington Irving et al., *Salmagundi; Or, the Whim-Whams and Opinions of Launcelot Langstaff, Esq. and Others, Volume I* (New York: Thomas Longworth and Co., 1820), 59–65; the quotation above appears on p. 63. In addition to newspaper reprints, Irving's Mustapha letters were also quoted in contemporary sources; see, for example, John Lambert, *Travels through Lower Canada and the United States of North America in the Years 1806, 1807, and 1808* (London: R. Phillips, 1810), 241. In later editions and sources, Irving's original "Keli Khan" is occasionally spelled instead as "Kali Khan."

3. For precedents upon which Irving's letter played, see Warren Walker, "Two- and Three-Tailed Turks in *Salmagundi*," *American Literature*, 53, no. 3 (1981): 477–478. Walker notes that Irving's Mustapha character would have immediately recalled "for contemporary readers [. . .] one of the seven Turkish prisoners-of-war [. . .] captured in August of 1804" and "brought to New York" (477). Marr also links Irving's Mustapha to these prisoners, highlighting "specifically one 'Mustaffa, Captain of the Ketch,'" while emphasizing too that Irving's letters were supposedly "translated from the 'Arabic-Greek'" (Marr, *Cultural Roots*, 67).

4. Irving, "A Letter," *Weekly Wanderer*, 2.

5. For Irving's Ichabod Crane as a "misfit," see, for instance, Jeffrey Weinstock, *Charles Brockden Brown* (Cardiff: University of Wales Press, 2011), 26.

6. This letter published in the *Richmond Enquirer*, which declared that "ingenuity is foiled," is quoted by Michael Drexler and Ed White in their *The Traumatic Colonel: The Founding Fathers, Slavery, and the Phantasmatic Aaron Burr* (New York: New York University Press, 2014), 162.

7. Kent Newmyer, *The Treason Trial of Aaron Burr: Law, Politics, and the Character Wars of the New Nation* (New York: Cambridge University Press, 2012), notes that on "April 1, 1807 [. . .] Marshall [found] sufficient evidence to hold Burr on the misdemeanor charge but not the treason charge" (9).

8. For Eaton "as the first witness for the prosecution," see Wright and Macleod, "William Eaton's Relations," 530. For Eaton's testimony, see David Robertson, *Trial of Aaron*

Burr for Treason: Printed from the Report Taken in Short Hand, 2 vols. (Jersey City: F. D. Linn, 1879), I:535 ff.

9. *The American Register, Or General Repository of History, Politics, and Science*, 7 vols. (Philadelphia: C. & A. Conrad, 1807–1809), I:110–114, features Eaton's pretrial deposition. See p. 110 for Eaton's claim of Burr "seem[ing] desirous of irritating resentment in my breast." This claim is also offered by Prentiss, *Life*, 397.

10. *The American Register*, I:110.

11. For Eaton's drinking, see Julius Pratt, "Aaron Burr and the Historians," *New York History*, 26, no. 4 (1945): 447–470, which cites Albert J. Beveridge's view that during Burr's trial Eaton deserved "the prize in drinking," as he "'spen[t] his time, when court was not in session, in the bar-rooms of Richmond'" (466).

12. John Adams to Benjamin Rush, February 2, 1807, *PJADE*.

13. See Wright and Macleod, *The First Americans in North Africa*, which notes that "upon" Hamet's "'commission' rests William Eaton's title of general, a rank which he treasured the rest of his life" (156).

14. For Burr as "the 'usurper,'" see Peter Charles Hoffer, *The Treason Trials of Aaron Burr* (Lawrence: University Press of Kansas, 2008), 80, as well as Wright and Macleod, "William Eaton's Relations," 526. Jefferson's refusal to act despite repeated warnings regarding Burr is frequently noted. For an early assertion of Jefferson taking "no action," see David Muzzey, *Thomas Jefferson* (New York: C. Scribner's Sons, 1918), 260. This same phrase surfaces in *The Treason Trial of Aaron Burr* as part of Newmyer's description of Eaton's initial warnings to Jefferson, recognizing that "Jefferson had good reason to doubt Eaton's warning [and] took no action" (122).

15. See Newmyer, *The Treason Trial*, which notes "Eaton's statement of October 20, 1806" regarding Burr's "order for several boats to be built" in Ohio—a statement that "came to Jefferson via Postmaster General Gideon Granger" and "carried real weight" (27).

16. These quotations derive from James Wilkinson to TJ, February 17, 1807, *PTJDE*. However, as Drexler and White note, Wilkinson had "revealed the infamous cipher letter to Jefferson in November [1806]" (*The Traumatic Colonel*, 158). This ciphered letter Wilkinson "revealed" to Jefferson is also widely understood to have been "altered," helping to hide Wilkinson's own complicity in Burr's plot (for the "altered" nature of the letter, and discussion of this allegation, see James Lewis, *The Burr Conspiracy: Uncovering the Story of an Early American Crisis* [Princeton: Princeton University Press, 2017], 207).

17. See Lewis, *Burr Conspiracy*, 43–44, which notes that the Cabinet agreed on October 24, 1806, "unanimously, to strengthen the naval detachment at New Orleans, both by sending Captains Edward Preble and Stephen Decatur 'to take command of the force'"; however, "the cabinet" subsequently "'rescind[ed]'" these orders, as Lewis also notes (45). This commissioning of Stephen Decatur—celebrated for his service in Muslim North Africa, and the burning of the *Philadelphia* in Tripoli's harbor—is especially ironic considering that Burr had also sought to recruit Decatur for his plot; see Stewart, *American Emperor*, 126.

18. For "Adair openly advocat[ing] western independence," see Stewart, *American Emperor*, 126. See also Samuel Wilson, "The Court Proceedings of 1806 in Kentucky against Aaron Burr and John Adair," *Filson Club History Quarterly* 10 (1936): 39–40.

19. For Clay as "a rising young Kentucky lawyer," see A. J. Langguth, *Union 1812: The Americans Who Fought the Second War of Independence* (New York: Simon & Schuster,

2006), 117. Clay's "agree[ing] to defend [Burr] pro bono" is recorded by James Klotter, *Henry Clay: The Man Who Would Be President* (New York: Oxford University Press, 2018), 214. Henry Clay partnered with fellow Kentucky lawyer John Allen to defend Burr (Lewis, *Burr Conspiracy*, 77).

20. See Walter Borneman, *1812: The War That Forged a Nation* (New York: HarperCollins Publishers, 2004), which notes that "on December 22, 1806, Burr left Nashville [. . . and] floated down the Cumberland" (17).

21. This is quoted from Pratt, "Aaron Burr and the Historians," which records that "[w]hen [Burr's] expedition gathered at the mouth of the Cumberland, there were nine flatboats and from sixty to one hundred men. At the end of December they swung into the Mississippi, and the Father of Waters bore them southward" (456).

22. See Robert Haynes, *The Mississippi Territory and the Southwest Frontier, 1795–1817* (Lexington: University Press of Kentucky, 2010), 158 for this date, as well as for Burr's stay in Natchez.

23. For recognition that Burr "quickly became a celebrity," see Haynes, *Mississippi Territory*, who emphasizes the warm reception enjoyed by the former vice president from local "Federalists," who received Burr by "entertaining him royally and throwing elaborate balls in his honor" (158). For early recognition of Marschalk, and his engagement with the Burr affair, see *Mississippi: Comprising Sketches of Towns, Events, Institutions, and Persons*, ed. Dunbar Rowland, 3 vols. (Atlanta: Southern Historical Publishing Association, 1907), which notes that the "train of bitter dissension" left in the wake of Burr's plot; even the governor of the Mississippi Territory, Robert Williams, was "openly charged [. . .] with Burrism and disloyalty to Jefferson," but was defended by "Andrew Marschalk's *Herald* [which] responded on behalf of the governor" (II:977). As Haynes notes, Marschalk was an "eccentric printer" who "came to the territory in the late 1790s as a lieutenant in the U.S. Army," and would eventually be "employed [. . .] to publish the territory's first laws" (*Mississippi Territory*, 158, 325).

24. Lyle Saxon, in his *Old Louisiana* (New Orleans: R. L. Crager, 1950), notes that "they were forced to try Burr out under big oak trees that are still standing" (274). For "the proceedings" against Burr being "moved [. . .] outdoors under a canopy of live oaks," see also David Hargrove, *Mississippi's Federal Courts: A History* (Jackson: University Press of Mississippi, 2018), 41.

25. For Osmun and his Windy Hill Manor, see Mary Carol Miller, *Lost Mansions of Mississippi* (Jackson: University Press of Mississippi, 1996), 5–6, as well as Haynes, *Mississippi Territory*, 158, who records that Burr "became Colonel Osmun's house guest at Windy Hill Manor. One of the territory's staunchest Federalists and a confirmed bachelor, Osmun had admired Burr since their days together in the Revolution." For Burr in Natchez, see also Buckner F. Melton, Jr., *Aaron Burr: Conspiracy to Treason* (New York: Wiley, 2002), 80 and ff.

26. R. B. Bernstein notes that Jefferson had "ordered Burr's arrest on charges of treason" on "November 26, 1806" (*Thomas Jefferson* [New York: Oxford University Press, 2005], 162). For Burr as a "wanted man" after his release from the grand jury in Mississippi, see Newmyer, *The Treason Trial*, 68, who also emphasizes Jefferson's "dramatic report to Congress on January 22, 1807, declaring Burr guilty of treason" (28). For "[t]he

grand jury of the Mississippi Territory, on a due investigation of the evidence brought before them, [being] of the opinion that Aaron Burr has not been guilty of any crime or misdemeanor," and for "Burr depart[ing] Natchez, riding eastward in disguise," see Kennedy, *Burr, Hamilton, and Jefferson*, 314 and 333, respectively.

27. Burr's arrest on February 19, 1807, "near Wakefield" (in present-day Alabama) is detailed in George Gaines, *The Reminiscences of George Strother Gaines: Pioneer and Statesman of Early Alabama and Mississippi, 1805–1843*, ed. James P. Pate (Tuscaloosa: University of Alabama Press, 1998), 5. Burr "first appeared before the United States Circuit Court in Richmond on March 30, 1807 for arraignment," as Zellar notes (*A Brave Man Stands Firm*, 87). However, it was on April 1, 1807, that Chief Justice John Marshall not only "dismissed the treason charge" against Burr, but found "probable cause" for his "conspiring to invade another country" (quotes from Nester, *The Jeffersonian Vision*, 77; see also note 7).

28. Stephen F. Knott, *Secret and Sanctioned: Covert Operations and the American Presidency* (New York: Oxford University Press, 1996), accents Eaton's characteristic "flair for the dramatic," linking this trait to "the idea to overthrow the pasha" in particular (208).

29. For "Eaton in Arab costume," see Newmyer, *The Treason Trial*, 70. According to Virginia Moore, the Richmond trial was not the first time that Eaton had adopted Middle Eastern dress to draw attention, detailing events surrounding December 1805. Moore's *The Madisons: A Biography* (New York: McGraw-Hill, 1979) records that "General William Eaton, brave in a Turkish sash, turned up to be fawned upon and feted" (199). For the "once redoubted Eaton," see Harman Blennerhassett, *The Blennerhassett Papers: Embodying the Private Journal of Harman Blennerhassett*, ed. William H. Safford (Cincinnati: Moore, Wilstach, Keys, 1891), 315–316.

30. Isenberg, *Fallen Founder*, notes that Eaton "was dressed as a Turkish prince and she [a prostitute] had donned a harem costume" (355). See also James Lewis, *The Burr Conspiracy: Uncovering the Story of an Early American Crisis* (Princeton: Princeton University Press, 2017), who notes that Eaton "injured his reputation with his activities outside of the courtroom—heavy drinking, betting on the trial, and swaggering about Richmond in a turban and with a cutlass" (579).

31. Although the "initial hearing" for Burr "was conducted in a back room of the Eagle Tavern in Richmond," the trial itself "convened in the larger House of Delegates Chamber on the second floor of the State Capitol" (Zellar, *A Brave Man*, 88 and 170 respectively).

32. Robertson, *Trial of Aaron Burr*, I:132.

33. I am indebted to Lewis, *The Burr Conspiracy*, 314, for these quotations from the *Virginia Argus*, labeling Burr "Mahomet Volpone, the Grand Imposter," due to his "low craft, his innumerable falsehoods, his callous effrontery, his remorseless treachery [. . .] and his strange tricks and manoeuvres." However, Burr's status as "Mahomet Volpone" has also been noted by Christine Heyrman in her *American Apostles: When Evangelicals Entered the World of Islam* (New York: Hill and Wang, 2016), 5.

34. For evidence of the enslaved "Muslim population in Louisiana" from such newspaper advertisements—for instance, in the "New Orleans' *Moniteur de la Louisiane*"

including one from "October 1807"—see Michael A. Gomez, *Black Crescent: The Experience and Legacy of African Muslims in the Americas* (New York: Cambridge University Press, 2008), 145. The Mississippi as "America's lifeline to the world" is quoted from David Heidler and Jeanne Heidler's *Washington's Circle: The Creation of the President* (New York: Random House, 2015), 201, who also note that the far West, when still in Spanish hands at the end of the eighteenth century, was a region known as "a haven for runaway slaves" facilitated by "agents" of Spain (201).

35. Ira P. Nash to TJ, October 5, 1807, *PTJDE*. Lacunae in this letter's original manuscript unfortunately make uncertain some of its content. While Nash's phrase "in the month of May" is certain (despite a slight obscuring to the phrase "the month"), the words that surround this phrase are interrupted by holes in the manuscript paper. In particular, just before Nash's "in the month of May" is a parenthetical phrase that the *PTJDE* transcribes as "(as w[. . .]ollect)"—a phrase that, in consulting of the original manuscript, appears possibly to have served as a qualifier to "May," perhaps signaling that Nash only tentatively identified this to be the specific "month" that the men were "taken up" (thereby leading to my "seemingly" above on page 132).

36. Ira P. Nash to TJ, October 5, 1807, *PTJDE*.

37. See William Cooper, *Jefferson Davis, American* (New York: Vintage, 2002), for Davis's birth "on June 3, 1808 in Christian County, Kentucky," being "named for his father's political hero, the sitting president of the United States, Thomas Jefferson" (10).

38. Unsurprisingly, records survive of fugitive slaves in Christian County, Kentucky, specifically during the first decades of the nineteenth century. For instance, in 1816, "Squire," a "bright mulatto," is recorded as escaping Hopkinsville itself, running north to Illinois in an advertisement published in the *Western Intelligencer* of Kaskaskia, Illinois (August 14, 1816), reprinted in Helen C. Tregillis's *River Roads to Freedom: Fugitive Slave Notices and Sheriff Notices Found in Illinois Sources* (Bowie, MD: Heritage Books, 1988), 51.

39. Ira P. Nash to TJ, October 5, 1807, *PTJDE*.

40. The 1807 US legislation that brought an end to the legal slave trade—and that went into effect on January 1, 1808—is treated further below (see especially Chapter 17, note 24).

41. As all quotations from the two Arabic manuscripts received by Jefferson, this selection is difficult to decipher due to flaws in spelling and script. The above selection— "سورة العاديات" ("The Chapter of the Runners," the title of Chapter 100 of the Qur'an) is my reconstructed quotation of materials spanning the end of line 5 and the beginning of line 6 of the larger Arabic manuscript received by Jefferson (i.e., "Page written in Arabic [October 1807]," MHS and Figure 1 above). While the first term of this phrase—"سورة," that is, "Chapter"—is relatively clear at the end of line 5, my reading of "العاديات" is speculatively construed from this term's context, as the Arabic term itself is nearly illegible, due both to its being divided over lines 5 and 6, as well as due to the omission of letters (orthographic slips have resulted in an Arabic term that appears as "العراة," or "الفراة"; however, "العادلة," which is nearly correct, seems intended). The targeted meaning of this title, however, is strongly suggested by the lines that precede these words, which do indeed form—although, again, with immensely irregular orthography—verses from Chapter 100 of the Qur'an. One final oddity that impacts this specific Arabic manuscript that Jefferson received is that it does not possess a clear

opening or ending, with its first and last words appearing instead as if they formed the middle of a longer authorial performance (unlike, for instance, the smaller Arabic manuscript that Jefferson also received, which ostensibly forms a single, continuous Qur'anic chapter, as treated below in Chapter 16). To render the Arabic term "العاديات," I have chosen "runners," which reflects this term's Arabic root (عدو); for prior translation of this titular term as "runners," see Angelika Neuwirth, *The Qur'an and Late Antiquity: A Shared Heritage*, trans. Samuel Wilder (New York: Oxford University Press, 2019), 432. However, English Qur'an versions tend to prefer to render this term in reference to the scriptural context of Chapter 100, offering equivalents that imply "running [horses]" (see, for instance, "Chargers," which is Arberry's choice).

Chapter 13

1. Although rarely receiving even cursory mention in contemporary studies, Ira P. Nash's life is detailed by several nineteenth-century histories of Missouri. See, for instance, William F. Switzler, *History of Boone County, Missouri: Written and Compiled from the Most Authentic Official and Private Sources*, 2 vols. (St. Louis: Western Historical Company, 1882), I:147, for Nash as an "eccentric." For Nash's birth as June 14, 1774, see his grave's epitaph at the Old Union Cemetery in Columbia, Missouri.

2. See *History of Howard and Cooper Counties, Missouri* (St. Louis: National Historical Company, 1883), 90, which notes that "[i]n 1800, Charles Dehault Delassus, lieutenant-governor of Upper Louisiana, granted Ira P. Nash a large tract of land in the present limits of Howard county."

3. See Phil. E. Chappell, "Floods in the Missouri River," *Kansas State Historical Society* 10 (1908): 533–563, who notes that Nash was "the first Anglo-American to ascend the Missouri river, he having preceded Lewis and Clark several months" (547). Chappell also includes a footnote to his article, however, citing a 1908 letter from a librarian at the Missouri Historical Society, who confesses their inability to verify this fact, but also notes that Nash was "employed at a Spanish fort on the Missouri" as early as 1798. For Ira P. Nash as the first to "set foot" into Howard County see Chancy Rufus Barns et al., *The Commonwealth of Missouri: A Centennial Record* (St. Louis: Bryan, Brand & Company, 1877), 177, which relays the report that "the first Americans who ever set foot within the present limits of Howard County [Missouri] were Ira P. Nash, (afterwards the founder of Nashville on the Missouri River, in Boone County,) a Deputy United States Surveyor, Stephen Hancock and Stephen Jackson" in 1804.

4. Nash's intended duel is treated by Dick Steward, *Duels and the Roots of Violence in Missouri* (Columbia: University of Missouri Press, 2000), 119, which describes Nash as a "Virginian emigre" who "had a flare for the dramatic" and who "challenged Gilpin S. Tuttle" to a duel; Nash's challenge, conveyed in a still-extant 1831 letter, sought to hide his intent, employing euphemisms, terming their prospective duel as "a short hunt." Prosecuted for his challenge, "Nash had the dubious honor of being the only man convicted of that offense in the county"; for further details on this legal proceeding—that is, "*State of Missouri v. Ira Nash*, circa August 1831"—see Steward, *Duels and the Roots of Violence*, 231.

5. Walter Williams, *A History of Northeast Missouri*, 2 vols. (Chicago: The Lewis Publishing Company, 1913), I:263, which notes that "Nash had considerable trouble with his first wife, Nancy, and she committed suicide in 1829, by hanging herself in the kitchen, probably the first suicide in the county."

6. Williams notes that the "suit of Nash vs. Nash was one of the first divorce suits in Boone county [. . .] Nash act[ed] as his own attorney"; after this first "divorce suit" was "dismissed," however, "another divorce suit was soon brought by [his] wife" (*A History of Northeast Missouri*, I:263).

7. Walter B. Stevens, *Centennial History of Missouri*, 4 vols. (St. Louis: S. J. Clarke Publishing Co, 1921), II:562 treats the "Will of Ira Nash," including his leaving of "instructions that he was to be buried standing on the highest hill in Cedar township. He said he wanted to be where he could look down on the neighbors."

8. For these contradictory quotes regarding Nash, see Stevens, *Centennial History of Missouri*, II:562 ("countless quarrels") as well as Switzler, *History of Boone County*, II:639 ("many a generous deed," "pugnacious"). For a report of Nash donating "land to the Morgan County Court" in his will to establish "a seminary of learning"—a seminary, however, that "was never built and the land was later sold for taxes"—see *The Evening Missourian* (Columbia, Missouri; March, 4, 1919), 2. Recognition that Nash was "among the very first slave owners in Boone County to manumit certain of his slaves" is offered also in Switzler, *History of Boone County*, II:639, and echoed by Steward, *Duels and the Roots of Violence*, 119.

9. For a report of Nash's behavior toward enslaved peoples entirely inconsistent with his repute for "generous deed[s]," see Williams, *Northeast Missouri*, I:263, which records that Nash was "charged" by "the second Mrs. Nash" for taking "a slave belonging to her, a negro named Sam, and hir[ing] him to a man in Mississippi, and then report[ing] to her that Sam ran off to Canada, whereas Sam had been sold and Nash had collected the money."

10. For these quotations—"men" and "momentous importance"—see Ira P. Nash to TJ, October 5, 1807, and Ira P. Nash to TJ, October 3, 1807, respectively (*PTJDE*).

11. For Nash's own parents—William Nash (1741–1822) and Mary Morgan (1737–1818), who married in Fauquier County on February 3, 1764—see, for instance, volume 1 of *Genealogies of Virginia Families: From Tyler's Quarterly Historical and Genealogical Magazine* (Baltimore: Genealogical Publishing Co., 1981), 205. Ira's father, William Nash, was the sixth William Nash in America, coming at the end of a long line that led back to the first William, born in 1613, who immigrated to colonial Virginia and died in Lancaster County in 1655.

12. For the name of Fauquier County, see H. C. Groome, *Fauquier during the Proprietorship: A Chronicle of the Colonization and Organization of a Northern Neck County* (Baltimore: Regional Publishing Company, 1969), 163. For Francis Fauquier and Jefferson, see Jon Meacham, *Thomas Jefferson: The Art of Power* (New York: Random House 2013), 43.

13. The Arabic term "*faqīr*"— that is, "فقیر‎," literally signifying "mendicant," but suggestive of a wandering mystic—was known in the nineteenth-century West, and would even be applied to Jefferson himself. William Travers Jerome—a New York

politician and lawyer who came to prominence at the end of the nineteenth-century—labeled the president satirically with this Arabic term, seemingly invoking "fakir" as a pun, signifying not only beggar, but "faker." See John Dunlap, *Jeffersonian Democracy: Which Means the Democracy of Thomas Jefferson, Andrew Jackson, and Abraham Lincoln* (New York: Jeffersonian Society, 1903), which quotes Jerome as declaring derisively: "[T]he great fakir Jefferson said men were born equal. I say that many are not born equal; and God forbid the time when there are not better, purer, wiser people than we are [. . .]" (107).

14. See Marie Louise Evans, *An Old Timer in Warrenton and Fauquier County, Virginia*, ed. Charles F. Knox (Warrenton: Virginia Publishing, 1955), 133, which records "[t]wo operettas, 'The Fakir' and 'The Wooing of Kishmush,' written and produced by S. A. Appleton."

15. For Nash as "founder of Nashville on the Missouri River," see *The Commonwealth of Missouri*, 177. Nash's death date on his grave at the Old Union Cemetery is given as November 11, 1844.

16. See Williams, *Northeast Missouri*, I, which records that "Nashville [Missouri] continued to be a town of some importance till 1844, the year of the high water, when all of it was washed into the Missouri river, except two or three houses which stood till 1865, when they were washed away" (235).

17. These names of Nash's three daughters—"Neppy," "Alpha," "Zarada"—are specified in *Reports of Cases Determined by the Supreme Court of the State of Missouri* (Columbia: Supreme Court Chambers & Knapp, 1886), LXXXVII:199. For literary usages of "Zarada," though spelled variously, see, for instance, Julia Douthwaite, *Exotic Women: Literary Heroines and Cultural Strategies in Ancien Régime France* (Philadelphia: University of Pennsylvania Press, 1992), which mentions "Zoraida, the Arabic woman who is led out of captivity in Cervantes's *Don Quixote*" (53). Perhaps most intriguing, the precise name chosen by Nash also appears during the ninenteenth century in Orientalist fiction. See, for instance, "Zozo and Zarada," a tale included in Edward Yardley's *Fantastic Stories* (London: Ward, Lock, and Tyler, 1865), 63–74. Zarada in this story merits a visit from "the prophet Mahomet" himself who "descended from the seventh heaven" to "behold" the "beauty of the princess Zarada" (70). For Orientalist usages that recall the name that Nash gave to his daughter, but appeared well before her birth, see, for instance, one of the Muslim-themed poems that Jefferson himself selected for inclusion in his scrapbook, namely "Osmam and Zorida" (Gross, ed., *Thomas Jefferson's Scrapbooks*, 434–435). In Arabic, the verb "زرد"—*zarada*—signifies to "strangle" or "choke."

18. Spellings for Nash's sons' names vary; his elder's name, for instance, appears alternately as "L. Man," and "Elman." For the former, see Stevens, *Centennial History of Missouri*, II:562, which notes that Nash's will "made bequests to two sons, one named Man L. Nash, the other named L. Man Nash," and Williams, *Northeast Missouri*, I:263, which records similarly that "in his will, Nash made a bequest to one son named Man L., and then a bequest to his other son named L. Man." However, see Nash's elder son's grave in Old Union Cemetery in Columbia, Missouri, which lists

his name instead as "Elman Nash" (1822–1862), while identifying Elman specifically as the son of Ira P. Nash.

19. This mystery of Nash's name is evident from nineteenth-century sources, including legal records. See, for instance, Williams, *Northeast Missouri*, I:263, which notes a plot of "land [whose claim was] under the name of 'H. Sanari', which is Ira Nash spelled backwards," adding that "this land described in Nash's will was entered under the name of H. Sanari, in February, 1837, and October, 1836." Nash's pseudonym would eventually prove problematic for his descendants, with land disputes rooted in his double name rising to the Supreme Court of the State of Missouri. See *Reports of Cases*, LXXXVII:199, which details a case in which the "[p]laintiffs base their claim of a title on a patent to H. Sanari, dated June 5, 1841. The evidence offered was insufficient in law to establish the title of the land in Ira Nash, the grandfather of Mrs. Long, the plaintiff." For yet another spelling of Nash's pseudonym as "H. San. Ari," see Robert Desty, ed., *Western Reporter* (Rochester, NY: Lawyers' Co-operative Publishing Company, 1886), II:131.

20. The accurate spelling of Nash's name has long proved problematic, and not merely due to his pseudonym. See, for instance, *American State Papers*, IV:824, which reflects the confusion caused merely by Nash's own handwriting, describing a plot whose "survey was made in the month of February, 1804" whose "record of the recorder's office [is signed by] R. L. Nash. This is evidently a mistake in the recording clerk [...] and must have proceeded from the singular manner in which Ira P. Nash signs his name, as Ira P. was certainly the person who made the survey." It is precisely such problems arising from Nash's own idiomatic signature that have helped obscure the story recounted in the present book, as emphasized below (see Chapter 22, note 13).

21. The precise spelling of Nash's last name pseudonym— "Sanari"— matches, for instance, the name of a prominent "Sudanese occultist" who engaged with Napoleon in Egypt. For this spelling of the name, see reference to the "House of Ibrahim Katakhda Al Sanari," in Peter Burke, ed., *History of Humanity: From the Sixteenth to the Eighteenth Century* (London: Routledge, 1999), 244. A more accurate English transliteration of the Arabic name linked to this Sudanese town— that is, "سنار," "*Sannār*"—would be "*Sannārī*," which is preferred in more recent sources, such as the 2009 English translation of 'Abd ar-Raḥmān ibn Ḥasan al-Jabarfi, *Al-Jabarfi's History of Egypt*, trans. Jane Hathaway (Princeton: Markus Wiener Publishers, 2009), 209.

22. John Ledyard to TJ, September 10, 1788, *PTJDE*.

23. For Jefferson's initial request for congressional funding for the Lewis and Clark expedition, and preparations for the voyage, see Stephen E. Ambrose, *Undaunted Courage: Meriwether Lewis, Thomas Jefferson, and the Opening of the American West* (New York: Simon & Schuster, 2005), 80 and ff.

24. This material is also quoted in E. W. Gilbert, *The Exploration of Western America, 1800–1850* (Cambridge: Cambridge University Press, 2013), 8.

25. For Ledyard being "expelled" by Catherine the Great, see Edward G. Gray, *The Making of John Ledyard: Empire and Ambition in the Life of an Early American Traveler* (New Haven: Yale University Press, 2007), 137.

26. For Jefferson's view of Ledyard as "a man of genius, of some science and of fearless courage and enterprise," see *The Papers of Thomas Jefferson*, XI:261.

27. For correspondence concerning this topic, see John Ledyard to TJ, September 10, 1788, in which Ledyard notes that "[w]ith regard to my Voyage, I can only tell you for any certainty that I shall be able to pass as far as the western boundaries of what is called Turkish Nubia, and at a Town called Sennar. You will find this town on any chart. It is on a branch of the nile: I expect to get there with some surety—but afterwards all is dark before me: my design and wishes are to pass in that parrelel across the Continent. I will write you from Sennar if I can." See also Thomas Paine to TJ, June 17, 1789, for Paine quoting "Sir Joseph Banks" who notes that " 'We have lost poor Ledyard—he had agreed with certain Moors to Conduct him to Sennar. The time for their departure was arrived when he found himself Ill and took a large dose of Emetic Tartar, burst a blood vessel on the operation which carried him off in three days[']." For Ledyard's destination as Sennar, see also Bill Gifford, *Ledyard: In Search of the First American Explorer* (Orlando: Harcourt, 2007), which notes that "[Ledyard] returned several times to the slave market [in Cairo], increasingly impatient, and by October 25th had found a merchant who would guide him to Sennar" (262).

28. See TJ, III. Report of the Committee, March 1, 1784, *PTJDE*, in which Jefferson invokes "the confluences of the rivers Wabash, Shawanee, Tanissee, Ohio, Illinois, Missisipi and Missouri" in deriving the name "Polypotamia."

29. See TJ, IV. Instructions for Meriwether Lewis, June 20, 1803, *PTJDE* for Jefferson's orders to Lewis that "[t]he object of your mission is to explore the Missouri river, & such principal stream of it, as, by it's course & communication with the waters of the Pacific ocean, may offer the most direct & practicable water communication across this continent, for the purposes of commerce."

30. This selection derives from the beginning of Joel Barlow's "On the Discoveries of Captain Lewis," which was published on p. 3 of the January 16, 1807, issue of *The National Intelligencer and Washington Advertiser*. For this quote and its relation to Jefferson specifically, see M. R. Montgomery, *Jefferson and the Gun-Men: How the West Was Almost Lost* (New York: Crown Publishers, 2000), 275.

31. This advertisement of the "LEWIS & CLARK EXPEDITION" was published by *The Universal Gazette* (Washington, DC: Samuel Harrison Smith), September 17, 1807, vol. 5, no. 502. This selection is also quoted by Paul Russell Cutright in his *A History of the Lewis and Clark Journals* (Norman: University of Oklahoma Press, 1976), 18.

32. See TJ, Table of Mileages, September 30, 1807, *PTJDE*.

33. TJ to Martha Jefferson Randolph, October 12, 1807, *PTJDE*.

34. For these details of Jefferson's itinerary, and those immediately following, see TJ, Table of Mileages, September 30, 1807, *PTJDE*.

35. See Smith, *First Forty Years*, 385, which mentions the maps on display at the President's House in particular.

36. The best overview of this particular "large scale" map of Africa (1802) by Aaron Arrowsmith is provided by Stein, *The Worlds of Thomas Jefferson at Monticello*, which notes that "[a]pparently satisfied with Arrowsmith's work, in 1805 Jefferson ordered maps of Europe, Asia, and Africa [. . .]. These three, along with the map of

the United States, were probably among the maps that hung in Jefferson's Cabinet at the President's House" (389). Jefferson's detailed map of Africa acquired in 1805 depicted not only "Sennar," but also "Futa Jallon"—the home of many of the Muslims who would become enslaved in America.

37. Ira P. Nash to TJ, October 3, 1807, *PTJDE*.

38. For previous, although entirely tentative, recognition of this particular quotation featured as part of Jefferson's Arabic document, see "Islamic manuscripts in North American collections, pt. 4." This article represents the only twentieth-century notice of Jefferson's original Arabic manuscript housed at the MHS (Figure 1); this article's author is, however, entirely unaware of this document's historic nature, not realizing that it was penned by Muslim Africans or by enslaved men. The reviewer does, however, note that "[p]arts of Koran 61:13 [are] identifiable in lines 5–7, although not without a stretch of imagination" (7); however, the reviewer credits this "identification [. . .] to Prof. Muhammad Bakir Alwān, of Brooklin." This passing and cautious recognition authored by an anonymous cataloguer in 1985 qualifies as the only published attempt to source the Arabic material contained in either of Jefferson's two manuscripts prior to the present study.

Chapter 14

1. For Jefferson's "accessib[ility]" during his second term especially, see Malone, *Jefferson and His Time*, V:122. Although reporting with "satisfaction" that Burr's "treasons & misdemeanors" had been "finally suppressed," Jefferson's report to the US House of Representatives (September 20, 1807, *PTJDE*) mentions specifically that "complaints have been heard that some of our citizens [. . .] in their uninformed zeal for bringing the offenders to legal punishment, have overstepped the limits of the law."

2. This is Ira P. Nash to TJ, October 5, 1807, *PTJDE*, which is quoted frequently below.

3. The size of Jefferson's larger Arabic manuscript—imaged as Figure 1—is "[f]olio" measuring "18.5 × 29.5 cm.," with its "written surface measur[ing] 14 × 20 cm." The much smaller size of the second Arabic manuscript delivered to Jefferson, reproduced as part of Patterson's facsimile, is evident from Figure 9 (see Chapter 16, note 7). Besides its Arabic content, the only noteworthy mark on this larger manuscript is a single English letter on its verso—a stylized "N"—which I judge to be Ira P. Nash's own handwriting, likely reflecting Nash's desire to inscribe his own initial on this historic Arabic document.

4. Ira P. Nash to TJ, October 5, 1807, *PTJDE*.

5. Ira P. Nash to TJ, October 5, 1807, *PTJDE*.

6. For this quotation, see the *PTJDE*'s V. The Declaration of Independence as Adopted by Congress, 11 June–4 July 1776.

7. Jefferson's early thought provided a "proof text" for the First Amendment, as Dreisbach traces (*Thomas Jefferson and the Wall of Separation*, 3); however, Jefferson also unsurprisingly regularly appealed to this amendment later in his career (see, for instance,

Jefferson's work on the Kentucky and Virginia Resolutions in 1798—I. Jefferson's Draft, [before 4 October 1798], *PTJDE*—in which the First Amendment is quoted).

8. Anonymous to TJ, October 4, 1807, *PTJDE*.
9. Ira P. Nash to TJ, October 5, 1807, *PTJDE*.
10. TJ to Martha Jefferson Randolph, October 12, 1807, *PTJDE*.
11. TJ to Robert Patterson, October 18, 1807, *PTJDE*.
12. TJ to John Wayles Eppes, October 8, 1807, *PTJDE*.
13. TJ to John Wayles Eppes, October 8, 1807, *PTJDE*.
14. TJ to Caesar Augustus Rodney, October 8, 1807, *PTJDE*.
15. TJ to George Hay, October 11, 1807, *PTJDE*.
16. George Hay to TJ, October 15, 1807, *PTJDE*.
17. TJ to Robert Patterson, October 18, 1807, *PTJDE*.
18. Philip S. Foner, *Essays in Afro-American History* (Philadelphia: Temple University Press, 1978), 19.
19. Patterson's service as this society's vice president is recorded by Edward Needles, *An Historical Memoir of the Pennsylvania Society for Promoting the Abolition of Slavery* (Philadelphia, 1848), 49.
20. TJ to Robert Patterson, 18 October, 1807, *PTJDE*.
21. TJ to Robert Patterson, 18 October, 1807, *PTJDE*.
22. TJ to Robert Patterson, 18 October, 1807, *PTJDE*.
23. TJ to Robert Patterson, 18 October, 1807, *PTJDE*.
24. For the "only two slaves Jefferson freed during his lifetime"—namely Robert Hemings and James Hemings—see Holland, *The Invisibles*, 76. In his own will, drafted March 1826, Jefferson also names "five slaves" selected to be released after his death (Hugh Howard, *Dr. Kimball and Mr. Jefferson: Rediscovering the Founding Fathers* [New York: Bloomsbury Publishing, 2006], 168). For Jefferson's "advice to" Edward "Coles not to emancipate his slaves," "counsel[ing] his neighbor against manumission because slaves 'of this color we know' were 'as incapable as children of taking care of themselves,'" see Paul Finkelman, *Slavery and the Founders: Race and Liberty in the Age of Jefferson* (New York: Routledge, 2014), 270.
25. I was fortunate to view the envelope that originally enclosed Jefferson's October 18, 1807, letter during my research at the American Philosophical Society (APS), which houses both the envelope as well as Jefferson's manuscript letter (Thomas Jefferson, Letter to Robert Patterson, October 18, 1807, B J35.p., held in box 3 of Mss.B.J35, Thomas Jefferson papers, 1775–1825). I quote from this envelope courtesy of the APS, and express my gratitude especially to Earle E. Spamer for initially alerting me not only to the survival of this envelope, but also to the markings that it bears, as quoted above.

Chapter 15

1. This date is visible on the same envelope referenced immediately above (Chapter 14, note 25), and is quoted courtesy of the American Philosophical Society.

2. Robert Patterson to TJ, October 24, 1807.

3. Jefferson himself admits that his naming of Patterson as head of the US Mint might seem an onerous role on top of Patterson's academic duties. See TJ to Robert Patterson, April 27, 1805, *PTJDE*, in which Jefferson notes that "I should be sorry to withdraw you from the college; nor do I conceive that this office need do it. it's duties will easily admit your devoting the ordinary college hours to that institution."

4. It is not clear when Jefferson's letter arrived to Patterson in Philadelphia. Although the manuscript's envelope is postmarked on the 19th, Patterson left no trace of date of receipt. Even assuming the letter arrived without delay, Patterson would not have possessed the Arabic manuscripts dispatched to him from Jefferson for more than four days before his October 24 reply.

5. For "the final tally" of fatalities struck down by the "epidemic of yellow fever" as "about 10 percent of Philadelphia's population," see Stephen Gehlbach, *American Plagues: Lessons from Our Battles with Disease* (Lanham, MD: Rowman & Littlefield, 2016), 18.

6. For O'Brien's service as consul, see Charles Stuart Kennedy, *The American Consul: A History of the United States Consular Service, 1776–1914* (New York: Greenwood Press, 1990), 32.

7. Suspicions of O'Brien's "espionage" harbored by Tripoli's "bashaw" following the *Philadelphia* affair are treated by Kilmeade and Yaeger, *Thomas Jefferson and the Tripoli Pirates*, 154. See also Allison, *The Crescent Obscured*, which notes much earlier mistrust of O'Brien, namely suspicions of his "conspiring" with local Tunisians harbored by his very own countryman, William Eaton (177).

8. Richard O'Brien to TJ, July 3, 1806, *PTJDE*.

9. For assertions regarding O'Brien's fluency in spoken Arabic, see H. G. Barnby, *The Prisoners of Algiers: An Account of the Forgotten American-Algerian War 1785–1797* (New York: Oxford University Press, 1966), 148, as well as Kennedy, *The American Consul*, 33.

10. Robert Patterson to TJ, October 24, 1807, *PTJDE*.

11. For Richard Van Lennep's "long voyage" undertaken "in order to establish commercial contacts with American firms," see Jan Schmidt, *From Anatolia to Indonesia: Opium Trade and the Dutch Community of Izmir, 1820–1940* (Istanbul: Netherlands Historisch-Archaeologisch Inst., 1998), 88. For the Van Lenneps' American engagements, also see Oliver, *American Travelers*, 338.

12. S. G. W. Benjamin, *The Life and Adventures of a Free Lance* (Burlington, VT: Free Press Company, 1914), 72.

13. Benjamin, *The Life and Adventures*, 72.

14. J. W. Henderson and Rodney Carlisle, *Jack Tar: Marine Art & Antiques: A Sailor's Life, 1750–1910* (Woodbridge, UK: Antique Collectors' Club, 1999), reproduces this "watercolor scene of men dancing aboard ship" from "*Richard Van Lennep Sketchbook*" (149).

15. See Henderson and Carlisle, *Jack Tar*, for these quotations; "the black musician" in Van Lennep's "watercolor" has his left foot raised, apparently keeping time to the

dance of four white men in front of him, with a fifth man standing behind the musician, but turned away from the scene.

16. Van Lennep's stay in Philadelphia lasted until around December 12, 1807. On that date, Charles Caldwell gifted him a copy of his own "Elegiac Poem" published in Philadelphia in 1807, which includes an inscription to Richard on his "leaving Philadelphia." This unique item is described within a 1922 auction inventory, namely *The Library of the Late George H. Hart of New York City: Americana, Order of Sale* (New York: Anderson Galleries, 1922), 22. For Richard's trip to the United States as helping to establish Van Lennep commerce in Philadelphia, as well as Boston, see Schmidt, *From Anatolia to Indonesia*, 89.

17. Robert Patterson to TJ, October 24, 1807, *PTJDE*. It is important to note, however, that the *PTJDE* version offers only a hesitant, and hence inaccurate, transcription of the name "Van Lennep," offered erroneously as "Mr. Sennup?"

18. For further deciphering of these same Arabic manuscripts which Van Lennep indicates to be indecipherable, see especially Chapter 16, below.

19. Mr. [Richard] Van Lennep to TJ, June 1, 1821, *PTJDE*.

20. For "the Smyrna firm of Jacob Van Lennep and Co." gifting "a mummy with its painted wood case" to Boston, see Oliver, *American Travelers*, 88. For a contemporaneous record of this gift's receipt in Boston, see the May 20, 1823, issue of the *American Watchman and Delaware Advertiser*, which records that "*An Egyptian Mummy* has been received at Boston, which is indeed to be exhibited [. . .] It is in high preservation, and was transmitted by Messrs. Jacob Van Lennep & Co. of Smyrna" (2).

21. TJ to Robert Patterson, 18 October, 1807, *PTJDE*.

22. Despite his influential career in Philadelphia, and especially philological accomplishments, Wylie rarely receives notice in early American historiography. However, his life is succinctly outlined in the first volume of *The National Cyclopedia of American Biography* (New York: James T. White, 1893), 348.

23. Robert Patterson to TJ, October 24, 1807, *PTJDE*. Wylie's love of classical languages, and their instruction, would even lead him to publish a Greek grammar, which is addressed briefly in note 27.

24. Robert Patterson to TJ, October 24, 1807, *PTJDE*.

25. Robert Patterson to TJ, October 24, 1807, *PTJDE*.

26. I am deeply grateful to Mitch Fraas, curator at the Kislak Center for Special Collections (Rare Books and Manuscripts, University of Pennsylvania Libraries), for bringing to my attention the marginalia featured in Wylie's autographed copy of the *Pantographia; Containing Accurate Copies of All the Known Alphabets in the World* (London: Printed by Cooper and Wilson, for John and Arthur Arch, 1799), 4, in advance of my visit to the Kislak Center in 2017, and his subsequent help in securing the image featured as Figure 8.

27. With his earliest studies of Arabic "spurred" by the arrival of Muslim slave documents, Wylie eventually rose to be appointed as the University of Pennsylvania's "chair of ancient languages," due partly to his repute as "an eminent Oriental scholar" (*The National Cyclopedia of American Biography*, I:348). Arabic also plays a role in the

Greek grammar that Wylie produced, that is, his *An Introduction to the Knowledge of Greek Grammar* (Philadelphia: J. Whetham, 1838), whose third page parallels the Greek and Arabic alphabets (an uncommon practice in Greek primers), printing a table with Arabic script preceding the Greek, offering the following comparisons in its first lines:

Arabic		Greek	
Elif	ا	Alpha	A α
Ba	ب	Beta	B β
Jim	ح	Gamma	Γ γ

28. For the University of Pennsylvania's "Arabic program [as] one of the most prominent in the country," see its homepage (http://ccat.sas.upenn.edu/arabic).
29. Robert Patterson to TJ, October 24, 1807, *PTJDE*.
30. Robert Patterson to TJ, October 24, 1807, *PTJDE*.

Chapter 16

1. TJ to Charles Willson Peale, October 5, 1807, *PTJDE*.
2. Silvio Bedini's *Thomas Jefferson and His Copying Machines* (Charlottesville: University of Virginia Press, 1984) has most comprehensively traced Jefferson's investment in early facsimile technology; for the stylograph technology, see especially p. 154 and ff.
3. For Jefferson's collaborations with Peale, as well as the friends they mutually shared— including Joel Barlow—see Charles Sellers, *Mr. Peale's Museum: Charles Willson Peale and the First Popular Museum of Natural Science and Art* (New York: Norton, 1980), 174 and 189. For Peale's 1791 oil on canvas *Thomas Jefferson*, see Alfred Bush, *The Life Portraits of Thomas Jefferson* (Charlottesville: Thomas Jefferson Memorial Foundation, 1987), 19. For Peale's portrait of Yarrow Mamout, see Austin, *African Muslims*, 31–32.
4. Jefferson marked his receipt of Patterson's October 24, 1807, letter, scribbling "rec[d] Oct. 26." at the very top right of this manuscript.
5. Robert Patterson to TJ, October 24, 1807, *PTJDE*.
6. In addition to thanking the Manuscript Division at the Library of Congress, Washington, DC, for facilitating my publication of this image, I acknowledge with especial gratitude Julie Miller, the library's resident historian of early American materials, who provided invaluable aid during my 2017 research at the library.
7. Patterson's oscillation of the smaller Arabic document on its side offers the means of fitting both manuscripts onto a single page, but perhaps also reflects his inability to read Arabic script. Patterson offers Jefferson no specifics as to his "*fac simile*" process; however, it is clear from comparing the documents imaged as Figure 9 and Figure 1 that the latter is indeed the original, and the former is Patterson's "*fac simile*," featuring material "added" via a method of reproduction, resulting in a single document that synthesizes the "two little manuscripts" Nash delivered to Jefferson in October 1807.

8. Despite extended searches among the surviving manuscripts possessed by participants in this story—not only Thomas Jefferson and Robert Patterson, but also Samuel B. Wylie and Richard O'Brien—I have been unable to recover the original of the smaller Arabic manuscript (unlike the larger Arabic manuscript, whose original is imaged as Figure 1). As a result, it is only Patterson's *"fac simile,"* housed at the Library of Congress, that bears witness to this smaller Arabic manuscript—a manuscript that is nearly illegible, but which, as I argue below, appears to contain the last chapter of the Qur'an.

9. Although the illegibility of the two manuscripts is extreme, demanding inference and construing meaning often through context, the script and spelling challenges presented by Jefferson's Arabic manuscripts are not at all unique among West African Muslim slave writings. In this regard, most notorious is "the case of the famous *Ben Ali's Diary"*—a manuscript penned by a Muslim enslaved on Sapelo Island. For the "indeterminate" character of *"Ben Ali's Diary,"* see Ronald A. T. Judy, *(Dis)forming the American Canon: African-Arabic Slave Narratives and the Vernacular* (Minneapolis: University of Minnesota Press, 1993), 187. For a published image from this nearly illegible Arabic manuscript, and for its "featur[ing] excerpts from a tenth-century text by the Tunisian scholar Abu Zayd al Qairawani," see Sylviane A. Diouf, *Servants of Allah: African Muslims Enslaved in the Americas* (New York: New York University Press, 2013), 152.

10. This description is quoted from the anonymous "Jefferson Papers: Number Two," *Knickerbocker Magazine* 6 (1835): 537–540 (540), which is discussed in-depth further below (Chapter 21, notes 12 and 14).

11. Robert Patterson to TJ, October 24, 1807, *PTJDE.*

12. Robert Patterson to TJ, October 24, 1807, *PTJDE.*

13. Considering that the Arabic material I identify as the Qur'an's Chapter 114 derives from a small manuscript witnessed only once, and merely oscillated in *"fac simile,"* not in its original, it is a marvel that it is legible at all. However, one of the reasons why this Arabic material is somewhat simpler to identify than the material inscribed as part of Jefferson's larger Arabic manuscript—imaged as Figure 1—is that it seems to constitute one continuous Qur'anic chapter (and not verses from discrete chapters, as is the case with the larger Arabic manuscript). The keyword I found essential for deciphering this smaller Arabic manuscript's lines is "الوسواس" (*"al-waswās,"* "the whisperer")—a term (relatively) identifiable in the Arabic above, and which is highly idiomatic, occurring only once in the Qur'an. Identifying this term in conjunction especially with a cognate verb "يوسوس" (*"yuwaswisu,"* "whispers") helped clarify that these lines are meant to inscribe the Qur'an's Chapter 114. Perhaps most unmistakable in the four lines of this smaller Arabic document is simply its last word—that is, "سورة" (*"sūra,"* "chapter")—a term signaling not only that this material represents a Qur'anic "chapter," but also marking the conclusion to the chapter copied. As above, the phraseology of my provided translation of this Qur'anic material draws on Arberry's *The Koran Interpreted*; however, rather than Arberry's "the slinking whisperer" for the Arabic "الوسواس الخناس," I offer the more literal and conventional "the withdrawing whisperer."

14. For Jefferson "summon[ing] this special session," see Arthur Scherr, *Thomas Jefferson's Image of New England: Nationalism Versus Sectionalism in the Young Republic*

(Jefferson, NC: McFarland & Company, 2016), 109; for Jefferson's congressional address, see TJ to United States Congress, October 27, 1807, *PTJDE*.

Chapter 17

1. Ira P. Nash to TJ, November 8, 1807, *PTJDE*.
2. Although he lived until 1844, participating in events pivotal to the nation—including the War of 1812, serving in the Missouri Militia—there are no additional extant letters exchanged between Nash and Thomas Jefferson after November 8, 1808.
3. The original manuscript of Nash's November 8, 1808, letter bears Jefferson's own mark on its second page, recording that the letter was "rec^d. Jan. 6." Housed as part of the Library of Congress's Thomas Jefferson Papers, this item—incorrectly catalogued as "Frank Nash to Thomas Jefferson, November 8, 1807"—is imaged at www.loc.gov/item/mtjbib017864.
4. This characterization of Christian County, Kentucky—that is, as a "sparsely settled part of the western frontier"—is offered by Cooper, *Jefferson Davis, American*, 10.
5. For "Southern states enact[ing] legislation barring black literacy," and "South Carolina and Georgia proscrib[ing] formal schooling for their African American population in 1740," see Ronald E. Butchart, *Schooling the Freed People: Teaching, Learning, and the Struggle for Black Freedom; 1861–1876* (Chapel Hill: University of North Carolina Press, 2010), 15.
6. Aptly, this quote reflecting American prejudice is quoted from an overview of another literate Muslim enslaved in America—'Abd ar-Raḥmān—who is addressed further below. For this quotation see "Abduhl Rahahman, the Unfortunate Moor," *The African Repository* 4, no. 8 (October 1828): 243–250 (246), which asserts that "[a]s christians [*sic*] we must especially rejoice that an opportunity will be afforded [by the return of freed slaves] for diffusing the blessings of christianity [*sic*] to that dark and benighted region"—a region in which "the Alcoran had [already] given the people a curiosity to see the Bible."
7. For these quotations, see Henry Adams, *History of the United States of America*, 9 vols. (New York: Charles Scribner's Sons, 1921), I:323.
8. See, for instance, the October 19, 1807, issue of *The National Intelligencer and Washington Advertiser*, p. 2, whose coverage of the Burr trial notes that "*Mr. Wirt* observed that he had understood the gentlemen who had opened the cause on the part of the defendants, had asserted that a system of espionage had pervaded the transactions in the Western Country."
9. William Henry Harrison, *Governors' Messages and Letters: Messages and Letters of William Henry Harrison*, 2 vols. (Indianapolis: Indiana Historical Commission, 1922), I:261.
10. Harrison, *Governors' Messages*, I:261.
11. This quote derives from John Marshall, *The Papers of John Marshall*, eds. Herbert A. Johnson et al., 12 vols. (Chapel Hill: University of North Carolina Press, 1974–2006), VII:148.

12. Adair's petition is quoted from the March 4, 1807, issue of *The National Intelligencer and Washington Advertiser*, p. 1. Adair's words are framed within a foregoing discussion, in which he was "told in the public room" of an inn "that Wilkinson had denounced [Adair] as a traitor, and declared [him] at the head of an army coming to attack that city."

13. I supply the question mark at the conclusion to this quotation, which in the original—cited immediately above—continues with a dash after which Adair declares, "I have said every citizen of the west, because on them was this bill intended to operate."

14. See Zellar, *A Brave Man Stands Firm*, who notes that after being sent to Baltimore, John Adair was released "on the writ of *habeas corpus*" and "later sued Wilkinson for wrongful arrest and was awarded $2,500, later paid by Congress on Wilkinson's behalf" (53).

15. This detail is offered by Nash in his second letter to Jefferson, on October 5, 1807; however, this letter is slightly mutilated, and I provide the reconstructed portions in the above, which is offered in the *PTJDE* transcript as follows: "they are still kept in con[fineme]nt and are ma[de to] labour daily." As emphasized above, Nash's assertion to Jefferson that "[t]hose men, are by some supposed to be Spys" is offered at the end to his November 8, 1807, letter, after the men had already escaped from Christian County, Kentucky, and reached Tennessee. Nash does not specify from where he is authoring his November 8 letter. He does, however, mention to Jefferson that he is "so far past that place," seemingly implying that he is already "far" west of where the "two men" were "taken up" in Tennessee. If this is correct, it would suggest that Nash's information, including these "spy" rumors, derives from Kentucky, perhaps from Christian Country itself, where Nash would have naturally expected to find the two men during his return trip home to Missouri.

16. For this Qur'anic verse—Chapter 100:7—see the second line of "Page written in Arabic [October 1807]," housed at MHS and imaged as Figure 1. My reading of this manuscript material as representing Qur'an 100:7 is consistent with my claim above that the top five lines of this Arabic document—the larger of the two delivered to Jefferson—appear to represent a quotation from the conclusion of the Qur'an 100 (i.e., this chapter's verses 6–11). As all of the material in both of the two Arabic documents, it is context, rather than individual characters, that is the best guide to revealing the intent of the transcriber, as the written lines are made nearly illegible due to slips in orthography.

17. Lon Arneld Bostick, *Family History Book, Christian County, Kentucky*, 2 vols. (Paducah: Turner Publishing Company, 1991), II:10.

18. Bostick, *Family History Book*, II:10.

19. The precise date on which the two men escaped Hopkinsville in 1807 is unclear. However, in light of surviving records from Christian County, it is perhaps not a coincidence that 1807 saw the county continue to be plagued with security concerns. During this same year it was "[o]rdered that Michael Cravens be allowed the sum of six dollars for sundry service by him performed as a smith in making hand cuffs as per account filed" (Bostick, *Family History Book*, II:11).

20. Ira P. Nash to TJ, November 8, 1807, *PTJDE*.

21. See Nicholas Dungan, *Gallatin: America's Swiss Founding Father* (New York: New York University Press, 2010), 165.

22. Ira P. Nash to TJ, November 8, 1807, *PTJDE*.

23. Ira P. Nash to TJ, November 8, 1807, *PTJDE*.

24. For Daniel Smith as "an experienced surveyor, possibly the only man in the whole west who could draw a map with any degree of accuracy," see Harriette Arnow, *Seedtime on the Cumberland* (Lincoln: University of Nebraska Press, 1995), 327.

25. Larry Miller, in his *Tennessee Place Names* (Bloomington: Indiana University Press, 2001), is able to shed little light on the background to Carthage as a name for this seat of Smith County, but does confirm that "[t]his label was inspired by the famed North African city of antiquity" (39).

26. See Newmyer, *The Treason Trial*, 4, who notes that it was Marshall who decided to "commit Burr for trial in Ohio"; Newmyer also recognizes on p. 174 that this Ohio trial never took place. The above quote, identifying Burr as being "bound over for a trial at Chillicothe in January, 1808," is from Rowland Rerick, *History of Ohio* (Madison, WI: Northwestern Historical Association, 1902), 175.

27. For this letter see Aaron Burr, *Aaron Burr: A Biography Compiled from Rare, and in Many Cases Unpublished, Sources*, eds. Samuel Wandell and Meade Minnigerode, 2 vols. (New York: Knickerbocker Press, 1925), II:231—a page that also notes that this "mysterious" letter by Burr to Theodosia is "abounding in cipher names and blanks."

28. This quotation derives from Aaron Burr, *The Private Journal of Aaron Burr during His Residence of Four Years in Europe with Selections from His Correspondence*, ed. Matthew Davis, 2 vols. (New York: Harper, 1838), I:21.

29. Considering his "grand Hegira" reference, it is interesting to note that Burr's own adventurous insurgency into the American west has also been termed a "hegira"; see, for instance, Isaac Cox, "The Burr Conspiracy in Indiana," *Indiana Magazine of History* 25, no. 4 (1929): 257–280, which notes that "[s]hortly after the Eighth Congress closed its session, Burr started on his enigmatic western hegira" (262).

30. For "the legend of Theodosia Burr" as a "favorite legend of the Carolina dune country," see John Harden, *The Devil's Tramping Ground: And Other North Carolina Mystery Stories* (Chapel Hill: University of North Carolina Press, 1997), 74.

31. For Theodosia as the subject of "[a]nother legend [that] relates that she was captured by the Barbary pirates," see *The Nelson Gallery & Atkins Museum Bulletin* 4, no. 10 (1969): 53.

32. For this declaration, see "Piracy on the Seas," which appears on p. 6 of the June 7, 1901, edition of *The San Francisco Call*.

33. See Hugh Thomas, *The Slave Trade: The Story of the Atlantic Slave Trade, 1440–1870* (New York: Simon & Schuster, 1997), 552, as well as Malone, *Jefferson and His Time*, who emphasizes in particular that "all the states had outlawed the foreign slave trade on their own authority and only South Carolina had reopened it" (V:541). Although illegal, the slave trade did not stop entirely in 1807, but lingered on for a half century, ending finally with *The Wanderer*, a ship that landed on November 28, 1858, on Jekyll Island, Georgia—an essential home in the Golden Isles for the Demere family itself. I first learned of *The Wanderer* from a permanent historical exhibit on Jekyll Island;

this voyage has also, however, been treated by Erik Calonius in his *The Wanderer: The Last American Slave Ship and the Conspiracy That Set Its Sails* (New York: Saint Martin's Press, 2006), which credits the Jekyll Island Museum specifically (see p. x).

34. Robert Williams to TJ, January 6, 1808, *PTJDE*.

35. TJ to John Taylor, January 6, 1808, *PTJDE*.

36. For the Gullah background to "bene," see Adrian Miller, *Soul Food: The Surprising Story of an American Cuisine, One Plate at a Time* (Chapel Hill: University of North Carolina Press, 2013), 24.

37. See Dorothea Bedigian, "African Origins of Sesame Cultivation in the Americas," in *African Ethnobotany in the Americas*, eds. John Rashford and Robert Voeks (New York: Springer, 2013), 67–120, and specifically 102–104, which address Jefferson's use of these seeds.

38. Ira P. Nash to TJ, November 8, 1807, *PTJDE*.

39. Ira P. Nash to TJ, November 8, 1807, *PTJDE*.

Chapter 18

1. Ira P. Nash to TJ, November 8, 1807, *PTJDE*.

2. For Hayes's recognition that many of Jefferson's possessions—and his books specifically—were sent forward to Monticello well before the president's retirement, see *The Road to Monticello*, 515 (and my Prologue, note 2).

3. It is, of course, difficult to ascertain precisely where any one piece of paper owned by Jefferson was housed during his years of retirement. What is clear, however, is that after his death, at least one of his two Arabic manuscripts from Kentucky—the single extant original, imaged as Figure 1—was archived together with his personal papers, retained alongside the bulk of his private correspondence, where it was first evaluated in 1835 (see Chapter 21, note 14).

4. For the "three thousand-volume Library of Congress" that was "burned by the British around 9 p.m. [on] August 24, 1814," see Ralph Eshelman, *A Travel Guide to the War of 1812 in the Chesapeake* (Baltimore: Johns Hopkins University Press, 2011), 225. For this collection as "a promising congressional library," see Paul Pruitt, David Durham, and Sally Hadden, *Traveling the Beaten Trail: Charles Tait's Charges to Federal Grand Juries, 1822–1825* (Tuscaloosa: University of Alabama School of Law, 2013), 14.

5. These quotations derived from TJ to Samuel H. Smith, September 21, 1814, *PTJDE*.

6. John Adams to TJ, October 28, 1814, *PTJDE*.

7. See Oliver, *American Travelers*, who notes that "[a]mong the first Americans to take advantage of the peace to travel to Europe were Edward Everett and George Ticknor" (58). However, severe hardships were still experienced by travelers abroad, due to European warfare; see Steve Batterson, *American Mathematics 1890–1913: Catching Up to Europe* (Washington, DC: The Mathematical Association of America, 2017), which notes that to reach Germany, the Americans elected to "cros[s] the Channel to Holland where, after another month of sometimes arduous overland travel, Everett and Ticknor reached Göttingen" (24).

8. Everett is only rarely and cursorily treated in studies of Jefferson, despite the significant intersections between their respective careers and convictions. See, however, Scherr's mention of Everett in his *Thomas Jefferson's Image of New England*, especially 301–303.

9. This quotation is from Paul Varg, *Edward Everett: The Intellectual in the Turmoil of Politics* (Selinsgrove, PA: Susquehanna University Press, 1992), who implies that it was Everett's plans to meet Jefferson specifically that prompted his "congregation" to become "upset," and dispatch their complaint, recalling him to New England (18).

10. John Adams to TJ, December 20, 1814, *PTJDE*.

11. For the view that Jefferson's library contained "too many books in foreign languages," as well as the purchase's "authoriz[ation]" on January 26, 1815, see Annette Melville, *Special Collections in the Library of Congress, a Selective Guide* (Washington, DC: Library of Congress, 1980), 189.

12. For the Arabic grammars acquired as part of the 1815 sale of Jefferson's library, see Green's 1830 *Catalogue of the Library of Congress*, 248 and 250, which records respectively the transfer to Washington of Jefferson's copies of *Erpeniii Rudimenta linguae Arabicae*, as well as Vieyra's *Specimina Arabica et Persica* (see also Chapter 7, notes 19 and 20).

13. TJ to John Adams, June 10, 1815, *PTJDE*.

14. For these two quotes, see *Jefferson in His Own Time: A Biographical Chronicle of His Life*, ed. Kevin J. Hayes (Iowa City: University of Iowa Press, 2012), 80.

15. TJ to John Adams, June 10, 1815, *PTJDE*.

16. This quotation appears denuded of its context—that is, Jefferson's praise of Ticknor—for instance in Thomas Jefferson, *The Quotable Jefferson*, ed. John P. Kaminski (Princeton: Princeton University Press, 2006), 25.

17. This quote surfaces in Carl Diehl's *Americans and German Scholarship: 1770–1870* (New Haven: Yale University Press, 1978), 95. This phrase, however, arises within Everett's self-reflective critique of Americans who insufficiently benefit from experiences abroad, noting that "when our pilgrimage is over [in Europe, Americans tend to return] to our wallowing in the professional mire" (95).

18. Lord George Byron, *Childe Harold's Pilgrimage, a Romaunt: And Other Poems* (London: John Murray, 1815), 113.

19. For Byron's statement "I was very near becoming a Mussulman" as recorded by his wife—with whom he had a notoriously contentious relationship—as well as his Islamic interests expressed by his best-selling *Turkish Tales*, see my *Islam and Romanticism: Muslim Currents from Goethe to Emerson* (London: Oneworld Publications, 2014), 113–131 (esp. 113–114).

20. For Byron as the "martyr of Missolonghi," see David Roessel, *In Byron's Shadow: Modern Greece in the English & American Imagination* (Oxford: Oxford University Press, 2003), 3.

21. For Everett and Ticknor's stopover in England and their engagements with Byron specifically, see Oliver, *American Travelers*, 58–59. For Ticknor's own record of their encounter with Byron, and their discussion of Ali Pasha in particular, see George Ticknor, *Life, Letters, and Journals of George Ticknor*, eds. George Stillman Hillard

et al., 2 vols. (Boston: J. R. Osgood, 1877), I:64, 68. Byron's letter from London—dated June 25, 1815—addressed to the "Vizir Ali Pasha of Albania, Joannina" is printed in Lord George Byron, *Letters and Journals, 1814–1815, Vol. 4*, ed. Leslie Marchand (Cambridge, MA: Harvard University Press, 1975); see especially Byron's notice to Ali Pasha that "[a]n American Gentleman (Mr Ticknor) has promised to deliver from me to your Highness a curious pistol (the properties and management of which he will explain) which I shall feel honored by your accepting" (299).

22. Never before published, this quotation derives from folder 12, p. 110 of Edward Everett, "Letterbook and Journal [photocopies], 1815–1842" (Ms. N-2226), Massachusetts Historical Society.

23. As above, I quote here from Edward Everett, "Letterbook and Journal [photocopies], 1815–1842" (Ms. N-2226), Massachusetts Historical Society, but from folder 12, p. 111. For Ticknor's parallel impressions of this 1815 encounter with Goethe, see Anna Ticknor and George Ticknor, *Two Boston Brahmins in Goethe's Germany: The Travel Journals of Anna and George Ticknor*, eds. Thomas Adam and Gisela Mettele (Lanham, MD: Lexington Books, 2009), 61–62. Ticknor also notes Goethe's understated presence, and his speaking "in a quiet, simple manner," which, Ticknor suggests, had caused "bitter [. . .] disappointment" to other pilgrims (62).

24. The piratical ethos of Byron's *Turkish Tales*—and especially his *Corsair*, which was so beloved by Goethe—has most recently been explored by William Davis, *The Pirates Laffite: The Treacherous World of the Corsairs of the Gulf* (Orlando: Harcourt, 2005), whose preface aptly implies New World links for Byron's mix of Orientalism and pirate romance (xi).

25. Never before published, this quotation derives from folder 13, pp. 127–128, of Edward Everett, "Letterbook and Journal [photocopies], 1815–1842" (Ms. N-2226), Massachusetts Historical Society.

26. The "Persian manner" of Goethe's late poetics is exemplified most conspicuously by his *West-östlicher Divan*—an 1819 verse collection shaped by classical Persian poetry that opens with a dual-language frontispiece, pairing together stylized Arabic calligraphy and German script. For this frontispiece, and Goethe's Persianate poetry more broadly, see my "The Genesis of *Weltliteratur*: Goethe's *West-Ostlicher Divan* and Kerygmatic Pluralism," *Literature and Theology* 19, no. 3 (2005): 238–250 (especially 241–243).

27. TJ to George Ticknor, July 4, 1815, *PTJDE*.

28. Jefferson was already familiar with this work, as it was one of the volumes that he had owned before the "translation" of his Monticello library to Washington; see Thomas Jefferson, *Thomas Jefferson's Library: A Catalog with the Entries in His Own Order*, eds. James Gilreath and Douglas Wilson (Clark, NJ: Lawbook Exchange, 2008), 123. The edition that Jefferson owned until his library's sale in 1815—that is, Richard Hakluyt, *The Principal Navigations, Voiages, Traffiques and Discoueries of the English Nation, Made by Sea or Overland* (London: G. Bishop, R. Newberie & R. Barker, 1589)—is recorded within the early Library of Congress catalogue offered by Green (*Catalogue of the Library of Congress*, 198).

29. Aptly for Jefferson, Hakluyt not only harbored broad Orientalist interests, but specifically engaged with Christian captivity in Muslim Africa, printing the testimony of one "John Fox," who "deliver[ed] 266 Christians out of the captivity of the Turks at Alexandria" in "1577"; see Daniel Vitkus and Nabil Matar, *Piracy, Slavery, and Redemption: Barbary Captivity Narratives from Early Modern England* (New York: Columbia University Press, 2001), 58 and ff.

30. Richard Hakluyt, *The Principal Navigations Voyages Traffiques and Discoveries of the English Nation*, 12 vols. (Glasgow: James MacLehose and Sons, 1903–1905), V:356.

31. See Richard Rush's Account of a Visit to Montpellier and Monticello, October 9, 1816, *PTJDE*.

32. These two quotations, characterizing the content of Rush's 1812 speech—that is, *An Oration, Delivered in the Hall of the House of Representatives, at the Capitol, Washington, July 4, 1812* (Washington, DC: 1812)—are supplied as part of the annotations to Richard Rush to TJ, July 18, 1812, as printed in Thomas Jefferson, *The Papers of Thomas Jefferson, Retirement Series*, ed. J. Jefferson Looney, 15 vols. to date (Princeton: Princeton University Press, 2004–2019), V:259.

33. See Richard Rush's Account of a Visit to Montpellier and Monticello, October 9, 1816, *PTJDE*.

Chapter 19

1. For this figure of "6,487" books, see Alan Pell Crawford, *Twilight at Monticello: The Final Years of Thomas Jefferson* (New York: Random House, 2008), 119.

2. George Ticknor to TJ, October 14, 1815, *PTJDE*.

3. Eichhorn's Arabic studies are often explored in relation to Goethe's own amateur Orientalism; see, for instance, Katharina Mommsen, *Goethe and the Poets of Arabia*, trans. Michael Metzger (Rochester, NY: Camden House, 2014), for Eichhorn not only as a "Jena theologian," but also as an "Arabist," with Mommsen identifying "Eichhorn's *Repertory*" as "a valuable source regarding questions of Arabic culture [for Goethe]" (13).

4. This quotation derives from Edward Everett, "Diaries, 1815–1865" (Ms. N-1201), Edward Everett Papers, Massachusetts Historical Society, specifically from this item's Box 1814–1816 (vols. 123–126), unpaginated, December 14, 1815, entry.

5. Although his stay in Göttingen receives regular mention, Everett's sustained study of Arabic has been almost entirely overlooked. See, for example, the latest book-length studies of Everett—Richard Katula's *The Eloquence of Edward Everett: America's Greatest Orator* (New York: Lang, 2010), and Matthew Mason, *Apostle of Union: A Political Biography of Edward Everett* (Chapel Hill: University of North Carolina Press, 2016)—which both neglect his study of Arabic altogether, despite attending to Everett's other scholarly pursuits. Most importantly, Everett's manuscript journals and scholarly papers, evidencing his reading of Arabic, have never previously been discussed in print.

6. Ticknor, *Life, Letters, and Journals of George Ticknor*, I:70.

7. Louis Menand, Paul Reitter, and Chad Wellmon, eds. *The Rise of the Research University: A Sourcebook* (Chicago: University of Chicago Press, 2017), 372.

8. *A Memorial of Edward Everett from the City of Boston*, ed. James M. Bugbee (Boston: Printed by order of the City Council, 1865), 174.

9. Edward Everett, "Edward Everett Diaries, 1815–1865" (Ms. N-1201), Massachusetts Historical Society. This quotation derives from Box 1814–1816 (vols. 123–126), unpaginated, October 30, 1815, entry.

10. For Eichhorn's Arabic edition, see Abū 'l-Fidā', *Abvlfedæ Africa. Cvravit Io. Godofredvs Eichhorn M. Britanniæ Regi a Consiliis Avlicia Et Professor P.o. Georgiæ Avgvstæ* (Gottingæ Typis Io. Christ. Dieterich, 1791).

11. This quotation derives from folder 6, p. 39, of Edward Everett, "Letterbook and Journal [photocopies], 1815–1842" (Ms. N-2226), Massachusetts Historical Society, where Everett notes that it was the "found[ing]" of the original "African Institution" in "England" that helped select "Africa" as the choice to be "given out as a prize question, in the University," which in turn prompted Eichhorn to undertake his editorial work on Abū 'l-Fidā'. Although Eichhorn's editing of "Africa" was conducted when England's antislavery organization was still known as "Society for the Abolition of the Slave Trade" (1787–1807), Everett instead invokes the name that was current in 1815 (i.e., England's "African Institution"), a society whose interests had turned from abolition to colonization in 1807—a shift that aptly anticipates future applications of Everett's own interests in Arabic, later to encounter a freed US Muslim slave on his way home to Africa, aided by America's own colonization society, as explored below.

12. *Rules and Regulations of the African Institution: Formed on the 14th April, 1807* (London: Printed by W. Phillips, 1807), 4.

13. TJ to George Ticknor, [before 6 June 1817], *PTJDE*.

14. For Jefferson's longtime "drea[m] of establishing in his own home county an institution of higher learning to rival Harvard or the College of New Jersey at Princeton," see Crawford, *Twilight at Monticello*, xxiii.

15. Thomas Jefferson to de Bure Frères, June 6, 1817, *PTJDE*.

16. See Charles H. Hart, *Memoir of George Ticknor, Historian of Spanish Literature* (Philadelphia: Collins Printer, 1871), which notes that Ticknor "took warm letters of introduction [authored by Jefferson] to Lafayette, Dupont De Nemours, Say, and others, which, together with his own polished and agreeable manners, gained for him such an entrance into Parisian and European society as few of his age and country could gain" (9).

17. This quotation derives from Edward Everett, "Letterbook and Journal [photocopies], 1815–1842" (Ms. N-2226), Massachusetts Historical Society, and specifically from Letterbook, folder 201–220 (December 3, 1817, letter to "President Kirkland," dated "Paris 3 Decr. 1817").

18. Katula notes that Everett in 1815 "accepted the post of professor of Greek studies at Harvard [which] brought with it a large grant to study abroad" (*The Eloquence of Edward Everett*, 13).

19. "Memoir of Edward Everett. Communicated by William Everett," *Proceedings of the Massachusetts Historical Society* 18 (December 1903): 91–117 (100).

20. See Edward Everett, *Selections from the Works of Edward Everett: With a Sketch of His Life* (Boston: J. Burns, 1839), 16, and "Memoir of Edward Everett. Communicated by William Everett," 100.

21. For this appointment in "French and Spanish," and Ticknor's 1818 Spanish sojourn, see Oliver, *American Travelers*, 58. See also Anna Ticknor and George Ticknor, *Two Boston Brahmins*, which notes that "[i]n November 1816, while Ticknor was still abroad, the president of Harvard University John T. Kirkland [. . .] offered him a teaching position in modern languages and literatures at Harvard effective upon his return" (5).

22. "Memoir of Edward Everett," 100.

23. Edward Everett's lengthy description of "the performances of a company of Dervises" derives from his unpaginated "Journal of Italy, Greece, and Constantinople, 21 Mar.– 2 July 1819," which forms vol. 135 of the "Edward Everett Diaries, 1815–1865" (Ms. N-1201), Massachusetts Historical Society.

24. Everett, "Journal of Italy, Greece, and Constantinople, 21 Mar.–2 July 1819," Massachusetts Historical Society.

25. Edward Everett, *Orations and Speeches on Various Occasions*, 4 vols. (Boston: C. C. Little and J. Brown, 1850–1868), III:626.

26. Everett, *Orations and Speeches*, III:627.

27. For Everett's touring of mosques in Constantinople, and viewing these "sentences from the Koran," see his unpaginated "Journal of Italy, Greece, and Constantinople, 21 Mar.–2 July 1819," vol. 135 of the "Edward Everett Diaries, 1815–1865" (Ms. N-1201), Massachusetts Historical Society.

28. This image derives from Edward Everett, Edward Everett Papers, 1675–1910 (Ms. N-1201), Massachusetts Historical Society, and specifically Vol. 247A, "Manuscript: 'An Introduction to the Old Testament,' undated," p. 3.

29. George Ticknor to TJ, May 27, 1819, *PTJDE*.

30. See Edward Bauer, *Doctors Made in America* (Philadelphia: Lippincott, 1963), who characterizes "Ezra Stiles Ely" as "a devoutly religious man and equally practical [whose] father, the Reverend Zebulon Ely, named him after Ezra Stiles, a famous president of Yale" (22).

31. TJ to Ezra Stiles Ely, June 25, 1819, *PTJDE*.

32. TJ to Ezra Stiles Ely, June 25, 1819, *PTJDE*.

33. Steven Waldman, *Founding Faith: How Our Founding Fathers Forged a Radical New Approach to Religious Liberty* (New York: Random House, 2009), emphasizes that Jefferson "excise[d] the miracles from the Bible" and quotes his gospel conclusion without the resurrection, noting that "[i]n Jefferson's Bible, Jesus never rises" (79).

34. For this quote, see Thomas Jefferson, *The Jefferson Bible: The Life and Morals of Jesus of Nazareth* (Mineola, NY: Dover Publications, 2012), 92.

35. The many Eichhorn volumes ordered for the University of Virginia are listed as part of the *PTJDE*'s Bill of Lading for Books shipped from Hamboro' for the University of Virginia, 24 Mar. 1825, 24 March 1825, which records the acquisition of Eichhorn publications including: *Geschichte der Litteratur* (11 vols.); *Litterar Geschichte* (2 vols.); *Allgemeine Geschichte der Cultur und Litteratur* (2 vols.); *Repertorium für*

biblische Litteratur (18 vols.); *Allgemeine Bibliothek der biblisch. Litteratur* (10 vols.); *Einleitung in der alte Testament* (5 vols.); *Einleitung in du Apocryph. Schriften des alten Test*; [*Einleitung in*] *neue Testament* (3 vols.); *Geschichte der drey letzten Jahrh* (6 vols.); *Urgeschichte* (2 vols.); and *Weltgeschichte* (5 vols.).

36. See James Madison to TJ, September 10, 1824, *PTJDE*, which concerns "the subject of a Theological Catalogue for the Library of the University," listing books including "*The Koran*." Even more significant than Madison's letter itself are the annotations offered by the *PTJDE*, which note that the "Koran" mentioned by Madison itself reflects "Jefferson's [own] list," which had not only stipulated the Muslim scripture for their prospective "Catalogue," but specified a particular edition for acquisition (namely George Sale, trans., *The Koran; Commonly Called The Alcoran of Mohammed: Translated from the Original Arabic. With Explanatory Notes*, 2 vols. [London, 1812]).

37. See TJ to James Madison, February 17, 1826, *PTJDE*, for Jefferson's (perhaps playful) reference to the university as a "seminary," noting specifically that "it is in our Seminary that that Vestal flame is to be kept alive."

Chapter 20

1. For this "Act Establishing the University" being passed on January 25, 1819, see Appendix K to Nathaniel Cabell and Joseph Cabell, *Early History of the University of Virginia* (Richmond: J. W. Randolph, 1856); see p. 452, specifically, for Jefferson's signature, together with those of James Madison, David Watson, and John H. Cocke.

2. In the last weeks of his life, Jefferson was still writing letters regarding the renovation and repair to university buildings; see TJ to Arthur S. Brockenbrough, May 5, 1826, *PTJDE*.

3. Jefferson's status as "*Pater almae matris*" ("Father of our *alma mater*") was enshrined, for instance, in an 1875 ode sung at a University of Virginia alumni dinner. See "*Collegiana*," *The Virginia University Magazine* 14, no. 1 (1875): 19–53 (45).

4. John Adams to TJ, January 22, 1825, *PJADE*.

5. For John Quincy Adams's service in 1817 as secretary of state, and its relation to his anti-slavery views, see John Quincy Adams, *John Quincy Adams and the Politics of Slavery: Selections from the Diary*, eds. David Waldstreicher and Matthew Mason (New York: Oxford University Press, 2017), 45 and ff.

6. TJ to William Short, April 13, 1820, *PTJDE*. Jefferson's anxieties, provoked by "the Missouri question" and its subsequent "compromise," are addressed by Robert Forbes, *The Missouri Compromise and Its Aftermath: Slavery & the Meaning of America* (Chapel Hill: University of North Carolina Press, 2007), 103 and ff.

7. John Quincy Adams, *Memoirs: Comprising Portions of His Diary from 1795 to 1848*, ed. Charles Francis Adams (Philadelphia: J. B. Lippincott & Company, 1875), 492–493.

8. See Lonnie Speer, *Portals to Hell: Military Prisons of the Civil War* (Lincoln: University of Nebraska Press, 2006), 1.

9. The attempt to maintain a "balance of power" with concurrent admission of Missouri and Maine is treated by Mark Graber, *Dred Scott and the Problem of Constitutional Evil* (Cambridge: Cambridge University Press, 2006), 123–126.

10. For the "debate over Missouri" inspiring Adams with a "romantic wish to step forward," as well as his "dreaming" of a "champion" for his own views, see James Traub, *John Quincy Adams: Militant Spirit* (New York: Basic Books, 2016), 242–243.

11. TJ to Edward Everett, April 8, 1826, *PTJDE*.

12. I find the word "slavery" occurring nowhere else in Jefferson's extant letters during the nearly three months between his April 8, 1826, letter to Everett and his death on July 4, 1826. Enslaved persons are specified by Jefferson in his own personal documents related to his estate in the lead-up to his death (see immediately below); intriguingly, however, the final time that the term "slave" emerges in a letter authored by Jefferson is at the end of TJ to James Madison, January 13, 1821, *PTJDE*—a letter that concludes with Jefferson discussing the "Missouri question" and the threat it posed to the Union.

13. In her *Free Some Day*, Stanton notes that "[b]etween 1774 and 1826, Jefferson owned in any one year from 165 to 225 slaves, the total number usually fluctuating around 200" (18). For documents reflecting Jefferson's designation of specific enslaved persons, see Thomas Jefferson's List of Slave Vaccinations, 17 Mar. 1826, 17 March 1826, *PTJDE*, as well as his own will (Chapter 14, note 24).

14. Edward Everett to TJ, March 29, 1826, *PTJDE*. Everett's speech was delivered in response to a "motion" by George McDuffie, which was subsequently published as "Speech of Mr. M'Duffie, on the Proposition to Amend the Constitution of the United States" (Washington: Gales & Seaton, 1826). Although concerned with domestic politics, George McDuffie's "proposition" gestures to foreign affairs as well, aptly making specific reference to the Ottoman occupation of Greece, addressing the "Turks" and their dominion over "seven millions of Greeks" (12).

15. For Clay's implication in the supposedly "backroom bargain" that led to the election of John Quincy Adams, see H. W. Brands, *Heirs of the Founders: The Epic Rivalry of Henry Clay, John Calhoun, and Daniel Webster, the Second Generation of American Giants* (New York: Doubleday, 2018), 119.

16. Scherr has previously noted this irony, while also emphasizing that Jefferson "was probably shocked at Everett's blatant proslavery sentiments" (*Thomas Jefferson's Image of New England*, 302).

17. For Jefferson's repute as "a founding father of colonization," as well as "his long advocacy of and copious writings on the proposal," see David Kazanjian, *The Colonizing Trick: National Culture and Imperial Citizenship in Early America* (Minneapolis: University of Minnesota Press, 2003), 101. For Jefferson's views as influencing the foundation of the American Colonization Society, and for Henry Clay's service as this society's second president, see Nicholas Guyatt, *Bind Us Apart: How Enlightened Americans Invented Racial Segregation* (Oxford: Oxford University Press, 2016), 4.

18. TJ to Edward Everett, April 8, 1826, *PTJDE*.

19. TJ to Edward Everett, April 8, 1826, *PTJDE*.

20. Edward Everett to TJ, April 16 1826, *PTJDE*.

21. The name of this enslaved Muslim is spelled in several ways, both in nineteenth-century sources, as well as present-day treatments. Identified often via the patrilineal

"Ibn Sori," which recalls his father, "'Abd ar-Raḥmān" constitutes a marker of Ibrāhīm's Muslim identity, forming an Arabic phrase variously transliterated into English, sometimes inaccurately, and even abbreviated, including by Everett himself, as will be seen further below.

22. As mentioned earlier (Prologue, note 5), it is Terry Alford's 1977 biography, entitled *Prince among Slaves*, that was most responsible for publicizing the story of Ibrāhīm 'Abd ar-Raḥmān ibn Sori in the twentieth century. However, 'Abd ar-Raḥmān was already "a celebrity" in the nineteenth century (Dickson D. Bruce, *The Origins of African American Literature, 1680–1865* [Charlottesville: University of Virginia Press, 2001], 149), even coming to play a role in the "vitriolic campaign being waged against [Adams] by Andrew Jackson, his challenger for the presidency," as Jill Lepore has noted, in her superb recounting of the 'Abd ar-Raḥmān story within *A Is for American: Letters and Other Characters in the Newly United States* (New York: Knopf, 2002), 113.

23. See Jon Sensbach, "'The Singing of the Mississippi': The River and Religions of the Black Atlantic," in *Gods of the Mississippi*, ed. Michael Pasquier (Indianapolis: Indiana University Press, 2013), 17–35 (27), who notes the arrival of Ibrāhīm 'Abd ar-Raḥmān in 1790, in the wake of "Spain" taking "over Louisiana from French control in 1766" and "reopen[ing] the Atlantic slave trade."

24. For early recognition of Jefferson being "unremitting in his efforts" as "Secretary of State" to "gain the right of navigation of the Mississippi by treaty [which] had at length been attained in 1795," see R. M. Lovett, "Thomas Jefferson and the Louisiana Purchase," *New England Magazine* 7 (1890): 569–577 (575).

25. For Abiel Holmes writing to Stiles, noting that 'Usman authored his Arabic document in 1788 "in my presence," see Chapter 5, note 33.

26. See Henry Clay, *The Papers of Henry Clay, 1797–1852*, 11 vols., ed. James F. Hopkins et al. (Lexington: University of Kentucky Press, 1959–1992), VI:352, for a transcription of Marschalk's letter to Clay, as well as Clay marking this letter "[t]o be submitted to the President."

27. See Clay, *Papers*, VI:352, where Clay personally notes to the president "[t]he propriety of a purchase of the Slave & of sending him home is respectfully recommended," signing his own name as "HC."

28. This quotation is offered in Mildred Bain and Ervin Lewis, eds., *From Freedom to Freedom: African Roots in American Soil* (New York: Random House, 1977), 157.

29. A summary of the process by which 'Abd ar-Raḥmān gained release has most recently been supplied by Spellberg, *Thomas Jefferson's Qur'an*, which notes that "the U.S. government began to correspond with Morocco on the slave's behalf via the U.S. consul in Tangier" and recognizes Henry Clay's role in "recommend[ing]" the release, despite being "a slaveholder himself" (189).

30. For this January 12, 1828, letter from Clay to Marschalk see Clay, *Papers*, VII:30–31. Clay notes on p. 31 that "[t]he object of the President being to restore" 'Abd ar-Raḥmān "for the purpose of making favorable impressions in behalf of the United States," but cites "one difficulty in acceding to the conditions prescribed by Mr. Foster, which I understand to be, that ['Abd ar-Raḥmān] shall not be permitted to enjoy his liberty in this country" (31).

31. For these quotations see James Horton and Lois Horton, *Slavery and the Making of America* (Oxford: Oxford University Press, 2006), 127.

32. For these details see Austin, *African Muslims*, 66.

33. I quote this entry from Alford, *Prince among Slaves,* 128.

34. Although this chapter reveals for the first time an 'Abd ar-Raḥmān Arabic document in Everett's possession, the meeting of the two men has attracted prior notice; in addition to Alford, cited immediately above, see also Lepore, *A Is for American,* 221, as well as Austin, *African Muslims,* 79.

35. Everett, *Orations and Speeches*, III:189.

36. I discovered this document, previously owned by Edward Everett, in 2015 at the Department of Special Collections of the Hesburgh Libraries of Notre Dame, and am grateful for the gracious aid of George Rugg, curator, during my research at the university. This Figure 12 image represents the first time this manuscript authored by 'Abd ar- Raḥmān has appeared in print. The image features the first five Arabic lines inscribed by 'Abd ar- Raḥmān, with two following Arabic lines, which are largely indecipherable, not pictured. Although indebted to a foregoing rendition of this document, which was included in the file alongside the manuscript at Hesburgh Libraries, the above represents my own rendition, reconstructed from what I take to be the intended significance of 'Abd ar-Raḥmān's text. Featuring ellipses, as well as orthographic and grammatical irregularities, I have filled in material where necessary that seems to be signified (e.g., "[may God bless] Muḥammad"), as well as construed words that are unclear (e.g., reading "الفقيه"—*faqīh,* "jurist"—to be the third word of the fourth line, which, however, is unclear in the Arabic original). At the end of the second line of Arabic text, there is a term that seems to be a place name—the name of the "land" in which resides "Imām Ibrāhīm"—which is sufficiently unclear that I do not offer a candidate translation. In line 5, the successive repetition of "Allah"—perhaps an act of *dhikr,* or pious "remembrance" of God's name—is somewhat unclear, especially its conclusion, where the terms that follow this divine invocation are uncertain. Finally, there are two additional undated lines of English at the bottom of this manuscript, speculating as to its provenance. Linking this document to "E. Everett" in "1828," these penciled lines also mention "Boston"— a town 'Abd ar-Raḥmān did indeed visit after Washington (see Alford, *Prince among Slaves,* 139). However, whereas their Washington encounter is regularly recounted, and was recorded by Everett himself (see above), I have been unable to find any evidence that Everett and 'Abd ar-Raḥmān met again in Boston. As a result, I believe that it is most likely that this manuscript was received by Everett sometime during the reliably documented time that they were both together in Washington, DC; I acknowledge, however, that the precise occasion of this Arabic document's donation to Everett is not certain.

37. For 'Usman's third-person autograph, see Chapter 6, note 11.

38. This material regarding the "Shaikh" derives from line 4 of 'Abd ar-Raḥmān's manuscript; this identity is linked to "Mecca" and "Medina," but with questionable clarity, with the manuscript's irregular usages making it difficult to ascertain the precise relation between the "Shaikh" and these cities (thereby giving rise to my tentative "the

Mecca[n] and Medina[n]"). ʿAbd ar-Raḥmān's appeal to this "Shaikh" is, moreover, not at all unique; see Lepore, *A Is for American*, 131, which features a section simply entitled "Saith the Sheikh to Mecca," quoting another ʿAbd ar-Raḥmān manuscript that seemingly invokes this same authority.

39. Austin, *African Muslims*, 73.

40. This diary entry is quoted from Adams, *Politics of Slavery*, 143.

41. See Spellberg, *Thomas Jefferson's Qurʾan*, which has previously drawn this link between John Quincy Adams's meeting with Mellimelni in 1805 and his encounter with ʿAbd ar-Raḥmān, noting especially that "Ibrahima was not the first Muslim Adams had met" (190).

42. Austin, *African Muslims*, 73.

43. For this date of February 7, 1829, see Diouf, *Servants of Allah*, 168. For their ship—the *Harriet*—and its Virginia departure, see Alford, *Prince among Slaves*, 175.

Chapter 21

1. This passage is quoted from Everett, *Orations and Speeches*, I:149. This selection has also appeared more recently in Katula, *The Eloquence of Edward Everett*, 37.

2. The oratorical response to the same-day deaths of Adams and Jefferson amounted to entire published volumes, such as the 1826 *A Selection of Eulogies Pronounced in the Several States: In Honor of Those Illustrious Patriots and Statesmen, John Adams and Thomas Jefferson* (Hartford: D. F. Robinson & Co, 1826). The "wonderful coincidence of events" is remarked by several of these collected speeches; see *A Selection of Eulogies Pronounced in the Several States*, 88, 117, 295, 302, 385, 425. For this extensive eulogist tradition, see also Robert McDonald, *Confounding Father: Thomas Jefferson's Image in His Own Time* (Charlottesville: University of Virginia Press, 2017), 226 ff.

3. Featuring a prologue that begins with the concurrent eulogies for the two founders, Gordon Wood, *Friends Divided: John Adams and Thomas Jefferson* (New York: Penguin Books, 2017), recognizes that "this equality of eminence did not last. In fact, even some of the eulogists suggested that Jefferson possessed something that Adams lacked. Two of the southern speakers practically ignored Adams" (4).

4. For the entire eulogy, see Everett's "Eulogy on Adams and Jefferson," in *Orations and Speeches*, I:131–149.

5. William Bruce, *John Randolph of Roanoke, 1773–1833; A Biography Based Largely on New Materials*, 2 vols. (New York: Putnam's, 1922), I:283.

6. For the memorial of Everett as "American Cicero" after his own death, see *A Memorial of Edward Everett*, 46.

7. Everett, *Orations and Speeches*, III:189–190.

8. Immediately before the quotation that begins above, Everett had declared that ʿAbd ar-Raḥmān "[e]arly in 1830 [. . .] embarked with his wife for Liberia," thereby mistaking the year of his departure and subsequent death (see Chapter 20, note 43, for the correct date of departure as February 7, 1829).

9. Everett, *Orations and Speeches*, III:192.

10. Everett's "'Abdul" transliterates merely the Arabic noun "عبد" ("'abd," "slave") together with the Arabic definite article, yielding "slave of the." This truncation reflects
a more general trend of imprecisely referring to 'Abd ar-Raḥmān's Arabic name;
Everett's own memorial is to "Abdul Rahaman" (note the extra "a" in "Rahaman").

11. "Jefferson Papers: Number Two," *Knickerbocker Magazine* 6 (1835): 537.

12. For the first part of this two-part series, see "Jefferson Papers: [Number One],"
Knickerbocker Magazine 6 (1835): 394–400.

13. One cursory exchange between the two men has survived, namely: Alexander
H. Everett to TJ, September 4, 1816, and TJ to Alexander H. Everett, September
19, 1816—an exchange that took place while Alexander Everett was serving as the
"Secretary of Legation in Holland."

14. For both Alexander Everett's 1835 publication and his 1836 oration, which was soon
thereafter published, see "Character of Jefferson," *North American Review* 40 (January
1835): 170–232, and *A Defence of the Character and Principles of Mr. Jefferson*
(Boston: Beals and Greene, 1836). From these efforts, Alexander Everett emerges as
uniquely invested in the study of Jefferson's life and legacy at precisely the time that
the two *Knickerbocker* articles were produced. This exclusivity is also emphasized by
the sweeping bibliography, compiled by Richard Holland Johnston, included at the
conclusion to the turn-of-the-century edition of *The Writings of Thomas Jefferson*;
according to this bibliography, it is only Alexander Everett who produced attributable published work on Jefferson during 1835–1836, with the *Knickerbocker*'s two-
part "Jefferson Papers" series (1835) enveloped in between Alexander Everett's
1835 "Character of Jefferson" and his 1836 *A Defence* (see *The Writings of Thomas
Jefferson*, 20 vols., eds. Andrew A. Lipscomb et al. [Washington, DC: The Thomas
Jefferson Memorial Association, 1903–1905], XX:44).

15. "Jefferson Papers: Number Two," 540.

16. For the Islamic contexts of Othello being "sold to slavery," see Julia Lupton, *Citizen-
Saints: Shakespeare and Political Theology* (Chicago: University of Chicago Press,
2005), 112.

17. Edward Everett, "Address of the Hon. Edward Everett: at the Anniversary of
the American Colonization Society, January 18, 1853" (Boston: Massachusetts
Colonization Society, 1853), 9.

18. For this quotation, see the April 30, 1848, entry from Edward Everett, "Diary
[Memoranda of My Youngest Child William]"; Papers of Edward Everett, 1807–
1864, Harvard University Archives (UAI 15.884), 52; quoted courtesy of the Harvard
University Archives.

19. For William Everett living at the Holmes house, and for this quotation—"gambrel-
roofed old house"—see Charles Francis Richardson, "Cambridge on the Charles,"
Harper's Magazine (January 1876): 191–208 (203).

20. Everett, *Orations and Speeches*, III:193.

21. For "Everett [speaking] for about two hours, Lincoln for approximately two
minutes" at Gettysburg, see Ronald Reid, *Edward Everett: Unionist Orator*
(New York: Greenwood Press, 1990), 1.

22. Everett, *Orations and Speeches*, IV:623–624.

23. For this quote from Byron, see Chapter 18, note 18.

24. See Douglas Wilson, *Lincoln before Washington: New Perspectives on the Illinois Years* (Urbana: University of Illinois Press, 1997), for echoes of Jefferson in Lincoln's iconic address (178).

25. For Lincoln's "ten complicated sentences," see Allen Guelzo, "Little Note, Long Remember: Lincoln and the Murk of Myth at Gettysburg," in *The Gettysburg Address: Perspectives on Lincoln's Greatest Speech*, ed. Sean Conant (Oxford: Oxford University Press, 2015), 147–174 (161).

Chapter 22

1. Video of Albert Gore Jr.'s June 16, 1999, speech, announcing himself "a candidate for the Democratic nomination for president in the 2000 election," is archived on CSPAN's website, available at www.c-span.org/video/?125103-1/gore-announcement. A polished transcript of this speech, from which I quote here and throughout this chapter, is archived on cnn.com as "Gore Launches Presidential Campaign" (June 16, 1999).

2. For Albert Gore Sr.'s death on December 5, 1998, see Anthony Badger, *Albert Gore Sr: A Political Life* (Philadelphia: University of Pennsylvania Press, 2018), 272.

3. Just ten days after Gore's June 16 speech in Carthage, Burt Solomon and W. John Moore published a piece simply entitled "Hometown Boy" (*National Journal*, June 26, 1999, 1872–1878)—a piece that mentions Gore's Carthage appearance, noting that "Gore is insistent and (understandably) a little defensive on the subject of his rural bona fides" (1873).

4. Ira P. Nash to TJ, November 8, 1807, *PTJDE*.

5. I am thankful for the generous reception I received at the Carthage Courthouse in January 2017, searching for traces of the two West African Muslims taken to the town in the autumn of 1807. John Waggoner Jr. was especially helpful during my review of the courthouse's nineteenth-century records, which, however, did not yield evidence of either their arrival or their fate.

6. This "deadlock," and its February 1801 congressional resolution, is treated in John Ferling, *Adams vs. Jefferson: The Tumultuous Election of 1800* (Oxford: Oxford University Press, 2004), 186.

7. For Al Gore's attempt to frame himself as a "native son," see David Maraniss and Ellen Nakashima, *The Prince of Tennessee: The Rise of Al Gore* (New York: Simon & Schuster, 2000), 85.

8. The "judicial intervention" that decided the closely contested 2000 election is considered by Robert Post, "Sustaining the Premise of Legality: Learning to Live with *Bush v. Gore*," in *Bush v. Gore: The Question of Legitimacy*, ed. Bruce Ackerman (New Haven: Yale University Press, 2002), 96–109 (especially 103).

9. Links between these two sites of incarceration are offered by Josh White, "Abu Ghraib Tactics Were First Used at Guantanamo," *Washington Post* (July 14, 2005): A1.

10. Gore Sr.'s "refusal to sign" the Southern Manifesto is treated by Badger, *Albert Gore Sr.*, 121–122.

11. For Gore Sr.'s failed re-election bid in 1970, see Badger, *Albert Gore Sr.*, 246–251.

12. According to *Politico*'s "2016 Tennessee Presidential Election Results," Donald Trump received 5,485 votes in Smith County, totaling 74 percent of the vote (see www.politico.com/2016-election/results/map/president/tennessee).

13. For the misidentification of Ira P. Nash as either "Frank Nash" or "J. Nash," see the Library of Congress entries for two of his critical 1807 letters to Jefferson, namely: i) "J. Nash to Thomas Jefferson, October 5, 1807, Mutilated" (www.loc.gov/item/mtjbib017739), the follow-up letter in which Nash summarizes for Jefferson the situation of the two fugitives in Kentucky whose Arabic writings he had delivered the day before; and ii) "Frank Nash to Thomas Jefferson, November 8, 1807" (www.loc.gov/item/mtjbib017864), the letter in which Nash informs Jefferson of the two fugitives' latest escape, their staggered run eastward to Tennessee, and their final capture in Carthage. Simply from their catalogue entries, it is not apparent that the author of these two pivotal letters is indeed the same man: Ira P. Nash. To confuse matters further, Jefferson *was* in contact with an actual Frank Nash, who wrote three incoherent letters to Jefferson during his first term, before perishing at sea in 1804; this Frank Nash was deemed, from the strangeness of his writings, by Jefferson to be "probably an idiot" (see Frank Nash to TJ, November 29, 1803, *PTJDE* and Frank Nash to TJ, February 4, 1804, *PTJDE*).

Index